History and Philosophy of the Language Sciences

Editor: James McElvenny

In this series:

1. McElvenny, James (ed.). Form and formalism in linguistics.

Form and formalism in linguistics

Edited by

James McElvenny

language
science
press

McElvenny, James (ed.). 2019. *Form and formalism in linguistics* (History and Philosophy of the Language Sciences 1). Berlin: Language Science Press.

DOI:10.5281/zenodo.2654375
Source code available from www.github.com/langsci/214
Collaborative reading: paperhive.org/documents/remote?type=langsci&id=214

Cover and concept of design: Ulrike Harbort
Typesetting: James McElvenny
Proofreading: Agnes Kim, Andreas Hölzl, Brett Reynolds, Daniela
Hanna-Kolbe, Els Elffers, Eran Asoulin, George Walkden, Ivica Jeđud, Jeroen
van de Weijer, Judith Kaplan, Katja Politt, Lachlan Mackenzie, Laura Melissa
Arnold, Nick Riemer, Tom Bossuyt, Winfried Lechner
Fonts: Linux Libertine, Libertinus Math, Arimo, DejaVu Sans Mono
Typesetting software: XƎLATEX

Language Science Press
Unter den Linden 6
10099 Berlin, Germany
langsci-press.org

Storage and cataloguing done by FU Berlin

Freie Universität Berlin

Contents

Preface

James McElvenny

University of Edinburgh

Notions of "form" have a long history in Western thought on language. When linguistics emerged as an institutionalized discipline in the early decades of the nineteenth century, its practitioners could look back on a multitude of senses and uses of "form", embedded in a variety of conceptual schemes. Even though many nineteenth-century linguists sought to emphasize the novelty of their work and imagined a radical break with the "pre-scientific" past (see Morpurgo Davies 1998: chap. 1), both their everyday practice and their theoretical views were permeated by an intellectual inheritance stretching back over centuries, in which "form" occupied a central place.

On a practical level, "form" has long been employed in a general sense to refer to the perceptible outer appearances of linguistic expressions, especially in connection with the inflectional variants of words. On a deeper theoretical level, there has often been an effort to find underlying motivations for these appearances and so conceive of "form" in senses loaded with metaphysical and epistemological significance. This was the path taken by such movements as the medieval Scholastics and the Enlightenment-era General Grammarians (see Law 2003: chaps. 8 and 11), whose successors in the ninetenth century – despite often disavowing their predecessors – were similarly engaged in a search for the cognitive, biological or aesthetic bases of linguistic form.

A particularly prominent figure in nineteenth-century discussions of form in language was Wilhelm von Humboldt (1767–1835), whose writings served as the point of departure for many later scholars. For Humboldt and his followers, there is a sense in which all language is form and nothing else, in that language is the representation we make of the world which, in Kantian fashion, we shape according to our perceptive faculties. "The essence of language", writes Humboldt (1905 [1820]: 17), "consists in pouring the material of the phenomenal world into

James McElvenny. 2019. Preface. In James McElvenny (ed.), *Form and formalism in linguistics*, iii–viii. Berlin: Language Science Press.
DOI:10.5281/zenodo.2654347

the form of thoughts." (*Das Wesen der Sprache besteht darin, die Materie der Erscheinungswelt in die Form der Gedanken zu giessen.*) A commonplace among the Humboldtians was to claim that each language has its own characteristic form of representation discernible in the form of its expressions. The task of the linguist is to capture these forms and analyse them for what they reveal about the mental, cultural and physical life of language speakers (see Morpurgo Davies 1998: chap. 5; Trabant 1986; McElvenny 2016).

The centrality of form to linguistic scholarship continued into the structuralist era. The *Cours de linguistique générale* of Ferdinand de Saussure (1857–1913) famously contains the assertion that "language is a form and not a substance" (*la langue est une forme et non une substance*) (Saussure 1922 [1916]: 169). Following on from the earlier Humboldtian position, a fundamental tenet of structuralism is to conceive of languages as self-contained structures imposed on the material substrate of the world. In describing phonological, grammatical and semantic apparatuses of languages, the structuralist is engaged in an investigation of linguistic form (for a classical structuralist account couched in these terms, see Lyons 1968: 54–70).

In the generativist era, Noam Chomsky's (b. 1928) efforts to construct an intellectual genealogy for his work involved an attempted appropriation of Humboldtian "form", which rekindled awareness of these ideas in mainstream linguistics. In his *Cartesian linguistics*, Chomsky (2009 [1966]: 69–77) sought to assimilate Humboldtian form to his own innovation of generative rules as the underlying system that allows for the creative use of finite means to produce an infinite array of expressions.

The fecundity of "form" is visible not only in its polysemy, but also in the family of derivatives it has brought into the world, including such terms as "formal", "formalized" and "formalist/formalism". Like their parent, these terms defy concise definition, although when applied as labels to directions in linguistic research they generally imply concentration on internal systematicity to the exclusion of external explanatory factors alongside an inclination to abstraction and axiomatization – two tendencies that may in fact manifest independently of one another (cf. Newmeyer 1998). As is explored in several contributions to this volume, formalism as a research mindset is at home in many fields – such as logic, mathematics, aesthetics and literary studies – and represents an area of rich historical cross-pollination between linguistics and other disciplines.

In a separate but related sense, "formalism" as a count noun refers to the devices employed in the representation and analysis of phenomena. Various formalisms in this sense, along with the theoretical views to which they are tied, are also examined in the following chapters.

In composing this volume, we have come together as historians of science and philosophers of language and linguistics to take a critical look at notions of form and their derivatives, and the role they have played in the study of language over the past two centuries. We investigate how these notions have been understood and used, and what this reveals about the way of thinking, temperament and daily practice of linguists.

The first contribution to our volume is Judith Kaplan's examination in Chapter 1 of the role of visual formalisms in representing genealogical relationships between languages. Engaging with some of the latest literature on material culture in the history of science, Kaplan explores how visual diagrams and metaphors helped in grasping relationships between languages in comparative-historical grammar, from the nineteenth century up to the present day. She finds that the tensions between the dominant models of language relationship – "tree" versus "wave" models – were typically conceived in a visual mode, whether this was explicitly represented in a diagram or initially described only as a visual metaphor. She observes shifting commitments to the realism of representations and mutual influences between linguists and those working in neighbouring sciences.

In Chapter 2, James McElvenny compares competing nineteenth-century accounts of "alternating sounds" – a cover term for the apparent unstable phonological variation found in "exotic" languages – for the different attitudes towards linguistic form that they reveal. The traditional view took alternating sounds to be a feature of "primitive" languages, which were assumed to have not attained the levels of formal arbitrariness characteristic of European languages. Franz Boas (1858–1942) famously refuted this view by insisting that all languages have fully developed phonologies and ascribed alternating sounds to perceptual error on the part of outside observers. Georg von der Gabelentz (1840–1893), on the other hand, embraced the phenomenon and wielded it against Neogrammarian doctrine, the leading formal theory of his day. Both Boas' and Gabelentz' positions can claim a measure of theoretical sophistication and at the same time contain obvious faults. McElvenny places these positions in their historical context and considers why Boas' view was so well received in linguistics while Gabelentz' was not.

Chapter 3 turns to the links between linguistic, psychological and, above all, aesthetic theory in the work of Edward Sapir (1884–1939). In this chapter, Jean-Michel Fortis provides a detailed exposition of Sapir's writings on form in language, concentrating in particular on Sapir's notion of "form-feeling" and following the trail – in some places explicitly marked by Sapir himself and in others reconstructed by Fortis through terminological and conceptual detective work

– to identify his sources of inspiration. Fortis places Sapir in a finely interlaced intellectual network spanning across contemporary *Gestalt* psychology and German art theory, with a heritage extending at least as far back as the Romantic period around the turn of the eighteenth to the nineteenth century.

The focus on Sapir continues in Chapter 4, where Els Elffers critically compares Sapir's philosophy of science to that of Jerry Fodor (1935–2017) and examines the implications of their views for the treatment of linguistic form. Looking at Sapir's arguments against the "superorganic" in language scholarship and Fodor's proposal for "token physicalism", she finds striking similarities between the two, despite their very different intellectual contexts: Sapir was responding to ideas in anthropology emerging from debates about the nature of the *Geisteswissenschaften* in contrast to the *Naturwissenschaften*, whereas Fodor was responding to logical positivism. Both scholars, however, concerned themselves with how best to demarcate the individual sciences, with the specific example of linguistics in mind, and settled on the principle of demarcating the sciences not according to their subject matter but the way in which that subject matter is conceived.

In Chapter 5, Bart Karstens undertakes a re-examination of the genesis of linguistic structuralism and its early interaction with Russian Formalism, a school of literary analysis from the early twentieth century. Karstens engages in a detailed investigation of the scholarly network around Roman Jakobson (1896–1982) and his role as a vector for the transmission of Russian Formalism first to the Prague School of structuralism in the 1920s and then later to the United States. While formalist doctrine was often heavily criticized by the early structuralists, Karstens shows that various formalist views informed elements of early structuralism.

A similar story of "resistant embrace" is told in Chapter 6, where John Joseph reconsiders the place of structuralism in French linguistics of the mid-twentieth century, before the onset of the "post-structuralist" period. Focusing on such figures as Émile Benveniste (1902–1976), Henri Meschonnic (1932–2000), Aurélien Sauvageot (1897–1988) and their closest contemporaries, Joseph demonstrates that each of these figures has a complex relationship to structuralism: at times criticizing the apparent premises of the approach while employing recognizably structuralist forms of analysis, or publicly avowing structuralism while straying away from its principles in their own work.

In Chapter 7, Ryan Nefdt surveys some of the radical changes in theory that generative linguistics has undergone in its short history and derives from them positive lessons for the philosophy of science. Amid the turbulence and instability that has characterized generative theory, he identifies one constant: the formal structures in language that generative linguists describe. With the durability of this constant in mind, he advocates for a position of structural realism in the philosophy of linguistics. Such a position, he argues, would allow linguists to escape pessimistic meta-induction – that is, the notion that we must necessarily expect our theories to one day be refuted and superseded – and allows them to step away from the ontology of natural languages, thereby securing the epistemological basis of the formal approach to language.

The gaze of the last two chapters in our volume is largely directed towards current questions in the philosophy of linguistics, specifically the role of normativity and authority in language description. After first tracing the origins of generative grammar in formalist approaches to logic, Geoffrey Pullum, in Chapter 8, develops a new perspective on the classical distinction between prescriptivism and descriptivism. He contends that the value of a grammatical description lies in the precise, formalized account it provides of a particular set of linguistic practices, which can guide those who may wish to participate in those practices. In serving as a guide, every grammar has normative force, but is not necessarily prescriptive: the grammar-reader may follow its advice but is not compelled to do so.

In Chapter 9, Nick Riemer identifies the ideologies of language he sees embodied in the "unique form hypothesis", the assumption that every linguistic expression can be reduced to a single, universally agreed underlying representation. While linguists might seek to distance themselves from this hypothesis and its implications, it is, argues Riemer, a recurring motif in linguistics, especially prominent in the teaching of the discipline. Its effects in education are particularly pernicious, since teachers, due to the exigencies of pedagogy, can usually offer no justification for the unique forms they present to their students other than arbitrary authority, a practice that reinforces unreflective submission to authority of all kinds, both at university and in life. Acknowledging that most linguists would shudder at such consequences, Riemer pleads for greater open-mindedness among linguists towards critique of the discipline's foundations.

Although dealing with a broad range of topics from diverse perspectives and in different styles, this volume is the product of concerted collective effort. Each of us came to this project with existing ideas about form and formalism in linguistics. These ideas we set out in draft chapters, which we discussed in person at a meeting in Edinburgh in August 2018. After our meeting, we revised the chapters to reflect the insights gained through our discussion. It is these revised chapters, shaped and harmonized by our dialogue, that are contained in this volume.

James McElvenny

References

Chomsky, Noam. 2009 [1966]. *Cartesian linguistics: A chapter in the history of rationalist thought.* Cambridge: Cambridge University Press. Edited by James McGilvray.

Humboldt, Wilhelm von. 1905 [1820]. Über das vergleichende Sprachstudium in Beziehung auf die verschiedenen Epochen der Sprachentwicklung. In Albert Leitzmann (ed.), *Wilhelm von Humboldts gesammelte Schriften*, vol. IV, 1–34. Berlin: Behr.

Law, Vivien. 2003. *The history of linguistics in Europe from Plato to 1600.* Cambridge: Cambridge University Press.

Lyons, John. 1968. *Introduction to theoretical linguistics.* Cambridge: Cambridge University Press.

McElvenny, James. 2016. The fate of form in the Humboldtian tradition: The *Formungstrieb* of Georg von der Gabelentz. *Language and Communication* 47. 30–42.

Morpurgo Davies, Anna. 1998. *History of linguistics: Nineteenth-century linguistics.* London: Longman.

Newmeyer, Frederick J. 1998. *Language form and language function.* Cambridge, Mass.: MIT Press.

Saussure, Ferdinand de. 1922 [1916]. *Cours de linguistique générale.* Paris: Payot. Edited by Charles Bally and Albert Sechehaye.

Trabant, Jürgen. 1986. *Apeliotes, oder der Sinn der Sprache: Wilhelm von Humboldts Sprach-Bild.* München: Fink.

Chapter 1

Visual formalisms in comparative-historical linguistics

Judith Kaplan

University of Pennsylvania

This paper examines visual formalisms in comparative-historical linguistics from the perspective of the history of science. It shows that visual aids representing key understandings of language relationship have followed on pre-existing visual metaphors. Using this observation to pry open canonical metaphors of language relationship, it traces the ways in which these "visualizations" have both consolidated existing research programs and opened up new lines of inquiry for students and recent advocates of phylogenetic methods.

1 Introduction

From the interiority of brain atlases to the distant topography of Mars, from the intimate realm of nano-images to the global modelling of climate data, a recent swell in computerized visualization techniques is transforming the face of scientific research, pedagogy, and generalist publications. Commenting on this trend in 2014, Lorraine Daston judged computer simulations to be "the greatest revolution in scientific empiricism since the canonization of observation and experiment in the late seventeenth century" (Daston 2014: 321). These developments, moreover, have had a profound impact on scholarship in Science and Technology Studies: many have hailed the growing sophistication of digital visual culture as an opportunity to re-think classical theories of scientific representation. Crucially, their efforts have emphasized the *materiality* of scientific representation in a turn away from questions of truth-as-correspondence and social infrastructure. For this new generation, the "material enactments" of scientific images are to be taken just as seriously as the embodied practices and community norms

Judith Kaplan. 2019. Visual formalisms in comparative-historical linguistics. In James McElvenny (ed.), *Form and formalism in linguistics*, 1–33. Berlin: Language Science Press. DOI:10.5281/zenodo.2654349

surrounding them, and a good deal more seriously than any quest to faithfully represent the natural world (Coopmans et al. 2014: 3; see also Kusukawa 2016).

How might these conversations relate to the formalisms of comparative-historical linguistics?[1] Like economics, chemistry, and molecular biology, to name a few arenas, diachronic linguistics has embraced and disseminated a raft of colourful and complex data visualizations since the early 2000s (see, e.g., Gray et al. 2009). Thoughtful critics have entertained the possibility that a belated turn to phylogenetic modelling (an iterative statistical approach to genealogical classification thought to have revolutionized biological systematics during the 1970s) has made "tree thinking" viable again (Lopez et al. 2013). But we may equally well use the opportunity occasioned by this surge in tree thinking to reflect on the status of visual culture and epistemology in the language sciences more generally. Looking at canonical visual topoi for understanding language relationship over roughly the last 150 years, my chapter attempts to do just that.

Two points emerge from this line of questioning. First, it shows that well-known diagrams of language relationship derive from pre-existing verbal descriptions: words came first and were subsequently elaborated by pictures.[2] This chronology illuminates George Lakoff's distinction between "conceptual" and "image" metaphors in complicated ways (Lakoff 1987), where "metaphor" itself is defined basically as a way of "understanding and experiencing one kind of thing [...] in terms of another" (Lakoff & Johnson 1980: 455). First, it shows that conceptual metaphors – understood to be systematic, quotidian, and extendable – and image metaphors – more limited in scope, hewn from conventional mental images, and characterized by "one-shot mapping" – often interact and define one another. This helps to explain the layering of arboreal and genealogical metaphors of language relationship, for instance, in comparative-historical linguistics. This double representation shows an inclination to capture the relatively abstract (the genealogical) with the relatively concrete (the arboreal). Furthermore, it helps us to understand that the fundamental metaphor here for conceptualizing relationship is LANGUAGE IS A LIVING THING. But even beyond this framework, the example suggests that image metaphors can become progressively conventional over time, to the point where they *are* systematic, quotidian, and extendable over a wide range of phenomena. This point takes on extra significance in the context

---

[1] See James McElvenny's preface to this volume. This chapter takes formalisms to be those "devices employed in the representation and analysis of phenomena" (p. iv), as he elaborates.

[2] This point generalizes to the history of biology. Here, Peter Simon Pallas (1741–1811) is credited with originating the tree of life (see his *Elenchus Zoophytorum*, 1766), though the visual was at that point purely descriptive, not diagrammatic. The diagrammatic rendering of Pallas' idea came some 63 years later (Eichwald 1829).

of science, where the extension of conventional mental images has contributed to the development and communication of theories about the way the world actually works (see Boyd 1979: 357).

In these respects, historical linguistics looks very much like molecular biology. Natasha Myers, tackling the latter tradition, traces the mechanical interventions of structural biology and bio-engineering back to the circulation of machinic metaphors for life during the 1870s (Myers 2015, "Introduction"). They provided Thomas Henry Huxley, analogizing between the "protoplasmic theory of life" and the "'horology' of a clock", with a bridge from the "visible tangible and manipulable world" of everyday life to an "invisible, intractable world of biological molecules" (Huxley 1880; Myers 2014: 157). Myers ultimately presents the idea of the "molecular machine" as a powerful "material-semiotic actor" capable of directing practitioners – initiates, especially — to travel certain lines of experimental inquiry (Haraway 1991; Myers 2014: 165–168).

The development and persistence of foundational metaphors for vertical (LANGUAGE IS A LIVING THING, entailing a genealogical concept of relationship) and horizontal (LANGUAGE IS A PHYSICAL THING, entailing a proximity theory of relationship) transfer in linguistics exhibit characteristics that are like the ones Meyers describes. They are hybrid in nature (both verbal and visual) and they feature prominently in texts that have served the consolidation of disciplinary knowledge. Attending to these similarities points up the enduring significance of texts, alongside material culture, in the history of science.

To focus on trees alone — rumoured to be the "most universally widespread of all great cultural symbols" (Pietsch 2012: 1) – might sustain conclusions on the specific conceptual ramifications of "biosystematic iconography" (see, e.g., Pulgram 1953: 69) and illuminate large scale patterns of change over time – from realism to anti-realism, and lately back again. Indeed, numerous studies of these phenomena already exist (see, e.g., Southworth 1964; Hoenigswald & Wiener 1987). Instead, by drawing together trees and their alternatives in what follows, I hope to show how such representations highlight certain notions of relationship while removing others from view.

This, then, is the second point of the paper: visual metaphors and visual aids of language relationship matter a great deal because they constrain objects and programmes of research. I aim to establish this point by showing how difficult it has been for linguists to visualize vertical and historical relationships at the same time. While the advent of algorithms like NeighborNet in 2003 purported to give researchers the tools needed to see variation within hierarchy – forests and trees – there is a much longer history of failed attempts to capture both kinds of relationship in a single visualization (Bryant & Moulton 2004). Select examples of this tension are woven throughout my discussion of canonical types in what follows.

These points are developed over the next five sections. In §2, I consider classificatory diagrams lacking figural elaboration, in other words, lists and tables (on diagrams, see Bigg 2016). My hope is that this starting point will de-naturalize the turn to tree thinking in the second half of the nineteenth century. §3 then introduces the dominant visualizations for understanding historical relationship – trees and waves – manifest in works that have gone on to have canonical status in pedagogy and historiography. Complementing previous studies of these texts, this part of the paper emphasizes the relationship between words and images and highlights conceptual problems that were encountered during the 1870s in bringing trees and waves meaningfully together. Next, in §4, I look at the uptake of these visualizations in twentieth-century textbooks. How were they introduced, drawn, and qualified? What attempts, if any, were made to see "the wave process and the splitting process" simultaneously? §5 entertains the possibility that computational models offered a new bifocal lens on these processes of linguistic differentiation. The conclusion, in §6, offers a few ideas about the benefits of integrating the historiography of science and linguistics when it comes to specifically *visual* formalizations.

2 From tables to trees

MultiTree is a "digital library of language relationships" that was launched in 2006, funded by the United States National Science Foundation in 2012, and hosted by Linguist List as recently as 2018 (http://new.multitree.org). The stated aim of the project is to facilitate research in historical linguistics, "representing the most complete collection of language relationship hypotheses in a user-friendly, visually-appealing, and interactive format". As with many such projects, it is a resource with ambitions vis-à-vis expert, interdisciplinary, and public audiences alike. While the visualizations presented on the site may be young (among other innovations, users can "climb" branches to view trees from individual nodes in rectangular and radial layouts), the data is often rather old. A search on "Mayan", for instance, retrieves a potentially interactive visualization of a classificatory note composed by the Swiss-American ethnologist Albert Samuel Gatschet in the mid-1890s, shown in Figure 1. The entry is quite simple: it pictures Mayan as a root node linked to six sub-groups (Huastec, Maya proper, Tzental, Mam, Quiché, and Pokom).

What is curious about this presentation is how unmotivated it makes the tree actually seem. Whereas science studies scholars have directed painstaking attention to the implications of rooted (versus unrooted) trees, top-to-bottom (versus left-to-right) orientation, branching patterns, and the like, the manipulability of MultiTree undercuts all authorial intentionality on such fronts. Moreover, the original publication of Gatschet's account of the "Maya Linguistic Family" holds nary a tree – a hierarchical outline format using Roman and Arabic numerals sufficed just as well for his classificatory purposes (Gatschet & Campbell 1973: 250–251). As Pietsch and others have noted, early arboreal representations merely translated tables into trees, perhaps explaining some authors' preference for their growth from the left-hand margin of a printed page (Wells 1987: 51; Pietsch 2012: 7–10; Archibald 2014: 57).[3]

Why bother layering the biosystematic metaphor on top of the familial (see Wells 1987: 49 on "mixed metaphors", 53–54 on biological imports)? When it comes to MultiTree, this choice not only fosters comparability across the database, it also reflects architects' stated commitments to aesthetics, access, and "fun". In other words, the visual is second nature to those already familiar with the techniques of comparison and sub-grouping, and it recruits potential newcomers to those particular methodological approaches.

This brief example is meant to suggest that tree thinking did not have a necessary or inevitable trajectory in comparative-historical linguistics. Trees were not the only means available for the organization of information on ancestor-descendant relations.[4] Rather, they have served additional rhetorical purposes, taken up in the next section.

---

[3]This is to say nothing of the local influence from stemmatics in linguistics, dating back to the sixteenth century, where trees typically drop down in a branching pattern from an original manuscript positioned at the top of the page (see e.g. Maher 1966; Hoenigswald 1975; Cameron 1987). Setting questions of priority aside, Müller (1913 [1891]: vol. I, 537) encourages reflection on the visual culture of linguistics in the late nineteenth-century, as his *Lectures on the Science of Language* includes both genealogical trees and tables. In this example, the table gives Müller more space for textual elaboration – allowing him to differentiate, for instance, between "living" and "dead" languages, and to layer vertical groupings, reflecting geography, on top of horizontal brackets, reflecting genetic affiliation.

[4]The case in biology on this point is somewhat different. In the case of Lamarck's diagrams, for example, the shift from tables (e.g. 1778) to trees (e.g. 1809) coincided with a definite conceptual shift (re. species mutability). The recognition of variation and change over time did not correspond with the visual in linguistics (Archibald 2014: chap. 3).

Cakchiquel
Tz'utujil
Kiché proper
Tzotzil
Chañabal
Quiché group
Chol
Maya proper
Tzental group
Huastec
Tzental
Mayan
Chontal
Mam-group
Mam
Pokom group
Aquacatan
Pokomchí
Ixil
Uspantec
K'ek'chi
Pokomam
Chorti

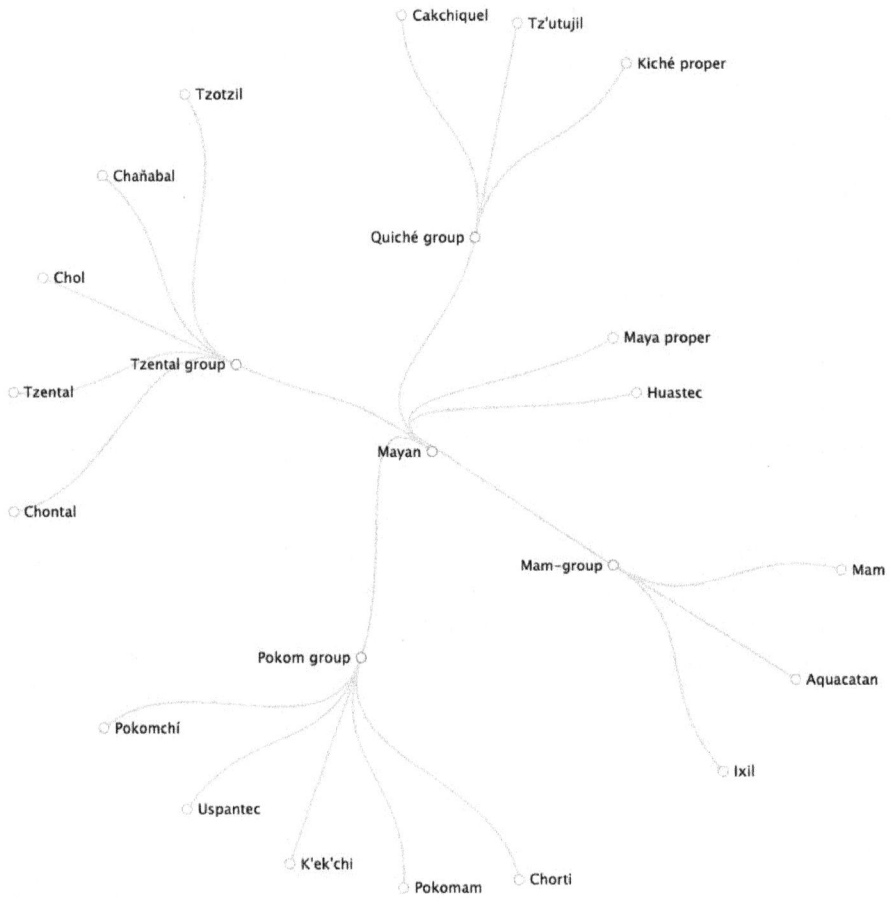

Figure 1: Gatschet (1895), according to Gatschet & Campbell (1973). This is the radial view with descendants expanded. Available at: http://new.multitree.org/trees/id/21186

3 Canonical visual metaphors

1853 was a pivotal year with regard to the visualization of language relationship — two of the earliest known language family trees were published that year.[5] The first, posthumously attributed to the Czech poet and translator Frantiek Ladislav Čelakovský (1799–1852), depicted the historical differentiation of the Slavic language family (Čelakovský 1853: 3; Priestly 1975). But Čelakovský's contribution has been overshadowed by the trees of August Schleicher (1821–1868). His first such visualization depicted the Indo-Germanic family with thick branches and weighty arboreal realism (see Maher 1966; Hoenigswald 1975; Koerner 1987). Significantly, Geisler and List suggest that this diagram was a formalization, after the fact, of Schleicher's first published reflections on the comparative history of languages some five years earlier (Schleicher 1848). Identifying relationship with descent, and pinning that conception on the tree, they assert, Schleicher's "new theory of vertical language relations [was] directly reflected in the tree model" that has since become so familiar (Geisler & List 2013: 114).

What more did Schleicher invest in his "schema" than a procedure for classification by two-way splits? Historians have emphasized notions of parsimony, regularity (Geisler & List 2013: 117, 114–115), organicism (Wells 1987: 56), and programmatic ambition (Koerner 1975: 755). More concretely, Schleicher told readers directly that branch length served as an indicator of "duration" and that the distance between branches was meant to indicate "degrees of relationship", left otherwise undefined (Schleicher 1853: 8). Going further, Schleicher emphasized the importance of his trees for training newcomers to the field, and their projected departure from older philological traditions:

> In the present work an attempt is made to set forth the inferred Indo-European original language side by side with all extant derived languages. Besides the advantages offered by such a plan, *in setting immediately before the eyes of the student the final results of the investigation in a more concrete form, and thereby rendering easier his insight into the nature of a particular Indo-European language*, there is, I think, another advantage of no less importance, namely that it shows the baselessness of the assumption that the non-Indian Indo-European languages were derived from Old-Indian (Sanskrit), an assumption which has not yet entirely disappeared. (Schleicher 1967 [1871]: 94; my emphasis)

---

[5]In fact, the "Arbre Généologique" by Felix Gallet (ca. 1807) is often cited as the first tree of language relationship (Hellström 2012: 242). This chronology roughly aligns with the biological context, where the first known tree diagram of relationship was published by Augustin Augier in 1801.

Judith Kaplan

My emphasis on the first "advantage" described in this passage, the pedagogical advantage, presents the tree diagram as tool for summing up and disseminating research findings to those just entering the field — for Schleicher it was decidedly *not* a means to new linguistic knowledge. References to the "eyes" and "insight" of the student recall Daston's (2008) depiction of the "all-at-once-ness" of disciplined perception, seen here to be very much in the making through the association between pedagogy and disciplinary differentiation. That said, phylogeny does not appear to be a primary goal, in and of itself. Rather, it is celebrated as a means to better understand a "particular" language under investigation. Schleicher's philosophy of science did not necessarily demand knowledge of a general sort (Nyhart 2012). His visual epistemology appears to have involved a kind of inward tendency, from sight to insight, both in the cultivation of the student and the discipline.

By the early 1870s, the outlines of the Indo-European family had been drawn, giving comparativists considerable cause for celebration. Nevertheless, exceptions persisted. As a young professor of German and Slavic at the University of Bonn, Johannes Schmidt (1843–1901), a student of Schleicher's, tackled these difficulties head-on. In a 31-page monograph on *The Relationships of the Indo-Germanic Languages* [*Die Verwandtschaftsverhältnisse der indogermanischen Sprachen*], he demonstrated that unique resemblances can be identified between any two Indo-European branches, and that these tend to increase with geographic proximity. In light of this observation, he argued that linguistic changes spread horizontally like waves on a pool of geographically distributed speech, rather than vertically, through a process of strict cleavage and differentiation. With each change propagated individually, he projected an image of successive waves moving out and interacting from a variety of centres – a network of linguistic features differentiated through space.

Though Schmidt did not give readers a diagram of his *Wellentheorie* in 1872, he did picture it in words.[6] With the following passage, Schmidt invited readers to join him in an image metaphor:

> If we want now to represent the relationships of the Indo-Germanic languages in a picture that illustrates the origin of their diversity, then we must completely abandon the idea of a family tree. I would like to *put a*

---

[6]The critique of Schleicher's tree thinking through alternative visual metaphors came even earlier in Hugo Schuchardt's 1870 lecture "On the Classification of the Romance Dialects", where he speaks of killing the tree by binding together numerous branches and twigs with "horizontal lines" (Schuchardt 1928 [1870]: 11).

8

picture of a wave in its place, which diffuses concentrically with the distance from the mid-point in ever weaker rings. It does not matter that our language area makes no circle, rather a circle-sector at best, with the most primitive language at one end, not the centre [...]. There were not initially any boundaries between languages within this domain, two arbitrarily distant dialects, A and X, were connected to each other by continuous varieties, B, C, D, etc. [...]. (Schmidt 1872: 27–28; my emphasis)[7]

With references to "pictures", geometry, and dialect labels, this passage reads as though it were captioning a printed diagram, though Schmidt did not provide one at first to accompany the text. Indeed, he went on to challenge the visual altogether – asserting the priority of linguistic data over any such formalization. As far as he was concerned, "[p]ictures have only marginal value in science, and if the one chosen here is displeasing to someone, he can replace it at will with something better without changing the results of the foregoing analysis" (Schmidt 1872: 28).[8]

Perhaps this attitude partly explains why his first attempt to provide a visual aid, as reproduced in Figure 2, lagged some three years behind his introduction of the image metaphor. Perhaps this reluctance derived from problems inherent to the visualization of horizontal relationship. Geisler & List (2013: 116–117) suggest as much through their side-by-side presentation of several "fruitless" attempts to draw an alternative to Schleicher's trees – from overlapping circles (Hirt 1905), to the spokes of a wheel (Meillet 1908), to early networks (Bonfante 1931), and alternating boundaries (Bloomfield 1933). I turn now to the challenging case of another visual metaphor that attempted to capture vertical and horizontal relationship simultaneously.

Johann Heinrich Hübschmann (1848–1908) heeded Schmidt's call to data-driven analysis in his comparative work on Armenian. Like Schmidt, Hübschmann

---

[7]"Wollen wir nun die verwantschaftsverhältnisse der indogermanischen sprachen in einem bilde darstellen, welches die entstehung irer verschidenheiten veranschaulicht, so müssen wir die idee des stammbaumes gänzlich aufgeben. Ich möchte an seine stelle das bild der welle setzen, welche sich in concentrischen mit der entfernung vom mittelpunkte immer schwächer werdenden ringen ausbreitet. Dass unser sprachgebiet keinen kreis bildet, sondern höchstens einen kreissector, dass die ursprünglichste sprache nicht im mittelpunkte, sondern an dem einen ende des gebietes ligt, tut nichts zur sache [...]. Sprachgrenzen innerhalb dises gebietes gab es ursprünglich nicht, zwei von einander beliebig weit entfernte dialekte des selben A und X waren durch continuierliche varietäten B, C, D, u. s. w. mit einander vermittelt."

[8]"Bilder haben in der wissenschaft nur ser geringen wert, und missfallen jemand die hier gewälten, so mag er sie nach belieben durch treffendere ersetzen, an dem ergebnisse der vorstehenden untersuchung wird dadurch nichts geändert."

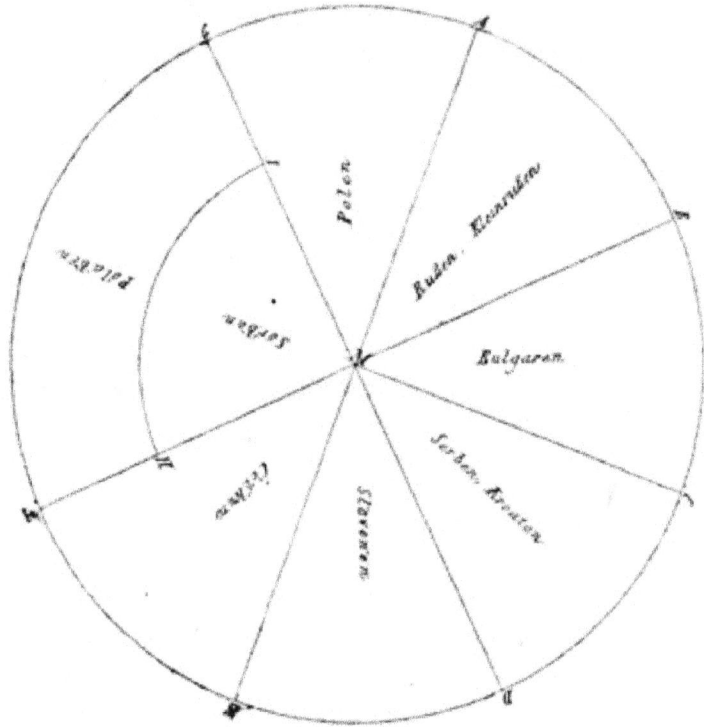

Figure 2: Schmidt (1875: 199). The text goes on to tell readers that the radia between lettered points should be read as isogloss lines, carving out dialects like pieces of a pie.

studied with Schleicher at the University of Jena, though he later completed his degree under the Iranian philologist Martin Haug (1827–1876) at the University of Munich. Having defended a dissertation on Avestan and Old Persian philology in 1872, he turned in the next three years to an investigation of the relationship between Iranian and Armenian in pursuit of his Habilitation at the University of Leipzig. Initially, Hübschmann was only interested in Armenian insofar as it contributed to an understanding of the internal phylogeny of the Iranian family of languages. In line with the general consensus of the day, Hübschmann had, up to this point, taken a high degree of shared vocabulary as evidence of the fact that Armenian was part of Iranian (Schmitt 1976).

His postdoctoral studies culminated in the 1967 [1875] paper "On the Position of Armenian in the Circle of the Indo-Germanic Languages" ["Ueber die Stellung des Armenischen im Kreise der indogermanischen Sprachen"]. Here Hübschmann sorted out non-native parts of the lexicon and analysed the remaining "native" words, which allowed him to identify strata in the historical development of the language. His findings compelled his colleagues to recognize Armenian as an independent branch of the Indo-European family — not a sub-group of Iranian after all.

In the 1967 [1875] essay, Hübschmann demonstrated an extensive political history of contact and exchange between native Armenian-speaking and Iranian-speaking groups, suggesting that the similarities traditionally invoked in support of the "prevailing" view of common descent were in fact derived from the sector of borrowed, not inherited, vocabulary. Working back and forth between etymological and phonological evidence, Hübschmann next established provisional sound laws unique to Armenian, which undermined long-standing confidence in what were thought to be cognates between the languages in question. From the lexicon, Hübschmann then moved to grammatical considerations – the inflectional morphology of Iranian and Armenian, which exhibited many surface similarities. He attributed these to processes of analogical change – a psychological process of association tending to regularize words with similar meanings or inflectional paradigms, a mechanism of convergence.

Adding further phonological evidence to the balance against family relationship in this case, Hübschmann came to a fairly radical position, one that prioritized horizontal over vertical relationship:

> Through the last part of our investigation, such a tight bond has without question been constructed between Armenian and European that it would be easier to tear Armenian from Aryan than from European. Among the European languages it stands closest to Balto-Slavic [...]. In this situation, friends of the family tree [...] will certainly be inclined to separate Armenian completely from Aryan and make it a purely European language. Against this view I might first refer to the fact that Armenian does not take part completely in the split of *a* and *r* [...].

> If further research makes this conclusion definitive, then the impossibility of setting up a family tree of the Indo-European languages would be strikingly demonstrated. For Armenian would be the connecting ring of both parts in the chain of the Aryan-Balto-Slavic languages, not a branch between two branches. And then too the family tree, which Johannes Schmidt's vigorous might has overturned, would remain lying forever [...].

> But if Armenian is to be the connecting member between Iranian and Balto-Slavic, between Aryan and European, then in my opinion it must have played the role of an intermediary at a time when they were still very similar to

one another, when the historical period had not yet drawn the present sharp boundary between them, but when they were still related to one another as dialects. (Hübschmann 1967 [1875]: 183)

Like all the examples encountered thus far, Hübschmann appealed first to a visual metaphor in this passage rather than a visual aid. Further, his discussion highlights inherent difficulties in drawing vertical and horizontal relationship together. To see Armenian as a link in the chain between Aryan and European, it was necessary to focus in on "*a time* when they were still very similar". If trees lacked, fundamentally, a feeling for spatially distributed variation, waves were completely without a sense of timing.

Though this painstaking work secured Hübschmann's reputation as the "father" of modern Armenian linguistics – a doubly genealogical claim – previous accounts have not had much to say about the degree to which his positivism paradoxically threatened to topple his faith in the comparative method. In a paper "On the pronunciation and transcription of Old Armenian", published the following year, Hübschmann pushed Schmidt's visual metaphor still further:

> [I]t seems that languages can have similar sound systems without being related to one another, that the sound system of a language can be conditioned by outside influences, i.e. local influences, leading one to infer the congruencies between the sound systems of two languages less from their origin as from their local gathering. This statement seems to me for the determination of the genealogy of languages to be important and in linguistics to reward further success than heretofore was the case [...] if Iranian languages on the border of India show Indic sound similarities, must one therefore believe that they stand nearer to the Indic than the other Iranian languages? (Hübschmann 1876: 73)[9]

Evidently, the dictates of historical fidelity required taking vertical *and* horizontal relationship into consideration. But this proved remarkably difficult to capture visually. Hübschmann's best practice was to toggle back and forth between the two.

---

[9] "Aus alledem ergiebt sich, dass Sprachen das gleiche Lautsystem haben können, ohne miteinander verwandt zu sein, dass das Lautsystem einer Sprache von äusseren, d. h. localen Einflüssen bedingt sein kann, und man aus der Gleichheit des Lautsystems zweier Sprachen weniger auf ihre Verwandtschaft als auf ihr locales Beisammensein zu schliessen hat. Dieser Satz scheint mir für die Beurtheilung der Verwandtschaftsverhältnisse der Sprachen wichtig zu sein und in der Linguistik mehr Beachtung zu verdienen als es bisher der Fall war. [...] wenn iranische Sprachen an der Grenze Indiens indische Lauteigenthümlichkeiten [...] zeigen, hat man darum zu glauben, dass sie dem Indischen näher als die andern iranischen Sprachen stehen?"

4 Metaphors and visual aids in twentieth-century textbooks

The canonical topoi just considered enjoyed a hearty afterlife in the *Disziplingeschichte* of the late nineteenth century, and its review in textbooks thereafter. This section looks at the deployment of visual aids in that genre, building on previous studies of print and pedagogy in the history of chemistry, physics, and biology (Bertomeu-Sánchez et al. 2002; Kuhn 1962; Hopwood 2015). This literature has shown how scientific textbooks specialized from the late eighteenth century on, emphasizing their "use in formal teaching and their pedagogical and scientific authority"; their significance for disciplinary self-fashioning; and their "major role" in the making of *interactional expertise*, that is "the worldviews of citizens, what they know, what they do, what they are" (Simon 2016: 475, 479; Johns 1998: 406–408).[10]

Leonard Bloomfield's *Language* met all of these criteria: it served as a provocative introduction to descriptive linguistics in 1933, asserting a new program while disciplining perception (Bloomfield & Hoijer 1965: v-vi). Comparative-historical material, notably, bookends the text: it appears first as a kind of "preface history", recounting progress towards the modern "scientific" study of language and, in the second half of the book, aligning with Bloomfield's priorities and programmatic vision. Far from a straightforward reproduction of earlier works, the presentation of historical research in the later part was designed for American students – those just beginning linguistics "who often d[o] not have the background in Indo-European languages" necessary to "understand texts that present methodology very largely in terms of concrete problems drawn from the older Indo-European languages" (Bloomfield & Hoijer 1965: vi). Put differently, the update shifted from exemplars to models, in line with what could reasonably be assumed of a new generation of students.

What, then, was textually self-evident, and what did Bloomfield think needed elaboration through the use of visual aids? By far the most common diagram in *Language* is the table, followed by maps (eight), and only then abstract visualizations of the sort laid out in the previous section. Interestingly, Bloomfield

---

[10]Josep Simon (2016) contends that "textbook" had come to mean a book conceived for instructional purposes within formal education by the middle of the nineteenth century, picking up on the earlier convention of designating canonical works, excerpted with spaces for students' interlineal notes, as *texts*. Thus, he implies a direct connection between the history of note-taking practices and the development of formal, printed textbooks. This contextualizes John Joseph's (2017) compelling discussion of the ambiguous relationship between pictures and words in Saussure's *Cours de linguistique gén015éale* within a broader history of science and education.

identifies visual metaphors and visual aids in teasing out the implications of the former. Students read:

> The comparative method assumes that each branch or language bears independent witness to the forms of the parent language, and that identities or correspondences among the related languages reveal features of the parent speech. This is the same thing as assuming, firstly, that the parent community was completely uniform as to language, and secondly, that this parent community split suddenly and sharply into two or more daughter communities, which lost all contact with each other. Often enough, the comparative method assumes successive splittings of this sort in the history of a language [...]. The comparative method thus shows us the ancestry of languages in the form of a family tree, with successive branchings [...]. (Bloomfield 1933: 311)

This passage rehearses standard criticisms of the tree model — namely, ancestral uniformity and clean two-way splits — showing it to have heuristic power despite being unrealistic. Thus, it signals an advance over nineteenth-century understanding. "The earlier students of Indo-European did not realize that the family-tree diagram was merely a statement of their method; they accepted the uniform parent languages and their sudden and clear-cut splitting as historical realities" (Bloomfield 1933: 311). In this way, Bloomfield subordinated Schleicher's visual aid to a method of inference. Translating this into Lakoff's terminology, he moved an "image metaphor" towards the "conceptual" register.

This shift was reflected in the highly idealized visual that accompanied the text, shown in Figure 3. The lengths and distances between branches are not particularly measured, and the labels refer to groupings and periods rather than specific language entities. Bloomfield was an anti-realist tree thinker, to be sure: the diagrams above depict relations but not relatives.

In the text, Bloomfield persistently refers tree thinking to "older scholars", setting off his positive variationist approach. To complement a series of examples highlighting exceptions to the assumption of clean two-way splits, he adapted a visual aid from the Germanist and linguistic palaeontologist Otto Schrader (1855–1919), shown in Figure 4.

The citation to Schrader may at first seem surprising, given that the authors differ in their selection of "special resemblances", hence, group assignments (Bloomfield 1933: 317). However, both authors allow that the groups could be drawn differently depending on the forms taken into consideration. Bloomfield explained his image in Figure 5 – containing elements of uniformity and variation – in

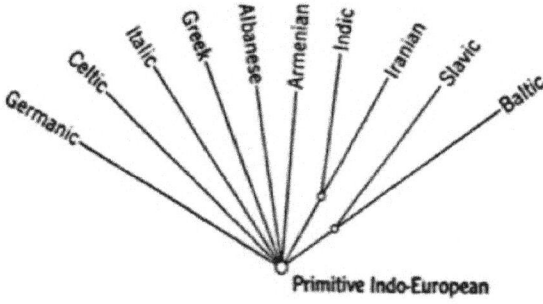

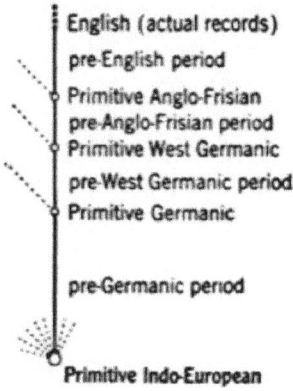

Figure 3: Bloomfield (1933: 312)

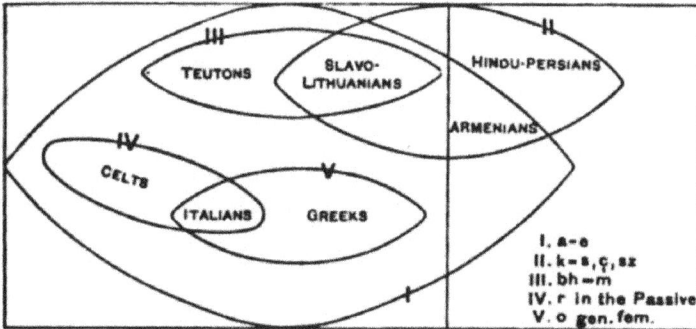

Figure 4: Schrader (1890: 65)

Judith Kaplan

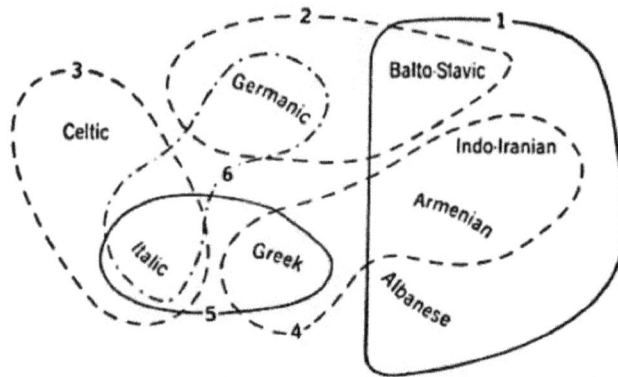

FIGURE 3. Some overlapping features of special resemblance among the Indo-European languages, conflicting with the family-tree diagram. — Adapted from Schrader.
1. Sibilants for velars in certain forms.
2. Case-endings with [m] for [bh].
3. Passive-voice endings with [r].
4. Prefix ['e-] in past tenses.
5. Feminine nouns with masculine suffixes.
6. Perfect tense used as general past tense.

Figure 5: Bloomfield (1933: 316)

terms of Schmidt's "*wave-hypothesis*", which he endorsed. "Indeed", he wrote favourably, it is "the picture presented by the local dialects in the areas we can observe" (Bloomfield 1933: 317). Charles Hockett (1916–2000), writing in a more richly visual idiom some twenty-five years later, would refer a reprint of the same image to overlaid notions of vertical and horizontal relationship (cf. Hübschmann 1967 [1875]).

Bloomfield's influence can be seen throughout the pages of Hockett's textbook, *A Course in Modern Linguistics* (1959 [1958]). Hockett introduced his subject in rigorous terms: "Linguistic research can accomplish nothing unless it is strictly inductive" (Hockett 1959 [1958]: 7). Such primacy of "actual usage, as determined by observation" was born out in the sequence of chapters, which proceed from the smallest units of synchronic observation – defined through examples and presented with rules for exacting description – to the more complex, with chapters on language diachrony and other unobservables saved for the end. Indeed, he did not even mention the distinction between synchronic and diachronic linguistics in the book until Chapter 36.

There are clues to Hockett's visual epistemology throughout the text, with bearing on the way he called upon diagrams of language relationship. First, the text shows a remarkable tolerance for the kind of idealization any visualization of

16

language relationship would require. Elaborating on the "design of a language" through its five subsystems, he allowed, for instance, that no description "can claim more than a kind of by-and-large accuracy" (Hockett 1959 [1958]: 139). He similarly flagged the underdetermined and heuristic nature of grammatical description in connection with immediate constituents a few pages later. The following passage is perhaps unexpected behaviourist fare:

> [...] grammatical analysis is still, to a surprising extent, an art: the best and clearest descriptions of languages are achieved not by investigators who follow some rigid set of rules, but by those who through some accident of life-history have developed a flair for it [...]. Consequently, the reader will find in these sections many an example which the writer has handled in one way, but which might also be handled in some other way [...]. Indeed, the reader should be alert for possible instances where conciseness of statement has unintentionally concealed uncertainty. (Hockett 1959 [1958]: 147)

Reflections like these contextualize his use of visual metaphors (e.g., the persistent reference to phonemic "shape") and visual aids in the text (Hockett 1959 [1958]: 130–132). With respect to the latter, Hockett's use of two-dimensional abstract representations involved explicit pedagogical aims. For example, in the notes to his chapter on "Canonical Forms and Economy", Hockett taught students *how to see* the three diagrams in Figure 6, which were most often used to represent complex morphological systems — the "maze", "freightyard", and "rollercoaster" (Hockett 1959 [1958]: 290–292; Harris 1951; Hoenigswald 1950).

Hockett told readers that the example provided was derived from the inflection of gendered Spanish adjectives, a pattern "too simple to need diagrammatic display", thus a "good one with which to demonstrate the diagramming techniques". The words accompanying these images train students in the techniques of visual analysis – navigating the maze, for example, one proceeds "from left to right, never crossing any lines"; once in the freightyard, there is "no turning back"; and while riding the rollercoaster, "one can turn down wherever there is a curved top, but not an angle". Thus, Hockett formalized morphological rules, rendered them exhaustive, and made them intelligible for beginners. The penultimate paragraph on the matter provides lessons in *critical* visual analysis. Here Hockett pointed out that vertical alignment in the first two diagrams can be "read" as indicating "a single positional class", whereas the "rollercoaster has the advantage of listing all the inflectional affixes along the bottom for ease of checking against inadvertent duplications". The discussion concludes with an exercise that recruits students to

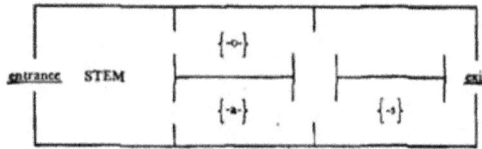

FIGURE 34.1. THE MAZE

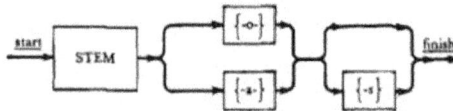

FIGURE 34.2. THE FREIGHTYARD

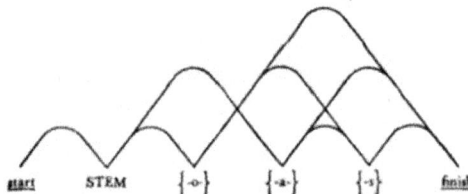

FIGURE 34.3. THE ROLLERCOASTER

Figure 6: Hockett (1959 [1958]: 291)

the practice of diagrammatic visualization, suggesting that this was not merely a means of summing up, but rather an active part of research practice.

How was this visual epistemology brought to bear on questions of language relationship? Hockett defined relationship in terms of common origin: divergence being the key factor, not time. Accordingly, he made a sharp distinction between linguistic and biological phylogeny – "languages do not 'reproduce' either sexually or asexually", instead, they "simply *continue*" (Hockett 1959 [1958]: 369; Hockett's emphasis). For this reason, familial metaphors to do with parenthood and ancestry appeared "shaky" in his estimation. "At a given point in time," he concluded,

> a set of related languages is merely what would be a set of dialects of a single language except that the links between the dialects have become very tenuous or have been broken [...]. The mere fact of relationship thus becomes of secondary importance. More important is the *degree* of relationship. (Hockett 1959 [1958]: 369; Hockett's emphasis)

The first tree diagrams to appear in the text serve methodological rather than representational ends. Grouping together Proto-Germanic and its descendants without concern for sub-grouping, two sets of arrows in Figure 7 instead illustrate the logic of traditional and inverted reconstruction.

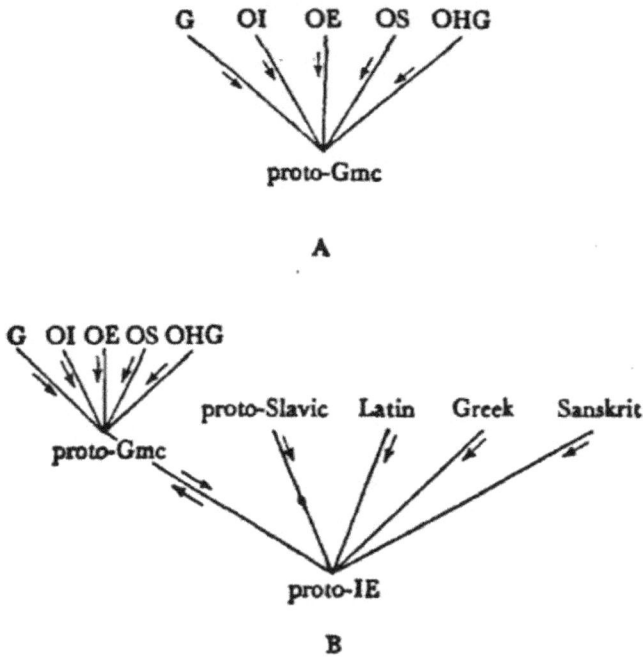

Figure 7: Hockett (1959 [1958]: 514)

A more realistic tree diagram, reproduced in Figure 8, appears a few pages later, qualified, with tips on interpretation.

Of this canonical image, Hockett wrote:

> The vertical dimension represents time, increasing as one goes from bottom to top. G[othic] has been placed earlier than the other four languages because our records of it date from an earlier century. Read literally, the diagram would suggest that, after Proto-Germanic, first the speakers of what was to become G split off from the rest [...], that somewhat later the speakers of what was to become O[ld] I[celandic] moved away from the rest, and that, finally, the remaining group split three ways — the splits, in each case, being more or less sudden. Now such literal interpretation is not contrary to what sometimes happens in history. But it is dangerous to assume that this is always what happened, because there are other ways in which divergence can come about. (Hockett 1959 [1958]: 519–521)

This passage begins with extremely rudimentary visual directives, a reminder of the pedagogical aim of the work. It also says something — through reference

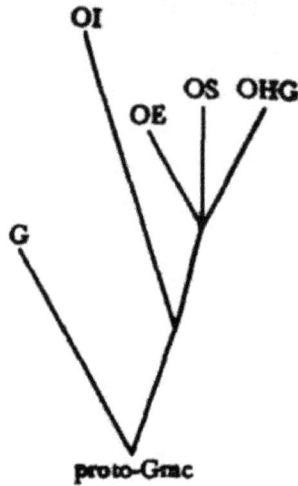

FIGURE 60.2

Figure 8: Hockett (1959 [1958]: 519)

to "our records" – about the research labour that goes into "cooking" the data summarized by the family tree. From there, readers are directed through a "literal" reading of the tree. The important point here is that insights on historical *process* are being extracted from a given *pattern* of historical relationship. While a bracketed table might capture a similar classification of language relationship, it would be harder to read in such a richly narrative way. This is because it would lack the "entailments" of the underlying image and conceptual metaphors we have been tracing. Ultimately, Hockett concluded, the tree was a possible, but unrealistic way of representing relationship. "It is imperative for us to remember that our reconstruction wears a disguise of greater preciseness than can validly be ascribed to it, but to throw it out for this reason would be folly" (Hockett 1959 [1958]: 523). He proposed the alternative illustrated in Figure 9 instead.

The diagram in Figure 9, in effect, zooms in on the base of the previous tree, looking at it through a series of cross-sectional slices like a flip-book. A succession of slices was Hockett's best effort to visualize relationship simultaneously in space and time. It culminated in the recapitulation of Bloomfield's diagram of dialect geography, formulated here in the context of a methodological argument rather than a list of discrepant data. This reflects another step away from exemplary towards formal instruction.

In his overview of scientific textbooks, Josep Simon calls for a transdisciplinary exploration of the genre, beyond a traditional emphasis on disciplines and dis-

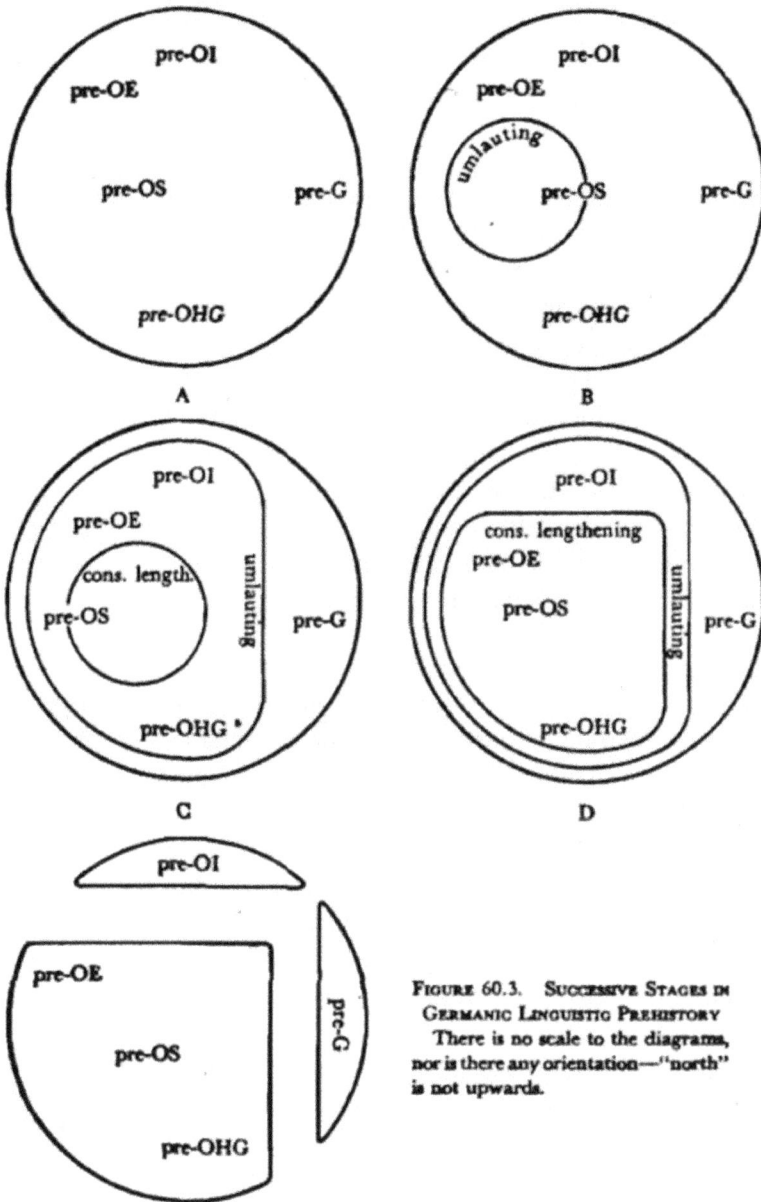

A

B

C

D

pre-OI

pre-OE

pre-OS

pre-G

pre-OHG

FIGURE 60.3. SUCCESSIVE STAGES IN GERMANIC LINGUISTIC PREHISTORY
There is no scale to the diagrams, nor is there any orientation—"north" is not upwards.

Figure 9: Hockett (1959 [1958]: 520)

21

cipline-formation in connection with this site of "normal science" (Simon 2016: 475). In partial fulfilment of that call, the final example in this section pivots from general introductions to a textbook devoted specifically to the sub-discipline in question, Theodora Bynon's *Historical Linguistics* (1977). Significantly, Bynon introduces the twentieth-century organization of linguistic knowledge with an extended image metaphor:

> The representation of the evolution of a language as consisting in a succession of discrete states is no more a true reflection of the situation than is the representation of a circle by a number of straight lines connecting successive points around its circumference. For, however large a number of such points are taken the resulting figure will never be a genuine circle and, in the same way, however many language sates are considered over a given period their succession will never provide a true picture of the unbroken *continuity* of a language in time. It is thus due to the limitations of our methodology that we are faced with the rather absurd situation that language evolution, although observable retrospectively in its *results*, appears to totally elude observation as a *process* while it is actually taking place. (Bynon 1977: 2; Bynon's emphasis)

So much for any attempt to comprehend, let alone visualize or represent, historical products and processes realistically. Accepting this fate, Bynon accordingly opts for a "two-fold strategy". First, she presents models of linguistic development from the neogrammarians to the transformational-generative school. "We must study [the] results [of language change] as abstracted from the grammatical descriptions of successive language states and [...] of related languages" (Bynon 1977: 6). Second, she turns to the "question of the connection between language change and social and geographical space" (Bynon 1977: 6). Rather than worry about the historical fidelity of either approach to the study of relationship and differentiation, this text holds them apart schematically, as shown in Figure 10.

According to this overall scheme, questions of the linear development of language through time – and, with them, trees – are isolated from those pertaining to internal variation and contact. Trees appear in her narrative as a bridge from the consideration of change within individual languages to changes between them. For Bynon, trees are not primary, they do the work of summing up the "rules" of differentiation – a sign of her times. That said, she emphasizes their visual interpretation more than either Bloomfield or Hockett. Describing a downward branching tree linking English, German, the Greek dialects, Persian and

Time   **Space**

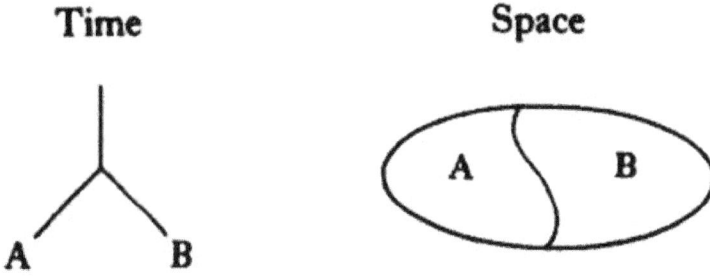

Figure 10: Bynon (1977: 173)

Sanskrit back to Proto Indo-European through a series of innovations, students read:

> In the tree diagram the horizontal dimension [...] represents "space" in a much idealized form – not in an absolute geographical sense but rather in terms of contact or absence of contact between speech communities – whereas the vertical dimension represents time. The branches of the tree then represent channels of transmission, that is the paths along which innovations have been transmitted, and whenever a branch divides into two or more this implies the splitting up of a speech community indicated by the fact that subsequent innovations are no longer shared. (Bynon 1977: 66)

Clearly, Bynon embraced anti-realistic tree thinking, though here she invests more words in training students to see this model than her structuralist predecessors. Notably, she resists the urge to conclude her discussion with an all-inclusive diagram of the Indo-European family, opting for a two-page chart instead, shown in Figure 11.

This diagram, she concludes, has the advantage of not overstating putative relationships, designed, as it was, to bring "together loosely according to branches and periods the main languages of the Indo-European family for which actual material survives." As for the tree model, Bynon states, it should be reserved for "the display of rules relating successive systems" (Bynon 1977: 70). At roughly the same time as phylogenetic modelling was taking off in biology, Bynon was relinquishing the analogy between languages and biosystematics entirely.

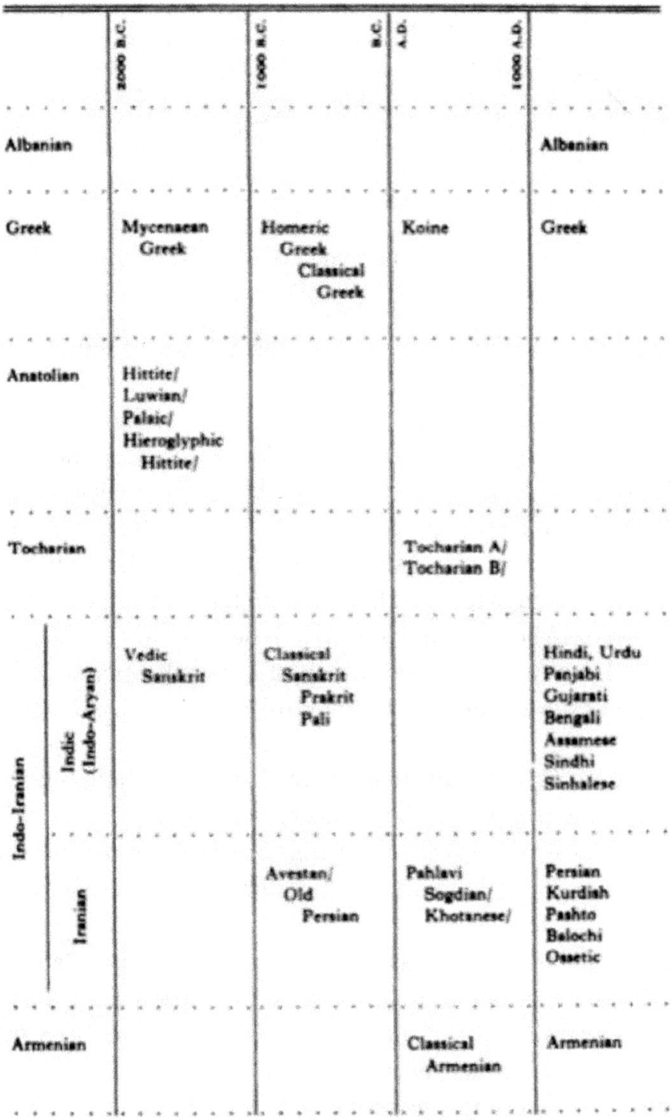

	2000 B.C.	1000 B.C.	B.C. / A.D.	1000 A.D.
Albanian				Albanian
Greek	Mycenaean Greek	Homeric Greek Classical Greek	Koine	Greek
Anatolian	Hittite/ Luwian/ Palaic/ Hieroglyphic Hittite/			
Tocharian			Tocharian A/ Tocharian B/	
Indo-Iranian — Indic (Indo-Aryan)	Vedic Sanskrit	Classical Sanskrit Prakrit Pali		Hindi, Urdu Panjabi Gujarati Bengali Assamese Sindhi Sinhalese
Iranian		Avestan/ Old Persian	Pahlavi Sogdian/ Khotanese/	Persian Kurdish Pashto Balochi Ossetic
Armenian			Classical Armenian	Armenian

Figure 11: Bynon (1977: 68). This is half of the chart, which stretches over two pages.

5 From anti-realism to realism in the digital era

At a 1973 conference on the topic of "Lexicostatistics in Genetic Linguistics", con-
vened in Montreal, Paul Black presented a paper on the adaption of Multidimensional Scaling (MDS) to historical linguistics, which built on a prior collaboration
with Isidore Dyen and Joseph Kruskal of Bell Labs. His work was an early attempt
to model hybrid transfer computationally using data collected by others. Black
endorsed the controversial use of statistics in comparative-historical linguistics,
stating by way of introduction that metrical analysis of linguistic distance "per-
mits a multidimensional recognition of relations" (Black 1973: 43–92). Thus, Black
adapted canonical metaphors of language relationship – forged on the basis of
Indo-European data in a two-dimensional environment – to a new geographic
and conceptual space.

Carried over from the world of marketing, psychology, and political science,
Black described MDS as a way to see continuous variation ("cline structure")
within a hierarchy of discrete classes (the evolutionary tree). The objective was
hybrid in nature:

> While a "family tree" diagram or some other representation of a hierarchi-
> cal subgrouping is an obviously appropriate way of describing the tempo-
> ral hierarchy of linguistic splits through which a group of languages may
> have evolved from a common ancestral protolanguage, multidimensional
> scaling can be used to investigate and describe the spatial variation which
> originates in the wave-like spread of linguistic innovations within a single
> language, and which may also persist within the evolutionary tree to an
> extent sufficient to hamper the correct inference of this tree. (Black 1973:
> 43)

According to Black's discussion, the method was new in that it began by *testing*
– rather than assuming or imposing – the fit between tree classifications, wave
models, and the actual language data (in this case, pertaining to Bikol, Lower
Niger dialects, Konsoid, and Salish) they were meant to represent. From there, distances between each of the entities under consideration (dialects or languages)
were scaled so as to approximate "actual physical distances". Looking at Bikol
dialects, for example, one might figure percentages of lexicostatistical retention,
subtract each from one hundred percent, and map each percentage point of difference as a distance of one tenth of an inch. A common retention of 79%, as in
the case of Sorsogon and Masbate, for instance, might yield a one-dimensional
distance of 2.1 inches according to this method. Black continued,

Oas might then be added to the picture by placing it 3.1 inches (corresponding to 69%) from Sorsogon and 4.2 inches (corresponding to 58%) from Masbate; these relationships would then be well represented in two-dimensional space as a triangle. (Black 1973: 52)

This was reasonably straightforward. But, as Black pointed out, the procedure becomes increasingly unwieldy as more dimensions are added to the mix, such that the representation "might prove to be difficult to visualize and interpret" should dimensionality not be "restricted to some very small number" (Black 1973: 53). With these words, Black was confronting the difficulty of reconciling language data with formalized relationships, fidelity with the "all-at-onceness" of disciplined perception. Even if MDS was escaping the constraints of the printed page as a research tool, Black was still bound to two dimensions when it came to the communication of research findings. In order to flatten a full set of distance measures into a two-dimensional representation with some degree of intelligibility, it was necessary to adjust the original percentages in a rationalized way that might be traced back to the original data. Electronic computers were thought to have the power needed to pull this off. Using the KYST program,[11] Black specified the range of possible dimensions, a rule for scaling, and the lexicostatistc data, ultimately yielding images like those in Figure 12.

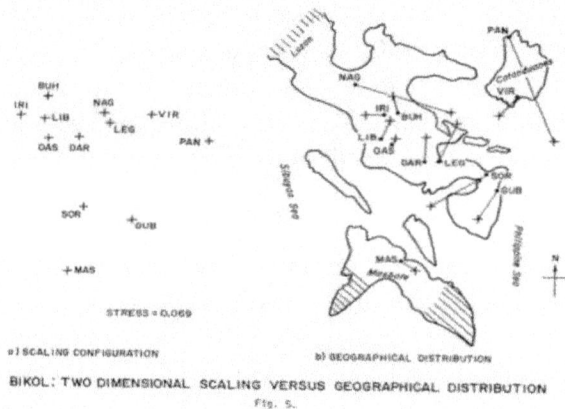

Figure 12: Black (1973)

---

[11]KYST, pronounced "kissed", was one of several MDS programs available in the 1970s. The name derives from those of its architects: Kruskal, Young, Shepard, and Torgerson (see Kruskal et al. 1973).

On the left-hand side of Figure 12, we have the distances (inverse percentage agreements) between twelve dialects scaled down to two dimensions from a potential total of eleven. The stress index given (.069) is a measure of how far these adjusted values differ from the original data fed into the program. The right-hand side shows these values projected into geographic space, with arrows indicating differences between scaled values and places where the dialects were actually observed.

This last point highlights the extent to which representational validity was of concern to those working with MDS. The iterative nature of this method – tinkering with dimensions and scaling to preserve fidelity to the data – foregrounded the issue of realism in a way that pre-computational diagramming did not. If earlier examples primarily served rhetorical, didactic, or programmatic functions, MDS thus can be seen to align with the advent of a new period of experimental visualization in comparative-historical linguistics.

In this respect, MDS looks like a forerunner of the use of phylogenetic networks in linguistics (Stevens 2013). Russell Gray, for instance, a self-described "evolutionist" and the newly appointed director of the Max Planck Institute for the Science of Human History in Jena, has zealously promoted the use of such probabilistic modelling techniques in linguistics, linking their powers of discovery to new scientific frontiers (e.g., http://www.mpi.nl/events/nijmegen-lectures-2014/lecture-videos, accessed 2 August 2018). Cheerfully labelling this work *lexomics*, Gray has sought to model and test tacit assumptions about comparative-historical methods, in addition to reconstructing family trees.

One of the programs commonly used in such work is SplitsTree, a tool for producing visualizations of phylogenetic networks (Greenhill et al. 2010), as in Figure 13. The idea, according to architects Daniel Huson (a specialist in bioinformatics at Tübingen University) and David Bryant (a mathematician from the University of Auckland) is to "use split networks, which are not trees, to represent phylogenetic signals that, for the most part, originate from trees" (Huson & Bryant 2006: 254–267). Through an iterative modelling process, this program prioritizes fidelity to the givens – acknowledging the realistic complexity of historical relationship while revealing the presence of latent trees to "plain sight".

6 Conclusion

This paper has surveyed visual metaphors and visual aids of language relationship and divergence from the mid-nineteenth century to the early 2000s. It has shown that, until recently, visual metaphors took priority over visual aids. In

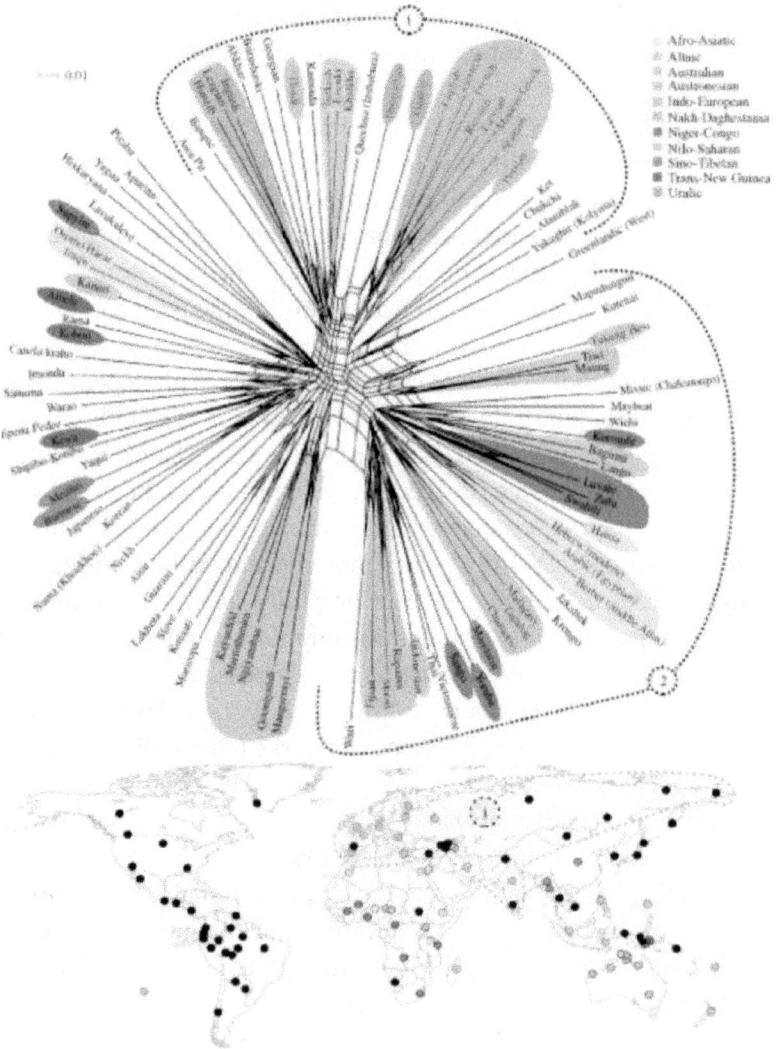

Figure 13: Greenhill et al. (2010: 2445)

some cases – Schmidt's most notably – we have seen the very utility of visual aids called fundamentally into question. The complicated overlay of mental images and concepts in this history suggests that there may be movement between these categories of metaphoric expression, accounting for both disciplinary consolidation and the open-endedness of linguistic practices. This emphasis on metaphor provides an interesting counterpoint to the recent material turn in Science and Technology Studies scholarship on practices of scientific representation. Highlighting the difficulties linguists have encountered in their efforts to comprehend the "all-at-once-ness" of language relationship in both time and space, I have suggested that canonical visualizations (whether presented in words or pictures) matter a great deal in pedagogy and practice. Phylogenetic modelling has offered new hope to those in pursuit of a "natural classification" insofar as it offers this kind of dual vision.

References

Archibald, J. David. 2014. *Aristotle's ladder, Darwin's tree: The evolution of visual metaphors for biological order.* New York: Columbia University Press.

Bertomeu-Sánchez, José-Ramon, Antonio García-Belmar & Bernadette Bensaude-Vincent. 2002. Looking for an order of things: Textbooks and chemical classifications in nineteenth century France. *Ambix* 49(3). 227–250.

Bigg, Charlotte. 2016. Diagrams. In Bernard Lightman (ed.), *A companion to the history of science,* 557–571. Malden, MA: Wiley, Blackwell.

Black, Paul. 1973. Multidimensional scaling applied to linguistic relationships. In Isidore Dyen & Guy Jucquois (eds.), *Lexicostatistics in genetic linguistics II: Proceedings of the Montreal conference,* 2–78. Leuven: Peeters.

Bloomfield, Leonard. 1933. *Language.* New York: Henry Holt.

Bloomfield, Leonard & Henry Hoijer. 1965. *Language history: From* Language *(1933 ed.).* New York: Holt, Rinehart & Winston.

Bonfante, Giuliano. 1931. I dialetti Indoeuropei. *Annali del R. Instituto Orientale di Napoli* 4. 69–185.

Boyd, Richard. 1979. Metaphor and theory change: What is "metaphor" a metaphor for? In Andrew Ortony (ed.), *Metaphor and thought,* 356–408. Cambridge: Cambridge University Press.

Bryant, David & Vincent Moulton. 2004. Neighbor-net: An agglomerative method for the construction of phylogenetic networks. *Molecular Biology and Evolution* 21(2). 255–265.

Judith Kaplan

Bynon, Theodora. 1977. *Historical linguistics.* Cambridge: Cambridge Textbooks in Linguistics.

Cameron, H. Don. 1987. The upside-down cladogram: Problems in manuscript affiliation. In Henry Hoenigswald & Linda Wiener (eds.), *Biological metaphor and cladistic classification: An interdisciplinary perspective*, 227–242. Philadelphia: University of Pennsylvania Press.

Čelakovský, František Ladislav. 1853. *Čtení o srovnávací mluvnici Slovanské na Universitě Pražské.* Prague: F. Řivnáče.

Coopmans, Catelijne, Janet Vertesi, Michael Lynch & Steve Woolgar. 2014. *Representation in scientific practice revisited.* Cambridge, MA: MIT Press.

Daston, Lorraine. 2008. On scientific observation. *Isis* 99(1). 97–110.

Daston, Lorraine. 2014. Beyond representation. In Catelijne Coopmans, Janet Vertesi, Michael Lynch & Steve Woolgar (eds.), *Representation in scientific practice revisited*, 319–322. Cambridge, MA: MIT Press.

Eichwald, Carl Eduard von. 1829. *Zoologia specialis quam expositis animalibus tum vivis, tum fossilibus potissimum rossiae in universum....* Vilnius: Josephus Zawadzki.

Gatschet, Albert S. & Lyle Campbell. 1973. Gatschet's classification of Mayan languages. *International Journal of American Linguistics* 39(4). 250–252.

Geisler, Hans & Johann-Mattis List. 2013. Do languages grow on trees? The tree metaphor in the history of linguistics. In Heiner Fangerau, Hans Geisler, Thorsten Halling & William Martin (eds.), *A companion to the history of science*, 111–124. Stuttgart: Franz Steiner.

Gray, Russell, Alexei Drummond & Simon J. Greenhill. 2009. Language phylogenies reveal expansion pulses and pauses in Pacific settlement. *Science* 323(5913). 479–483.

Greenhill, Simon J., Quentin D. Atkinson, Adam Meade & Russell D. Gray. 2010. The shape and tempo of language evolution. *Proceedings of the Royal Society B* 277. 2443–2450.

Haraway, Donna. 1991. *Simians, cyborgs, and women: The reinvention of nature.* New York: Routledge.

Harris, Zellig. 1951. *Methods in structural linguistics.* Chicago: Chicago University Press.

Hellström, Peter. 2012. Darwin and the tree of life: The roots of the evolutionary tree. *Archives of Natural History* 39(2). 234–252.

Hirt, Herman. 1905. *Die Indogermanen: Ihre Verbreitung, ihre Urheimat und ihre Kultur I.* Strassburg: Trübner.

Hockett, Charles. 1959 [1958]. *A course in modern linguistics.* New York: Macmillan.

Hoenigswald, Henry. 1950. Morpheme order diagrams. *SiL* 8. 79–81.

Hoenigswald, Henry. 1975. Schleicher's tree and its trunk. In Werner Abraham (ed.), *Ut videam: Contributions to an understanding of linguistics: For Pieter A. Verburg*, 157–160. Lisse & Holland: P. de Ridder.

Hoenigswald, Henry & Linda Wiener (eds.). 1987. *Biological metaphor and cladistic classification: An interdisciplinary perspective.* Philadelphia: University of Pennsylvania Press.

Hopwood, Nick. 2015. *Haeckel's embryos: Images, evolution, and fraud.* Chicago: Chicago University Press.

Hübschmann, J. Heinrich. 1876. Ueber Aussprache und Umschreibung des Altarmenischen. *Zeitschrift der Deutschen Morgenländischen Gesellschaft* 30. 53–73.

Hübschmann, J. Heinrich. 1967 [1875]. On the position of Armenian in the sphere of the Indo-European languages. In Winfred P. Lehmann (ed.), *A reader in nineteenth century historical Indo-European linguistics*, 164–189. Bloomington: Indiana University Press. Original: "Ueber die Stellung des Armenischen im Kreise der indogermanischen Sprachen", *Zeitschrift für vergleichende Sprachforschung auf dem Gebiete der indogermanischen Sprachen*, 23: 5-49.

Huson, Daniel & David Bryant. 2006. Application of phylogenetic networks in evolutionary studies. *Molecular Biological Evolution* 23(2). 354–367.

Huxley, Thomas H. 1880. Biology. In *Encyclopaedia Britannica. 9th edition*, vol. III, 679–696. New York: Scribner.

Johns, Adrian. 1998. *The nature of the book: Print and knowledge in the making.* Chicago: Chicago University Press.

Joseph, John E. 2017. The arbre-tree sign: Pictures and words in counterpoint in the *Cours de Linguistique Générale. Semiotica* 217. 147–171.

Koerner, E. F. Konrad. 1975. European structuralism: Early beginnings. In Thomas A. Sebeok (ed.), *Historiography of linguistics* (Current Trends in Linguistics 13), 717–827. The Hague: Mouton.

Koerner, E. F. Konrad. 1987. On Schleicher and trees. In Henry Hoenigswald & Linda Wiener (eds.), *Biological metaphor and cladistic classification: An interdisciplinary perspective*, 109–114. Philadelphia: University of Pennsylvania Press.

Kruskal, Joseph, Forrest Young & Judith Seery. 1973. *How to use kyst: A very flexible program to do multidimensional scaling and unfolding.* http://www.netlib.org/mds/kyst2a_manual.ps. Bell Laboratories Unpublished Manuscript.

Kuhn, Thomas S. 1962. *The structure of scientific revolutions.* Chicago: University of Chicago Press.

Kusukawa, Sachiko. 2016. Classics from this journal: Martin Rudwick's "The emergence of a visual language for geological science, 1760-1840", History of Science, xiv: 3, 1976, pp. 149-95. *History of Science* 54(1). 98–104.

Lakoff, George. 1987. Image metaphors. *Metaphor and Symbolic Activity* 2(3). 219–222.

Lakoff, George & Mark Johnson. 1980. Conceptual metaphor in everyday language. *The Journal of Philosophy* 77(8). 453–486.

Lopez, Philippe, Johann-Mattis List & Eric Bapteste. 2013. A preliminary case for exploratory networks in biology and linguistics: The phonetic network of Chinese words as a case study. In Heiner Fangerau, Hans Geisler, Thorsten Halling & William Martin (eds.), *Classification and evolution in biology, linguistics, and the history of science*, 181–196. Stuttgart: Franz Steiner.

Maher, John P. 1966. More on the history of the comparative method: The tradition of Darwinism in August Schleicher's work. *Anthropological Linguistics* 8(3). 1–11.

Meillet, Antoine. 1908. *Les dialectes indo-européens*. Paris: La Société de Linguistique de Paris.

Müller, F. Max. 1913 [1891]. *The science of language*. New York: Charles Scribner's Sons.

Myers, Natasha. 2014. Rendering machinic life. In Catelijne Coopmans, Janet Vertesi, Michael E. Lynch & Steve Woolgar (eds.), *Representation in scientific practice revisited*, 153–175. Cambridge, MA: MIT Press.

Myers, Natasha. 2015. *Rendering life molecular: Models, modelers, and excitable matter*. Durham: Duke Univerity Press.

Nyhart, Lynn. 2012. Wissenschaft and Kunde: The general and the special in modern science. *Osiris* 27(1). 250–275.

Pietsch, Theodore. 2012. *Trees of life: A visual history of evolution*. Baltimore: Johns Hopkins University Press.

Priestly, Tom. 1975. Schleicher, Čelakovský, and the family-tree diagram: A puzzle in the history of linguistics. *Historiographia Linguistica* 2. 299–333.

Pulgram, Ernst. 1953. Family tree, wave theory, and dialectology. *Orbis: Bulletin International de Documentation Linguistique* 2(1). 67–72.

Schleicher, August. 1848. *Sprachvergleichende Untersuchungen*. Bonn: H. B. Koenig.

Schleicher, August. 1853. Die ersten Spaltungen des indogermanischen Urvolkes. *Allgemeine Zeitung fuer Wissenschaft und Literatur* (August 1853). 786–787.

Schleicher, August. 1967 [1871]. Introduction to a *Compendium of the comparative grammar of the Indo-European, Sanskrit, Greek and Latin languages*. In Winfred

P. Lehmann (ed.), *A reader in nineteenth century historical Indo-European linguistics*, 87–96. Bloomington: Indiana University Press. Original: *Compendium der vergleichenden Grammatik der indogermanischen Sprachen*. Weimar: Böhlau.

Schmidt, Johannes. 1872. *Die Verwantschaftsverhältnisse der indogermanischen Sprachen*. Weimar: Böhlau.

Schmidt, Johannes. 1875. *Zur Geschichte des indogermanischen Vocalismus II*. Weimar: Böhlau.

Schmitt, Rüdiger. 1976. Einführung. In Rüdiger Schmitt (ed.), *Heinrich Hübschmann: kleine Schriften zum Armenischen*, ix–xiv. Hildesheim & New York: Georg Olms.

Schrader, Otto. 1890. *Prehistoric antiquities of the Aryan peoples: A manual of comparative philology and the earliest culture*. Trans. by F. B. Jevons. London: Charles Griffin.

Schuchardt, Hugo. 1928 [1870]. Über die Klassifikation der romanischen Mundarten: Probe-Vorlesung, gehalten zu Leipzig am 30. April 1870. In Leo Spitzer (ed.), *Hugo Schuchardt Brevier*, 166–188. Tübingen: Niemeyer.

Simon, Josep. 2016. Textbooks. In Bernard Lightman (ed.), *A companion to the history of science*, 400–413. Malden, MA: Wiley, Blackwell.

Southworth, Franklin. 1964. Family-tree diagrams in comparative linguistics. *Language* 40(4). 557–565.

Stevens, Hallam. 2013. *Life out of sequence: A data-driven history of bioinformatics*. Chicago: University of Chicago Press.

Wells, Rulon. 1987. The life and growth of language: Metaphors in biology and linguistics. In Henry Hoenigswald & Linda Wiener (eds.), *Biological metaphor and cladistic classification: An interdisciplinary perspective*, 39–80. Philadelphia: University of Pennsylvania Press.

Chapter 2

Alternating sounds and the formal franchise in phonology

James McElvenny

University of Edinburgh

A matter of some controversy in the intersecting worlds of late nineteenth-century linguistics and anthropology was the nature of "alternating sounds". This phenomenon is the apparent tendency, long assumed to be characteristic of "primitive" languages, to freely vary the pronunciation of words, without any discernible system. Franz Boas (1858–1942), rebutting received opinion in the American anthropological establishment, denied the existence of this phenomenon, arguing that it was an artefact of observation. Georg von der Gabelentz (1840–1893), on the other hand, embraced the phenomenon and fashioned it into a critique of the comparative method as it was practised in Germany.

Both Boas and Gabelentz and indeed also their opponents – were well versed in the Humboldtian tradition of language scholarship, in particular as developed and transmitted by H. Steinthal (1823–1899). Although the late nineteenth-century debates surrounding alternating sounds were informed by a number of sources, this chapter argues that Steinthal's writings served as a key point of reference and offered several motifs that were taken up by his scholarly successors. In addition, and most crucially, the chapter demonstrates that the positions at which the participants in these debates arrived were determined not so much by any simple technical disagreements but by underlying philosophical differences and sociological factors. This episode in the joint history of linguistics and anthropology is telling for what it reveals about the dominant mindset and temperament of these disciplines in relation to the formal analysis of the world's languages.

James McElvenny. 2019. Alternating sounds and the formal franchise in phonology. In James McElvenny (ed.), *Form and formalism in linguistics*, 35–58. Berlin: Language Science Press. DOI:10.5281/zenodo.2654351

James McElvenny

1 Introduction

Phonology is in many ways the promised land of formal conceptions of language. The apparent orderly transmutation of sounds over time stimulated the mechanical minds of historical-comparative linguists, ultimately inspiring the Neogrammarians to their postulation of exceptionless sound laws. The vanguard of linguistic formalism in subsequent generations continued to look to sound patterns – although now chiefly in their synchronic aspect – as the pristine embodiment of the self-contained systems they sought. In this way, the classical American structuralist grammar sets out from the firm ground of phonology and ascends to increasingly less regular linguistic levels.

But a question that remained controversial into the last decades of the nineteenth century was just how far the formal franchise in phonology should be extended. Do the sound systems of all languages of the world meet the standards of arbitrariness and regularity identified in the Indo-European languages? An apparent phenomenon prevalent in the "primitive" languages of the Americas, Africa and the South Seas suggested limits to law-governed language. European scholars and adventurers who tried to learn and transcribe the words of these languages were frequently frustrated by the way in which native informants would seemingly change the pronunciation of the same word from utterance to utterance. From the perspective of present-day phonological theory, this phenomenon would be considered variously a manifestation of free variation, allophonic variation and difficulty perceiving articulations markedly foreign to the recorder's own phonological system. Nineteenth-century scholars, by contrast, conceptualized this phenomenon in a number of different, competing ways. These differences in conceptualization led to terminological instability, but a common cover term, also adopted here, was "alternating sounds".

This chapter explores some responses from prominent language scholars in the mid- to late nineteenth century to the phenomenon of alternating sounds, and looks at what these responses reveal about the underlying philosophical commitments and sociological structure of the intersecting fields of anthropology and linguistics in this era. The investigation spans the intellectual worlds of America and Germany which, although closely intertwined, were organized around different disciplinary structures. The figures featured here who were active in America described themselves as anthropologists, for whom linguistic research was one of the "four fields" of American anthropology.[1] The corresponding German dis-

---

[1] The essays contained in Kuklick (2008) provide an excellent comparative overview of the history of anthropology in America and Europe, including their disciplinary structures.

cussion, on the other hand, took place largely within the discipline of linguistics, in which the study of "exotic" languages was a niche pursuit. The exception is the work of H. Steinthal (1823–1899), who is put forward in this chapter as an inspiration to – and therefore link between – both the German and American worlds. His *Völkerpsychologie*, developed with his collaborator M. Lazarus (1824–1903), strove to offer an all-encompassing scientific account of human culture, history and society.[2]

The starting point for this chapter, in §2, is the 1889 paper "On alternating sounds" by Franz Boas (1858–1942), a milestone marking the way to modern explanations of alternating sounds and modern views on the equality of all languages. Here Boas rebutted the received position of the American anthropological establishment, represented in particular by such luminaries as Daniel Garrison Brinton (1837–1899) and John Wesley Powell (1834–1902), which held that the alternating sounds observed in American languages were a manifestation of their alleged primitiveness. Boas argued, by contrast, that the alternating sounds were an illusion caused by the conflicts of incommensurable phonological systems in informant and ethnographer.

From a present-day perspective, this episode may seem like a simple case of science triumphing over naivety and prejudice. But arguments presented on both sides of the American debate could claim some degree of theoretical sophistication. Indeed, Brinton and Boas shared a key source of theoretical inspiration in the work of Steinthal, whose views were in turn anchored in the linguistic writings of Wilhelm von Humboldt (1767–1835). While phonological issues occupy at most a peripheral place in Steinthal's work, aspects of his linguistic and psychological theory would seem to have informed the later debate. §3 offers an account of the nuanced views advanced by Steinthal and their possible links to later arguments.

Despite its now canonical status, the American debate was not the only reconsideration of principles of phonological regularity around the turn of the nineteenth to the twentieth century. In Germany, Georg von der Gabelentz (1840–1893), also drawing on the Humboldtian tradition as transmitted by Steinthal, affirmed the existence of alternating sounds, in a turn that could be seen as prefiguring key features of later phonemic theory. Like Boas, Gabelentz fashioned his treatment of alternating sounds into a critique of the linguistic establishment. But unlike Boas, Gabelentz' goal was not to extend the formal franchise to all languages, but rather to redefine it and thereby challenge the comparative method

---

[2]For a detailed account of *Völkerpsychologie* from its beginnings with Steinthal and Lazarus to its later developments and ultimate fate, see Klautke (2013).

as it was practised at the time. §4 looks at Gabelentz' proposals for alternative methods in historical-comparative linguistics and their rather unfavourable reception.

Finally, §5 brings the American and German debates together to discuss what they reveal about the dominant mindset and temperament in the intersecting fields of linguistics and anthropology in relation to questions of the nature and correct treatment of linguistic form.

2 Alternating sounds in America

Boas' (1889) "On alternating sounds" occupies a prominent place in the standard disciplinary narrative of linguistic anthropology as a text that helped to establish the scientific foundations of the field. According to this story, Boas overcame contemporary evolutionary prejudice by demonstrating that an alleged characteristic of "primitive" languages was in fact nothing more than an artefact introduced by insufficiently trained observers.[3] Alternating sounds, in various guises, were a recurring motif in the description of exotic languages throughout the nineteenth century, but the two key figures against whom Boas developed his position were Brinton and Powell, the leading anthropologists of the previous generation.[4]

In the year before Boas' seminal article appeared, Brinton reaffirmed several tropes about "primitive" languages in an 1888 address to the American Philosophical Society, "The Language of Palæolithic Man", which in an 1890 volume of his collected papers became "The earliest form of human speech, as revealed by American tongues" (Brinton 1890 [1888]). As the titles suggest, Brinton sought insights into the nature of the earliest stages of human language evolution through an examination of the supposedly characteristic features of American languages. While much of Brinton's paper focuses on the lexical and grammatical properties of these languages, it begins with a discussion of their phonological features.

Primitive speech, in Brinton's assessment, has not yet attained the levels of arbitrariness and fixedness that characterize the more developed languages: in European languages individual sounds carry no sense, words have fixed sound

---

[3]"Evolutionary prejudice" was the term later used by Boas' student Edward Sapir (1884–1939) to describe the assumption that the world's languages can be categorized according to their putative level of grammatical development (see Sapir 1921: 130–132).

[4]On the relationship between Boas, Brinton and Powell in the context of late nineteenth-century American anthropology, see Darnell (1988) and Darnell (1998). See also Laplantine's (2018) preface to her translation of Boas' (1911) *Handbook of American Indian Languages* for a succinct summary of his life and work in context.

forms, and the articulated word alone is enough to convey its meaning. American languages, by contrast, frequently attach meaning to individual phonetic segments (Brinton 1890 [1888]: 394), word meaning is often modified by such devices as "[t]one, accent, stress, vocal inflection, quantity and pause" (Brinton 1890 [1888]: 399) that are not reducible to graphic writing, and sounds in words can vary freely: "In spite of the significance attached to the phonetic elements, they are, in many American languages, singularly vague and fluctuating" (Brinton 1890 [1888]: 397). His concluding observation is that "[t]he laws of the conversion of sounds of the one organ into those of another have not yet been discovered; but the above examples, which are by no means isolated ones, serve to admonish us that the phonetic elements of primitive speech probably had no fixedness" (Brinton 1890 [1888]: 398–399).

Under the name of "synthetic sounds", this same phenomenon of apparent fluctuating phonology in American languages found a place in Powell's (1880 [1877]) *Introduction to the Study of Indian Languages.* Given Powell's influential position as director of the Bureau of American Ethnology, which was founded on his initiative in 1879, the *Introduction* achieved widespread use in the recording of American languages, not only in projects officially sponsored by the Bureau, but also in the efforts of other researchers and amateurs, including Boas and his students (see Darnell 1998: 50–51).

Powell was very conscious of the difficulties associated with capturing the phonology of American languages. His commitment to scientific rigour led him to commission the noted Sanskrit scholar and general linguist William Dwight Whitney (1827–1894) to devise a standardized alphabet for recording American languages. Despite Powell's efforts to encourage its use, the alphabet was generally considered inadequate and impractical by many of those who worked for the Bureau. Whitney himself felt no great attachment to the alphabet, regarding its design and implementation not as a theoretical task but merely a matter of expedience (see Darnell 1998: 50–51). For Powell, however, the alphabet was a foundational element of language description: his *Introduction* opens with a sophisticated discussion of articulatory phonetics and the principles of accurate transcription, which observes a number of phonological peculiarities of American languages still recognized today, such as ejective consonants ("interrupted sounds") (Powell 1880 [1877]: 1–16).

"Synthetic sounds" appear in this discussion as another characteristic of American phonologies. Powell (1880 [1877]: 12) speaks of the "indefinite character of some of the sounds of a[n American Indian] language", although this is not due to the chaotic variation imagined by Brinton but rather because the sounds are "made by the organs of speech in positions and with movement comprehending in part at least the positions and movement used in making the several sounds to which they seem to be allied". That is, Powell believes these "synthetic" sounds are insufficiently "differentiated" – they are produced by articulating several simple sounds at once. Through historical sound change, such synthetic sounds have been simplified and disappeared from the European languages, but this is a process yet to take place in the American languages. In their present undifferentiated state, these sounds "will be heard by the student now as one, now as another sound, even from the same speaker." There is, however, a trace of humility in Powell's approach to the American languages, an admission that science may not yet have fully grasped the principles underlying this phenomenon: "When the phonology of our Indiàn tongues is thoroughly understood, much light will be thrown upon the whole science of phonology [...]" (Powell 1880 [1877]: 13).

In response to views of the kind put forward by Brinton and Powell, Boas argued that such sounds are not a peculiarity of primitive languages at all, but rather the result of perceptual error on the part of the language researcher. All languages, European and American alike, make use of a fixed and finite repertoire of the total range of sounds that can be produced by the human articulatory organs. When an observer encounters a sound in a foreign language that is not present in their native repertoire, they will "apperceive" it as a similar sound that is in their repertoire. A term with a long history and a diverse range of uses, "apperceive" became in the early nineteenth century part of the technical apparatus of Johann Friedrich Herbart's (1776–1841) associational psychology, from where it was taken up into the *Völkerpsychologie* of Steinthal and Lazarus, and later into the *Bewusstseinspsychologie* of Wilhelm Wundt (1832–1920).[5] Boas' invocation of "apperception" is too fleeting and off-hand to align him with any specific school of psychology at the time, but his usage attests to a familiarity with contemporary psychological jargon and a desire to dress his own work in the latest technical garb.

According to Boas, the mapping from foreign to native sound that results through the process of apperception may vary from occasion to occasion, creating the illusion of alternating sounds. The presence of this perceptual filter on the part of the observer is demonstrated by the fact that "the nationality even of well-trained observers may be readily recognized" in the transcriptions they make of foreign sounds (Boas 1889: 51). Boas sums up his argument with the following words:

---

[5]For a recent survey of approaches to what can retrospectively be called "psycholinguistics" in this period, including the work of Lazarus, Steinthal and Wundt, see Levelt (2013).

I think, from this evidence, it is clear that all such misspellings are due to a wrong apperception, which is due to the phonetic system of our native language. For this reason I maintain that there is no such phenomenon as synthetic or alternating sounds, and that their occurrence is in no way a sign of primitiveness of the speech in which they are said to occur; that alternating sounds are in reality alternating apperceptions of one and the same sound. A thorough study of all alleged alternating sounds or synthetic sounds will show that their existence may be explained by alternating apperceptions. (Boas 1889: 52)

Boas was no doubt correct to impugn the perception of his colleagues in many cases where they accused American languages of phonetic fluctuation. But it must be acknowledged that the potential for cross-linguistic phonological interference was already well recognized in the literature of the time. Powell (1880 [1877]: 2) noted this difficulty in his own guide to transcription:

[T]here are probably sounds in each [Indian language of North America] which do not appear in the English or any other civilized tongue; [...] and further, [...] there are perhaps sounds in each of such a character, or made with such uncertainty that the ear primarily trained to distinguish English speech is unable to clearly determine what these sounds are, even after many years of effort. (Powell 1880 [1877]: 2)

As is shown in the following sections, this awareness of cross-linguistic interference is clear in many other contemporary and antecedent sources, where it co-existed with a range of different attitudes towards alternating sounds. A scholar's stance in relation to these questions was therefore shaped to a very large degree by beliefs and commitments beyond the immediate language data.

A key motivation for Boas was of course to subvert the then current discourse of primitive languages and language evolution. But this was not his only aim, and indeed this subversion was at least in part beholden to other goals. Although he enjoyed mostly respectful and collegial relations with both Brinton and Powell, Boas was always engaged in a project to proclaim his superior scientific expertise and secure institutional support for his coterie of students and adherents. The chief and most valid source of data in Boasian anthropology were the descriptions made and texts recorded by the scientifically trained observer in a fieldwork situation. By contrast, Brinton, the doyen of the previous generation, relied mainly on the critical philological analysis of written documents that had been collected and compiled by others (see Darnell 1988: 21–24). By diminishing existing written documentation, Boas' critique undermined the legitimacy of the mode of research employed by Brinton and boosted his own fieldwork-oriented approach.

Even among confirmed fieldworkers, Boas' critique helped to assert the exclusive expertise of his own school. In later years, Boas developed a reputation for his domineering role in the world of Americanist anthropology, freely blocking the work of researchers who did not meet his frequently quite arbitrary standards (see Darnell 1998). Pointing out the technical inadequacies of his predecessors, as in the case of alternating sounds, served this end well. In his 1911 *Handbook of American Indian Languages*, which was explicitly intended to supersede Powell's (1880 [1877]) *Introduction*, Boas' doctrine of the conditioned apperception of foreign sounds is incorporated as part of the propaedeutic guide to the correct recording of American languages, as a simple and uncontroversial methodological principle (see Boas 1911: 16–18).

That assertions of expertise are a decisive factor in Boas' campaign is demonstrated by his enduring commitment to the possibility of objective observation in language documentation. While previous transcribers of American languages may have been afflicted with a phonological filter, the goal of the Boasian anthropologist must be to eliminate this interference altogether. Even after the importation and elaboration of phonemic theory in America, Boas maintained a preference for fine-grained phonetic transcription. It was not enough for the observer to simply enter the foreign phonological system; they had to step outside phonology and record the given phonetic datum as accurately as possible.[6] Boas' zeal extended to correcting written texts from one of his native speaker informants, which were essentially phonemic in nature, to include as much phonetic detail as possible (see Anderson 1985: 204–208). Even the phonemic testimony of the native speaker did not pass Boasian muster.[7]

---

[6] Another perspective from which Boas' position should perhaps be explored is that of contemporary debates on the "personal equation" in recording data, which were prominent across the natural sciences (see Schaffer 1988) and also played a role in attitudes to fieldwork in anthropology (see Kuklick 2011). I thank Judith Kaplan for drawing my attention to these debates.

[7] A further piece of circumstantial evidence is perhaps Boas' work on a revised standard alphabet for American languages. After Powell's death in 1902, Boas was asked by William John McGee (1853–1912), Powell's successor at the Bureau of American Ethnology, to form a committee to update the Bureau's alphabet. The resulting system, published 1916, clearly contains many compromises between various conflicting constraints, but the overall Boasian impulse towards greater phonetic detail and specialist exclusivity is quite apparent (see Darnell 1998: 195–197).

3 Steinthal and the Humboldtian tradition

The American debate on alternating sounds was shaped by a number of influences: the three figures mentioned in the previous section – Brinton, Powell and Boas – all had broad backgrounds spanning the natural sciences and humanities that informed their attitudes and approaches (see Darnell 1998). But a central point of reference – in particular for Brinton and Boas – was the Humboldtian tradition of linguistic scholarship as it was interpreted and propagated by Steinthal. Boas had met Steinthal personally in Berlin and freely acknowledged Steinthal's influence on his linguistic research. Brinton was the leading Humboldt scholar in America and frequently cited Steinthal (see Bunzl 1996: 63–69; Trautmann-Waller 2006: 289–292). Although the questions of phonology and language documentation that lay at the heart of the American debate on alternating sounds are addressed only at the periphery of Steinthal's work, we see in his texts several threads unpicked and woven into the later accounts.

Steinthal's great achievement in linguistics was to construct a monolithic theoretical edifice dealing with issues ranging from the mental processes underlying individual language use to language evolution and typology, and to attempt an empirical demonstration of these principles through detailed investigations into the languages of the world. Through his collaboration with Lazarus from the 1850s onwards, Steinthal's linguistics became a central component of the broader project of *Völkerpsychologie*.[8]

Following Humboldt, Steinthal imagined an "idea of language" (*Sprachidee*), an ideal form towards which linguistic expression strives. The evolution of language passes through three stages on the way to the full realization of this ideal; these stages are recapitulated in child language acquisition and can be discerned in the contours of "primitive" languages (cf. Bumann 1965: 81–93). The first stage consists in self-awareness, the psychological attainment that distinguishes humans from animals. Unlike animals, humans can represent, share and understand their "intuitions" (*Anschauungen*), which they "apperceive" (*appercieren*) in their consciousness. Here Steinthal invokes the core notion of "apperception" from Herbartian associational psychology; this is the same term that Boas would later use in generic form (see §2 above).

At the first stage language is made up of nothing more than "reflex sounds" (*Reflexlaute*), which merely represent and communicate intuitions in an unanalysed

---

[8]Trautmann-Waller (2006) is a comprehensive intellectual biography of Steinthal, which examines his linguistic work and *Völkerpsychologie* in depth. For studies of Steinthal's linguistics, see Bumann (1965) and Ringmacher (1996).

way. These sounds are brought forth through unreflected action and are solely mimetic in character. The further development of language occurs as speakers become increasingly aware of the thoughts they entertain in consciousness and begin to analyse them. At the second stage, language progresses beyond reflex sounds to a proper conscious analysis of thoughts. It is at this point that sentence structure develops, with a distinction between subject and predicate and individual words that can be abstracted from the sentence as a whole:

> It is therefore already at the point where language first appears in its true quality, where it achieves its full intellectual character, that it breaks through onomatopoeia. And *words in their true conception develop only with the development of the sentence form; that is, simultaneously with the opposition of subject and predicate*, which soon establishes itself as the difference in the naming of things and expressions for circumstances and changes. The logical character of words seems to be decisively hostile to their onomatopoeic origin. (Steinthal 1881 [1871]: 424–425)[9]

At the third stage of evolution, language continues its ascent from its mimetic origins: the etymological bond between words and their meanings fades from consciousness and the connection between them becomes truly arbitrary.

For Steinthal, the crucial moment in language evolution is the second stage, as this is the point at which "inner linguistic form" (*innere Sprachform*) emerges (Steinthal 1881 [1871]: 425–426). "Inner linguistic form" is a term that first appears in Humboldt's (1998 [1836]) introduction to his work on the Kawi language of Java. The term is therefore generally associated with Humboldt, even though, as Borsche (1989) definitively demonstrated, its elaboration into a theoretical construct is the later work of Steinthal. In Steinthal's hands, inner form became a wide-ranging concept covering all aspects of the immanent structure of languages. Like "apperception", "inner form" grew in the second half of the nineteenth century into a favourite but rather indefinite term in linguistic and philosophical scholarship. Despite the explosion of senses attached to the term in this period, its ultimate origin in Humboldt's essay and its deep association

---

[9]Original: "Also gerade schon da, wo die Sprache zuerst in ihrer wahren Eigentümlichkeit auftritt, wo sie ihren vollen intellectuellen Charakter gewinnt, durchbricht sie die Onomatopoie; und *das Wort in seinem wahren Begriff entsteht erst mit der Satzform, also zugleich mit dem Gegensatze von Subjekt und Prädikat*, der sich bald zu dem Unterschiede der Benennung von Dingen und der Ausdrücke für Zustände und Veränderungen festsetzt. Der logische Charakter des Wortes scheint dem onomatopoetischen Ursprunge desselben entschieden feindlich zu sein." Italics in this quotation renders *Sperrung* in the original.

with Steinthal's work remained foremost in the minds of those who employed it. Both Brinton and Boas keenly spoke this idiom and acknowledged the tradition with which it was aligned: Brinton constantly advocated for attention to the inner form of languages and Boas (1911: 81) set capturing the unique inner form of each language as the goal of the language sketches in his *Handbook* (cf. Darnell 1988: 98–105).

Steinthal's typological efforts were aimed at assessing how far towards the "idea of language" the inner form had progressed in different languages and at identifying the grammatical means – such as morphological or syntactic structures – in which it manifests itself. His 1860 *Charakteristik der hauptsächlichsten Typen des Sprachbaues* provided a survey and classification of the world's languages, in which the primary division is between those language with properly developed inner form (*Formsprachen*) and those without (*formlose Sprachen*). This work was followed by his 1867 *Mande-Neger-Sprachen*, which subjected several Mande languages of Africa – Mandingo, Bambara, Soso and Vai – to a detailed examination that revealed alleged developmental deficiencies in all aspects of their inner forms. This examination is based on a philological analysis of existing written sources, similar to the preferred research practice of Brinton. The analysis proceeds from both a "phonetic" (*phonetisch*) perspective, which looks at the grammatical apparatus of the languages, and a "psychological" (*psychologisch*) perspective, which investigates how expressions are formed.[10]

In his "phonetic" examination of the Mande languages, Steinthal found no way to distinguish individual words from the sentences in which they appear: there are allegedly no phonological processes observed to operate only at the word level distinct from the sentence as a whole. In their grammars, the languages supposedly rely on mechanisms that are not truly arbitrary, such as the "interjectional" process of reduplication, used for a variety of purposes in the languages. The grammatical affixes and particles that can be identified in the languages all seem to have transparent etymologies that link them to "material" words, which keep them bound to their mimetic origins.

From the "psychological" perspective, the Mande languages did not fare any better. Steinthal's assessment of how various meanings are rendered using the lexical and grammatical means available in the languages reveals that the Herbartian processes of "isolation" (*Isolirung*) and "condensation" (*Verdichtung*) of "representations" (*Vorstellungen*) in the minds of speakers are not carried out properly. The inevitable conclusion for Steinthal (1867: 255) is that the speakers of

---

[10]For a discussion of the historical background to this dual-perspective approach to language description, see McElvenny (2017: 2–6).

Mande languages have not completely raised their "intuitions" to the level of "representations": "in the consciousness of the Mande negro the concrete intuition with its material relations is still dominant, and its conversion into representations is not carried out completely".[11]

Up to this point, Brinton's account of the "primitive" phonological features of American languages accords well with Steinthal's story of language evolution. The alleged lack of arbitrariness and fixedness Brinton identified in the sounds of American languages are features that could be expected of languages at Steinthal's first stage of evolution. Steinthal in fact considered the possibility that a lack of arbitrariness in the earliest languages could lead to greater variability, since the sounds produced by reflex are bound to the mental moment and subject to all of its modifications:

> We may think that language, as long as it is still the immediate creation of the excited soul, shares in the fluctuations and inequalities of these excitations. So just as the representation, even though its content is the same, is not always the same in its psychological behaviour – e.g. not always as lively and energetic to the same degree, vivid, strongly concentrated – the word, as the reflex of this representation, is not always the same. The energy of thinking expresses itself most immediately in intonation, then also in the sharpness of articulation, i.e. the clearness and definiteness of the sound. And both together most certainly influence the quality or even the content of the sound, the way in which it is articulated. (Steinthal 1867: 3–4)[12]

But such questions remained hypothetical for Steinthal. According to Steinthal (1867: 3–4), the "uncivilized peoples" (*culturlose Völker*) living today are not the *Natur-Völker* of the earlier stages of human evolution. He accepted a greater degree of variation in the sounds of the languages of "uncivilized peoples" because

---

[11] Original: "im Bewußtsein des Mande-Negers ist die concrete Anschauung mit ihren materiellen Verhältnissen noch vorwiegend, und ihre Umsetzung in Vorstellungen ist unvollständig vollzogen."

[12] Original: "Wir dürfen uns denken, daß die Sprache, so lange sie noch die unmittelbare Schöpfung der erregten Seele ist, auch an den Schwankungen und Ungleichheiten dieser Erregungen Theil hat. Wie also die, obschon ihrem Inhalte nach gleiche und selbe, Vorstellung doch in ihrem psychologischen Verhalten nicht immer gleich ist, z. B. nicht immer gleich lebendig und energisch, gleich anschaulich, gleich kräftig concentrirt: so lautet auch das Wort, als der Reflex dieser Vorstellung, nicht immer gleich. Die Energie des Denkens drückt sich am unmittelbarsten in der Weise der Betonung aus, dann auch in der Schärfe der Articulation, d. h. der Klarheit und Bestimmtheit des Lautes; und beides zusammen beeinflußt sicherlich die Qualität oder den Inhalt selbst des Lautes, die Weise seiner Articulation."

these languages lacked the stabilizing and standardizing influence of an orthography, but even before the invention of writing, human language will "have established itself in the consciousness" and "its word forms [will] have crystalized in definite shape" ([...] *hat sich die Sprache im Bewußtsein gefestigt, sind ihre Wortformen in bestimmter Gestalt krystallisirt*; Steinthal 1867: 4–5).

In Steinthal's estimation, the Mande languages find themselves in this situation: they stand uneasily on the threshold to the second stage of evolution, but their apparent phonetic inconstancy in comparison with European languages is not due to enduring mimetic reflexes but simply anarchy arising from the absence of a regulating instance. Steinthal (1867: 257–266) discounts the fact that the Vai do indeed possess a native writing system, since it is an imitation of European scripts fashioned without proper understanding of those scripts' underlying principles. The result is a massive syllabary – of over 200 characters – lacking system and internal order, which is chiefly used by distinguished members of the community to write books containing "tales from the life of their authors, sayings, observations and fables – without any unity" (Steinthal 1867: 260).[13] While the Vai may have a script, they do not have an orthography: they simply transcribe whatever pronunciation occurs to them as they write (Steinthal 1867: 264–266), and this can vary even within the same text.[14]

The perceptual problems to which Boas (1889) attributed alternating sounds in American languages were acknowledged by Steinthal in the case of the Mande languages. Steinthal (1867) critiqued the transcriptions found in all of his sources, commenting, among other observations, that the influence of the transcriber's native phonology and writing habits had to be taken into consideration. On his English sources, he remarked:

> Since we frequently have to rely on English works, the influence of the English ear and English orthography must be taken into account. However, although this influence may be responsible for some things, it is hardly responsible for everything. The same sources offer at times, both consciously and unconsciously, double forms, e.g. *bombong* and *bambang*, "hard" [...].

---

[13] Original: "Der Inhalt dieser Bücher besteht in der Erzählung von Ereignissen aus dem Leben ihrer Verfasser, in Sittensprüchen, Betrachtungen und Fabeln – ohne alle Einheit."

[14] Steinthal (1852) presented an account of the development of writing from ideographic systems to alphabets. Like his language typology, this represented an evolutionary scheme in which language users became progressively more aware of the structure of their languages. The Vai syllabary has reached the upper echelons of a pure phonetic script – i.e. a script without ideographic elements – but has not reached the highest point of a full alphabetic script (Steinthal 1867: 262–264). The place of the Vai script in this hierarchy does not bear directly on the question of its consistency.

James McElvenny

The most frequent alternation is perhaps that between *i* and *e*. (Steinthal 1867: 9)[15]

While phonology as such was never among Steinthal's core concerns, in his empirically oriented researches he was inevitably confronted with the practical difficulties that arise in reducing to writing the sounds of exotic languages with no native orthographic tradition. The dangers he identified in written materials produced by European observers were precisely those that Boas would later turn into the fatal failures of perception on the part of his predecessors. On the other hand, the corroboration Brinton provided for existing accounts of phonetic fluctuation in American languages could in principle be licensed by Steinthal's scheme of language evolution, although Steinthal explicitly denied that any language spoken today would still find itself at this most elementary stage. Steinthal accepted greater degrees of variation in the languages of "uncivilized peoples", but only because they lacked a standard imposed by authority.

4 Phonetic latitude and sound laws

Around the same time that Boas launched his attack against alternating sounds – but independently of the American debate – Georg von der Gabelentz marshalled related phonetic phenomena to mount a critique of the linguistic establishment in Germany. His opponents were the Neogrammarians, whose work was built upon an insistence on the exceptionless nature of sound change, and Gabelentz embraced the prospect of relative regularity in languages as a means to undermining this fundamental Neogrammarian tenet. As in the American context, a key theoretical reference in Germany – in particular for Gabelentz – was the work of Steinthal.

In his magnum opus, *Die Sprachwissenschaft*, Gabelentz (2016 [1891]: 341–384) undertakes an extensive investigation into contemporary linguistic typology that is essentially organized around the principles espoused by Steinthal.[16] Gabelentz rejected the strong distinction between "formal" and "material" elements in language hypothesized by Steinthal and used by him to demonstrate the alleged infe-

---

[15]Original: "Da wir mehrfach auf englische Arbeiten angewiesen sind, so darf hierbei der Einfluß des englischen Ohrs und der englischen Orthographie nicht unberücksichtigt bleiben. Indessen, er mag manches verschulden, schwerlich alles. Dieselben Quellen stellen zuweilen unbewußt und bewußt doppelte Formen auf; z. B. *bombong* und *bambang*, hart [...]. Am meisten vielleicht wechseln *i* und *e* mit einander."

[16]Gabelentz (1889) had already presented key parts of this section of his book in an address to the Saxon Academy of Sciences. An English translation can be found in McElvenny (2019).

48

rior mental development of speakers of the Mande and other languages. Instead, argued Gabelentz (2016 [1891]: 380–384), linguistic form is the product of an aesthetic drive to achieve subjective self-expression.[17] In his view, all shaping of linguistic expression, regardless of how transparently its origin shows through, is formal in nature (see McElvenny 2016). Gabelentz (2016 [1891]: 406–408) accepted, however, that in the most primitive stages linguistic forms would have been created spontaneously and freely, and only over time become constrained and fixed through force of collective habit.

Given the dominance of historical-comparative grammar in the disciplinary linguistics of his day, Gabelentz dedicates an entire "book", or primary section, of his *Sprachwissenschaft* to this approach to language study. He finds that the principle of gradual fixing of the linguistic system applies also on the phonetic plane, and uses this principle both to critique the supposed exceptionless nature of sound change as promulgated by the Neogrammarians and as a means to explain how sound change can occur at all. "Fluctuating articulations" (*schwankende Articulationen*), according to Gabelentz (2016 [1891]: 196), are a very real part of languages, and indeed they are the force driving sound change in the first place. If, as the Neogrammarians argued, sound change proceeded according to inviolable rules then everyone would always speak the same way. For sound change to occur, one speaker has to innovate a new pronunciation and then it has to spread to the rest of the speaker community. Gabelentz (2016 [1891]: 196–197) is very clear that he means not only variation in pronunciation between speakers, but also variation in the same speaker over the course of their lives and even from utterance to utterance.

The way in which Gabelentz describes the range of variation that each language allows in fact seems to evince an inchoate concept of the phoneme as an ideal sound which may have multiple realizations:

> But languages, even the smallest dialects, distinguish only a certain number of sounds, which are related to individual phonetic phenomena like species to individuals, like circles to points; a language draws the boundaries more broadly or narrowly, but it always tolerates a certain degree of latitude. (Gabelentz 2016 [1891]: 35).[18]

---

[17]Jean-Michel Fortis, in Chapter 3 of this volume, examines similar aesthetic ideas in the work of Edward Sapir, and their possible connection to Gabelentz' work.

[18]Original: "Die Sprache aber, und wäre es die kleinste Mundart, unterscheidet nur eine bestimmte Anzahl von Lauten, die sich zu den lautlichen Einzelerscheinungen verhalten wie Arten zu Individuen, wie Kreise zu Punkten; sie zieht die Grenzen weiter oder enger, immer aber duldet sie einen gewissen Spielraum."

The "degree of latitude" allowed may vary from language to language, according to Gabelentz (2016 [1891]: 197–198), and this greater or lesser latitude provides the theoretical basis for countenancing the possibility of alternating sounds of a more extreme kind outside the familiar European languages.

A similar recognition of variation within limits is also a feature of Boas' (1911) account of alternating sounds in the officially codified version of the *Handbook*. Here Boas admits variations in the realization of sounds in languages, but crucially he denies that the range or latitude of variation can vary from language to language: the American languages admit neither more nor less variation in their sounds than any other languages, and certainly no more than European languages. Taking the example of a sound in Pawnee, Boas (1911: 17) insists:

> Thus the Pawnee language contains a sound which may be heard more or less distinctly sometimes as an *l*, sometimes an *r*, sometimes as *n*, and again as *d*, which, however, without any doubt, is throughout the same sound, although modified to a certain extent by its position in the word and by surrounding sounds. [...] This peculiar sound is, of course, entirely foreign to our phonetic system; but its variations are not greater than those of the English *r* in various combinations, as in *broth, mother, where.* (Boas 1911: 17)

Gabelentz' theoretically grounded belief in varying degrees of latitude in pronunciation leads him, in contrast to Boas, to accept and repeat several well-known cases of alternating sounds from the corners of the world: Gabelentz (2016 [1891]: 202–204) offers examples from Samoan, Malay languages, Australian languages and of course various American languages. Gabelentz is willing to trust the data on alternating sounds delivered by scholars in the field, insisting that they are fully qualified observers who through extended immersion in the foreign language have had the opportunity to overcome the interference of their native phonology. Indeed, it is because they have become so accustomed to the phonological systems of the languages they record that they have developed the feeling for the languages that allows them to perceive the subtle alternating articulations:

> We could raise the following objection: most of our informants were not schooled in the scientific observation of sounds; they judge the foreign sounds according to their native language, and intermediate grades between these sounds seem at one moment to tend to one side and in another moment to another side. We may retort that at least some of these men

have lived long enough among the aborigines that their ear has become as accustomed to the foreign language as it was previously to their native language. It is to this, or rather to their multilingual schooling, that they owe precisely this fine ability to hear that allows them to perceive those uncertain, fluctuating articulations. (Gabelentz 2016 [1891]: 204–205)[19]

In an inversion of the assignment of expertise effected by Boas, Gabelentz endorses the data and uses them to undermine the theoretical edifice of the Neogrammarians. Rather than refining sound laws to explain away exceptions, Gabelentz (2016 [1891]: 198) advocated statistical surveys that would embrace all variants observed, the deviants as well as the well-behaved regular forms. Gabelentz' model for this endeavour was perhaps the statistical analyses undertaken by William Dwight Whitney (1827–1894) of variant forms throughout the history of Sanskrit and in modern English dialects (Whitney 1874; Whitney 1896 [1875-1878]; cf. Silverstein 1971: vix-xx, xxii-xxiii).[20] Wilhelm Wundt similarly suggested that a statistical approach to the study of sound change may prove more fruitful than the absolutism of the Neogrammarians (see Formigari 2018).

Gabelentz' first steps towards applying a statistical method were taken in an 1893 address to the Berlin Academy of Sciences in which he tried to prove a genealogical relationship between the Basque and Berber languages.[21] As Gabelentz (1893: 593–594) himself noted, the hypothesis that the Basques of southern Europe, whose language could not be aligned with any known family, were in some way related to the "Hamites" of North Africa was not a novel idea. That no linguistic proof of this relationship had yet been given, he contended, was due to the inflexibility of the comparative method as it was practised at the time. The comparative method needed to be ramified to accommodate the radical mutability of linguistic form that had been discovered in regions beyond the familiar Indo-European context, as in Indo-Chinese and Melanesian sources:

---

[19]Original: "Folgenden Einwand könnte man erheben: Die meisten Gewährsmänner waren nicht zu wissenschaftlicher Lautbeobachtung geschult; sie beurtheilten die fremden Laute nach denen ihrer Muttersprache, und Zwischenstufen zwischen diesen schienen ihnen bald nach der einen, bald nach der anderen Seite zu neigen. Darauf ist zu entgegnen, dass mindestens ein Theil jener Männer lange genug unter den Eingeborenen gelebt, um ihr Ohr an die fremde Sprache so zu gewöhnen, wie es vordem an die Muttersprache gewöhnt gewesen. Dieser, oder richtiger ihrer mehrsprachigen Schulung, verdankten sie eben das feinere Gehör, das sie jene unsicheren, schwankenden Articulationen empfinden liess."

[20]Gabelentz (1894b) also later proposed using a statistical approach for the typological study of languages. McElvenny (2018) offers an English translation of this text.

[21]For a comprehensive account of this episode, including Gabelentz' initial address, the subsequent book-length publication (Gabelentz 1894a), and the reaction of Gabelentz' colleagues, see Hurch & Purgay (2019).

The belief in the constancy of the outer and inner linguistic form is among the achievements to which our science clings most tenaciously, and the facts that could shake this belief are for their part newly acquired and poorly known, since they are in the territory of Indo-Chinese and Melanesian. (Gabelentz 1893: 594)[22]

Looking across Basque dialects, Gabelentz (1893) postulated extremely irregular sound correspondences between apparently cognate words, leading him to the conclusion that "they offer a picture of phonetic wildness which, as far as I know, must be one of a kind in the world of languages" (*sie geben ein Bild lautlicher Verwilderung, das meines Wissens in der Sprachenwelt kaum Seinesgleichen hat*; Gabelentz 1893: 596). He found a similar situation in the Berber languages. On this basis, Gabelentz (1893: 604) assumed the existence of a "prehistoric period of the most uncertain articulation" (*vorgeschichtlichen Periode der unsichersten Articulation*) in these languages, "where the phonetic images appeared before the soul only in vague outlines, as if they were drawn with a mop or paint-roller" (*wo die Lautbilder der Seele nur in vagen Umrissen vorgeschwebt haben, als wären sie mit dem Wischer gezeichnet oder mit dem Vertreiberpinsel gemalt*). To bring order into this chaos, Gabelentz employed his statistical method, tabulating the frequencies of putative correspondences across the Basque dialects, the Berber languages and between these two groups.

The extraordinarily large latitude in pronunciation of the kind attributed to Basque and Berber is, Gabelentz (1893: 606) argued, characteristic of languages "at a lower level of culture" (*auf niederer Culturstufe*). At this cultural level, articulated forms are only rejected when they cannot be understood. This lack of constraint on variation leaves linguistic forms subject to the temperamental and corporeal contingencies of the moment, as in Steinthal's conception of the first stage of language evolution. Distant analogues of such cases can even be observed in Indo-European languages, claimed Gabelentz, offering the example of an uneducated Saxon from Germany (the same example with a more moderate moral occurs also in Gabelentz 2016 [1891]: 398):

In this way a strange thing can happen, that a very indefinite sound image appears before the soul, and yet the mouth produces a very clearly articu-

---

[22]Original: "Der Glaube an die Beständigkeit der äusseren und inneren Sprachform gehört zu den Errungschaften, an denen unsere Wissenschaft am zähesten festhält, und die Thatsachen, die ihn erschüttern könnten, sind ihrerseits neuer Erwerb und wenig bekannt, da sie auf indochinesischem und melanesischem Gebiete liegen."

lated sound, although not always the same one, but rather at one moment this one and then at another that one, depending on chance and mood. [...] I can offer an example of an at least distant analogue of this from our own languages. The Saxon, who does not distinguish between *d* and *t*, between *i* and *ü*, *e* and *ö*, *ei* and *eu*, *äu*, can in the heat of the moment pronounce the *d* as *t* and – when he is talking about deep, dark, terrible things – turn all *i*, *e* and *ei* into *ü*, *ö*, *eu* in a kind of onomatopoeia. (Gabelentz 1893: 606–607)[23]

Needless to say, Gabelentz' attempted reform of the comparative method did not gain a foothold. The exceptionless dismissal of Gabelentz' approach may not, however, have been so much due to his underlying premises as to his cavalier treatment of his sources. Even among those who could be expected to sympathize with Gabelentz' proposal, the criticism was widespread that he had not properly curated or analysed the Basque and Berber data, which led him to obvious errors in presentation and interpretation (cf. Hurch & Purgay 2019). Brinton (1894), for one, in his brief review of the 1894a expanded book version of Gabelentz' Basque and Berber studies, did not criticize Gabelentz' underlying views on variation, but did note that he had not properly distinguished between cognates and loan words in his analyses.

Hugo Schuchardt (1842–1927) – one of the most prominent contemporary opponents of the Neogrammarians, as he acknowledged himself (see, e.g., Spitzer 1928 [1922]) – was similarly unimpressed by Gabelentz' methodological laxness, despite being sympathetic to the motivating idea of the radical mutability of linguistic forms. In a review of Gabelentz (1894a), he questioned the wisdom of taking such an adventurous course in comparing these languages when the more conventional and uncontroversial methods had yet to be tried properly:

The Kabyle and Tuareg words that the author [Gabelentz] compares to the Basque words differ from these greatly for the most part. He does indeed attempt to explain this on the basis of muddled and washed out phonetic confusion. However, even if I do not dispute this possibility in general, it

---

[23]Original: "So kann das Seltsame geschehen, dass der Seele ein sehr unbestimmtes Lautbild vorschwebt, und doch der Mund ein sehr scharfes hervorbringt, aber nicht immer dasselbe, sondern bald dieses bald jenes, je nach Zufall und Stimmung. [...] Aus unserem Sprachkreise wüsste ich wenigstens entfernt Analoges anzuführen. Dem Obersachsen, der zwischen *d* und *t*, zwischen *i* und *ü*, *e* und *ö*, *ei* und *eu*, *äu* nicht unterscheidet, kann es geschehen, dass er im Affecte jedes *d* wie *t* ausspricht, und dass er, wo es sich um tiefe, dunkele, grausige Dinge handelt, alle *i*, *e* und *ei* lautmalend in *ü*, *ö*, *eu* verwandelt."

still seems to me that we should for the time being – that is, as long as
further and more careful examinations of Basque phonetic history are not
available – not seek refuge in this "last resort". (Schuchardt 1893: 334)[24]

Gabelentz' freewheeling approach, commented Schuchardt (1893: 334), offers
no credible way to navigate language history. It could just as easily be used to link
Basque to the languages of the Caucasus or the Ural as to those of North Africa.
Although there were linguists dissatisfied with the rigid system-building of the
Neogrammarians and prepared to face the messiness of the raw data, Gabelentz'
scheme did not present a viable alternative for them.

5 Conclusion

In the last decades of the nineteenth century, the phenomenon of alternating
sounds was instrumentalized in different ways by scholars hoping to advance
their various academic and disciplinary agendas. In America, Boas denied the
reality of the phenomenon as part of a project to assert the scientific superiority
of the anthropological school he was busily building up. In Germany, Gabelentz
moved in the opposite direction, embracing the phenomenon as a means to undermine the hegemony of Neogrammarian linguistics. The positions of both Boas
and Gabelentz – and indeed also their rivals – were informed in no small way
by the mid-nineteenth-century writings of Steinthal, who developed a unified
theory of the psychological basis and evolution of language with a strongly empirical accent.

Although both Boas and Gabelentz indulge in exaggeration and caricature in
their critiques, and exhibit obvious faults in elaborating their own positions, their
views have had very different fates in the received histories of linguistics and
anthropology. External factors no doubt play a role here: Boas achieved institutional dominance and is feted as the founding father of modern American anthropology, while Gabelentz died early and disappeared into relative historical
obscurity.

The different fates of their views on alternating sounds are perhaps also indica-
tive of the temperament of linguistics and anthropology as disciplines. Despite

---

[24]Original: "Die kabylischen und tuaregischen Wörter, die der Verf. zu baskischen Wörtern stellt,
weichen von diesen zum grossen Theil sehr stark ab. Zwar sucht er das aus einer verworrenen
und verwaschenen Lautirung zu erklären: aber wenn ich auch im Allgemeinen die Möglichkeit
einer solchen nicht bestreite, so dünkt mich doch, wir sollten vorderhand, d. h. so lange nicht
mehr und sorgfältigere Untersuchungen über die baskische Lautgeschichte vorhanden sind,
hier nicht zu dieser 'ultima ratio' unsere Zuflucht nehmen."

his apparent hostility to later conceptions of the phoneme, Boas' attack on the notion of alternating sounds is celebrated for expanding the formal franchise, making all languages equal subjects under the laws of linguistics. Gabelentz' efforts to problematize the comparative method, by contrast, could find no supporters: his dismembering of current historical linguistics offered no practical alternative. Boas is more welcome than Gabelentz in fields that place a premium on technical progress, conceived positivistically as the ability to capture and catalogue phenomena within a universalizing system. This case study offers informative parallels to the "resistant embrace" of structuralism in France that John Joseph (Chapter 6, this volume) sketches and the "unique form hypothesis" that Nick Riemer (Chapter 9, this volume) imputes to present-day linguistics.

Acknowledgements

Clemens Knobloch, Chloé Laplantine, H. Walter Schmitz and Manfred Ringmacher all provided useful feedback on earlier versions of this chapter which led to its improvement.

References

Anderson, Stephen R. 1985. *Phonology in the twentieth century: Theories of rules and theories of representations.* Chicago: University of Chicago Press.

Boas, Franz. 1889. On alternating sounds. *American Anthropologist* 2(1). 47–54.

Boas, Franz. 1911. Introduction. In *Handbook of American Indian Languages, Part I*, 1–83. Washington DC: Government Printing Office.

Borsche, Tilman. 1989. Die innere Form der Sprache. Betrachtungen zu einem Mythos der Humboldt-Herme(neu)tik. In Hans-Werner Scharf (ed.), *Wilhelm von Humboldts Sprachdenken. Symposion zum 150. Todestag*, 47–65. Essen: Reimer Hobbing.

Brinton, Daniel Garrison. 1894. Basque and Berber. *Science* 23 (26 January 1894). 43.

Brinton, Daniel Garrison. 1890 [1888]. The earliest form of human speech, as revealed by American tongues. In *Essays of an Americanist*, 390–409. Philadelphia: Porter & Coates.

Bumann, Waltraud. 1965. *Die Sprachtheorie Heymann Steinthals. Dargestellt im Zusammenhang mit seiner Theorie der Geisteswissenschaft.* Meisenheim am Glan: Hain.

Bunzl, Matti. 1996. Franz Boas and the Humboldtian tradition: From *Volksgeist* and *Nationalcharakter* to an anthropological concept of culture. In George W. Stocking Jr. (ed.), Volksgeist *as method and ethic: Essays on Boasian ethnography and the German anthropological tradition*, 17–78. Madison: University of Wisconsin Press.

Darnell, Regna. 1988. *Daniel Garrison Brinton: The 'fearless' critic of Philadelphia.* Philadelphia: Department of Anthropology, University of Pennsylvania.

Darnell, Regna. 1998. *And along came Boas: Continuity and revolution in Americanist anthropology.* Amsterdam: John Benjamins.

Formigari, Lia. 2018. Wilhelm Wundt and the *Lautgesetze* controversy. *History and Philosophy of the Language Sciences.* https://hiphilangsci.net/2018/01/17/wundt-lautgesetze/.

Gabelentz, Georg von der. 1889. Über Stoff und Form in der Sprache. *Berichte über die Verhandlungen der königlich-sächsischen Gesellschaft der Wissenschaften zu Leipzig, philologisch-historische Classe* 21. 185–216.

Gabelentz, Georg von der. 1893. Baskisch und Berberisch. *Sitzungsberichte der königlich-preußischen Akademie der Wissenschaften zu Berlin.* 593–613.

Gabelentz, Georg von der. 1894a. *Die Verwandtschaft des Baskischen mit den Berbersprachen Nord-Africas, nachgewiesen von Georg von der Gabelentz.* Braunschweig: Richard Sattler. Edited by Albrecht Conon Graf von der Schulenburg.

Gabelentz, Georg von der. 1894b. Hypologie [Typologie]: Eine neue Aufgabe der Linguistik. *Indogermanische Forschungen* 4. 1–7.

Gabelentz, Georg von der. 2016 [1891]. *Die Sprachwissenschaft, ihre Aufgaben, Methoden und bisherigen Ergebnisse.* Berlin: Language Science Press. Edited by Manfred Ringmacher and James McElvenny.

Humboldt, Wilhelm von. 1998 [1836]. *Über die Verschiedenheit des menschlichen Sprachbaues und ihren Einfluß auf die geistige Entwicklung des Menschengeschlechts.* Paderborn: Ferdinand Schöningh. Edited by Donatella Di Cesare.

Hurch, Bernhard & Katrin Purgay. 2019. The Basque-Berber connection of Georg von der Gabelentz. In James McElvenny (ed.), *Gabelentz and the science of language*, 57–97. Amsterdam: Amsterdam University Press.

Klautke, Egbert. 2013. *The mind of the nation:* Völkerpsychologie *in Germany, 1851-1955.* New York: Berghahn Books.

Kuklick, Henrika (ed.). 2008. *A new history of anthropology.* Malden: Blackwell.

Kuklick, Henrika. 2011. Personal equations: Reflections on the history of fieldwork, with special reference to sociocultural anthropology. *Isis* 102(1). 1–33.

Laplantine, Chloé. 2018. Préface. In Chloé Laplantine & Andrew Eastman (eds.), *Introduction du* Handbook of American Indian Languages *(1911).* Limoges: Lambert-Lucas.

Levelt, Willem J. M. 2013. *A history of psycholinguistics: The pre-Chomskyan era.* Oxford: Oxford University Press.

McElvenny, James. 2016. The fate of form in the Humboldtian tradition: The *Formungstrieb* of Georg von der Gabelentz. *Language and Communication* 47. 30–42.

McElvenny, James. 2017. Grammar, typology and the Humboldtian tradition in the work of Georg von der Gabelentz. *Language and History* 60(1). 1–20.

McElvenny, James. 2018. Typology – a new task of linguistics. *History and Philosophy of the Language Sciences.* https://hiphilangsci.net/2018/09/05/typology/.

McElvenny, James (ed.). 2019. *Gabelentz and the science of language.* Amsterdam: University of Amsterdam Press.

Powell, John Wesley (ed.). 1880 [1877]. *Introduction to the study of Indian languages.* Washington, D. C.: Smithsonian Institution.

Ringmacher, Manfred. 1996. *Organismus der Sprachidee: H. Steinthals Weg von Humboldt zu Humboldt.* Paderborn: Ferdinand Schöningh.

Sapir, Edward. 1921. *Language: An introduction to the study of speech.* San Diego / New York / London: Harcourt, Brace & Co.

Schaffer, Simon. 1988. Astronomers mark time: Discipline and the personal equation. *Science in context* 2(1). 115–145.

Schuchardt, Hugo. 1893. Review of G. von der Gabelenz, *Baskisch und Berberisch. Literaturblatt für germanische und romanische Philologie* 14. 334–338.

Silverstein, Michael (ed.). 1971. *Whitney on language: Selected writings of William Dwight Whitney.* Cambridge, MA: MIT University Press.

Spitzer, Leo (ed.). 1928 [1922]. *Hugo Schuchardt-Brevier: Ein Vademecum der allgemeinen Sprachwissenschaft.* Halle (Saale): Max Niemeyer.

Steinthal, H. 1852. *Die Entwicklung der Schrift.* Berlin: Ferdinand Dümmler.

Steinthal, H. 1860. *Charakteristik der hauptsächlichsten Typen des Sprachbaues.* Berlin: Ferdinand Dümmler.

Steinthal, H. 1867. *Die Mande-Neger-Sprachen, psychologisch und phonetisch betrachtet.* Berlin: Ferdinand Dümmler.

Steinthal, H. 1881 [1871]. *Einleitung in die Psychologie und Sprachwissenschaft.* Berlin: Ferdinand Dümmler.

Trautmann-Waller, Céline. 2006. *Aux origines d'une science allemande de la culture: Linguistique et psychologie des peuples chez Heymann Steinthal.* Paris: CNRS Editions.

Whitney, William Dwight. 1874. The elements of English pronunciation. In *Oriental and linguistic studies*, vol. II, 202–276. New York: Scribner, Armstrong & Co.

Whitney, William Dwight. 1896 [1875-1878]. *A Sanskrit grammar, including both the classical language, and the older dialects, of Veda and Brahmana.* Leipzig: Breitkopf & Härtel.

Chapter 3

On Sapir's notion of form/pattern and its aesthetic background

Jean-Michel Fortis

CNRS, Université Paris Diderot

> "I find that what I most care for is beauty of form, whether in substance or, perhaps even more keenly, in spirit. A perfect style, a well-balanced system of philosophy, a perfect bit of music, the beauty of mathematical relations — these are some of the things that, in the sphere of the immaterial, have most deeply stirred me."
> Sapir, letter to Lowie, 29 September 1916 (cited in Silverstein 1986: 79)

On Sapir's view, units of cultural behaviour (such as linguistic units) can only be identified through the relations they maintain to other elements of the same kind. This set of interrelations is what Sapir calls a "pattern", or refers to simply as "form". The chapter begins by examining Sapir's notion of pattern in his analysis of phonological systems. It is shown that, to a certain extent, Sapir conflated the notion of pattern with that of *Gestalt*, yet his own conception was idiosyncratic insofar as it placed much emphasis on the purely formal potency of patterns, understood as aesthetic configurations existing for form's sake and independent from functional motivations.

The second part of the chapter is devoted to Sapir's description of how patterns are formed and grasped. Complex interrelations are not laid bare in ordinary conscious

Jean-Michel Fortis. 2019. On Sapir's notion of form/pattern and its aesthetic background. In James McElvenny (ed.), *Form and formalism in linguistics*, 59–88. Berlin: Language Science Press. DOI:10.5281/zenodo.2654353

thinking; they can only be accessed through an intuition that Sapir characterizes as a "form-feeling". Form-feeling, as Sapir himself tells us, takes its origin from art theory. It is argued that the source of this notion is to be found in German-speaking art theory, specifically the notion of *Formgefühl*. In the course of the discussion, the hypothesis is set forth that Sapir's "form drive", which underlies the elaboration of patterns for form's sake, might also have its source in German thought, notably in Humboldt and Schiller.

1 Introduction[1]

The vast range of scholarly interests which Sapir nurtured during his life far exceeds what would fall under our current conception of linguistic matters. In particular, psychology, especially Gestaltist, psychoanalysis, as especially represented by Carl Jung (1875–1961), music and aesthetics were to him concerns of prime importance. As we shall see, his interests are reflected in the general conceptions he entertained about culture and language, and more precisely about linguistic form, or, in terms also used in his writings, linguistic pattern or configuration.

In what follows, it will be shown that the aesthetic leitmotiv running through many of Sapir's writings is essential to understand what is idiosyncratic in his notion of form or pattern. The aesthetic viewpoint, as will be argued, is fundamental for understanding how Sapir conceived of an individual's relation to cultural and linguistic patterns; it also helps us see in what ways Sapir's ideas about the constitution of patterns and their diachrony deviated from anything we are familiar with. Further, the theoretical connections of Sapirian form with Gestaltist ideas and psychoanalysis might be best appreciated by, again, following the aesthetic thread.

What about the historical roots or inspirations of Sapir? Their very heterogeneity and the fact that they were not always disclosed by him appear to have produced a gap, or an indecision, in Sapirian studies. Were we to suggest probable influences beyond the well-attested ones, this gap could be at least partially filled and our comprehension of Sapir deepened. Any attempt in this direction is certainly worthwhile and we will do our best to offer proposals on this historical context throughout the discussion and particularly in the last part of this chapter.

---

[1]Parts of this chapter have already appeared as a post of the multi-author blog *History and Philosophy of the Language Sciences* (Fortis 2014) and in an extended French version (Fortis 2015).

2 An example of pattern: the phonological system

Sapir's conception of a phonological system is a good entry point for his notion of pattern. As early as *Language* (1921), phonemes are said to be "points" of an "underlying phonetic pattern". A potential simplifying misconception should first be dispelled: we may be tempted to read into Sapir's analysis of a phonological pattern the idea that phonemes are merely identified by their distinctive features, in effect, then, by the contrastive relations they hold to other phonemes of the language. Sapir's conception is more complex. In a phonological pattern, the relative distance of elements is also determined by the degree to which they share common contexts of occurrence and partake of the same functional/semantic role. See, for example, the fact that a Nootka speaker conflates /p'/ and /'m/ into a single phonological structure /C'/ (Sapir 1951 [1933]: 55–57). There can be no other reason, as Sapir explains, than the fact that the occurrences of /p'/ and /'m/ are sufficiently similar to warrant the assimilation of their phonological structure. This assimilation, in other words, manifests the fact that the occurrences of /p'/ exert an attraction on /'m/ which results in a levelling out of their phonological structure. The relative proximity of elements in the system is also determined by functional and semantic factors. For instance, in English /f/ contrasts with /v/, as /p/ contrasts with /b/, but /f/ is closer to /v/ than /p/ to /b/ for the reason that /f/ and /v/ belong to common paradigms, such as *wife/wives*. In turn, /f/ and /v/ form with /θ/-/ð/ and /s/-/z/ what we may call a subsystem or subpattern, in view of parallel voicing contrasts like *sheath/sheathe* and *mouse/mouses* (Sapir 1951 [1933]: 48). The very existence of idiosyncratic patterns, and the fact that the relational feelings of speakers have an effect on phonetic change, do not make it permissible "to look for universally valid sound changes under like articulatory conditions" (Sapir 1951 [1933]: 48). This is not to reject the search for regularities, nor is it in contradiction of the neogrammarian assumption of the inviolability of sound laws, rather it is an implicit restriction of their validity to a family of languages. In fact, Sapir occasionally points out the perpetuation of patterns or subpatterns within a language or genetically related languages.

On several points, it should be noted, Sapir's view is in line with Hermann Paul (1846–1921) in his *Prinzipien* (1880–1920): linguistic elements form dynamic groups which absorb or repulse elements that are, respectively, similar or dissimilar in their form, function and semantics. The series *wife/wives = sheath/sheathe = mouse/mouses* would constitute, in Paul's parlance, a *stoffliche Proportionengleichung*, a "material equation" (Paul 1920 [1880]: 86). In the German context, such views on representations acting as groups can be traced back to Johann Friedrich

Herbart (1776–1841), whose psychology of the unconscious appears to have furnished theoretical tools to many thinkers, not only to Paul. By contrast with Paul, however, Sapir isolates phonemes from morphemes, an abstraction which Paul might have found implausible from a psychological point of view. In addition, Sapir's aesthetic conception of patterns strongly colours his interpretation of Herbartian groups, as we shall see later.

Again in conformity with Paul and much of the linguistic literature of the time, for Sapir the organization of groups is *unconscious*. Latent factors can be brought to light in a variety of ways: through the conflation of phonemic structures, as in the Nootka example; through the filling in of phonemes which reflect co-occurrences latent in the speaker's knowledge (Sapir 1951 [1933]: 52–53); or through what Herbartian psychology and Boas (1858–1942) had described as apperceptive phenomena, for example, in English speakers, the illusory addition of a weak consonant in syllables ending with a short vowel (Sapir 1951 [1933]: 58–59).[2] More generally, unconscious patterning gives rise to what we would characterize as "categorial perception"; that is, the perception of forms that is consonant with their position in a pattern and abstracts away from physical features. Such perception, as Sapir (1951 [1933]: 46) points out, is a general trait of human cognition; indeed, the distinction between physical features and their position in a cultural or linguistic pattern, and the psychological primacy of the latter, is a point repeatedly emphasized in Sapir's texts. Lastly, and this brings us back to aesthetics, in Sapir's (1951 [1925]) "Sound patterns in language", the ability to access and use this sytem of positions, in other words *speech*, is characterized as an "art". This rather surprising characterization, undeveloped and allusive as it is in the text, will hopefully be made more understandable when Sapir's notion of form (or pattern) and the aesthetic motif are more closely examined.

3 Patterns as Gestalten

Most remarkable is the very salient fact that Sapir does not speak of a network of groups but of patterns of elements. This shift of emphasis only underlines the action of unconscious patterns on forms surfacing as conscious elements, for only elements are conscious, not groups. Speaking of "pattern" or, at times, of "con-

---

[2]"A new sensation is apperceived by means of similar sensations that form part of our knowledge" (Boas 1889: 50). Apperception is one of those notions which belong to the stock-in-trade of Herbartian psychology. The concept of apperception was presumably passed on to Boas through Steinthal. Its application to the issue of "alternating sounds" in Native American languages is discussed by McElvenny in Chapter 2 of this volume.

figuration" also reveals the connection Sapir established between unconscious organization and configurations designated as *Gestalten* in the psychology of the same name.

We do not know for certain when Sapir became acquainted with *Gestalt* psychology. Several testimonies (including a letter by Sapir himself) have revealed Sapir's admiration for Kurt Koffka (1886–1941) and more specifically his book *The Growth of the Mind* (1924), which he appears to have read in 1924.[3] We know the book lay at hand's reach in the family house, and that it was recommended reading for Sapir's seminars on the impact of culture on personality and on the psychology of culture at Yale (years 1933–34 and 1935–36; Sapir 1999 [1933]: 677). It is also a matter of historical record that Sapir met Koffka personally in a symposium on the unconscious in 1927.

There is certainly a kinship between the Gestaltist rejection of elementist psychological accounts and its holistic view of perception and behaviour and, on the other hand, Sapir's idea that all units of culturally determined behaviour are pyschologically active only as "points in a pattern", not as bundles of physical features. The "psychological reality of phonemes" (the title of Sapir's famous paper) has its match in the Gestaltist affirmation that "sensations" do not have phenomenal reality. The contexts of the two theories were vastly different, but this common point shoud be highlighted.[4]

Perhaps most congenial to Sapir was Koffka's definition of a configuration (*Gestalt*) which, although it occurred in the context of a discussion of figure/ground organization, was of the widest generality. A configuration (or *Gestalt*),[5] said Koffka (1924: 146), was definable as a "co-existence of phenomena, in which each member possesses its peculiarity only by virtue of, and in connection with, all the others". In a similar vein, Sapir explained that a linguistic sound

> is not only characterized by a distinctive and slightly variable articulation
> and a corresponding acoustic image, but also — *and this is crucial* — by

---

[3] Sapir's positive judgment of the book is conveyed with particular elation in a letter to Benedict (cited in Sapir 2002 [1928-1937]: 121). David Sapir's testimony is cited in Cowan et al. (1986: 478). These testimonies alone suffice to show that Murray (1981), who denies any influence of Gestaltist ideas on Sapir, has seriously misjudged the influence of *Gestalttheorie* on Sapir's thinking.

[4] Sapir's view was also an argument in favour of a minimalist position in the debate on the phonetic notation most suited to Amerindian languages: should one complexify or simplify it? See Darnell (1990: 285).

[5] Mead had lent Koffka's book to Sapir in its English version, where "configuration" translates *Gestalt/Struktur* (Darnell 1990: 185). Koffka explains that the translation as "structure" was not retained for fear that in an American context it might be interpreted in connection with structural psychology (i.e. the Wundtian-style analysis of mental states promoted by Titchener in the United States).

> a psychological aloofness from all the other members of the system. [...]
> A sound that is not unconsciously felt as "placed" with reference to other
> sounds is no more a true element of speech than a lifting of the foot is a
> dance step unless it can be "placed" with reference to other movements
> that help to define the "dance". (Sapir 1951 [1925]: 35; Sapir's emphasis)

Sapir's allusion to an organized sequence of actions (dancing), in this passage
and elsewhere (Sapir 2002 [1928-1937]: 104–105), might point to the fact that patterned behaviour was appreciated as a major step towards an enlargement of the
notion of configuration. This enlargement was especially noticeable in the way
Koffka described Köhler's experiments with apes: learning how to solve a task
is, says Koffka, the establishment of a new configuration in which an element
of the field – for example, a stick – comes to find a role in an action sequence
with a beginning and an end; that is, a configuration which has the property of
closure (a term significantly reused by Sapir in *The Psychology of Culture*, 2002
[1928-1937]: 104). Further, the apprehension of something as a tool is configura-
tional insofar as a chimpanzee, when putting together a thicker and a thinner
stick, is sensitive to their relative length, not to their absolute size; in another
situation, the thinner stick may thus play the role of the thicker one.

The vicarious character of units of behaviour and their identification through
the configuration of which they partake is precisely the point being made in
the initial example of Sapir's (1951 [1925]) "Sound patterns of language": the ex-
piration *wh* that blows a candle gets entirely reconfigured when it becomes a
linguistic gesture.

An essential property of formal patterns is their transposability. By "transpos-
able" is meant here the capacity for a system of relations to remain unaltered under a change in physical implementation. Language furnishes several instances
of transposability. Thus, the formal patterning of language is said to underlie the
possibility of "linguistic transfers"; that is, the possibility of resorting to various
(de)coding techniques, such as writing, lip-reading or gestural systems; or again,
the system of initial consonants in English is a historical transfer from the Indo-
European one (Sapir 1921: 200). The latter kind of transposition, which involves
a phonological system, will be further elaborated through an artificial example
in "Sound patterns of language".

Now, transposability, in *Gestalt* thought, furnished evidence for the existence
of qualities not reducible to sums of sensations. Indeed, from the very beginning
of *Gestalt* psychology, in the seminal work of Christian von Ehrenfels (1859–
1932), transposability was played upon as a favourite theme: "proof of the existence of Gestalt qualities", said Ehrenfels (1988 [1890]: 90), "is provided, at least

in the sphere of visual and aural presentations, by the similarity-relations [...] which obtain between melodies and figures having different tonal or positional foundations". Note that the transposability of melodies as "systems of relations" was cited as a universal of human musical cultures by Carl Stumpf (1848–1936) in *Die Anfänge der Musik* (1911), a book Sapir reviewed at an early stage of his career. Gestaltist ideas thus came to Sapir at least in part through the mediation of aesthetic theory, and much earlier than 1924. There remains, however, a point on which Sapir is at variance with the Gestaltists: whereas a *Gestalt* quality is phenomenally more directly accessible than its elements, the structure of a pattern is, for Sapir, unconscious. However, its units are grasped in a way which, because it does not lay its structure bare, Sapir most often describes as a "feeling". We shall now turn our attention to this feeling for form.

4 The form-feeling

In many places, Sapir refers to the grasping of patterns of all kinds, be they phonological, morphological and syntactic, or behavioural and social, as a "feeling" or, less frequently, as an "intuition" of the same order. This view, as far as I know, makes its first appearance in *Language* (1921), where it is applied to linguistic patterning. For example, we read that "both the phonetic and conceptual structures show the instinctive feeling of language for form" (Sapir 1921: 56) or that every language has a definite feeling for its inner phonetic system and "also a definite feeling for patterning on the level of grammatical formation" (Sapir 1921: 61). The notion of a feeling for form/pattern recurs in different guises which we may assume to carry the same meaning: "relational feeling", "form intuition", "feeling for form/relations/patterning/classification into forms", "to feel a pattern/form" etc. These expressions are used in various contexts: quite generally, as above, to refer to the phonological/morphosyntactic apparatus of a language, as in discussing the unconscious direction imparted to thinking by the forms a language has laid down (Sapir 1951 [1924]: 153); more specifically, while speaking of vocalic alternations in English (*goose-geese, sing-sang-sung*; Sapir 1921: 60–61), active constructions (Sapir 1921: 84–85, 111), of which the speaker is said to feel the SVO structure, possessive pronouns, the animate/inanimate distinction (Sapir 1921: 156), case-marking on the English interrogative pronoun (Sapir 1921: 159), the semantic relation between *boy* and *man* (Sapir 1951 [1929]: 61), the meaning of *est-ce que* in French and of verbal stems in Athabaskan languages (Sapir 1991 [1923]: 147), causative forms (Sapir 1951 [1924]: 154), which are an unconscious, unreflective mode of the mental representation of the concept of causation; French reflexive verbs (Sapir 1951 [1931]: 116), which, to French speakers, induce a "formal feeling", a sense of belonging together, although from an external perspective semantic homogeneity is hard to find. Of all these texts, the notion of "form-feeling" is probably most frequently referred to in "Sound patterns" (1951 [1925]).

A passage from "The unconscious patterning of behavior in society" (1951 [1927](b)) provides a good illustration of the issues intertwined with the notion of form-feeling.

> To most of us who speak English the tangible expression of the plural idea in the noun seems to be a self-evident necessity. Careful observation of English usage, however, leads to the conviction that this self-evident necessity of expression is more of an illusion than a reality. If the plural were to be understood functionally alone, we should find it difficult to explain why we use plural forms with numerals and other words that in themselves imply plurality. "Five man" or "several house" would be just as adequate as "five men" or "several houses." Clearly, what has happened is that English, like all of the other Indo-European languages, has developed a *feeling* for the classification of all expressions which have a nominal form into singulars and plurals. So much is this the case that in the early period of the history of our linguistic family even the adjective, which is nominal in form, is unusable except in conjunction with the category of number. (Sapir 1951 [1927](b): 550; my emphasis)

The example brings home the point that a structural feature is, as it were, "exercised" in actual speech in a way that is not of the order of conscious knowledge. Such a feature gives form to experience and may perpetuate itself by the sheer force of the unconscious pattern which imposes itself on the speaker. Their thoughts being channelled in these formal grooves, speakers may resist the elimination of what, in the eyes of cool reason, would appear to be non-functional or a superfluous luxury.

Note too that the form-feeling has implications for the way diachrony should be conceived. In the passage just cited, and in other places, Sapir seems to be engaged in an implicit dialogue with Otto Jespersen (1860–1943), who had famously argued that languages evolve toward greater economy and analyticity (1894, 1965 [1924]; see e.g. 1965 [1924]: 207ff for the example of plurality). Against Jespersen, yet not in complete disagreement with him, Sapir apparently claims that languages may not evolve toward the complete elimination of superfluities and toward absolute or near absolute analyticity, for speakers' unconscious attachment to formal patterns carries with it an inertia which resists this evolution. We shall return to the issue of diachrony shortly.

A clue to the understanding of Sapir's "form-feeling" may be found in the following excerpt, which clearly points to the aesthetic source of the notion:

> Probably most linguists are convinced that the language-learning process, particularly the acquisition of a feeling for the formal set of the language, is very largely unconscious and involves mechanisms that are quite distinct in character from either sensation or reflection. There is doubtless something deeper about our feeling for form than even the majority of *art theorists* have divined, and it is not unreasonable to suppose that, as psychological analysis becomes more refined, one of the greatest values of linguistic study will be in the unexpected light it may throw on the psychology of intuition, this "intuition" being perhaps nothing more nor less than the "feeling" for relations. (Sapir 1951 [1924]: 156; my emphasis)

There are two possible ways of interpreting the reference to aesthetics: our feeling for linguistic form can be conceptualized in analogy with its counterpart in aesthetic theory; or both feelings reflect a common ability, the intuitive grasp of complex patterns. From what we have said so far, from the way Sapir conflates phonological intuition with art (Sapir 1951 [1925]: 34), or seems to equate *Gestalten* with aesthetic forms (Sapir 2002 [1928-1937]: 145–150), we may gather that aesthetic intuition was for him a general ability exceeding the bounds of the perception of artistic forms as such (see too, in this respect, the epigraph to this chapter). Such an interpretation would allow us to draw a parallel between this formal linguistic play which is supposed to reflect an innate striving for formal elaboration and, on the other hand, the Boasian idea that artistic creation begins with the purely formal, unrepresentative exercising of technical skills (Boas 1927 [1922]). In the realm of aesthetic thought, Sapir would have as counterparts those theorists granting pride of place to ornamentation, decorative arts; that is, to formalist considerations. In the same way, linguistic change becomes comparable to stylistic change, at that time an all-important question of aesthetic theory. It is now time to see the relation of linguistic change to the aesthetic perspective.

5 Diachrony

We may wonder if Sapir's concepts of pattern and form-feeling have important consequences for his descriptive linguistic work. They certainly do in phonology.

It is suggested here that his view of diachronic processes might furnish another illustration and demonstrate again the relevance of the aesthetic perspective.

In *Language*, diachronic change is described as a "drift", a notion which Sapir (1921: 155) defines as follows: "The drift of a language is constituted by the unconscious selection on the part of its speakers of those individual variations that are cumulative in some special direction".[6] This view of change can be made more palpable through an illustration, Sapir's account of the progressive disappearance of *whom* in favour of *who*. According to Sapir, four causes have contributed to the decline of *whom*. They are summarized in Table 1.

Table 1: Sapir's causes for the decline of *whom*

Cause	Phenomenon	Consequence
1	The forms marking the non-subject ("objective forms") are *me/him/her/us/them/whom*. In this group *whom* is isolated. The functional class of *whom* comprises *which/what/that* but these are not inflected.	The isolation of *whom* causes its weakening.
2	Interrogative words like *where/when/how*, are invariable, except *who/whom*	The isolation of *whom* causes its weakening.
3	Objective forms are strongly associated with the post-verbal position (cf. *he told him, it's me*), while interrogative ones are strongly associated with pre-verbal positions.	*whom* belongs to two groups whose members are associated with distinct positions. *Who* is not associated with distinct positions and is thereby favoured over *whom*.
4	*whom* is followed by a slight hesitation in *Whom did you see?*	*whom* is often "clumsy", from a rhythmical point of view, which weakens it.

---

[6]On the meanings of "drift", and its reception after Sapir, see Malkiel (1981). Malkiel suggests that drift may have its source in the continental drift (*Verschiebung* in German) of Wegener. The idea seems outlandish to me. Hermann Paul, like other authors, speaks of drift (also *Verschiebung*) when dealing with those slight variations which cause constant linguistic change. The definition of "drift" just cited would be perfectly in line with Paul.

Points 1 to 3 in Table 1 are faithful to Hermann Paul's style of explanation: elements which formally or functionally deviate from a group (*Isolierung*) are weakened, except if they are very frequent. However, Sapir's description has its own peculiarities. The frequency factor has disappeared and Sapir has his own way of accounting for the cause of isolation. For example, on the isolation of *whom* in situation 1, he suggests that "there is something unesthetic about the word. It suggests a form pattern which is not filled out by its fellows" (Sapir 1921: 158). He is a little more affirmative in case 2, when he adds: "it is safe to infer that there is a rather strong *feeling* in English that the interrogative pronoun or adverb, typically an emphatic element in the sentence, should be invariable" (Sapir 1921: 159; my emphasis). Apparently, a purely "mechanical" account of the formation and dissolution of groups of the kind advocated by Paul is not deemed sufficient. The form-feeling, with its aesthetic connotation, had to come into play.

As hinted at above, the aesthetic perspective on language made it possible to envisage a comparison of linguistic change and stylistic change. The similitude is explicitly endorsed in *The Psychology of Culture*:

> Practically all aesthetic patterns run through such a gamut: a rise from humble beginnings, an authoritative pinnacle, a prestige hangover — then down! The progress of an aesthetic cycle, then, means that there is aesthetic development within an aesthetic idea. [...] Even language forms have something like a cyclical development. Although the language's development is continuous, it is possible to define a certain set of linguistic forms — or point to a certain stage of development of a form — as classical. The classical stage would have a perfectly consistent and tightly-wrought use of forms. Now people participating in an aesthetic cycle are not conscious of it. (Sapir 2002 [1928-1937]: 132–133)[7]

Sapir then goes to explain that English has embarked on an evolution toward analyticity but, unlike Chinese, has not yet completed the cycle.

As already noted, the formal efficacy of entrenched patterns explains Sapir's qualifications on Jespersen's idea of a progress toward analytic forms.[8] English, says Sapir, still mixes up concrete and relational concepts in some limited domains, hence is not fully analytic. For example, the animate/inanimate distinction correlates with distinctive markings, since *I/me* and the possessive *'s* are

---

[7]It is difficult to find any originality in this cyclical view of history. Winckelmann is famous for having defended it in aesthetics.
[8]McElvenny (2013, 2017b) shows how Jespersen's views relate to the debate on the form of international languages.

associated with forms denoting animate entities. Through this convergence, formal configurations reinforce each other, with the consequence that "however the language strives for a more and more analytic form, it is by no means manifesting a drift toward the expression of 'pure' relational concepts in the Indo-Chinese manner" (Sapir 1921: 168). In other words, if we apply to this case the same reasoning as for *whom*, linguistic change is at least partly determined by an aesthetic feeling responding to the (dis)harmony of groups. This view leads to the rejection of purely "mechanical" (Paul) and teleological (Jespersen) accounts.

6 Form, function and formal play

The potency of a pattern is not determined by the function it might fulfil; we have seen that formal patterns have their own efficacy. Reciprocally, function may counteract a well-established pattern. An example of such a counteraction in the non-linguistic realm is given in "Anthropology and sociology" (Sapir 1951 [1927][a]). In many Indian tribes, Sapir observes, there is an entrenched social pattern according to which prestigious positions are a matter of inheritable privilege. This pattern may even extend to positions which should require special individual capacities, and thus may be transferred to domains in which it is clearly non-functional. However, some tribes resist this transfer, because "the psychic peculiarity which leads certain men and women ('medicine-men' and 'medicine-women') to become shamans is so individual that shamanism shows nearly everywhere a marked tendency to resist grooving in the social patterns of the tribe". In the present case, functionality (the exigencies of the craft) supersedes a dominant social pattern (the prevalence of inheritable privilege).[9] However, it is not clear that any such counteraction of function can be observed in the linguistic realm. Given what Sapir says about the greater insulation of language from conscious rationalization, it would be coherent to think that a counteraction of function is

---

[9]Sapir's notion of cultural/social pattern is in line with Boasian relativism, and its opposition to cross-cultural descriptive schemes appealing to race, evolution or environmental factors. Within diffusionist Boasian anthropology, some emphasized that a proper understanding of the diffusion and assimilation of cultural traits involved moving to the pattern level: substantively identical cultural traits are functionally different if placed within different patterns (Wissler 1917). A radical view holds that substantive traits are of little importance for characterizing some cultural patterns. Totemism, for example, is not to be defined by a substantive trait nor analysed as having originated from any particular trait (be it a guardian spirit, exogamy, taboo, the use of totemic names etc.). Rather, it is a classificatory social pattern, whose origin matters little; what matters is the totemic pattern spreading over a group (Goldenweiser 1912). The analogy with the purely structural Sapirian view of a phonological pattern is obvious.

perhaps only found in non-linguistic domains: language "forms a far more compact and inherently unified conceptual and formal complex than the totality of culture. This is due primarily to the fact that its function is far more limited in nature, to some extent also to the fact that the disturbing force of rationalization that constantly shapes and distorts culture anew is largely absent in language" (Sapir 1951 [1916]: 432–433).

This "largely" unilateral autonomization of form in the field of language would seem to imply that the aesthetic form-feeling plays a greater role in linguistic matters than in any other field. The action of this form-feeling would also be more coercive. In several texts, Sapir connects the potency of patterns with their being unconscious, saying for example that "we act all the more securely for our unawareness of the patterns that control us" (Sapir 1951 [1927][a]: 549).[10] In this respect, language has a special status since, explains Sapir (1951 [1912]: 100), "linguistic features are necessarily less capable of rising into consciousness of speakers than traits of culture". Though less radical, such an affirmation is in agreement with Boas' (1911: 67) claim that linguistic classifications, of all ethnological phenomena, are unique in being inaccessible to consciousness. For Sapir, the access point is obviously the form-feeling.

The relative independence of form and function also manifests itself in a process we may call the "semantic disinvestment" of form. By this term is meant that the "full" content of linguistic forms may not be activated in all of their occurrences, insofar as forms may be simply conventionally applied to ends to which they are not suited. An example from *Psychology of Culture* may illustrate this point (the square brackets indicate places where the reconstructed "manuscript" has been patched by significant additions from the editors):

> Consider, for example, verbs that are not entirely active [in their meaning but are treated as active in the linguistic structure:] in English the subject "I" is logically implied to be the active will in "I sleep" as well as "I run". [A sentence like] "I am hungry" might, [in terms of its content, be logically] better expressed with "hunger" as the active doer, as in [the German] *mich hungert* [or even the French] *j'ai faim*. In some languages, however, such as Sioux, a rigid distinction is made between truly active and static verbs. [...] [It seems, then, that] when we get a pattern of behavior, we follow that [pattern] in spite of [being led, sometimes, into] illogical ideas or a feeling of inadequacy. We become used to it. We are comfortable in a groove of behavior. [Indeed], it

---

[10]This conception, as noted by Joseph (2002), gives the linguist an important role in weakening the grip of linguistic patterns.

> seems that no matter what [the] psychological origin may be, or complex of psychological origins, or a particular type of patterned conduct, the pattern itself will linger on by sheer inertia. [...] Patterns of activity are continually getting away from their original psychological incitation. (Sapir 2002 [1928-1937]: 109–110)

In other words, the SV pattern is disinvested of its full significance when it gets applied to cases in which S is not an active doer and the verb is static (cf. also Sapir 1921: 14–15). In English, the generalization of this pattern conforms to the general observation that "all languages evince a curious instinct for the development of one or more particular grammatical processes at the expense of others, tending always to lose sight of any explicit functional value that the process may have had in the first instance, delighting, it would seem, in the sheer play of its means of expression" (Sapir 1921: 60). The description of this formal play is couched in terms that can hardly fail to evoke artistic activity. This step is taken most explicitly in "The unconscious patterning of behavior in society". In this text, the conception of language as an aesthetic product serves to capture two features of linguistic activity: the disconnection between form and function, yet the fact that the formal consistency of language seems to act as a surrogate of this functional demotivation:

> Purely functional explanations of language, if valid, would lead us to expect either a far greater uniformity in linguistic expression than we actually find, or should lead us to discover strict relations of a functional nature between a particular form of language and the culture of the people using it. Neither of these expectations is fulfilled by the facts. [... T]he forms of speech developed in the different parts of the world are at once free and necessary, in the sense in which all artistic productions are free and necessary. Linguistic forms as we find them bear only the loosest relation to the cultural needs of a given society, but they have the very tightest consistency as aesthetic products. (Sapir 1951 [1927][b]: 550)[11]

An important aspect of the Sapirian version of the so-called Sapir-Whorf hypothesis may well reside in this aesthetic view, besides, of course, those facets it owes to other motivations, well described in Joseph (2002), and which relate in particular to the publication of Ogden and Richard's *Meaning of Meaning* (1923).

---

[11]This interplay between freedom and necessity invites a comparison with what Sapir says of the rules of etiquette: etiquette "combines a strong moral necessity and tyranny and a felt element of choice" (Sapir 2002 [1928-1937]: 236).

In view of this aesthetic dialectic between the free and the necessary, Allen (1986: 462) is quite justified in stating that, for Sapir, the linguistic coercion of thought and the compliance of behaviour with cultural patterns "is not the grip of a master (culture) upon a slave (the individual) but is, instead, more closely analogous to the felt need of the member of an orchestra to play his instrument in accordance with a musical score".

The fact that forms may be disinvested of their semantic/psychological content finds its counterpart in Sapir's typology of symbols. In the entry "Symbolism", which was written for the *Encyclopedia of the Social Sciences*, Sapir (1951 [1934]) calls "referential symbolism" the kind of symbolism that has been divested of affective content, in contrast to those symbols that act as substitutes for emotionally charged behaviour, which are said to belong to the second main type, that of "condensation symbolism".[12] During the evolution of mankind, one symbolism has developed from the other:

> It is likely that most referential symbolisms go back to unconsciously evolved symbolisms saturated with emotional quality, which gradually took on a purely referential character as the linked emotion dropped out of the behavior in question. Thus shaking the fist at an imaginary enemy becomes a dissociated and finally a referential symbol for anger, when no enemy, real or imaginary, is actually intended. (Sapir 1951 [1934]: 565)

From a psychoanalytical point of view, this was a very neutral and agnostic way of describing the evolution of symbolism, without, for instance, the concept of repression. Quite significant in this respect is the *non-affective* factor adduced by Sapir to explain the development of referential symbolism, namely "the increased complexity and homogeneity of symbolic material"; that is, the evolution to more richly patterned symbols. This can be brought in relation to Sapir's examples of pattern extensions, and their "getting away from their original psychological incitation" (cf. the quotation above).

---

[12] The manifestly Freudian "condensation", a rendering of *Verdichtung*, only underlines the importance of affect in the way Sapir conceived of this symbolism, whose immediate emotional significance puts it at the origin of symbolization in mankind. There is a certain kinship between Sapir and some views defended by Ernest Jones (1879–1958) in his psychoanalytical essay on symbolism (Jones 1916), in particular a duality of symbolisms correlated with the unconscious/conscious distinction.

7 The form drive

Form for form's sake is the aesthetic motto for explaining the routinization of linguistic processes, against "mechanical" accounts which narrowly concentrate on low-level processes:

> It is usual to say that isolated linguistic responses are learned early in life and that, as these harden into fixed habits, formally analogous responses are made, when the need arises, in a purely mechanical manner, specific precedents pointing the way to new responses. We are sometimes told that these analogous responses are largely the result of reflection on the utility of the earlier ones, directly learned from the social environment. Such methods of approach see nothing in the problem of linguistic form beyond what is involved in the more and more accurate control of a certain set of muscles towards a desired end, say the hammering of a nail. I can only believe that explanations of this type are seriously incomplete and that they fail to do justice to a certain innate striving for formal elaboration and expression and to an unconscious patterning of sets of related elements of experience. (Sapir 1951 [1924]: 156)

The contrast between the hammering of a nail and speaking is reminiscent of that between blowing a candle and uttering the linguistic sound *wh*; it is, says Sapir (1951 [1925]: 34), what separates mere practical behaviour from art.

In the above passage, the mention of an "innate striving for formal elaboration and expression" echoes other declarations, such as the following one, in which the aesthetic leitmotiv reappears: "the projection in social behavior of an innate sense of form is an intuitive process and is merely a special phase of that mental functioning that finds its clearest voice in mathematics and its most nearly pure aesthetic embodiment in plastic and musical design" (Sapir 1951 [1927][a]: 344). Sapir's appeal to a sort of instinctual "form-craving" of the human mind and to an innate sense of form (e.g. Sapir 1951 [1924], Sapir 1951 [1927](a); see Handler 1986: 445) is not without antecedents. His form-drive is reminiscent of the Schillerian *Formtrieb*, which Friedrich von Schiller (1759–1805) characterized as a drive to a free expression of personality and toward insulating a permanent self from ever-changing worldly conditions (Schiller 1795, letters 12 to 16). The wedding of this "form-drive" to the flow of sensations is accomplished through an aesthetic impulse, the "play-drive" (*Spieltrieb*). Even if Schiller's *Formtrieb* was not on Sapir's mind when he wrote *Language*, Jung's (1921) *Psychological Types*, a book and a theory Sapir was very fond of, may have reminded him of it. For

Jung, however, the *Spieltrieb* was not interpreted as an essentially aesthetic attitude, nor as a systematization of formal patterns, but rather the conciliation of abstract thinking and sensation, of ego-centred vs object-centred orientation, and the source of symbolic creativity.

Sapir is not the only linguist of the time to speak of a form-drive. As McElvenny (2016) observes, Georg von der Gabelentz (1840–1893), in a passage of his *Sprachwissenschaft* (2016 [1891]), speaks of a drive towards the creation of forms (*Formungstrieb*) which would acccount for the formal lavishness (*Formengepränge*) of languages, whose profusion goes beyond functional needs. This *Formungstrieb* accounts for people's delight in formal play, says Gabelentz, who describes this human urge with Schiller's word *Spieltrieb*; that is, the play-drive which grounds the aesthetic attitude (Gabelentz 2016 [1891]: 381; no explicit reference to Schiller is made). The play-drive implies that the "little surplus of effort that I made on my work over and above bare utility was already a piece of love, and gave the dead material a breath of the personal for all time." Indeed, continues Gabelentz (2016 [1891]: 344), "precisely the same thing happened with language" (trans. McElvenny 2016: 35).

In an addition to the second edition of Gabelentz' text, and in the context of the present discussion, Gabelentz' nephew, Albrecht Graf von der Schulenburg, refers back to Wilhelm von Humboldt (1767–1835) (see also McElvenny 2017a). Especially praised are speakers of languages which systematize this formal play by resorting to obligatory inflections, that is, speakers of Indo-European languages; in them, says Schulenburg, one finds a specific sense of form (*Formensinn*, a word also found in texts on art) and an outstanding "aesthetic" gift (Gabelentz 2016 [1891]: 394). While the value judgement might not have been to Gabelentz' taste, I believe the reference to Humboldt puts us on the right track.

Although the term *Formungstrieb*, so it seems, is not used by Humboldt (Jürgen Trabant, p. c.), what we do find in Humboldt is the idea of a formative power which is especially active in some phases of language evolution, a power that Humboldt calls *Bildungstrieb*. The term can be found in two contexts: in texts about language, and in instances where the discussion revolves around biological questions (respectively Humboldt 1907 [1830-35], vol. VII: 95, 168, cf. Eng. trans. in Humboldt 1988 [1830–1835], p. 88, "constructive urge", and p. 150, "formative urge"; Humboldt 1903 [1794], vol. I: 328). The latter contexts point to the biological source of the *Bildungstrieb*, a concept borrowed from Humboldt's former teacher at Göttingen, Johann Friedrich Blumenbach (1752–1840). For Blumenbach (1781), the *Bildungstrieb* is a force creating and perpetuating organic forms (Jürgen Trabant, p. c.). In the linguistic domain, the stage at which language forms, as it were, "outgrow" the mind seem to be evaluated negatively (cf. *Über die Verschiedenheit*, Eng. trans. §20, in Humboldt 1988 [1830–1835]), which of course separates him from Sapir.

In short, linguistic structures are produced by an instinct which governs the creation of aesthetic objects through its formal play. I believe that by setting Sapir's aesthetic form-drive in the very German genealogy sketched above I am not going far beyond the bounds of decent speculation. This brief digression on the sources of the form-drive is not all the German lead has to offer, as we shall now see.

8 On the source of the form-feeling: Croce?

We have shown that the form-feeling has its origin in aesthetic theory. Aesthetics is a continent unto itself, and the potential sources are many. Let us first go back to what Sapir himself said about his influence(s). The crucial passage is repeated here:

> Probably most linguists are convinced that the language-learning process, particularly the acquisition of a feeling for the formal set of the language, is very largely unconscious and involves mechanisms that are quite distinct in character from either sensation or reflection. There is doubtless something deeper about our feeling for form than even the majority of *art theorists* have divined, and it is not unreasonable to suppose that, as psychological analysis becomes more refined, one of the greatest values of linguistic study will be in the unexpected light it may throw on the psychology of intuition, this "intuition" being perhaps nothing more nor less than the "feeling" for relations. (Sapir 1951 [1924]: 156; my emphasis)

In this passage, "intuition" is equated with "feeling for form". On the other hand, we have explicit statements by Sapir in *Language* in which he acknowledges his debt to Benedetto Croce (1866–1952); further, in one instance, Sapir (1921: 224) says he borrows the term "intuition" from Croce, who in his *Aesthetics* uses "intuition" in contrast to "logical knowledge". Altogether, this may be conducive to an adventurous syllogism: Sapir owes his notion of intuitive knowledge to Croce, intuitive knowledge = form-feeling, *ergo* Sapir's form-feeling is a version of Croce's intuition, or at least related to it. This conclusion is endorsed by Modjeska (1968: 347), who claims that in Croce Sapir "found a confirmation, if not the source of his own thoughts on formal pattern". Hymes (1969) agrees with Modjeska, while Hall (1969) begs to differ.

That Sapir borrowed "intuition" from Croce is acknowledged by Sapir himself, as we just saw. Whether the notion of form-feeling can be conflated with Croce's "intuition" is another matter. Croce's definitions of intuition, however hazy, show that intuition is for him a faculty essentially dedicated to the apprehension of individual objects. Further, Croce wields his notion of intuition against an intellectualist view of cognition and implicitly against Kant's concept of intuition; at any rate, his discussion shows he completely misses the Kantian doctrine of forms of intuition and categories, which certainly should detract from its interest for an informed reader.[13]

In the *Aesthetic*, there is no particular emphasis on the grasp of unconscious patterns. On the contrary, genius, as superlative intuition, is essentially conscious, and in the chapter on language (chap. 18), Croce makes clear that parts of speech, which might be taken here as building blocks of linguistic patterning, are dubious abstractions floating above linguistic intuition. Intuition is also, however, a faculty that is inherently expressive, insofar as its operation is fully realized (intuiting a geographical area is being able to draw it, says Croce); this aspect, at least, is consonant with the dynamic character of the Sapirian unconscious (see Allen 1986).

Given the philosophical context in which Croce introduces his notion of intuition, what was its relevance for Sapir? In *Language*, occurrences of "intuition" that may be considered to come close to Croce's notion appear in the section devoted to literary criticism; that is, when discussing the idiosyncrasy of writers. In this section, the irreducibly individual character of an artist's "intuition" is said to have its origin in personal experience, within "thought relations" which, says Sapir (1921: 239), "have no specific linguistic vesture". If this were not clear enough, shortly after this passage, a distinction is drawn between this personal intuition and the "innate, specialized art of language", an art that would seem to be exercised by the form-feeling.

When Sapir uses "intuition" in a sense that would appear to be more relevant to his own understanding of the term, he does not go back to Croce but to Jung. In this respect, the way he handles Jung's functional types of mental activity (thinking, feeling, sensation, intuition) is revealing. Of all these types, intuition is singled out. Intuition, he says, is not on a par with the rest of the functional types; it is rather a mode of apprehension which cuts across the other functional

---

[13] Against Kant, Croce says for instance that we have "intuitions without space and time": "Noi abbiamo intuizioni senza spazio e senza tempo: una tinta di cielo e una tinta di sentimento, un 'ahi !' di dolore e uno slancio di volontà oggettivati nella coscienza, sono intuizioni che possediamo, e dove nulla è formato nello spazio e nel tempo" (Croce 1908 [1902]: 6–7). Here, intuition is used in reference to Kant's *Anschauung* (which adds to the confusion, if anything).

types. Intuition is really an awareness of relations provided by a quick rate of apprehension, and the intuitive mind might be described as "an historical mind, aware of all the relations that are locked up in the given configuration" (Sapir 2002 [1928-1937]: 167). Thus, in the realm of abstract thinking, the quick glance of intuition is a privilege of the great mathematician, who sees the answer before it is proven (Sapir 2002 [1928-1937]: 167). In the realm of sensationist apprehension, intuition is the process which lies behind the ability of a cook to project the result of combining flavours (Sapir 2002 [1928-1937]: 168). Being thus generalized to all sorts of fields, Jungian intuition is redescribed by Sapir in a way that makes it come very close to the form-feeling.

The aesthetic aspect, however, is not essential in Jung's conception, except when the discussion leads him to find objections to it; for example, when he scrutinizes Schiller's *Spieltrieb*. On the other hand, in the preface to *Language* (1921: iii), a short eulogy praises Croce for being "one of the very few who have gained an understanding of the fundamental significance of language", and apparently expanding on what this significance consists in, Sapir goes on to say that Croce "has pointed out its [i.e. language's] close relation to the problem of art" and that he is "deeply indebted to him for this insight."

A glance at what Croce has to say about language, both simplistic and vague, suggests that Sapir, beyond this fundamental insight, could find little of value for his own concerns. First, the notion of "form-feeling" does not figure in the theoretical apparatus of Croce. Second, Sapir had reservations about Croce. Thus, in notes he jotted down on Croce he criticizes him for conceding too much to an individual's expressive capacity and not enough to formal conventions (Handler 1986). As a matter of fact, this is a recurring objection. It is for example levelled against Jung and Lévy-Bruhl: we should not transfer to individuals qualities which come from their complying with cultural patterns.

From this excursus on Croce, we may conclude, in agreement with Handler (1986: 441), that Sapir's analyses of linguistic patterning owe little to Croce, and we should take him at his word when he says that his debt to Croce is one fundamental insight, the connection of language to aesthetics. Further, even if Sapir borrowed "intuition" from Croce, his use of the term is his own and may at least as much reflect the influence of Jung.

9 Form-feeling and Formgefühl: Vischer and Wölfflin

We are left without an answer to the question of Sapir's sources in aesthetics. I suggest that "form-feeling" is in fact a translation of the German *Formgefühl*, a term commonly used by art theorists of the time. Note also that the plural in the quote above ("the majority of art theorists") points to a notion that is not the prerogative of a single author, and this is indeed the case for the *Formgefühl*. A few words need to be said about the historical background to this notion.

Formgefühl has various meanings. In the *Ästhetik*, the magnum opus of the "ponderous Hegelian" (Croce's words) Friedrich Theodor Vischer (1807–1887), the term is used abundantly without, however, being thematized as such. Its signification is essentially that of aesthetic sensibility, and it is most often used in connection with a people and a period. It may also characterize one of the opposed principles into which Vischer resolves styles, namely the painterly and the plastic (Vischer is one of the sources for the analyses of styles into opposing pairs; cf. for example the *Principles* of Wölfflin).

Since the psychological aspect of the *Formgefühl* is our first concern here, we should mention that early occurrences of the term in psychological literature can be found in the writings of the great mandarin of the field in Germany, Wilhelm Wundt (1832–1920). Wundt (1908–1911 [1874]) appears to employ *Formgefühl* in contradistinction to, on the one hand, sensations of (dis)harmony between elementary impressions and, on the other hand, "intellectual" contents associated with the perception of forms, including, for example, the functionality of body parts in representations of the human figure (cf. the 1902 edition, chap. 16, part 2). The *Formgefühl* is thus associated with the perception of organization and order.[14] In this "structural" meaning, its genealogy can be traced back to some of Herbart's followers, namely, to Nahlowsky (1812–1885) and his notions of "elementary feelings" and "group-feelings" (Nahlowsky 1862; Romand 2018), and to Waitz (1821–1864) and his observations on the aesthetic effect of *Form* and *Gestalten* (Waitz 1849; Romand 2015, Romand In press).

The notion of *Formgefühl* seems to gain a larger audience with the advent of an empathy-centred, psychological aesthetics. An important landmark in this tradition, which goes back to the Romantic era, is the work of Robert Vischer (1847–1933), son of Friedrich Vischer.[15] In a short treatise (his dissertation) entitled *On The Optic Feeling of Form* (*Über das Optische Formgefühl*, 1873), Vischer explains that contemplating and forming images always implies an active involvement of the body or a projection of bodily feelings and affects onto the object (a projection he calls *Nachfühlung/Einfühlung*, "concurring-feeling", as it were, and

---

[14]My thanks to David Romand for having called to my attention Wundt's *Grundzüge* and the Herbartians. According to Romand, the Wundtian concept was the one taken over by Lipps and Dessoir (Romand In press).

[15]For an English introduction to Robert Vischer, see Barasch (1998).

"empathy"). Thus, a rock facing a subject may appear to defy or challenge her, a road which widens awakens a triumphant feeling etc. This is not yet art, but its prelude: the artist's task consists in imbuing such projected feelings with a more general and spiritual meaning. In sum, the *Formgefühl* is for Vischer a projection of a feeling into a form.

Heinrich Wölfflin (1864–1945), in his first study Wölfflin (1886), pursues Vischer's line of thought, and applies it more specifically to the description of factors which condition the affective effect produced by an architectural style. In *Renaissance und Barock* (1888), Wölfflin explains that the features which define a style reflect a way of projecting inner feelings and corporeal habits, characteristic of a period, into forms. The tapering of Gothic forms, for example, reflects a muscular tension and an effort of the will that one does not find in the serene and vigorous equanimity of Renaissance constructions. Further, the *Formgefühl* offers a psychological definition of style which cuts across arts and thus unites architecture with painting, sculpture and decorative arts (e.g. clothing). This relative homogeneity of style is manifested in recurrent formal patterns (e.g. the pointed elongated shape of Gothic art), of which the *Formgefühl* is therefore both an intuition and a source.[16] Moreover, Wölfflin lays great importance on the idea that artistic forms cannot be determined by cultural-historical factors nor by functionality or technical necessity. And although the notion of *Formgefühl* is still framed in an empathy-based theory (or Wölfflin's own version of empathy, the *Lebensgefühl*), the *Formgefühl* itself circumscribes a relatively autonomous formal plane.

On the whole, Wölfflin's formalist style of analysis, which reflects an emphasis on non-representative art (such as architecture), resonates with the great interest of the time in ornamental design and decorative art, exemplified in particular by Alois Riegl (1858–1905; see e.g. Riegl 1893) and Gottfried Semper (1803–1879). The latter, for example, placed much emphasis on the role of decorative arts, small artefacts, costume, furniture and architecture (i.e. all objects close to the body; Semper 1884).[17] Such an emphasis could hardly be lost on anthropologists who often had to deal with everyday objects. Indeed, Boas does not seem far from Semper when he states that "so far as our knowledge of the works of art of primitive people extends the feeling for form is inextricably bound up with technical experience. Nature does not seem to present formal ideals, — that is fixed types that are imitated, — except when a natural object is used in daily life; when it is handled, perhaps modified, by technical processes" (Boas 1927 [1922]: 11).

---

[16] See, for example, Wölfflin (1888: chap. 3); the English translation has somewhat distorted the text, *Formgefühl* being variously rendered as "formal sensibility", "formal response" and, worse, "conception of form".

[17] On the relation of Wölfflin to Semper and Riegl, see Payne (2012).

In this way, the formalist perspective in aesthetic theory may be considered as a counterpart to Sapir's view on the potential autonomization of linguistic form.

10 Form-feeling and Formgefühl: Lipps and Dessoir

Perhaps most relevant for our concerns are the discussions of Theodor Lipps (1851–1914) and Max Dessoir (1867–1947), in view of their insistence on the structural features of form, and therefore their possibly greater proximity to Sapir's understanding of the form-feeling.

In his *Aesthetics of Space* (*Raumästhetik*), Lipps (1897) draws a parallel between, on the one hand, this form of unconscious and rule-driven knowledge, intuited by feeling, which we exercise when engaged in "mechanical activities" (such as riding a bicycle) and, on the other hand, the feeling which rules our speech productions, the "language-feeling" or *Sprachgefühl* (a term in common parlance at the time; cf. Tchougounnikov In press). Further, Lipps (1897: chap. 8) states that this "language-feeling" is akin to the "form-feeling" which is built from our bodily experience and our acquaintance with the world of physical objects, and which results in the grasp of general geometrical patterns. These various feelings, though rule-driven, do not rest on an exact memory of past events, since each new case which presents itself is different from the preceding ones; they constitute a *sui generis* kind of knowledge, unconscious and "amazingly sure", says Lipps.

In an introduction to his conception of psychological aesthetics, Lipps (1907) explains that the *Formgefühl* is a feeling assigning a value to the way in which parts are articulated into a whole; that is, to the structure of a pattern. The rules which govern this part-whole organization fall under two main principles: those related to the identification of global organization (e.g. rhythm), and those related to the hierarchical structure of the whole. For instance, in the Greek temple, because of the regular disposition of columns, the principle of rhythmic organization prevails, while in the Gothic cathedral the hierarchical principle is dominant. The beautiful is defined as a vital affirmation of the Ego (*Lebensbejahung*), an affirmation which results from a positive empathy, which Lipps attempts to define in not too nebulous terms. Finally, Lipps characterizes art as a formal language (*Formensprache*), and this formal language he identifies with a play with forms endowed with a functional role (e.g. a capital stylized into a vegetal form).

Close to some positions advocated by Lipps, Dessoir (1906) defines the *Formgefühl* as that feeling which arises from the structural features of proportion, harmony and rhythm, as well as from the quantitative and intensive aspects of forms. The *Formgefühl* itself is carefully distinguished from feelings associated with pure sensations and the content of aesthetic objects; it is therefore a feeling which revels in the organization of formal elements. Much of the discussion centres on rhythm and music and, in fact, the term *Formgefühl* surfaces from time to time, in addition to Dessoir's text, in discussions about the "new music" (*Neue Musik*), such as those of Schönberg and Webern (see e.g. Webern 1912). Given Sapir's intense interest for music and the similarity he perceived between music and language (Darnell 1990: 156), these discussions may have been a possible source too.

11 Conclusion

In a Sapirian spirit we may say that Sapir has assembled into a unique configuration ideas which he had found consonant with his own perspective. That linguistic structures are unconscious was almost a commonplace in the linguistics of the time. However, Sapir's notion of pattern has, to the best of my knowledge, no equivalent. On the one hand, patterns are formed out of groups which are formally and functionally/semantically defined, as in Paul's theory; on the other hand, the combinatorial potential of units, be they phonemes, morphemes or words, helps define unconscious groups, an aspect which brings him closer to Bloomfield. In contrast to Paul, the form-feeling is a window on unconscious structures; its intuitive grasp of linguistically relevant units attests to the psychological reality of forms which abstract away from physical features. The form-feeling warrants, perhaps makes possible, the linguist's labour.

Unconscious patterns were obviously connected in Sapir's mind with the notion of *Gestalt*, and the way Koffka conceived of *Gestalten* may have enticed him to generalize the notion of pattern-*Gestalt* to any culturally significant activity; that is, beyond linguistic behaviour. As to the unconscious structuring of linguistic units, this was not apprehended by Sapir in the "mechanical" fashion of Paul, but as the result of the creative facet of the form-feeling, or form-drive. The form-drive and the form-feeling operate in accordance with entrenched patterns, which may have lost their functional motivation. The conventionality or routinization of patterns invites a parallel with what aesthetics knows as style, and we have seen that for Sapir the creation and perception of linguistic pattern is fundamentally of the same order as the artistic attitude. This insight he said he owed to Croce, but, as we have shown, it can be doubted that Croce's influence went far beyond this very general idea.

If the form-feeling is an allusion to the German *Formgefühl*, as was suggested above, it seems legitimate to examine more closely this notion as it circulated in aesthetics, and ask what, among its various aspects in different authors, had seemed to answer to Sapir's concerns. In this respect, Lipps' theory seems to be especially relevant: like the Sapirian form-feeling, Lipps' aesthetic form-feeling is an unconscious form of knowledge which cannot be reduced to a kind of conceptual knowledge, yet it is rule-driven. Further, it is explicitly compared with that feeling for language which regulates speech production. Given his fame, Wölfflin may have come to Sapir's attention and may have suggested to him a parallel between language and style. Moreover, Wölfflin's formalist perspective and in the same respect that of Lipps and Dessoir was also potentially congenial to the Sapirian view of "form for form's sake". In addition, we may speculate that the problem of stylistic change, of major importance for Wölfflin, could suggest a comparison with the question of linguistic change. Finally, the interplay, in art productions, between functionality, stylization and convention, between emotion-laden and detached formal play may have reinforced the Sapirian view of language as an aesthetic form.

References

Allen, Robert J. 1986. The theme of the unconscious in Sapir's thought. In William Cowan, Michael K. Foster & E. F. Konrad Koerner (eds.), 455–481. Amsterdam/Philadelphia: John Benjamins.

Barasch, Moshe. 1998. *Modern theories of art 2. From Impressionism to Kandinsky.* New York/London: New York University Press.

Blumenbach, Johann Friedrich. 1781. *Über den Bildungstrieb und das Zeugungsgeschäfte.* Göttingen: Dietrich.

Boas, Franz. 1889. On alternating sounds. *American Anthropologist* 2(1). 47–54.

Boas, Franz. 1911. Introduction. In *Handbook of American Indian Languages, Part I*, 1–83. Washington DC: Government Printing Office.

Boas, Franz. 1927 [1922]. *Primitive art.* New York: Dover Publications Inc.

Cowan, William, Michael K. Foster & E. F. Konrad Koerner (eds.). 1986. *New perspectives in language, culture and personality. Proceedings of the Edward Sapir Centenary Conference (Ottawa, 1-3 oct. 1984).* Amsterdam/Philadelphia: John Benjamins.

Croce, Benedetto. 1908 [1902]. *Estetica come scienza dell'espressione e linguistica generale.* Florence: Sandron.

Darnell, Regna. 1990. *Edward Sapir: Linguist, anthropologist, humanist.* Lincoln/London: University of Nebraska Press.

Dessoir, Max. 1906. *Ästhetik und allgemeine Kunstwissenschaft.* Stuttgart: Verlag von Ferdinand Enke.

Ehrenfels, Christian von. 1988 [1890]. On "Gestalt qualities". In Barry Smith (ed.), *Foundations of Gestalt theory*, 82–117. Munich/Vienna: Philosophia Verlag.

Fortis, Jean-Michel. 2014. Sapir's form-feeling and its aesthetic background. *History and Philosophy of the Language Sciences.* http://hiphilangsci.net/2014/10/15/sapirs-form-feeling-and-its-aesthetic-background/.

Fortis, Jean-Michel. 2015. Sapir et le sentiment de la forme. *Histoire Epistémologie Langage* 37(2). 153–174.

Gabelentz, Georg von der. 2016 [1891]. *Die Sprachwissenschaft, ihre Aufgaben, Methoden und bisherigen Ergebnisse.* Berlin: Language Science Press. Edited by Manfred Ringmacher and James McElvenny.

Goldenweiser, Alexander A. 1912. The origins of totemism. *American Anthropologist* 14. 600–607.

Hall, Robert A. 1969. Sapir and Croce on language. *American Anthropologist* 71(3). 498–500.

Handler, Richard. 1986. The aesthetics of Sapir's "Language". In William Cowan, Michael K. Foster & E. F. Konrad Koerner (eds.), 433–454. Amsterdam / Philadelphia: John Benjamins.

Humboldt, Wilhelm von. 1903–1920. *Wilhelm von Humboldts gesammelte Schriften.* Berlin: B. Behr's Verlag. Edited by Albert Leitzmann. 13 vols.

Humboldt, Wilhelm von. 1903 [1794]. Über den Geschlechtsunterschied und dessen Einfluß aud die organische Natur. In *Wilhelm von Humboldts gesammelte Schriften*, vol. I, 311–334. Berlin: B. Behr's Verlag. Edited by Albert Leitzmann. 13 vols.

Humboldt, Wilhelm von. 1907 [1830-35]. Über die Verschiedenheit des menschlichen Sprachbaues und ihren Einfluß auf die geistige Entwicklung des Menschengeschlechts. In *Wilhelm von Humboldts gesammelte Schriften*, vol. VII, part 1, 1–349. Berlin: B. Behr's Verlag. Edited by Albert Leitzmann. 13 vols.

Humboldt, Wilhelm von. 1988 [1830–1835]. *On language. the diversity of human language-structure and its influence on the mental development of mankind.* Cambridge University Press. Trans. by Peter Heath of Humboldt (1907 [1830-35]).

Hymes, Dell. 1969. Modjeska on Sapir and Croce: A comment. *American Anthropologist* 71(3). 500.

Jespersen, Otto. 1894. *Progress in language.* London: Swan, Sonnenschein & Co.

Jespersen, Otto. 1965 [1924]. *The philosophy of grammar.* New York: W. W. Norton & Company.

Jones, Ernest. 1916. The theory of symbolism. *British Journal of Psychology* 9. 181–229.

Joseph, John E. 2002. The sources of the Sapir-Whorf hypothesis. In *From Whitney to Chomsky. Essays in the history of American linguistics,* 71–105. Amsterdam/Philadelphia: John Benjamins.

Jung, Carl G. 1921. *Psychologische Typen.* Zürich: Rascher.

Koffka, Kurt. 1924. *The growth of the mind.* London: Routledge & Kegan Paul.

Lipps, Theodor. 1897. *Raumästhetik und geometrisch-optische Täuschungen.* Leipzig: Barth.

Lipps, Theodor. 1907. Ästhetik. In Wilhelm Dilthey (ed.), *Systematische Philosophie,* 349–388. Berlin/Leipzig: B. G. Teuber.

Malkiel, Yakov. 1981. Drift, slope and slant: Background of, and variations upon a Sapirian theme. *Language* 57(3). 535–570.

McElvenny, James. 2013. Otto Jespersen and progress in international language. *History and Philosophy of the Language Sciences.* https://hiphilangsci.net/2013/05/15/otto-jespersen-and-progress-in-international-language/.

McElvenny, James. 2016. The fate of form in the Humboldtian tradition: The *Formungstrieb* of Georg von der Gabelentz. *Language and Communication* 47. 30–42.

McElvenny, James. 2017a. Grammar, typology and the Humboldtian tradition in the work of Georg von der Gabelentz. *Language and History* 60(1). 1–20.

McElvenny, James. 2017b. Linguistic aesthetics from the nineteenth to the twentieth century: The case of Otto Jespersen's 'progress in language'. *History of Humanities* 2(2). 417–442.

Modjeska, C. N. 1968. A note on unconscious structure in the anthropology of Edward Sapir. *American Anthropologist* 70. 344–348.

Murray, Stephen O. 1981. Sapir's Gestalt. *Anthropological Linguistics* 23(1). 8–12.

Nahlowsky, Joseph Wilhelm. 1862. *Das Gefühlsleben. In seinen wesentlichsten Erscheinungen und Bezügen dargestellt.* Leipzig: Veit.

Ogden, Charles K. & Ivor A. Richards. 1923. *The meaning of meaning: A study of the influence of language upon thought and of the science of symbolism.* London: Kegan Paul, Trench, Trubner & Co.

Paul, Hermann. 1920 [1880]. *Prinzipien der Sprachgeschichte.* Halle: Max Niemeyer.

Payne, Alina. 2012. Wölfflin, architecture and the problem of Stilwandlung. *Journal of Art Historiography* 7. 1–20.

Riegl, Alois. 1893. *Stilfragen: Grundlegungen zu einer Geschichte der Ornamentik*. Berlin: Georg Siemens.

Romand, David. 2015. Theodor Waitz's theory of feelings and the rise of affective sciences in the mid-19th century. *History of Psychology* 18(4). 385–400.

Romand, David. 2018. An unorthodox Herbartian in Graz: Joseph Wilhelm Nahlowsky's 'affective Herbartianism'. In Rainer Bolle & Jean-François Goubet (eds.), *Herbart als Universitätslehrer*, 203–220. Jena: IKS Garamond.

Romand, David. In press. More on formal feeling/form-feeling in language sciences. Heinrich Gomperz's concept of "formal logical feeling" (logisches Formalgefühl) revisited. *Histoire Epistémologie Langage*.

Sapir, Edward. 1951 [1912]. Language and environment. In *Selected writings of Edward Sapir in language, culture and personality*, 89–103. Berkeley/Los Angeles: University of California Press. Edited by David G. Mandelbaum.

Sapir, Edward. 1951 [1916]. Time perspective in aboriginal american culture: A study in method. In *Selected writings of Edward Sapir in language, culture and personality*, 389–462. Berkeley/Los Angeles: University of California Press. Edited by David G. Mandelbaum.

Sapir, Edward. 1921. *Language: An introduction to the study of speech*. San Diego / New York / London: Harcourt, Brace & Co.

Sapir, Edward. 1991 [1923]. A type of Athabaskan relative. In *The collected works of Edward Sapir*, vol. VI, 143–149. Berlin: De Gruyter. Edited by Philip Sapir et al. 14 vols.

Sapir, Edward. 1951 [1924]. The grammarian and his language. In *Selected writings of Edward Sapir in language, culture and personality*, 150–159. Berkeley/Los Angeles: University of California Press. Edited by David G. Mandelbaum.

Sapir, Edward. 1951 [1925]. Sound patterns in language. In *Selected writings of Edward Sapir in language, culture and personality*, 33–60. Berkeley/Los Angeles: University of California Press. Edited by David G. Mandelbaum.

Sapir, Edward. 1951 [1927](a). Anthropology and sociology. In *Selected writings of Edward Sapir in language, culture and personality*, 332–345. Berkeley/Los Angeles: University of California Press. Edited by David G. Mandelbaum.

Sapir, Edward. 1951 [1927](b). The unconscious patterning of behavior in society. In *Selected writings of Edward Sapir in language, culture and personality*, 544–559. Berkeley/Los Angeles: University of California Press. Edited by David G. Mandelbaum.

Sapir, Edward. 2002 [1928-1937]. *The psychology of culture. A course of lectures.* Berlin/New York: Mouton de Gruyter.

Sapir, Edward. 1951 [1929]. The function of an international auxiliary language. In *Selected writings of Edward Sapir in language, culture and personality*, 110–121. Berkeley/Los Angeles: University of California Press. Edited by David G. Mandelbaum.

Sapir, Edward. 1951 [1931]. The function of an international auxiliary language. In *Selected writings of Edward Sapir in language, culture and personality*, 110–121. Berkeley/Los Angeles: University of California Press. Edited by David G. Mandelbaum.

Sapir, Edward. 1951 [1933]. La réalité psychologique des phonèmes. *Journal de Psychologie Normale et Pathologique* 30. 247–265. Trans. as "The psychological reality of phonemes" in Sapir (1951: 46–50).

Sapir, Edward. 1999 [1933]. Sapir's lists of suggested readings for "the impact of culture on personality" (1933–1934) and "the psychology of culture" (1935–1936). In *The collected works of Edward Sapir*, vol. III, 677–678. Berlin: De Gruyter. Edited by Philip Sapir et al. 14 vols.

Sapir, Edward. 1951 [1934]. Symbolism. In *Selected writings of Edward Sapir in language, culture and personality*, 564–568. Berkeley/Los Angeles: University of California Press. Edited by David G. Mandelbaum.

Sapir, Edward. 1951. *Selected writings of Edward Sapir in language, culture and personality.* Berkeley/Los Angeles: University of California Press. Edited by David G. Mandelbaum.

Sapir, Edward. 1990–. *The collected works of Edward Sapir.* Berlin: De Gruyter. Edited by Philip Sapir et al. 14 vols.

Schiller, Friedrich von. 1795. *Über die ästhetische Erziehung des Menschen in einer Reyhe von Briefen.* Tübingen: J. G. Cotta.

Semper, Gottfried. 1884. *Kleine Schriften.* Berlin/Stuttgart: W. Spemann.

Silverstein, Michael. 1986. The diachrony of Sapir's synchronic linguistic description. In William Cowan, Michael K. Foster & E. F. Konrad Koerner (eds.), 67–110. Amsterdam/Philadelphia: John Benjamins.

Stumpf, Carl. 1911. *Die Anfänge der Musik.* Leipzig: Johann Ambrosius Barth.

Tchougounnikov, Serguei. In press. *Le "sentiment de la langue" (Sprachgefühl) dans la "linguistique psychologique" (fin du XIXème – début du XXème siècle).*

Vischer, Robert. 1873. *Über das optische Formgefühl. Ein Beitrag zur Aesthetik.* Leipzig: Hermann Credner.

Waitz, Theodor. 1849. *Lehrbuch der Psychologie als Naturwissenschaft.* Braunschweig: Vieweg.

Webern, Anton. 1912. Schönbergs Musik. In Alban Berg (ed.), *Arnold Schön-berg. Mit Beiträgen von Alban Berg, Paris von Gütersloh, K. Horwitz, Heinrich Jalowetz, W. Kandisky, Paul Königer, Karl Linke, Robert Neumann, Erwin Stein, A. v. Webern, Egon Wellesz*, 22–48. München: Piper.

Wissler, Clark. 1917. *The American Indian*. New York: Douglas C. McMurtrie.

Wölfflin, Heinrich. 1886. *Prolegomena zu einer Psychologie der Architektur*. Universität München dissertation.

Wölfflin, Heinrich. 1888. *Renaissance und Barock. Eine Untersuchung über Wesen und Entstehung des Barockstils in Italien*. Munich: Theodor Ackermann.

Wundt, Wilhelm. 1908–1911 [1874]. *Grundzüge der Physiologischen Psychologie*. Leipzig: W. Endelmann.

Chapter 4

Linguistics as a "special science": A comparison of Sapir and Fodor

Els Elffers

Independently of each other, the linguist-anthropologist Edward Sapir (1884–1939) and the philosopher of mind Jerry Fodor (1935–2017) developed a similar typology of scientific disciplines. "Basic" (Fodor) or "conceptual" (Sapir) sciences (e.g. physics) are distinguished from "special" (Fodor) or "historical" (Sapir) sciences (e.g. linguistics). Ontologically, the latter sciences are reducible to the former, but they keep their autonomy as intellectual enterprises, because their "natural kinds" are unlike those of the basic sciences. Fodor labelled this view "token physicalism". Although Sapir's and Fodor's ideas were presented in very different periods of intellectual history (in 1917 and 1974) and in very different intellectual contexts (roughly: *Geisteswissenschaften* and logical positivism), the similarity between them is striking. When compared in detail, some substantial differences can also be observed, which are mainly related to contextual differences. When applied to linguistics, Sapir's and Fodor's views offer a perspective of autonomy, albeit in different ways: for Fodor, but not for Sapir, linguistics is a subfield of psychology.

1 Introduction

In 1974, Jerry Fodor (1935–2017) introduced "token physicalism", a non-reductive variety of physicalism, which applies to "special sciences".[1] According to Fodor, special sciences, such as economics, psychology and linguistics cannot be entirely reduced to physics, which is a "basic science". Such a reduction would imply that special sciences actually disappear as autonomous sciences.

According to Fodor, special sciences retain their autonomy, because reduction is possible only with respect to the events they describe ("tokens"), not with

---

[1]Token physicalism belongs to a larger class of non-reductive types of physicalism. Supervenience physicalism and emergentism are other members. John Stuart Mill (1806–1873) is generally regarded as an early representative of non-reductive physicalism.

Els Elffers. 2019. Linguistics as a "special science". A comparison of Sapir and Fodor. In James McElvenny (ed.), *Form and formalism in linguistics*, 89–114. Berlin: Language Science Press. DOI:10.5281/zenodo.2654355

respect to properties or natural kinds ("types"). For example, economic events such as monetary exchanges are, ultimately, physical events, but, from a physical point of view, very heterogeneous ones. There is no single physical natural kind corresponding to the economic natural kind "monetary exchange", because such exchanges may involve "strings of wampum, [...] dollar bills, [...or] signing one's name to a check" (Fodor 1974: 103). Physics, according to Fodor the only "basic science", develops taxonomies of physical phenomena in terms of physical properties. Special sciences develop their own taxonomies of, ultimately, physical phenomena as well, but in other terms, not belonging to the vocabulary of physics.

In this chapter, I will compare Fodor's token physicalism with ideas of Edward Sapir (1889–1939), presented in an article published in 1917. I will argue that Sapir's ideas are highly similar to Fodor's. Despite differences, Sapir's "conceptual sciences" and "historical sciences" resemble Fodor's basic and special sciences to such a degree that, in this respect, Sapir can be regarded as Fodor's predecessor.

Historians, including historians of linguistics, apply the concept "predecessorship" in different and partially unfounded ways. In §2, I will briefly discuss this problem and present my own view of predecessorship, including its implications for the concept "predecessorship of token physicalism".

In the sections that follow, I will argue that this concept applies to Sapir. §3 will discuss Sapir's distinction of conceptual and historical sciences in detail. In §4, Fodor's token physicalism is further analysed. Together, these sections present a picture of similar theories, developed in different periods, intellectual contexts, and with different motivations. §5–§7 present a systematic comparison of both theories. In §8–§10, both theories will be discussed in a broader context, both chronologically and intellectually.

The views of both Sapir and Fodor were presented without any special focus on linguistics. In linguistic circles, their views are not well known. In §12, I will explore the linguistic implications of Sapir's and Fodor's varieties of token physicalism.

2 Pitfalls of predecessorship

"Predecessorship" belongs, together with some other concepts (e.g. "influence" or "source"), to the more dangerous instruments of the historian's toolbox. They are applied in multifarious and sometimes confusing ways. Present-day dangers of "predecessorship" can be partially attributed to the belated influences of older approaches to intellectual historiography:

1. The exegetical "history of ideas" approach, with its focus on isolated and quasi-immutable "ideas" or "themes", and their march through history.

2. The historicist approach (in one of many meanings of this term)[2] of interpreting chronological sequences of events in causal, teleological or developmental terms.

Unwarranted claims of predecessorship are corollaries of (1) and (2).[3] I mention an example of both, to be found in historiography of linguistics:

Ad 1. In Antal (1984), the entire history of linguistics is interpreted in terms of an alternation of two themes: "psychologism" and "objectivism". Hermann Paul (1846–1921) is thus presented as a "psychologistic" predecessor of Noam Chomsky (b. 1928). The term "psychologism" applied to approaches as far apart as those of Paul and Chomsky, is, however, almost meaningless, and so is the predecessorship conclusion based upon it.

Ad 2. In Chomsky's (2009 [1966]) well-known *Cartesian Linguistics*, the seventeenth-century Port-Royal Grammar is presented as a – still imperfect – predecessor of twentieth-century generative grammar. This claim has been amply criticized as being based upon an incorrect and biased interpretation of seventeenth-century grammar, and as a specimen of presentism, Whig history and ancestor hunt. All these defects are rooted in the historicist idea of chronology as a series of developmental steps towards the present.

Although pitfalls (1) and (2) are well known today, the danger of unwarranted claims of predecessorship still exist. It is natural for historians to compare phenomena over time. Discovering similarities easily creates "the temptation to discern and extract pervasive themes or patterns running through and manifested in the succession of events and activities" (Robins 1997 [1967]: 7–8). Moreover, historicism (conceived in the above manner) is still influential in the way it permeates our common historical vocabulary, which "presents history as a 'stream'

---

[2] The meaning of "historicism" applied here is related to the meaning of other "-ism" terms such as "psychologism" or "scientism"; these terms claim to reveal "where" the essence of things has to be looked for. This meaning of "historicism" has to be distinguished from, e.g., Popper's use of the term (cf. Elffers 1991: 43).

[3] Cf. Elffers (1991: chaps. 2 & 3) for a more thorough and comprehensive discussion of these influences in present-day intellectual historiography, and for more details of the alternative approach, briefly indicated on p. 92 of this chapter as reconstruction of earlier scientific ideas "as problem solutions within the context of the contemporary intellectual state-of-the-art".

which proceeds irresistibly [...]. Metaphors talking of 'progress' [...] constitute examples: 'avant-garde' art, advanced technique [...], locutions like 'keeping pace with' [...] or 'being in advance of' one's time as well as clock-metaphors, such as 'turning back' or 'stopping' the clock [...]" (van der Dussen 1986: 131, transl. E. E.)[4]

If the above pitfalls are avoided, the establishment of predecessorship relations in intellectual history may become a more complicated task, but it continues to be interesting and rewarding; indeed, even more so, because we are now disregarding superficial historical similarities as well as irrelevant later developments. Instead, we are thoroughly analysing and comparing the actual contents of scientific ideas, which are carefully reconstructed as problem-solutions within the context of the contemporary intellectual state of the art.

Following this approach, I assume that a predecessor of token physicalism was similar to Fodor with respect to the questions that Fodor answered by postulating token physicalism, and to the answers themselves.

Questions – predecessors of token physicalism are involved in:

a. Ontological questions concerning basic categories of entities.

b. Epistemological questions about the basic categories of separate disciplines.

Answers: Predecessors of token physicalism present theories which take into account questions (a) and (b) and assume that for one or more "basic" disciplines, the categories of (a)-answers and (b)-answers are identical. For other, "special", disciplines, the categories of (a)-answers and (b)-answers are non-identical.[5]

Predecessorship thus conceived is typically unconstrained by terminology. Terminological identity may conceal fundamental differences in content, and vice versa. Consequently, predecessors of token physicalism may apply quite different terms from those used in the above preliminary assumption. The only requirement is that the content of their statements can be interpreted in terms of this assumption. This also applies to Fodor himself: Fodor (1974) does not use the term

---

[4] "...waarbij de geschiedenis wordt voorgesteld als een 'stroom', die onweerstaanbaar [...] voortgaat. Metaforen waarin over een 'vooruitgang' wordt gesproken [...] zijn hier voorbeelden van: 'avant-garde' kunst, geavanceerde techniek [...] het spreken van een 'meegaan' met de tijd [...] of zijn tijd 'vooruit' zijn, evenals klok-metaforen, zoals de klok 'terugdraaien' of 'stilzetten' [...]"

[5] Against this background, I regard Seuren's (2016: 827–832) claim that a scholar much earlier than Sapir, Hyppolyte Taine (1828–1893), anticipated Fodor's token physicalism as unconvincing. Seuren presents quotations to support his view, but none of them suggests a distinction comparable to the distinction between (a) and (b).

"ontological" at all, and he sometimes gives the term "epistemological" a rather specific meaning.[6] But the content of his statements meets the requirement of being interpretable in the above terms, as I hope to show below.

3 Sapir: against a "superorganic"

Sapir's 1917 article is titled "Do we need a 'Superorganic'?" It is a reaction to the anthropologist Alfred Kroeber's (1876–1960) article "The Superorganic" (Kroeber 1917). Both articles were published in subsequent issues of *American Anthropologist*, an anthropological journal that is still quite prominent in the field.[7]

Both Kroeber and Sapir were students of Franz Boas (1858–1942), the "founding father" of American anthropology. Kroeber, who became an influential American anthropologist, argues in his 1917 article against the reduction of anthropology to biology. He states that human cultural behaviour, unlike animal behaviour, cannot be explained through an appeal to inheritance plus Darwinian adaptation, nor to personal psychology. The forces of culture, a superorganic and autonomously developing entity, are the main determinants. For anthropology, this superorganic is the actual object of research.[8]

When Sapir wrote his critical article, he was working as director of the Anthropological Division of the Geological Survey of Canada in Ottawa. This was a very productive period in his career. Anthropological linguistics, which included the investigation and description of American Indian languages never studied by academics before, was his main area of research. He exchanged correspondence with Kroeber over a period of many years.

In "Do we need a 'Superorganic'?", Sapir begins by welcoming Kroeber's "salutary antidote" to the trend of applying methods used by the exact sciences to the study of culture. But he also feels that Kroeber "has allowed himself to go further than he is warranted in going" on "two points of considerable theoretical importance" (Sapir 1917: 441). Although only the second point directly concerns our subject, I will also briefly discuss the first one, because there is, according to Sapir, a connection between them.

---

[6]"Epistemological" as used in Fodor (1974: 113) refers to the "context of discovery". This deviates from the usual reference, which is primarily to the "context of justification".

[7]Sapir's article appeared in the section "Discussion and correspondence". Another comment on Kroeber's article by A. A. Goldenweiser (1917) was included in the same section.

[8]Herbert Spencer (1820–1903) coined the term "super-organic" to focus on social organization, in the first chapter of his 1898 *Principles of Sociology*, entitled "Super-organic Evolution".

The first point concerns Kroeber's denial of any influence by individuals on the course of cultural history. Sapir admits that the influence of individuals is mostly highly exaggerated by historians. He fully recognizes that individual thought and action are very much moulded by cultural traditions, and that the cultural influence of most individuals is nil. If it is not nil, broader cultural conditions are necessary to trigger this influence. But this does not obviate the influence of at least some individuals – such as Napoleon, Jesus, Shakespeare or Beethoven – on cultural history, according to Sapir. A total social determinism goes too far.

The second point concerns the nature of social phenomena. Kroeber claims that they are built out of organic phenomena but are not reducible to organic phenomena, just as organic phenomena are built out of inorganic phenomena but are not reducible to them. A superorganic social "force" is assumed, which is manifested in social history.

Sapir regards the above analogy as false. The types of irreducibility are entirely dissimilar. Sapir's ontology is trialistic. He assumes three basic types of entities: inorganic, organic and psychic. Social phenomena are not a fourth type, as Kroeber feels they are, but "merely a certain philosophically arbitrary but humanly immensely significant *selection* out of the total mass of phenomena ideally resolvable into inorganic, organic and psychic processes" (Sapir 1917: 444, italics Sapir). Social phenomena are, therefore, not at all conceptually irresolvable but experientially irresolvable. Conceptual irresolvability is what separates inorganic, organic and psychic phenomena; these are, in Sapir's terms "true conceptual incommensurables" (Sapir 1917: 445). Experiential irresolvability is entirely different: it refers to classes of directly experienced phenomena, demarcated not in terms of ontology, but in terms of values that determine their selection. These classes are studied in historical sciences. Conceptually demarcated classes are studied in conceptual sciences.

Sapir illustrates his distinction between types of science using the example of geology:

> Few sciences are so clearly defined as regards scope as geology. It would ordinarily be classed as a natural science. Aside from paleontology, which we may eliminate, it does entirely without the concepts of the social, psychic or organic. It is, then, a well-defined science of purely inorganic subject matter. As such, it is conceptually resolvable, if we carry our reductions far enough, into the more fundamental sciences of physics and chemistry. But no amount of conceptual synthesis of the phenomena we call chemical or physical would, in the absence of previous experience, enable us to construct a science of geology. The science depends for its *raison d'être* on a

series of unique experiences, directly sensed or inferred, clustering about an entity, the earth, which from the conceptual standpoint of physics is as absurdly accidental or irrelevant as a tribe of Indians or John Smith's breakfast. The basis of the science is, then, grounded in the unique relevance of particular events. To be precise, geology looks in two directions. In so far as it occupies itself with abstract masses and forces, it is a conceptual science, for which specific instances as such are irrelevant. In so far as it deals with particular features of the earth's surface, say a particular mountain chain, and aims to reconstruct the probable history of such features, it is not a conceptual science at all. In methodology, strange as this may seem at first blush, it is actually nearer, in this respect, to the historical sciences. It is, in fact, a species of history, only the history moves entirely in the inorganic sphere. In practice, it is, of course, a mixed type of science, now primarily conceptual, now primarily descriptive of a selective chunk of reality. (Sapir 1917: 445)[9]

As examples of "chunks of reality" studied by historical sciences, Sapir also mentions, next to the earth, "France, the French language, the French Republic, the romantic movement in literature, Victor Hugo, the Iroquois Indians, some specific Iroquois clan, all Iroquois clans, all American Indian clans, all clans of primitive peoples." Sapir (1917: 446) stresses that none of these terms has any relevance in a purely conceptual world, whether organic, inorganic or psychic.

These examples are not selected arbitrarily. Sapir wants to show (i) that historical sciences apply to "history" in a much wider sense than the word ordinarily indicates, (ii) that historical sciences not only study directly experienced entities, but also more abstract entities.

Sapir elaborates on (ii) in order to explain two further differences between types of science: "such concepts as a clan, a language, a priesthood" might suggest a similarity with "the ideal concepts of natural science", which also "lack individual connotation" and appear in generalized laws. Logically, both sets of concepts are involved in similar operations such as observation, classification, inference, generalization etc. "Philosophically", however, the concepts are distinct, because, in actual fact, the social concepts are not "ideal" at all; they are "convenient summaries of a strictly limited range of phenomena, each element of which has real value":

---

[9]In this quotation, physics and chemistry are both mentioned as fundamental sciences of the inorganic. In 1917, reducibility of chemistry to physics was not at all as generally accepted as it is today (cf. Hettema 2012: 13, 17–18).

> Relatively to the concept "clan" a particular clan of a specific Indian tribe
> has undeniably value as a historical entity. Relatively to the concept "crys-
> tal" a particular ruby in the jeweler's shop has no relevance except by way
> of illustration. It has no intrinsic scientific value. Were all crystals exis-
> tent at this moment suddenly disintegrated, the science of crystallography
> would still be valid, provided the physical and chemical forces that make
> possible the growth of another crop of crystals remain in the world. Were
> all clans now existent annihilated, it is highly debatable, to say the least,
> whether the science of sociology, in so far as it occupied itself with clans,
> would have prognostic value. (Sapir 1917: 446–447)

A corollary of this difference is the different status of laws in both types of science. A sociological law is a generalization, an abbreviation for a finite number of
phenomena. Exceptions occur, and the laws become "more and more blurred in
outline with the multiplication of instances", whereas this multiplication makes
natural laws "more and more rigid" (Sapir 1917: 447). Natural laws cover an indefinitely large number of phenomena and have to be exceptionless: an exception
necessitates a new formulation of the law.

Sapir concludes his article by connecting his two criticisms of Kroeber: if the
nature of historical phenomena had been sufficiently clear to him, he would have
felt no need to invoke a "superorganic" force as a unique explanans in history,
and to deny individual force.

4 Fodor: against reductive physicalism

Fodor's article is titled "Special sciences (or: the disunity of science as a working
hypothesis)". It was published in 1974 in *Synthèse*, a well-known philosophical
journal that is still published. It takes as its starting point the "typical thesis of
positivistic philosophy of science [...] that all true theories in the special sciences
should reduce to physical theories in the long run" (Fodor 1974: 97). This thesis,
and its foundation in a materialist ontology, were the cornerstones of the Unity of
Science movement, to which Fodor's title alludes. This movement was narrowly
related to logical positivism during the first decades of the twentieth century.
Since those days, questions about the unity of science and about reductivism
have never disappeared from the philosophical agenda.

When Fodor wrote "Special sciences", he was a professor in the departments
of philosophy and psychology at the Massachusetts Institute of Technology. Philosophy of mind and language was his central subject of research. He had already

published widely on many themes related to this area. In 1975, his seminal book *The language of thought* would appear. In "Special sciences", psychology is by far the science that receives the most attention.

Fodor addresses a problem that results from the positivistic assumption that the subject matter of a special (i.e. non-physical) science, such as psychology, is part of the subject matter of physics. A generally accepted inference from this assumption is that psychological theories must reduce to physical theories. This causes methodological problems for psychology; the discipline should actually disappear as a separate science. Fodor (1974: 98) wants to "avoid the trouble by challenging the inference".

Assuming that sciences are about events, Fodor claims, in agreement with the physicalists, that "all events that the sciences talk about are physical events [...]" (Fodor 1974: 100). He calls this doctrine "token physicalism". But he rejects the stronger reductionist doctrine of "type physicalism", which claims that, in addition, every property mentioned in the laws of any science is a physical property. Token physicalism claims that, for example, every psychological event is identical to a neurological event, but not every psychological property is identical to a neurological property.

The reason why type physicalism is too strong a thesis is that interesting generalizations in special sciences are often about events whose physical descriptions have nothing in common. Moreover, the question "whether the physical descriptions have anything in common is, in an obvious sense, entirely irrelevant to the truth of the generalizations, or to their interestingness, or to their degree of confirmation, or, indeed, to any of their epistemologically important properties [...]" (Fodor 1974: 103). As an example of such a generalization, Fodor refers to Graham's Law, an economic law about monetary exchanges. In the above introduction, this example was already mentioned to illustrate the wildly different physical events which correspond to the concept of "monetary exchange" (transactions with bills, cheques etc.). These events do not correspond to a natural kind in physics. Similarly, although psychological events correspond to neurological events, "there are no firm data for any but the grossest correspondence between types of psychological states and types of neurological states, and it is entirely possible that the nervous system of higher organisms characteristically achieves a given psychological end by a wide variety of neurological states" (Fodor 1974: 105).[10]

---

[10]Fodor refers to the physiological psychologist Karl Lashley as a defender of this claim. He also acknowledges that there is much "psychology and brain" research throughout the world, which is based upon the assumption that psychological types correspond to neurological types (Fodor 1974: 105).

Fodor further supports his token physicalistic view by arguing that his view explains (i) that laws of special sciences have exceptions, (ii) why there are special sciences at all.

Ad i. Given the assumption that, in a special science law, physical counterparts of the antecedent as well as the consequent consist of heterogeneous disjunctions, the counterpart "law" cannot be a genuine physical law.[11] Exceptions occur when the physical counterpart of an instantiation of the antecedent of a special science law has no lawlike connection with one of the disjunctive physical counterparts of the consequent. According to Fodor, this is a common situation in a special science such as psychology: there are always exceptions to psychological generalizations which are "uninteresting from the point of view of psychological theory" (Fodor 1974: 111).

Ad ii. According to reductionists, special sciences exist for practical, "epistemological" (cf. footnote 6) reasons. If neurons were not so small and brains were on the outside of the head, we would do neurology instead of psychology. Fodor does not agree: even if brains were on the outside, we would not know what to look for, lacking "the appropriate theoretical apparatus for the psychological taxonomy of neurological events". Moreover, he assumes that such a corresponding taxonomy does not necessarily exist, that "quite different neurological structures can subserve identical psychological functions [...] In that case the existence of psychology depends not on the fact that neurons are so sadly small, but rather on the fact that neurology does not posit the natural kinds that psychology requires" (Fodor 1974: 113).

Special sciences exist autonomously, because other taxonomies are required alongside the taxonomy which suits the purpose of formulating exceptionless basic physical laws. The other taxonomies are necessary for the formulation of important generalizations in areas of knowledge such as psychology or economics.

5 Similarities and differences

The last two sections show two scholars struggling for a plausible philosophical reconstruction of science in general and its division into separate disciplines in

---

[11]This is a very brief and simplified presentation of a complex argument, presented in Fodor (1974: 109).

particular. Independently from each other and separated by nearly six decades, they devised a nearly identical theory.[12] According to this theory, boundaries between disciplines are not merely determined by the kind of stuff they investigate. Although some ("conceptual" or "basic") sciences can be demarcated along these lines, other ("historical" or "special") sciences are demarcated in a different way. Their object of investigation consists of heterogeneous stuff, but is homogeneous by its relevance to the purposes of the area of knowledge to which they belong.

For Sapir, the theory was a welcome alternative to Kroeber's ontological way of rescuing the autonomy of sociology and anthropology through the assumption of a superorganic force. For Fodor, the theory was a welcome alternative to reductive physicalism, with its problematic methodological requirements, especially for psychology.

Due to these different backgrounds, the theories have a different "appearance". In Fodor's discourse, subtle logical properties of scientific theories are taken into account, as was (and is) usual in positivistic-oriented philosophy of science. In Sapir's and Kroeber's discourse, this approach is entirely absent, also in conformity with what was (and is) usual in philosophy of non-exact sciences.

In the following sections, Sapir's and Fodor's theories will be compared in more detail. Their common basic idea is elaborated in partially different ways by both scholars. Part of these differences can be shown to be related to the intellectual context in which the theories were developed.

In the rest of this article, I will use Fodor's term "token physicalism" to refer to the common view of Sapir and Fodor.[13] In the same vein, I will adopt Fodor's terms "basic science" and "special science" for the similar types of sciences distinguished by both scholars.

My comparison is almost entirely based upon the articles just discussed. Neither Sapir nor Fodor elaborated their theory further in later publications. Fodor, however, returned to the subject in his article "Special sciences: still autonomous after all these years", published in 1997. This article consists of a defence of his view against the criticism of Kim (1992). In the course of this defence, some aspects of token physicalism are presented in more detail than before. An addition, which is relevant to our comparison with Sapir, is that special sciences are now explicitly described in functionalistic terms. Their physically heterogeneous natural kinds are functionally homogeneous, in the same way as physically het-

---

[12]Of course, Fodor *could* have read Sapir's article, but I regard this as improbable. As far as I know, Fodor never refers to Sapir. Moreover, Sapir's intellectual activities and viewpoints were unrelated to Fodor's area of interest, or even repugnant to him (cf. Pullum 2017).

[13]The literal meaning of the term has to be bracketed in Sapir's case, because of his trialistic ontology.

erogeneous types of artefacts (can openers, mousetraps) are functionally homogeneous (Fodor 1997: 160). This characterization was lacking in the 1974 article,
although "psychological functions" are mentioned. The term "functional" must
be interpreted in a very broad sense, because it is equally applied to biology,
psychology and geology. The last mentioned example of a special science is a
new one, and identical to Sapir's example. Like Sapir, Fodor (1997: 160) claims
that mountains are made "of all sorts of stuff", but that "generalizations about
mountains-as-such [...] serve geology in good stead".

Taking into account the 1997 additions to Fodor's theory, the views of Sapir
and Fodor, as presented in §3 and §4 can be schematically juxtaposed as in Table 1.

Table 1: Comparison of the views of Sapir and Fodor

| | Basic sciences | | Special sciences | |
	Sapir	*Fodor*	*Sapir*	*Fodor*
Sciences	Physics, Chemistry, Geology, Biology, Psychology	Physics	Sociology, Anthropology, Linguistics, Geology, (Cultural) History	Psychology, Linguistics, Biology, Geology
Demarcation	Ontological	Ontological	Experiential	Functional
Exceptions of laws?	No	No	Yes	Yes

Table 1 shows that Sapir's and Fodor's varieties of token physicalism are different at two points: (i) their selection of basic and special sciences, (ii) their characterization of special sciences. As to (i), we may ask how far the differences can be
related to contemporary ontological assumptions. As to (ii), we may ask how far
apart the standpoints actually are, given the similarity of both scholars' general
view of the special sciences. Likewise, we may ask how far their agreement about
the issue of exceptions to laws actually goes, given the different motivations of
these ideas, observed earlier. I will discuss these three issues in separate sections.

6 Which basic and special sciences?

Fodor recognizes one basic science, physics, which is in conformity with the positivistic discourse he connects with. In the same vein, he also mentions chemistry
as a science that has been successfully reduced to physics.

His most important example of a special science is psychology. The anti-reductionist defence of the autonomy of this science is his central aim, and directly relevant to his work as a cognitive psychologist. In his seminal book *The language of thought* (1975), the text of "Special sciences" is included in the introductory chapter, which presents the foundations of the psychological and linguistic approach described and applied in the rest of the book.[14]

Linguistics is not explicitly discussed in the 1974 article.[15] However, Fodor has always incorporated linguistics in psychology, following Chomsky's views and elaborating this connectedness in more detail than Chomsky did (cf., e.g., Fodor 1985: 149, quoted in footnote 26; and Loewer & Rey 1991: 278). *The language of thought* bears clear witness to this approach. So there can be no doubt that, for Fodor, linguistics is a special science. Other special sciences, such as economics and geology, are dealt with as instructive examples.

Sapir distinguishes three irreducible ontological categories: inorganic, organic and psychic. Inorganic sciences are physics, chemistry, and, partially, geology; psychology is the basic science of the psychic. Sapir does not mention examples of organic sciences, but we may assume that biology is the main, or even only, example of this category.

Sapir does not present arguments in favour of his trialistic ontology. He simply claims that "the organic can be demonstrated to consist objectively of the inorganic plus an increment of obscure origin and nature". There is "a chasm between the organic and the inorganic which only the rigid mechanists pretend to be able to bridge. There seems to be a unbridgeable chasm [...] between the organic and the psychic, despite the undeniable correlations between the two. Dr. Kroeber denies this *en passant* [...]" (Sapir 1917: 444).

These quotations show that Sapir is aware of the existence of divergent ontological ideas, but he does not feel obliged to supply arguments for his own view. This is not surprising when we take contemporary ontological thought into account. Vitalism, the idea that organic nature is created from chemical elements plus the action of a "vital force" had been waning over several decades, but was not at all extinct (cf. Beckner 1967). Psychology was, despite some reductionistic attempts, still largely regarded as studying purely mental entities. This applies, for example, to Gestalt psychology, an approach Sapir found appealing (cf. Sapir 2002 [1928-1937]: xvi).

---

[14]There are some minor differences between the article and the book section. The book section contains more notes and is extended by some final paragraphs.

[15]There is, however a note reference to Chomsky's (1965) statements about natural language predicates, to support Fodor's claim that natural kind predicates of the special sciences cross-classify the physical natural kinds.

An example of a special science is, for Sapir, in the first place, social science, including anthropology, the common discipline of Kroeber and himself. Other examples are history – cf. Sapir's term "historical sciences" – and, partially, geology. Given the above examples of "chunks of reality" studied by historical sciences, we can add linguistics (cf. "the French language") and literary history (cf. "the romantic movement in literature").

In summary, Sapir's and Fodor's examples as well as ideas about the position of separate disciplines in their dichotomy are partially different. This is mainly due to their different basic ontologies and their implications, especially for psychology. A remarkable conclusion about linguistics is that its status of special science has a different meaning for Sapir and Fodor. For Sapir, a language is an ontologically heterogeneous entity. So linguistics is not reducible to psychology, nor to any other basic science. Fodor includes linguistics in psychology, but for him, psychology is itself a special science, due to ontological irreducibility. In §12 I will return to this issue.

7 Characterizing special sciences

The categories/types/natural kinds of special sciences are ontologically heterogeneous, but they are "experientially" (Sapir) or "functionally" (Fodor) homogeneous. At first sight, these characterizations are dissimilar. Experiences are direct and unique, functions are conceptualized regularities. Therefore, when both scholars conclude that a certain discipline belongs to the special sciences, their reasons for the classification appear to be different. On the other hand, their common focus on areas consisting of human institutions (clans, economics) or "interesting" phenomena (mountains) suggests that they may share the same basic insight, but reconstruct it in different terms.

The shared example of geology may serve to clarify this point. For Sapir, geology is a special science, because it "depends, for its *raison d'être*, on a series of unique experiences, directly sensed or inferred, clustering about an entity (the earth, a mountain chain)" (Sapir 1917: 445). For Fodor, it is essential that mountains, however ontologically heterogeneous, enter into generalizations that "serve geology in good stead. [...] Unimaginably complicated to-ings and fro-ings of bits and pieces at the extreme *micro-level* manage somehow to converge on stable *macro-level* properties" (Fodor 1997: 160). On the next page, these macro-level properties are equated with functional properties, as in psychology and biology.

My hypothesis is that these different characterizations are connected to the different discourses in which both scholars are operating. Sapir conceives of "historical sciences" as comparable to *Geisteswissenschaften*, referring to Rickert

(1913 [1896]). This class of sciences is often characterized as "idiographic", and is contrasted with the "nomothetic" *Naturwissenschaften*. Hence Sapir's emphasis on particular, directly experienced events and on "the unique or individual, not the universal" (Sapir 1917: 446). At the same time, the above citation also refers to "inferred" experiences and later on, "such concepts as a clan, a language, a priesthood" are denied individual connotation and supposed to be involved in the same operations as natural science concepts: "observation, classification, inference, generalization, and so on" (Sapir 1917: 446), exactly the operations Fodor frequently refers to with respect to all sciences.

Fodor's suggestion that, in special sciences, the generalizations are all of the functional type has, in turn, to be taken with a grain of salt. When applied to geology, the term "functional" is almost meaningless. Sapir's appeal to "a certain philosophically arbitrary but humanly immensely significant selection out of the total mass of phenomena", quoted above, seems to be a more adequate, but for Fodor undoubtedly too subjective, characterization of what special sciences are about, although he does not eschew the term "interesting".[16] So Sapir and Fodor appear to appeal to the same insight, worded differently.

There is another difference between Sapir's and Fodor's ideas about special sciences. In Sapir's examples, ontologically heterogeneous features are simultaneously realized, for example in the earth, or a mountain chain. In Fodor's special sciences, they are realized in different events (the "tokens") at different moments, for example in various monetary transactions.[17] This difference is not entirely watertight, however. Sapir refers to events too (cf. the quotation on p. 95). His incorporation of history in the special sciences and examples such as "the French Republic, the romantic movement in literature, Victor Hugo" also suggest that the heterogeneous counterparts of special science entities may be events. Fodor's extension of the class of special sciences to geology and his comparison with artefacts, in turn, implies that he also recognizes the possibility of simultaneous presence of heterogeneous features.

Certainly Sapir and Fodor did not have *exactly* the same idea of special sciences in mind. But their ideas were more similar than their formulations suggest at first sight.

---

[16]In Fodor's "Special sciences", there are some references to the alleged "interestingness" or "importance" of the natural kinds of a special science. Compare the following passage about monetary exchange: "The point is that monetary exchanges have interesting things in common. But what is interesting about monetary exchanges is surely not their commonalities under physical description" (Fodor 1974: 103–104).

[17]Consequently, Fodor's presentation of the physical counterparts of a special science predicate as a disjunction does not apply to the physical counterparts in Sapir's examples. In these cases, they constitute a conjunction.

8 Laws and exceptions

Sapir and Fodor are both convinced that special science laws have exceptions. For both scholars, scientific practice is an important argument. Sapir describes this practice and contrasts it with natural science practice: "If, out of one hundred clans, ninety-nine obeyed a certain sociological 'law', we would justly flatter ourselves with having made a particularly neat and sweeping generalization; our 'law' would have validity, even if we never succeeded in 'explaining the one exception'" (Sapir 1917: 447). According to Fodor, the idea that laws of special science are exceptionless has to be rejected because it "flies in the face of fact. There is just no chance at all that all the true, counter-factual supporting generalizations of, say, psychology, will turn out to hold in strictly each and every condition where the antecedents are satisfied" (Fodor 1974: 111).

Both Sapir and Fodor thus take the requirement of *historical adequacy* (conformity to clear cases of scientific practice) for philosophy of science seriously and derive a strong argument for exceptions to special science laws from actual scientific practice. When it comes to *philosophical adequacy*, however, their arguments differ widely. Sapir appeals to his above-mentioned claim that special sciences are about particular events. "Laws" are actually abbreviations for a finite number of phenomena. Sapir admits that this is a complicated issue and adds here a footnote about Rickert for further reading.

Fodor's argument is entirely based upon the disjunctive character of the antecedent and the consequent of the physical counterpart of special science laws. The resulting physical "law" is not a genuine law (cf. §3 above) and this explains why special science laws have exceptions.

With respect to philosophical adequacy, Sapir's as well as Fodor's explanations appeal to the pseudo-lawlike character of special science "laws". However, the ways in which pseudo-lawlikeness is argued for are different.

Summarizing the last three sections, we may conclude that some aspects of token physicalism are elaborated in different ways by both scholars. These differences can be shown to be related to the temporal and intellectual context in which the theories were developed.

9 Getting involved

In the following three sections, Sapir's and Fodor's token physicalism will be embedded in a wider context. The rise and development of their theories can be further clarified in this way. There is, firstly, the preliminary question of how they got involved in the problem of relations between disciplines and, secondly, whether their similar solutions were based on any clues in their intellectual environments. Finally, we may ask what, in general, became of Sapir's and Fodor's token physicalism. Neither Sapir nor Fodor was a specialist in general philosophy of science. During his student years, Sapir did not follow a philosophy programme, but his education in Germanic philology certainly yielded some knowledge of German philosophy, the breeding ground for the distinction between *Naturwissenchaften* and *Geisteswissenschaften.* Fodor was educated in philosophy. He was a pupil of Hilary Putnam and acquired a thorough knowledge of philosophy of science, but philosophy of mind became his specialization. Like many scientists, especially in the humanities and the social sciences, both scholars became involved in the broader issue of relations between disciplines through problems in their scientific work or through reflection on this work.

In Sapir's case, his master thesis on Herder's *Ursprung der Sprache* (Sapir 1907) bears witness to an early interest in the foundations of linguistics, but he did not become involved in foundational issues again until 1917. Kroeber's article seems to have been the direct incentive for Sapir's development of token-physicalistic ideas. He must have been dissatisfied with Kroeber's ontological answer to the question of what social sciences are about. Sapir's title "Do we need a 'superorganic?' " reveals an Ockhamian approach: we must, if possible, avoid an unnecessary appeal to unknown and questionable entities such as Kroeber's superorganic force. Token physicalism supplied a promising alternative.

In Fodor's case, there is not, as far as I know, such a direct "external" occasion for his development of token physicalism. My hypothesis is that there was an "internal" occasion. As well as Putnam, Noam Chomsky, his MIT colleague, became very influential to Fodor's intellectual development. Fodor adopted Chomsky's mentalistic approach of claiming psychological reality for linguistic categories, rules etc. When Fodor wrote "Special sciences", he was probably simultaneously writing *The language of thought*, a book which went further than Chomsky in postulating mental, and even innate, entities, structures and operations in the cognitive systems of thinking and communicating humans. Token physicalism could furnish a foundation for this approach by emphasizing the autonomy of psychology. The fact that the text of "Special sciences" constitutes the second section of the introduction to *The language of thought* is an indication that Fodor saw it that way.[18] The final paragraphs of the introduction, absent in "Special sci-

---

[18] The introduction is titled "Two kinds of reductionism". Its two sections are named after views Fodor argues against: "Logical behaviorism" (about Wittgenstein's and Ryle's views of psychology) and "Physiological reductionism".

ences", confirm this suggestion. Compare the concluding sentences: "It has [...] been the burden of these introductory remarks that the arguments for [...] the physical reduction of psychological theories are not, after all, very persuasive. The results of taking psychological theories literally and seeing what they suggest that mental processes are like might, in fact, prove interesting. I propose, in what follows to do just that" (Fodor 1975: 26).

10 Clues to token physicalism

Both Sapir and Fodor present their varieties of token physicalism as new ideas. Indeed, there were no earlier theories with this content. But there certainly were ideas of others which functioned as substantive building blocks or as sources of inspiration for their views.

Both scholars refer only briefly to fellow scholars in their texts. Apart from Kroeber, Sapir only refers to Rickert, in the footnote reference mentioned above (the only footnote in the article). Sapir characterizes Rickert's *Die Grenzen der naturwissenschaftlichen Begriffsbildung* as "difficult but masterly" and continues: "I have been greatly indebted to it." This is understandable: Rickert's way of distinguishing *Geisteswissenschaften* and *Naturwissenschaften*, not in terms of their subject matter, as other philosophers would have it, but in terms of their ways of concept formation, appears to have inspired Sapir directly (cf. Anchor 1967). Therefore, I do not share Silverstein's doubts about this indebtedness to Rickert: "While Sapir, in his paper, expresses his debt to Rickert [...], it is clearly Boas' discussion of 1887, the very phraseology and terms of which he repeats, that underlies his discourse" (Silverstein 1986: 70, fn.5).

In any case, neither Rickert nor Boas developed anything comparable to token physicalism. Both scholars adopted the distinction between *Geisteswissenschaften* and *Naturwissenschaften*. But both assumed a much deeper chasm between the two types of science than Sapir did, by restricting *Geisteswissenschaften* to a "value-laden" (Rickert) or "affective" (Boas) focus on *individual* entities and regarding all generalizing thought as proper to natural sciences only.[19] We observed above that Sapir was also inclined to take into account the individuality of the phenomena described by special sciences. But he also recognized their clustering into abstract, generalized entities, which are subjected to operations such as "classification, inference, generalization, and so on" in these sciences. This view strongly deviates from Rickert's and Boas' views and is similar to Fodor's

---

[19] See Anchor (1967) and Silverstein (1986) for Rickert's and Boas' views, respectively.

view. Both Sapir and Fodor claim that special sciences share their general methodology with basic sciences.

Fodor does not mention any indebtedness. Nevertheless, token physicalism is often regarded as similar to Putnam's idea of "multiple realizability", presented in several publications in the nineteen sixties (cf. Putnam 1960, Loewer & Rey 1991: xiii). Multiple realizability is the thesis that the same mental property can be implemented by different physical properties. Actually, without mentioning the term, Fodor (1974: 105–106) refers to this idea. He explicitly mentions Putnam's reference to computers as possible providers of physical counterparts of psychical events. Connections are also observed with Davidson's "anomalous monism", which, like Fodor's theory, restricts the links of the physical and the psychical to the level of events (cf. Davidson 1970, Loewer & Rey 1991: xxxi). Fodor does not refer to Davidson's theory, but a reference to Davidson (1970) in *The language of thought* (p. 200) proves that he knew about it. So Fodor's idea of how psychology reduces to physics was clearly prepared by other philosophers he knew about. Fodor, however, extended Putnam's and Davidson's solutions to the mind-body problem to a thesis about sciences in general, their typology and their characteristics as intellectual enterprises.

11 What became of token physicalism?

Neither Sapir's nor Fodor's version of token physicalism was elaborated further by their authors after the publications discussed above. Two additional questions will be explored now:

a. Did token physicalism, as presented in these publications, play a role in their later work?

b. Did token physicalism play a role in the work of later scholars?

Answering these questions exhaustively is far beyond my limited state of knowledge, but this does not prevent me from making some tentative suggestions.

As to the first question, token physicalism, not surprisingly, "sets the stage" for Sapir's and Fodor's further research in their respective "special sciences". Sapir presents and practises linguistics and anthropology as autonomous sciences; Fodor's "psychosemantics" is also practised autonomously, without any appeal to specific brain states.[20] But in their writings, token physicalism is not

---

[20] *Psychosemantics* is the title of a 1987 book by Fodor. I apply the term here to the totality of Fodor's work on cognitive psychology and its relations to semantics.

at all prominent; it is a background framework rather than a major discussion theme.

For example, Sapir does not refer at all to his typology of sciences in his 1929 article "Linguistics as a science", although the main theme of this article is the relation between linguistics and other sciences.[21] The conclusions drawn – e.g. that linguistics is not "a mere adjunct of either biology or psychology" (Sapir 1929: 214) – are in line with those drawn in 1917, but they are attained without any appeal to the distinction between conceptual sciences and historical sciences. The same is true of the passage about the definition of language in the first chapter of Sapir's seminal book *Language* (1921). There, Sapir claims that language cannot be defined "as an entity in psycho-physical terms alone" and that language can be discussed "precisely as we discuss the nature of any other phase of human culture – say art or religion – as an institutional or cultural entity, leaving the organic and psychological mechanism back of it as something to be taken for granted" (Sapir 1921: 10–11).

A clear echo of Sapir's discussion with Kroeber can be found in Irvine's reconstruction of Sapir's lectures on the psychology of culture, presented in the 1930s (Sapir 2002 [1928-1937]). In a lecture on "difficulties of the social sciences", Sapir mentions the problem that "the culturalist [...] cannot be absolutely sure of the limits or bounds of what he is dealing with", unlike physicists, who "know what particular corner of the universe they are dealing with". Another difficulty is the essential uniqueness of cultural phenomena. Referring to Rickert, Sapir contrasts the physicist, who deals with a conceptual universe covering all possible phenomena in an abstract way allowing for one hundred percent accuracy, with the social scientist, who studies all actual and unique phenomena, without this same level of accuracy (Sapir 2002 [1928-1937]: 56–57). In another lecture, Sapir explicitly refers to his discussion with Kroeber. A sentence literally repeated from Sapir (1917: 444) concludes the passage: "Social science is not psychology, not because it studies the resultants of superpsychic or superorganic forces, but because its terms are differently demarcated" (Sapir 2002 [1928-1937]: 245). But again, none of these claims is argued for in terms of an explicit and general typology of sciences, as presented in Sapir (1917).

Fodor now and then refers to token physicalism after 1975. Like Sapir, he wrote an article which surprisingly omits the subject ("Some notes on what linguistics is about", 1985). In an article about the mind-body problem in *Scientific American*

---

[21]In Sapir (1929), linguistics is emphatically presented as a science aiming at generalization, explanation, laws etc., which is at odds with Silverstein's (1986) idea that the views presented in Sapir (1917), as he interprets them in Boasian terms (cf. p. 106), permeate Sapir's entire oeuvre.

(Fodor 1981), one paragraph is devoted to a brief explanation and defence of token physicalism as part of the solution to this problem. In his books *Psychosemantics* (Fodor 1987: 5–6) and *The elm and the expert* (Fodor 1994: 39), the "special science" status of psychology is mentioned but, as in Sapir's case, without a reference to the broader context of token physicalism and the issue of typology of sciences.

The inconspicuous role of token physicalism in Fodor's work cannot be better illustrated than by the obituaries that appeared after his death on 29 November 2017. Of the eight obituaries I read, all paying ample attention to the content of Fodor's scientific work, only one, Rey (2017), mentions token physicalism.

Our second question about the role of token physicalism in the work of later scholars receives a negative answer in Sapir's case. As far as I know, Sapir's token physicalism *avant la lettre* was not discussed by other scholars. His distinction between conceptual and historical sciences was neither adopted nor criticized by his linguistic or anthropological colleagues. Autonomy versus reducibility was an important and controversial issue for all humanities and social sciences, before and after 1917, but Sapir's solution does not seem to play any role in this multi-faceted discussion.[22]

Fodor's token physicalism, on the other hand, became a rather popular issue in philosophical discussions, and remains so up to the present day.[23] Many philosophers of science have analysed and commented on Fodor's views. A considerable portion of their reactions are critical and try to vindicate some variety of reductive physicalism. As an example of the broad impact of Fodor's token physicalism, I would mention *The Electric Agora* ("a modern symposium for the digital age"), which devoted a Special to "Jerry Fodor's 'Special sciences'" in 2015. After a brief introduction about "one of the most influential essays in the philosophy of science since the Second World War" (Kaufman 2015: 1–2), thirty comments follow.

In areas outside philosophy, I found very few reactions to Fodor's token-physicalistic ideas.[24] It is sometimes suggested that all practising cognitive scientists now adopt Fodor's line of thought and proceed without any appeal to neurology. For example, Jones (2004) claims that "this [token physicalism] has been the consensus view among cognitive scientists since at least the mid-seventies", due to Fodor's 1974 article. This is, however, an overstatement. In the same article, when talking about belief states, Jones claims that their reduction to physical

---

[22]This tentative conclusion is based on a search in Google and Google Scholar for "conceptual science". No items were found containing this expression in the Sapirean sense.

[23]The most recent article devoted to token physicalism I found is DiFrisco (2017).

[24]I found only six non-philosophical items via a Google Scholar search for "token physicalism".

neurological states "has been at the centre of numerous research projects in the behavioural and brain sciences for decades" (Jones 2004: 423). This recent observation shows the lasting validity of an earlier claim by Fodor himself that many psychologists are type physicalists who believe that every psychological kind predicate is lawfully related to a neurological kind predicate and that "there are departments of psycho-biology or psychology and brain science in universities throughout the world whose very existence is an institutionalized gamble that such lawful coextensions can be found" (Fodor 1974: 105, cf. footnote 10).

In summary, Sapir's token physicalism seems not to have left traces in the work of later scholars.[25] Fodor's token physicalism was only partially influential as a programme for research in cognitive science. But it did become the subject of a lively philosophical debate that is still ongoing.

12 Linguistics as a "special science"

Recently, a newly appointed professor of Dutch Linguistics at Leiden University claimed, in his inaugural lecture, that linguistics is in crisis because it is thought it may become superfluous fairly soon. Language, as a cognitive phenomenon, can now be investigated through brain research, so why should there be a separate discipline of linguistics alongside neurology? The answer is that the role of linguistics has not yet become entirely irrelevant because the help of linguists is still necessary for the correct interpretation of the neurocognitive data (Barbiers 2017).

This line of argument, which presupposes correspondences between linguistic and neurological natural kinds, is a clear example of reductive, type-physicalistic thought. Such a radically reductive view of linguistics is not new, but recent developments in neurolinguistics have made it much more prominent and much more applicable (and actually applied) in research practice. But it is not, and never was, the only view. On the contrary, there are many linguistic approaches that do not make any appeal to neurology, either because of a more autonomous psychologistic conception of cognitive-linguistic research, or because of a more radically autonomous, non-psychologistic view of linguistics (cf. Botha 1992; Elffers 2014).

Thus far, token physicalism does not play a role in discussions about these approaches. This might be due to the context in which it was introduced – an-

---

[25]There might be traces in work I did not consult: later publications by Kroeber, or his correspondence with Sapir, which lasted for several decades. On p. 106, Silverstein (1986) was mentioned for drawing attention to Sapir's token physicalism from the perspective of the history of linguistics.

thropology in Sapir's case, philosophy of science in Fodor's case. Neither Sapir (1917) nor Fodor (1974) explicitly refer to linguistics but, as was argued in §6, both scholars certainly incorporated linguistics in the category of special sciences, although this incorporation has a different meaning for Sapir's and Fodor's varieties of token physicalism. For Sapir, psychology is a basic science. Linguistics, as a special science, has a non-psychological status. Language belongs, with art and culture, to the category of "human institutions" (cf. the quotation on p. 108). For Fodor, only physics is a basic science; psychology is a special science. Given Fodor's psychologistic view of linguistics, linguistics is also a special science.[26]

Can token physicalism, if plausible at all, play a relevant role in the discussions of linguistic approaches examined above? A positive answer seems possible. The conception of linguistics as a "special science" can play a supportive role in the argumentation of both psychologists and non-psychologists. For psychologists, token physicalism can help to justify the fact that they do not appeal to neurology. Thus far this justification is often lacking or unconvincing. For example, many cognitive linguists (cf., e.g., Langacker 1999) make strong statements about mental architecture and processes, without discussing questions of neurological reality. Chomsky (1987: 5–6) claims that such discussions are unnecessary, because chemists, too, "have not stopped to discuss 'abstractly construed' molecule elements, the periodic system and so on". The analogy fails, because chemists *could* apply the vocabulary of atomic physics instead, whereas linguists are far from knowing what corresponds neurologically to their psychological-linguistic categories. Token physicalism provides a better justification for not discussing neurological equivalents of linguistic natural kinds.

For non-psychologists, the autonomy of linguistics often implies a rather problematic ontological status of language. Like Kroeber, they look for an ontological answer to questions of non-reducibility. For example, according to Cooper (1975), language belongs to a separate "linguistic reality", Itkonen (1978) assumes a non-empirical "social reality" which incorporates language, Katz (1981) localizes language in an abstract "Platonist" realm. In all cases, there is, apart from Ockhamian considerations, the problem of explaining the interaction of these separate realms with the psychological realm of actual use and knowledge of language. Without suggesting that token physicalism offers ready-made solutions, I feel that it has certain advantages: language use consists of (psycho-)physical events (tokens)

---

[26]Fodor (1985: 149) claims that "it is nomologically necessary that the grammar of a language is internally represented by speaker/hearers of that language". In itself, Fodor's token physicalism allows for an "institutional" interpretation of language as well (cf. his discussion of economics). Jones (2004: 422–423) regards multiple realizability as a typical feature of institutional facts in general.

and the linguist's constructs they instantiate (types, natural kinds) are epistemo-logically but not ontologically autonomous.[27]

Of course, this extension of the topic in the final paragraphs of this chapter is too fragmentary. But it may give an impression of how the idea of linguistics as a "special science" can play a role in discussions of linguistic approaches.

References

Anchor, Robert. 1967. Heinrich Rickert (1863–1936). In Paul Edwards (ed.), *The encyclopedia of philosophy*, vol. 7, 192–194. New York: Macmillan.

Antal, László. 1984. Psychologism, platonism and realism in linguistics. *Word* 35. 163–175.

Barbiers, Lambertus C. J. 2017. De zonnige toekomst van de nederlandse taalkunde. Inaugural lecture, Leiden University.

Beckner, Morton O. 1967. Vitalism. In Paul Edwards (ed.), *The encyclopedia of philosophy*, vol. 8, 253–256. New York: Macmillan.

Botha, Rudolf P. 1992. *Twentieth century conceptions of language: Mastering the metaphysical market*. Oxford: Blackwell.

Chomsky, Noam. 1965. *Aspects of the theory of syntax*. Cambridge: MIT Press.

Chomsky, Noam. 1987. Language in a psychological setting. *Sophia Linguistica: Working papers in linguistics* 22. 1–73.

Chomsky, Noam. 2009 [1966]. *Cartesian linguistics: A chapter in the history of rationalist thought*. Cambridge: Cambridge University Press. Edited by James McGilvray.

Cooper, David. 1975. *Knowledge of language*. London: Prism Press.

Cowan, William, Michael K. Foster & E. F. Konrad Koerner (eds.). 1986. *New perspectives in language, culture and personality. Proceedings of the Edward Sapir Centenary Conference (Ottawa, 1-3 oct. 1984)*. Amsterdam/Philadelphia: John Benjamins.

Davidson, Donald. 1970. Mental events. In Lawrence Foster & Joe Swanson (eds.), *Experience and theory*, 79–112. Amherst, Mass.: University of Massachusetts Press.

---

[27]For non-psychologists, Sapir's variety of token physicalism is, of course, a better example than Fodor's. Ironically, Itkonen is the only one of these more recent scholars who made a thorough study of Sapir's work, including his anthropological publications, but he seems to have missed Sapir (1917), and his interpretation of Sapir's view as identical to his own non-empirical view of linguistics is a mistake (cf. Itkonen 1978: 62–65).

DiFrisco, James. 2017. Token physicalism and functional individuation. *European Journal for Philosophy of Science* 8. 309–329.

Elffers, Els. 1991. *The historiography of grammatical concepts. 19th and 20th-century changes in the subject predicate conception and the problem of their historical reconstruction.* Amsterdam: Rodopi.

Elffers, Els. 2014. Earlier and later anti-psychologism in linguistics. In Vadim Kasevich, Yuri A. Kleiner & Patrick Sériot (eds.), *History of linguistics 2011: Selected papers from the 12th International Conference on the History of the Language Sciences (ICHoLS XII)*, 127–136. Amsterdam: Benjamins.

Fodor, Jerry A. 1974. Special sciences (or: The disunity of science as a working hypothesis). *Synthèse* 28. 97–115.

Fodor, Jerry A. 1975. *The language of thought.* New York: Crowell.

Fodor, Jerry A. 1981. The mind-body problem. *Scientific American* 244. 114–123.

Fodor, Jerry A. 1985. Some notes on what linguistics is about. In Jerrold J. Katz (ed.), *The philosophy of linguistics*, 146–160. Oxford: Oxford University Press.

Fodor, Jerry A. 1987. *Psychosemantics: The problem of meaning in the philosophy of mind.* Cambridge, Mass.: MIT Press.

Fodor, Jerry A. 1994. *The elm and the expert. Mentalese and its semantics.* Cambridge, Mass.: MIT Press.

Fodor, Jerry A. 1997. Special sciences: Still autonomous after all these years. *Philosophical Perspectives* 11. 149–163.

Goldenweiser, Alexander A. 1917. The autonomy of the social. *American Anthropologist* 19. 447–449.

Hettema, Hinne. 2012. *Reducing chemistry to physics. Limits, models, consequences.* Groningen University dissertation.

Itkonen, Esa. 1978. *Grammatical theory and metascience.* Amsterdam: Benjamins.

Jones, Todd E. 2004. Special sciences: Still a flawed argument after all those years. *Cognitive Science* 28. 409–432.

Katz, Jerrold J. 1981. *Language and other abstract objects.* Oxford: Blackwell.

Kaufman, Daniel A. 2015. Jerry Fodor's "special sciences (or: The disunity of science as a working hypothesis)". *The Electric Agora. A symposium for the digital age.* https://theelectricagora.com/2015/10/14/this-weeks-special-jerry-fodors-special-sciences-or-the-disunity-of-science-as-a-working-hypothesis/.

Kim, Jaegwon. 1992. Multiple realization and the metaphysics of reduction. *Philosophy and Phenomenological Research* 53. 1–26.

Kroeber, Alfred L. 1917. The superorganic. *American Anthropologist* 19. 163–213.

Langacker, Ronald. 1999. A dynamic use-based model. In Michael Barlow & Suzanne Kemmer (eds.), *Usage-based models of language*, 1–64. Stanford: CSLI Publications.

Loewer, Barry & Georges Rey (eds.). 1991. *Meaning in mind. Fodor and his critics.* Oxford: Blackwell.

Pullum, Geoffrey K. 2017. The man who hated relativism. *The Chronicle of Higher Education.* http://www.chronicle.com/blogs/linguafranca/2017/12/04/the-man-who-hated-relativism.

Putnam, Hilary. 1960. Minds and machines. In *Mind, language and reality (philosophical papers, vol.2 1975)*, 362–385. Cambridge: Cambridge University Press.

Rey, Georges. 2017. A remembrance of Jerry Fodor, 1935-2017. *Daily Nous.* http://dailynous.com/2017/12/01/remembrance-jerry-fodor-1935-2017-guest-post-georges-rey/.

Rickert, Heinrich. 1913 [1896]. *Die Grenzen der naturwissenschaftlichen Begriffsbildung; eine Einleitung in die historischen Wissenschaften.* Tübingen: Mohr.

Robins, Robert H. 1997 [1967]. *A short history of linguistics.* Abingdon: Routledge.

Sapir, Edward. 1907. Herder's *Ursprung der Sprache. Modern Philology* 5. 109–142.

Sapir, Edward. 1917. Do we need a "superorganic"? *American Anthropologist* 19. 441–447.

Sapir, Edward. 1921. *Language: An introduction to the study of speech.* San Diego / New York / London: Harcourt, Brace & Co.

Sapir, Edward. 2002 [1928-1937]. *The psychology of culture. A course of lectures.* Berlin/New York: Mouton de Gruyter.

Sapir, Edward. 1929. The status of linguistics as a science. *Language* 5. 207–214.

Seuren, Pieter A. M. 2016. Saussure and his intellectual environment. *History of European Ideas* 42. 819–847.

Silverstein, Michael. 1986. The diachrony of Sapir's synchronic linguistic description. In William Cowan, Michael K. Foster & E. F. Konrad Koerner (eds.), 67–110. Amsterdam/Philadelphia: John Benjamins.

Spencer, Herbert. 1898. *The principles of sociology, 3 vols.* New York: Appleton.

van der Dussen, Willem J. 1986. *Filosofie van de geschiedenis. Een inleiding.* Muiderberg: Coutinho.

Chapter 5

The impact of Russian formalism on linguistic structuralism

Bart Karstens

Vrije Universiteit Amsterdam

The aim of this chapter is to clarify the relation between Russian formalism, a movement in literary studies, and structuralism. Because leading structuralists such as Mukarovsky (linguistics) and Lévi-Strauss (anthropology) defined their approach in opposition to formalism, we may have the impression that structuralism and formalism are fundamentally different. However, on closer inspection, it turns out that Mukarovsky and Lévi-Strauss targeted specific articulations of formalism. There is a third major variant, namely systemic formalism, which escapes their criticism and can be shown to have influenced structuralism in its earliest phase. First, Tynjanov and Jakobson worked together and co-authored an important short programmatic paper. Second, the genesis of Prague School structuralism should be considered a merger of elements stemming from a multitude of directions. If we do so, we can see how ideas derived from systemic formalism fitted in with other constituents of linguistic structuralism, and hence how formalism influenced the latter to a significant degree.

1 Introduction

Since the very beginning of structuralism, its relation to Russian formalism has been a matter of dispute. Leading structuralists, such as Jan Mukarovsky (1891–1975) and Claude Lévi-Strauss (1908–2009), emphasized the differences between formalism and structuralism, and members of the Prague Circle even claimed that formalism was *passé* and in need of replacement, as it was marked too much by its mechanistic heritage. In this chapter, I will review the dismissive attitude of structuralists towards formalism. My conclusion is that this attitude applied to a number of articulations of formalism, but *not* to the so-called *systemic* variant, which itself was formulated in response to problems experienced within the

Bart Karstens. 2019. The impact of Russian formalism on linguistic structuralism. In James McElvenny (ed.), *Form and formalism in linguistics*, 115–139. Berlin: Language Science Press. DOI:10.5281/zenodo.2654357

formalist programme. From this it follows that a number of key notions of formalism must be considered as constitutive of the structuralist analysis of linguistic phenomena. In my interpretation these key notions include the application of the function concept, the recognition of the systematic recurrence of forms in language, the perspective on language as a system, as well as a system *within* systems, and the analysis of actual manifestations of language in speech and writing with reference to a deeper, underlying system.

I begin by discussing the reasons proponents of structuralism, such as Mukarovsky and Lévi-Strauss, had for their opposition to formalism. Mukarovsky is interesting because he put forward his critique of formalism during the formative days of structuralism in Prague and, according to Toman, Mukarovsky was the second most important representative of Czech structuralism after Roman Jakobson (1896–1982) (Toman 1995: 128). Lévi-Strauss carried structuralism into the social sciences. I focus on his infamous 1960 critique of Vladimir Propp (1895–1970) and his 1928 book *Morphology of the Folktale*, which met with a late reception in Europe and the United States. Despite the fact that more than 30 years elapsed, both scholars delivered similar forms of critique on formalism, which gives the impression of a clear-cut and deep rift between formalism and structuralism.

But it is essential to see that formalism was not a unitary movement at all. Following Steiner (1984), three main types of formalism can be identified, namely mechanical, organic and systemic formalism.[1] This classification probably does not even exhaust all possible varieties of formalism that have existed, but it is very useful for the present purposes. As will be made clear in what follows, Mukarovsky dismissed mechanical formalism while Lévi-Strauss targeted organic formalism. In my view, however, systemic formalism possessed a number of properties that escaped both these attacks.

The main proponent of systemic formalism was Yuri Tynjanov (1894–1943). Tynjanov co-authored a highly influential programmatic paper with Roman Jakobson, which was published in 1928. The nine theses defended in this paper are often referred to as crucial to the genesis of linguistic structuralism. This document thus forms a clear point of contact between systemic formalism and structuralism.[2] In addition, the work of Ferdinand de Saussure (1857–1913) served as an inspiration to both Tynjanov and Jakobson. It is true that formalism was

---

[1] These labels are based on Steiner's analytical terms. They were not actor's categories. Significantly, however, what is identified as systemic formalism was sometimes referred to as "neo-formalism" by contemporaries.

[2] In historiography, claims of influence always need to be made concrete either by pointing at references in texts or through an investigation of direct personal relations between historical actors. Still relevant in this respect is Koerner (1989).

an approach in literary studies and structuralism mainly applied to linguistics. However, the study of literature and the study of language were seen by Tynjanov and Jakobson as complementary parts of the same endeavour. Indeed, the formalism that inspired Jakobson must be embedded in the broader Russian revolutionary cultural climate of the 1910s which included modernist art and futurism (see Holenstein 1975: 32–33; see also Karstens 2017a).

It is in this context that scholars claimed a place for literary studies as a new independent science. They wanted to base this new science of literature on a set of facts that had to be established without presuppositions. Formalists were in constant debate amongst themselves on how best to pursue this aim. In doing so, different approaches came about, but what they shared was an eschewal of philosophical and psychological speculation. Instead they started to "borrow" models from natural sciences, such as biology and chemistry, and made use of technological metaphors to bolster their research programme. Thus, somewhat paradoxically, autonomy for literary studies was claimed through an alignment with science and technology.

A similar story applies to linguistics. Structuralism can be seen as a further step in the realization of Saussure's quest to establish an autonomous science of language, centred around the idea of treating languages as value systems of signs. In my view, the formation of structuralism is best studied as a merger of elements stemming from multiple directions.[3] The "merger" perspective allows us to see how systemic formalism provided constituents of early structuralism. Both formalism and structuralism may not have many adherents anymore; however, the systemic way of thinking continues to exert a strong influence on linguistics to this day. Hence it is important to clarify the historical ties between formalism and structuralism in its earliest phase.

2 Mukarovsky's definition of structuralism as opposed to formalism

Born in Pisek, Bohemia in 1891, Jan Mukarovsky was among the founders of the Prague Linguistic Circle in 1926. Mukarovsky developed an approach towards literary analysis in which the concepts of structure and structuralism played a

---

[3]For a hybridization perspective on discipline formation, see Karstens (2012). For the study of interdisciplinarity in terms of a merger of constitutive elements, see Graff (2015) and Bod et al. (In Press). For a contextual study of Jakobson as part of an age of synthesis, see Karstens (2017a).

central role.[4] He conceived of a structure as a set of elements, organized in a complex hierarchy in which one element dominated over the other elements. This dominant determined how other elements of the structure functioned. For example, in Charlie Chaplin's 1931 silent film *City Lights*, Mukarovsky identified "expressive gestures" as the dominant. Other bodily movements and auditory elements (like music) he interpreted as subordinate to the expressive gestures in the film. A literary work or film could thus be interpreted as a relational structure and the main task of the literary critic was to locate the dominant, and the relationships between the dominant and all other elements occurring in the structure. For Mukarovsky, this form of relationalism was holistic: "Structure is dynamic, containing both the tendencies of convergence and divergence, and its artistic phenomenon which cannot be taken apart since each of its elements gains value only in relationship to the whole" (Mukarovsky, quoted in Galan 1985: 30). Structure could thus also be defined as a whole "whose nature is determined by the parts and their reciprocal relationships, and which in turn determines the nature and the relationships of the parts" (Mukarovsky, quoted in Galan 1985: 35).

In an interview given to *Prague Weekly* in 1932, Mukarovsky appears to have used the term structuralism for the first time to refer to the new school of literary criticism.[5] In the interview he explicitly mentioned that this new school should be distinguished from formalism. In a 1934 review of the Czech edition of Viktor Shklovsky's (1893–1984) *Theory of Prose* (original edition 1925), it becomes clear how Mukarovsky viewed the opposition between structuralism and formalism. Mukarovsky gave the formalists credit for their polemical extremism and for their rejection of all extrinsic approaches to art that included all kinds of (contextual) interpretation and psychologizing.[6] According to Mukarovsky, this unqualified emphasis on content had to provoke a radical antithesis emphasizing the form of literary products.

This shift to form had, however, gone too far. For example, when in Shklovsky's analysis a change in form directly led to a change in content (such as in a passage in *Theory of Prose* on Cervantes's *Don Quixote*), this was accidental according to Mukarovsky. Shklovsky's research programme would not normally lead to such an analysis because form and content had to be strictly separated. The example demonstrates, however, that even Shklovsky could not avoid accidental identifications of form with meaning. From such examples Mukarovsky drew the con-

---

[4]What follows in the paragraphs below is by and large based on Galan (1985: 22–44).

[5]The first time structuralism was mentioned in print in relation to the study of language is in Jakobson (1929). I will give this citation below.

[6]If one thing united all formalists, it was their rejection of both psychologism and subjectivism in literary studies.

clusion that a synthesis was required between the intrinsic, formalist approach and the extrinsic, interpretative approach, and Mukarovsky explicitly claimed that structuralism provided this synthesis.

The difference between structuralism and its direct predecessor is nicely illustrated in the way Mukarovsky elaborated on one of the industrial metaphors for which Shklovsky is so well known. Shklovsky had pointed out that the literary critic should be interested in the "yarn and weaving techniques" that produce literariness and not in the "textile" that is produced and subsequently reaches consumers on the economic market. According to Mukarovsky, however, it is impossible to separate the "external" market from production techniques because the market mechanism of supply and demand conditions the very development of weaving techniques. While in structuralism the internal relations, and the laws that govern these relations, are still at the centre of investigation, external factors, which influence the course of literary evolution, are included too.

In Mukarovsky's interpretation, a structure has a dynamic, instead of a static, nature. Structures are not unique and unchangeable. The stability of the relations between the elements that make up the structure is temporary and represents a fragile equilibrium. The continuous regrouping of elements and permutations of functions is given by an evolutionary dynamic that involves interplay between the literary tradition and external factors. A literary work may thus reflect the tradition to which it belongs but diverge from it at the same time. This applies especially when the dominant shifts, owing to external changes. In the Chaplin case, this would, for example, be the change from silent films to films with audible dialogue; the literary work may assume a completely new appearance. The nature of the structure is therefore not univocally given by the work, as it must be perceived against the background of an external context. A form of empiricism that is too narrow, which does not move much beyond the literary facts as given by the work itself, as Mukarovsky found in Shklovsky, entirely misses this dynamic side of literature.

It is important to note that changes in Mukarovsky's view did not occur randomly. Quite the contrary, Mukarovsky thought that it was possible to uncover *laws* of modifications, and other alterations, of literary structures. If change were chaotic and not orderly, it would probably be unintelligible. We find the same consideration in the work of Russian futurists, who were aiming at language reform, often with the help of poetry.[7] They argued that it made no sense to create a new language from scratch. Instead, linguistic innovations should respect or-

---

[7]A clear example in this respect is Velimir Khlebnikov (1885–1922); see below.

derly codes and norms that a community of speakers of a language has built up during its history. It was only through a deeper understanding of the systematicity of a language that purposeful innovations could be won.

Clearly Mukarovsky was a dialectic thinker. Formalism had been a necessary stage in the development of literary criticism because without its theory of immanence the later synthesis with extrinsic approaches would not have been possible. With their theory of immanence, the formalists had created a realm of autonomy for literary works and for their study, yielding an independent science of literature. However, in order to mature, the science of literature had to acknowledge that this independence was a matter of degree. Poetics does not live in a vacuum; it should not be cut-off from social reality. Hence some of the intrinsic formalism remains in structuralism but it must be wed to extrinsic (i.e. sociological, cultural, historical) considerations. According to Galan (1985: 38), structuralists were formalists "only to the extent of holding that the primary causes for literary changes have to be sought within the literary series, and social scientists to the extent of recognizing that literature properly belongs to the wider realm of culture and society".

Given the synthetic position that structuralists sought to occupy, they had to strongly oppose any identification of structuralism with either the sociological or the formalist pole. This explains the repeated effort of structuralists, such as Mukarovsky, to draw boundaries between formalism and structuralism. However, because he was attacking a formalism that erected a strict barrier between art and social reality, his criticism applied only to the earliest expression of formalism, namely mechanical formalism.

Mechanical formalism had its starting point with Shklovsky's 1914 book *The Resurrection of the Word* and the subsequent creation of the OPOJAZ group in St. Petersburg in 1916. OPOJAZ is an acronym that translates to "Society of the Study of Poetic Language". The aim of the group was to put the study of poetics, metrics and folklore on a new scientific footing. The focus of literary criticism had to be on the "machines" or "devices" (rhythmic, stylistic, literary genre, etc.) with which the form or the medium of expression was created. Through such devices linguistic material could be transformed into a work of art. Devices thus essentially determine whether a work is literary or not, hence the emphasis of the early formalists on technology, craftsmanship and construction.

The OPOJAZ programme was of a positivistic nature. The guiding idea was that a basic set of literary devices could be uncovered. Art (poetry, fiction, *belles-lettres*) was separated from everyday language because the form of art works had to have no relation to the external world. OPOJAZ members thought this was essential to safeguard a realm of independent facts from which an autonomous science (and we might perhaps also say "technology") of literature could be built, fitting to the demands of the modern industrial world.

In this type of formalism, a work of art is not considered in holistic terms. Instead, it is viewed as an aggregate of loose parts. When these loose parts form a set of facts that can be discovered through empirical research, it becomes immaterial who in the end puts the aggregate together. As Osip Brik (1888–1945) once said: "*Evgeny Onegin* would have been written, also without Pushkin, just as America would have been discovered, even without Columbus" (Brik 1923: 213). This attitude is of course in tune with the view of science as a process of uncovering the world "as it is". The achievements of individual scientists in the process can be marvelled at, but in the end each individual is in principle interchangeable with someone else. The specific use of literary devices determines whether a work like *Evgeny Onegin* is a sign of the time in which it was written. In this sense, Shklovsky defended the view that a single man does not write and that it is instead the time, the school-collective, that writes. Change occurs through changes in the application of literary devices and this was seen as a completely immanent process.

This conception of immanent change was felt to be problematic by others. Can we really sufficiently explain the history of art if art at all times has to be disconnected from the rest of the world? And how do we capture the experience of the totality of an artwork if we can only consider it bottom-up, as an aggregate of basic elements? Such problems with mechanical formalism bothered contemporary formalists and led to exploration in new directions, while aiming to retain the basic premises of the formalist programme, namely to develop an autonomous science of literature and to do so without the *a priori* assumption of analytical schemes or modes of interpretation. If we take this into account, Mukarovsky's dialectical analysis, in which structuralism is the synthesis of intrinsic and extrinsic approaches, comes across as overly schematic. Even before Mukarovsky published his critique of Shklovsky, other types of formalism had been put forward in which form and content were connected and in which external factors were integrated in explanations of historical change. One example is Propp's organicist formalism. It is this articulation of formalism that was, however, severely criticized by Lévi-Strauss in 1960 – interestingly enough, on roughly the same grounds as those invoked by Mukarovsky in his earlier attack on mechanical formalism.

3 Lévi-Strauss's voicing of structuralism contra Propp's organicist formalism

Although Propp was also from St. Petersburg, he was *not* a member of the OPO-JAZ group. In reaction to the problems experienced with mechanical formalism, he developed his own variant: organicist formalism. What this entailed is best illustrated by considering his main work, *Morphology of the Folktale* (1928). This book was based on an empirical investigation of a collection of Russian fairy tales compiled by Alexander Afanasyev (1826–1871) in the mid-nineteenth century, of which Propp selected 100 tales. In comparing this material Propp found that 31 functions (for example, "trickery", "mediation", "departure" and "return") and seven character types (for example, "hero", "villain", "princess") were constantly recurring. He labelled these the basic elements of all folk tales.

Contrary to his expectations, Propp also found that the order in which the functions occur in the tales was always the same. Thus, a tale always starts with an injury of a victim or a lack of an important object, which immediately gives the end result of the story, retribution for the injury or the recovery of the lost object. The hero is then introduced, who must accomplish the main task. He meets a donor who supplies him with a magical agent (ring, horse, lion, etc.), which enables him to achieve his goal. Then they meet the villain, who will engage him at some point in a decisive battle, and so on. This led Propp to the conclusion that all fairytales are of one type in regard to their structure (Propp 1968 [1928]: 23). He provided an algebraic representation of this general structure, shown in Figure 1.

$$\text{ABC}{\uparrow}\text{DEFG}\,\frac{\text{HJIK}{\downarrow}\,\text{Pr-Rs}^{\circ}\,\text{L}}{\text{LMJNK}{\downarrow}\text{Pr-Rs}}\,\text{Q Ex TUW} \; *$$

Figure 1: Propp's generalized fairytale with the set of functions ordered in a compositional scheme. Copied from Propp (1968 [1928]: 105).

In Figure 1 we see that a fairytale starts at A on the left and proceeds to G on the right. It can then either go up first, then down, and then proceed from Q to the end; or it can go up first and then directly to the end part; or down first then to the end part; or skip the middle part and move to the end part right away. Hence, not all functional elements have to be present in every story but, when they are, they always occur in the order given by the general type. It is also immaterial how and by whom the functions are performed. What matters is that these functions are performed in the story, and that this happens in a fixed order. Sequencing the functional elements is thus like establishing word order in a sentence and so it is possible to arrive at a grammar of stories.

Propp created a new method of description, which he clearly hoped would raise the prestige of literary studies: "What matters is not the amount of material, but the methods of investigation. At a time when the physical and mathematical sciences possess well-ordered classification, a unified terminology adopted by special conferences, and a methodology improved upon by the transmission from teachers to students, we have nothing comparable" (Propp 1968 [1928]: 4). The morphological method of classification Propp introduced was inspired by the biological writings of Johann Wolfgang von Goethe (1749–1832). This involved the notion that we can identify fundamental ideas or archetypes (*Urtypen*) underlying natural phenomena. The study of common patterns of development and modifications of the archetype was called "morphology" by Goethe.[8]

The generalized fairytale of Figure 1 can be considered the *Urtyp* of all fairytales. Moreover, the word "morphology" in the title of Propp's book is a direct reference to Goethe; every chapter in the original publication is in fact preceded by an epigraph from Goethe's work. Following Goethe, Propp had an organicist understanding of functions: a function is an activity seen from the perspective of the relevance of this activity for the total course of action; that is, the story that is being told (Steiner 1984: 84). With Propp, functions can never be studied in relation to an isolated task or goal. Each tale is thus perceived as a functionally integrated whole, and this distingishes him from members of the OPOJAZ group, who saw works of art as mere aggregates of constituting elements.

Propp was very much focused on the description of the structure of the stories available in the present: "We shall not speak at present about the historical study of the tale, but shall speak only about the description of it, for to discuss genetics, without special elucidation of the problem of description as it is usually treated, is completely useless. Before throwing light upon the question of the tale's origin, one must first answer the question as to what the tale itself represents" (Propp 1968 [1928]: 5). But the analytical result that all folktales were basically of the same structure made Propp speculate about their origin. Could they all come

---

[8] According to Steiner (1984: 257–258), the return to Goethe was more widespread and stemmed from a growing dissatisfaction with positivism, which led scholars to explore scientific models that had existed before positivism became dominant. Oppel (1947: 13) argues that the appearance of the Russian translation of Wilhelm Troll's (1897–1978) book *Goethes morphologische Schriften* in 1926 paved the way for the acceptance of morphology as a respectable method. Alongside Propp, Petrovskij (1927) also adopted the term. For the long-lasting influence of Goethe on the study of language and literature, see also Cassirer (1945).

from the same source? Moreover, he was well aware that *Morphology of the Folk Tale* left open the crucial issue of how to get from the general type to the actual tales that occur in reality. What kind of transformations exist? And what explains their occurrence?

Pressed by these issues, Propp devoted a separate essay to the subject, "Fairy Tale Transformations", which was first published separately and then as an appendix to the book (the original publication is Propp 1928). He argued that synchronic comparative analysis and diachronic genealogical analysis could be undertaken separately, but in the end complemented each other. In the complementary paper, Propp discussed affinities that exist between the fairy tale and religion (myth and ritual) and various social institutions at different stages of their evolution. According to his analysis, the basic forms of fairy tales are religious. Changes into derived forms occur through ethnological and social processes. Hence, in order to understand the transformations (of which Propp specified 20 kinds) we must include external factors. But Propp did not make clear if a similar analysis can apply to all literary products. In his view, folk narratives were the products of collective creativity and came about through long-term social processes. They may thus differ in crucial respects from other literary works, such as novels and poems. The morphological approach was, however, tried on other literary genres as well, for example by Michael Petrovsky (1887–1940) and Aleksandr Skaftymov (1890–1968).

Morphology of the Folktale met with a late and peculiar reception in the West. Initially the work was not noticed internationally. This was probably an effect of the rise of Stalinism, which cut off intellectual exchange. The first translation into English, and to my knowledge into any Western language, appeared in 1958 with Indiana University Press.[9] This translation was however full of deficiencies. It also did not include the "Fairy Tale Transformations" appendix, and the Goethian epigraphs that preceded chapters in the original edition were conspicuously left out.[10]

Since structuralism was in full swing in 1958, the publication of *Morphology of the Folktale* prompted a reaction from Lévi-Strauss in the form of a long review, which was published in French in 1960. Lévi-Strauss praised Propp for seeing through the rich semantic variety of fairy tales and for penetrating into the for-

---

[9] Such delayed reception due to the political turmoil of the 1930s and 1940s occurred often. Emigrant scholars could make a "second" career in the United Kingdom or the United States. A well-known example is the sociologist Norbert Elias (1897–1990). In this context, it must be noted that the first translation of Propp's work into English is accompanied by an introduction written by Svatava Pirkova-Jakobson, the wife of Roman Jakobson.

[10] The 1968 second edition was of much better quality but still without the Goethian epigraphs, which were considered to be "non-essential" (preface by Louis A. Wagner).

mal regularity of the stories. But he called it an error of formalism to disconnect syntax from the vocabulary (or lexicon). According to Lévi-Strauss, it is not possible to do formal analysis and content analysis separately:

> For formalism, the two areas must be absolutely separate, as form alone is intelligible, and content is only a residual deprived of any significant value. For structuralism, this opposition does not exist; structuralism does not treat one as abstract and the other as concrete. Form and content are of the same nature, amenable to the same type of analysis. Content receives its reality from its structure, and what is called form is a way of organizing the local structures that make up this content. (Lévi-Strauss 1984: 179)

As an illustration, he provided the example of bird names to stand for formal oppositions. According to Lévi-Strauss, the morphological approach cannot deal with the fact that the same bird names can be used to stand for multiple formal oppositions. This becomes especially problematic when in one case two bird names are in opposition, but in another case they together form one pole to oppose something else. As an example Lévi-Strauss gave "day" vs. "night", as expressed by an "eagle" vs. an "owl", and "predators" vs. "scavengers", which can be expressed by "eagle + owl" vs. "crow" or even "sky-land" vs. "sky-water"; that is, "eagle + owl + crow" vs. "duck". Structural oppositions framed in this way involve the use of lexical meaning. For this reason, the formal opposition can only be understood when content is taken into account. In my view, the point Lévi-Strauss makes here resembles Mukarovsky's point that structuralism involves a synthesis between formal text analysis and meaningful interpretation through relating the text to the external context.

In addition to this, Lévi-Strauss also declared structuralism superior to formalism in that it did not have to stick to a linear basic structure but could shift from a syntagmatic (or temporal) order to a paradigmatic general structure. This paradigmatic structure is based on the recognition of a number of fundamental oppositional patterns and abstracts away from the temporal ordering of the story. In my view, the idea of making a distinction between a surface level and deeper levels of linguistic structure, with corresponding rules of transformation between them, is crucial to the structuralist approach to the study of language.[11] But even this does not yield a fundamental distinction between structuralism

---

[11]Deep structure, surface structure and transformation are of course Chomskyan terms, and used here somewhat anachronistically. But they are not far off the mark: according to Joseph (2001: 1899–1900), Chomsky's transformational grammar must be interpreted as a direct continuation of European structuralism (to contrast it with the significantly different American, Bloomfieldian structuralism which was challenged by Chomsky).

and formalism. Lévi-Strauss may have been correct in his assessment that organicist formalism lacked the means to abstract away from temporal order, but in the next section I will argue that the assumption of multiple levels of analysis in structuralism was inspired by another formalist variant, namely systemic formalism.

Propp reacted to Lévi-Strauss' critical reception. This reaction was translated into Italian in 1966 and published together with an Italian version of *Morphology of the Folk Tale*, accompanied by Lévi-Strauss' critical review of it. In his rebuttal Propp blamed the American translator:

> Professor Lévi-Strauss knows my book only in the English translation. But its translator allowed himself an impermissible liberty. Not understanding the function of the epigraphs which at first glance do not seem to be explicitly connected to the text, he considered them useless ornaments and barbarously omitted them [...] all these epigraphs [...] had the purpose of expressing what was left unsaid in the text of my book. (As translated in Steiner 1984: 81)

Propp also lamented that Lévi-Strauss had completely missed the importance of the plot for the understanding of a text as a functionally integrated whole. In this respect it is perhaps even more significant that the "Fairy Tale Transformations" complementary paper was not translated at all and only became available in English in 1971. The complementary paper demonstrates even more clearly that Propp had a profound interest in historical and ethnographic investigation and that he was willing to include "content" as an explanation for changes in the structure of fairy tales. It could even have become clear that Propp viewed this type of research as complementary to formalist analysis.

The aim of Propp's two-way publishing strategy was to optimize clarity of presentation, but the reception of Lévi-Strauss shows that this strategy may have had the opposite effect. Still, had the references to Goethe and "Fairy Tale Transformations" been known to Lévi-Strauss, I think that he would have maintained the two main points of his critique. For a structuralist to assume that formal and contextual analysis are complementary is insufficient; the two must be *integrated*, since form and content simultaneously inform and determine each other. Mukarovsky charged mechanical formalism with neglect of external factors. While organic formalism in Propp's approach no longer did this, it still did not achieve the synthesis structuralists were seeking. Hence Lévi-Strauss could deliver a similar critique on Propp, even though the latter represented a different kind of formalism. Systemic formalism could, however, not be targeted in this way. This I will show in the next section.

4 Systemic formalism and its points of contact with structuralism

According to Steiner (1984: 112), systemic formalism represented the most advanced stage of the formalist movement. Significantly, it was called "neo-formalism" by contemporaries. Steiner connects the label systemic formalism for the most part to the work of Tynjanov, who put forward a dynamic, relationist understanding of literary structures. The literary theorist – or, as the case may be, linguist – had to account for the fact that linguistic structures are continuously unfolding, but at the same time that the recurrent systematic appearance of forms is what makes a language intelligible and understandable. In order to capture this double aspect of language, Tynjanov argued that a focus on experience alone is insufficient. Shklovsky counted as a formalist anyone whose analyses did not move beyond the sensory stratum, with a rather static theory as a result. According to Tynjanov, good science had to proceed both from taking direct experience into account *and* from the assumption of a system, or deeper structure, that governs the way experiences come about.

In this respect he was clearly inspired by Saussure's *langue-parole* distinction. The actual appearance of utterances (*parole*) is a manifestation of the underlying linguistic system (*langue*). For a number of reasons, Tynjanov very much liked the analogy between language and chess that Saussure had drawn. The positions we see on the chessboard depend on an unchangeable set of rules that exist before the game even begins. The analogy supports the relationist stance, because each piece receives its identity due to the system of rules *and* its value is relative with respect to the other pieces on the board. The system of rules is strict, but it allows for a great degree of freedom of choice in the actual execution of moves. Finally, the social aspect of the analogy was attractive to Tynjanov: the system of rules has to be shared by players of the game, otherwise they cannot play. As written in Chapter 4 of the *Cours*, the socially shared linguistic code "is necessary if speaking is to be intelligible and produce all its effects" (Saussure 1922 [1916]: 37). The analogy thus showed that both creative expression and human communication rest on a governing system.

Yet, as Steiner explains, there was a "deep-seated difference" between Saussure's and Tynjanov's thought about the autonomy of the *langue* (Steiner 1984: 112). While both wanted to establish an autonomous science of language (Saussure) and literature (Tynjanov, very much like *all* the formalists), Saussure had insisted on absolute autonomy, but for Tynjanov autonomy was a relative notion.

Bart Karstens

Tynjanov argued that any literary system was always part of an overall cultural system. This stance "effected a gradual relativization of the original formalist position on the autonomy of the literary system" (Steiner 1984: 111). Where other formalists had made a sharp distinction between what was immanent to literature and what was not, Tynjanov started to blur this distinction and replaced it with a multi-layered conception of systems within systems.

A theory of relative autonomy was put forward in a 1928 paper co-written by Tynjanov and Jakobson titled "Problems in the Study of Literature and Language" (Tynjanov & Jakobson 1928).[12] In this ground-breaking paper they presented nine theses on the historical development of language and literature and the relation between them. The eighth thesis reads:

> The discovery of the immanent laws of literature (language) permits us to characterize every concrete change in literary (linguistic) systems but does not permit us either to explain the tempo of evolution or to determine the actual selection among several theoretically possible evolutionary paths. This is because the immanent laws of literary (linguistic) evolution are indefinite equations which, while limiting the number of solutions, do not necessarily leave only a single one. Which pathway, or at least which dominant, is chosen can be determined only through an analysis of the correlation among the literary and other historical series. This correlation (the system of systems) has its own structural laws which should be studied. (Quotation given in English in Steiner 1984: 128)

Tynjanov and Jakobson saw the entire culture as a complex system of systems. Each subsystem has its own immanent set of rules but is also determined by the larger system of which it is part, which can lead to a change in rules in the subsystem itself.

The authors perceived a deep relation between language and literature, and hence also between the science of language and the science of literature. These two formed more than just a continuum: both disciplines had to be based on the same principles. The literary genre of poetry provides a good illustration of this commutativity (see Jakobson 1981b,a). Poetry is made of language; therefore linguistics directly informs the writing of poems. But structuralists also investigated poetry as a special function of language. Because in poetry it is possible to break the natural ties between signifier and signified, it is also possible to experiment

---

[12]For the importance of this text in the genesis of structuralism, see Holenstein (1975: 17).

in poetry and self-reflexively develop the language that is being used.[13] The 1928 paper established a connection between formalism, which pertained to literary studies, and structuralism, which mostly pertained to linguistics. From this it becomes understandable that Jakobson, the linguist, and Mukarovsky, the literary scholar, could collaborate in the development of structuralism in the context of the Prague Linguistic Circle.

Systemic formalism differed from mechanical formalism in that it no longer searched for an unchanging literary essence. It also did not explain the history of literature as an immanent process. Systemic formalists analyzed both the structural relations within a single literary product *and* the relations of this work with the rest of literature and with the whole culture of the time in which the work was written and published. All of these realms were conceived as systems containing sets of interdependent variables. In this way, a literary work was itself seen as a variable in a system of higher order.

The difference between organic formalism and systemic formalism was subtler, yet very significant. Like the systemic approach, the morphological approach was also anti-positivistic and had a functional understanding of the role elements play in relation to the purpose (artistic goal) of the whole. The whole is a system because of the interplay of functional elements that work together to achieve the common goal. But in systemic formalism the notions of system and function got a different definition. A function in systemic formalism is seen as a relation of two interdependent variables and a system was conceived as a hierarchical set of interdependent variables. To call literature a system in this sense was extremism or radicalism to adherents of the morphological approach.

In my view, a highly important difference is at stake here. In historiography of linguistic structuralism, we often confront the "standard" interpretation that the organic way of thinking of 19th century historical and comparative linguistics, with August Schleicher's (1821–1868) morphology perhaps as the most distinctive representative, paved the way for the systematic/structural way of thinking of the 20th century.[14] To conceive of languages as structures is then simply the continuation of the application of the organism metaphor; that is, to conceive of a language as a living organism. What matters in both structuralist and comparative linguistics is to unravel the (reciprocal) relations between parts and the whole of the linguistic structure/organism. Fitting to this account would be a ref-

---

[13]On the redefinition of the notion of function in semiotic terms and the use of functions in Jakobson's structuralism, see the next section.

[14]A clear example of this interpretation, which even reached the major handbook of the history of the language sciences, is Kohrt & Kucharczik (2001).

erence to organic formalism as a source of inspiration for linguistic structuralism. But, as we have seen above, it is systemic formalism that mostly influenced linguistic structuralism and not the morphological approach. In my view, it follows that the "standard" continuity interpretation must be seriously questioned.

Notwithstanding the similarity between organic formalism and structuralism with respect to holistic analysis, the morphological approach does not dig to a deep level of systematic analysis. It remains quite closely tied to the empirical "sensory stratum"; if we were to think, for example, of the skeleton as a structure of bones. In this sense organic formalism was still relatively close to mechanical formalism. Systemic formalism, on the other hand, involved a fundamental shift in thinking. The approach rested on the recognition of multiple systems, hierarchically ordered in levels. This conception did not only apply to a view of the system of language within broader cultural systems, but also to the study of language itself. I believe this helped to pave the way for the distinction structuralists made between a surface, or manifest, level of actual occurring written or spoken speech, and a deeper level of structural relations that underlie occurrences at the manifest level.

This of course had to be accompanied by a theory of the transformations from one level to another. Such theories became customary in postwar linguistics, even if not always under the banner of structuralism, and sometimes even opposed to it. Given this long-lasting impact, the final section of this chapter explores how the ideas of systemic formalism were incorporated as elements of a larger merger of constituents of structuralism.

5 Structuralism as a merger of multiple constituents

The historiography of structuralism has been dominated by the so-called "French model" (cf. Flack 2016). In this model, structuralism starts with the Swiss, but French-speaking, Saussure and after a brief intermediary phase is further developed by Lévi-Strauss and via him disseminated in many fields of study. I agree with two recent papers that this model is at best incomplete and should be replaced by a model that involves a much wider circulation perspective *and* that makes the figure of Roman Jakobson occupy centre stage (see Percival 2011; Flack 2016). This central position is justified because Jakobson was part of both the Moscow formalism and futurism of the 1910s and the Prague Circle in the 1920s and 1930s. He was the first to use the very term structuralism in linguistics and contributed significantly to developing it, in the early years first and foremost in the area of phonology. Due to his exile in the United States, he directly influenced

Lévi-Strauss, who was also exiled for a while in New York, and after the war his thought had an impact on important linguists such as Morris Halle (1923–2018) and Noam Chomsky (b. 1928).

The study of the circulation of knowledge should investigate the crossing of temporal, geographical as well as disciplinary boundaries. The latter is especially relevant when it comes to providing an account of the genesis of structuralism. Jakobson was an extremely versatile scholar who fused together constituents of structuralism from a variety of sources.[15] Among these are the concepts of *Gestalt* from psychology, "invariance" from mathematics, "limited variation" from biology, "periodicity" from chemistry, and from phenomenology the central role of "expression", the importance of the notion of "opposition" and the anti-positivist stance.[16] Members of the Prague School were therefore not as hostile to philosophical "speculation" as the Russian formalists had been, as they aligned their core anti-positivist stance to phenomenology and to the philosophically informed Gestalt psychology.[17] However, as in formalism, we find the inclusion of ideas from the natural sciences, which the practitioners of structuralism could use to claim a respectable place in the disciplinary landscape. But, significantly, Jakobson, took this alliance a step further. The very first time he mentioned the term structuralism he did not connect it to linguistics only, but immediately raised it to the status of a *science générale*:

> Were we to comprise the leading idea of present-day science in its most various manifestations, we could hardly find a more appropriate designation than structuralism. Any set of phenomena examined by contemporary science is treated not as a mechanical agglomeration but as a structural whole, and the basic task is to reveal the inner, whether static or developmental, laws of this system. What appears to be the focus of scientific preoccupations is no longer the outer stimulus, but the internal premises of development; now the mechanical conception of processes yields to the question of their functions. (Jakobson 1929: 11)

---

[15]"Das Werk [of Jakobson, like that of Leibniz] ist gekennzeichnet durch eine breitgefächerte Forschungstätigkeit, die ans Unglaubliche grenzt" (Holenstein 1975: 17). In Karstens (2017a), I argue that the pursuit of a number of key virtues helped Jakobson to fuse together a variety of elements to a more or less coherent approach to the study of language. In this respect, see also Karstens (2017b).

[16]For the influence of phenomenology on structuralism, the main point of reference has for quite some time been Holenstein (1975), but see also Flack (2016).

[17]The widespread anti-psychologism of the time did not involve a complete rejection of psychology, but a rejection of "bad" psychology and of an ill-founded connection between linguistics and psychology that members of the Prague circle, for example, found in the work of Wilhelm Wundt (1832–1920). See Toman (1995: 139).

Two things are striking in this citation. The first of these is the distinction that is drawn between two levels, namely "the outer stimulus" and an inner system, seen as a structural whole. The second is the importance that Jakobson attached to the investigation of functions of this structural whole. As was discussed above, both the concepts of system and function played a central role in systemic formalism. Here I want to investigate how to place these concepts in the broader amalgam of structuralism.

An important idea that structuralists took over from systemic formalism is that, in order to be intelligible, language has to have recurrent properties. That is, the regular appearance of linguistic forms is what makes language understandable and hence apt as a medium of communication. Russian futurists had made a similar point in their call for cultural *and* linguistic reform in the 1910s and 1920s.[18] Their approach must be contrasted with Italian futurism. The difference became apparent when Filippo Marinetti (1876–1944), the author of the "Manifesto del Futurismo" (1909), paid a visit to Moscow in 1914.[19] In a lecture he gave there, Marinetti proposed to liberate speech by freeing words from the bonds of grammatical rules and by using onomatopoetic and emotive interjections to create expressions that appeal directly to the senses (Gasparov 2014: 87–88).[20] The Russians found this approach extremely shallow. They argued that meaningful variation is only possible given the structure of a language and the existing tradition of language use in a community of speakers. Successful reform could only be achieved by gaining a deeper understanding of the systematic aspects of the language and by effecting meaningful and lasting reform from such knowledge. Hence the advancement of the investigation of a deeper-level system behind surface-level occurrences of linguistic expressions.

The Russian avant-garde explored relations between constituents of music, painting and poetry. They wanted to know which constituents were basic or "invariant", and explored the limits set on combinations of constituents. Their goal was to create a basis for free creativity, without any utilitarian purpose. It was generally thought that elementary forms that appealed to everyone would provide such a basis (Toman 1995: 238–239). When Jakobson said, "we learned from the poets", he was referring in particular to Khlebnikov, the futurist poet who was influential in the Moscow Linguistic Circle, the Moscow counterpart

---

[18]There were many connections between futurism and formalism; this is one of the main themes of Toman (1995).

[19]Interestingly, the young Jakobson acted as an interpreter at this event. See Toman (1995: 17).

[20]Such ideas about language reform were not uncommon at the time. Both in Dada and other surrealist movements, spontaneous language use, freed from rules and "formulas", was promoted. See, for example, van Spaendonck (1977).

of the Petersburg OPOJAZ group (see Jakobson 1979).[21] Khlebnikov thought that knowledge of basic structural relations could show unused realms for the expressions of meaning and help to determine the scope of meaningful variation. But this knowledge still had to be won. He drew inspiration from chemistry in this respect: "The entire language is to be divided into its fundamental elementary truths, whereafter it would be possible to build for sounds something similar to Mendeleev's law, that last pinnacle of chemical thought" (Khlebnikov as translated in Gasparov 2014: 95). This "law" states that chemical and physical properties of the elements recur periodically. By analogy, Khlebnikov expected that periodicity could also be found when the basic elements of language were arranged in systematic order.

Jakobson and his fellow structuralists took up Khlebnikov's challenge. Since phonemes are the smallest units of sound capable of distinguishing units of meaning in language, a basic set of phonemes could be the basic elements of language that Khlebnikov was looking for.[22] It is therefore not a coincidence that Prague structuralists focused on phonology, the area that studies the systematic organization of sounds in languages; that is, the system of phonemes. Phonology was simply seen as the most basic science of language. Jakobson's research yielded an integral system of sets of minimal oppositions between the phonemes of a language. The system of minimal pairs sets limits on the possible sound combinations out of which words can be created and which eventually occur on the surface level in language use.

We can therefore see how ideas about systematic organization from formalism connected to Russian futurism and found their way into structuralist phonology. The mathematical concept of "invariance" and the somewhat offbeat biological concept of "limited variation" fitted in here too. The concept of invariance allowed structuralists to express linguistic relations in mathematical terms. In Leo Berg's (1876–1950) evolutionary theory limits are set on variation, as variation was thought to be strongly contained by morphological forms. This theory thus differs from Charles Darwin's (1809–1882) idea of random variation and selection through environmental pressures. Jakobson was attracted to Berg's theory because it corresponded to limits set on word formation through a system of basic forms of language.

---

[21]Toman (1995: 10–11) mentions an early interest by Jakobson in the formal aspects of folkore, Russian dialects and poetry. One of the first major papers he wrote was an essay on Khlebnikov.
[22]In fact, the great breakthrough was to go one layer deeper and consider phonemes as bundles of constitutive features. These features then are the real basic elements of language.

The idea of distinguishing between a surface level and a deeper system was most probably drawn directly from the work of Saussure.[23] According to Joseph (2010: 237), Saussure achieved the conceptual leap to consider phonemes not as sound as such, but as units within a system: "Saussure's impact on 20th century linguistics would include the simplification brought about by the reorientation away from sound as such, and toward systems and the units that compose them. This would be the basis for the movement known as structuralism." It is not entirely clear where the conceptual leap of Saussure came from. Some have suggested that he was inspired by an analogy with economics, others see an impact of the periodic system of Mendeleev (1834–1907) on Saussure too.[24] But in the absence of concrete references the case is hard to make.

The distinction between surface structures and a deeper governing system Jakobson most likely took over from Tynjanov's systemic formalism, Khlebnikov's futurism *and* directly from Saussure. Moreover, Jakobson liked to draw analogies between linguistic structures and biological or physical structures which included those found in geology (earth layers) or meteorology (isolines) (see Holenstein 1975: 74, 188–194). For him all these links could only confirm the hypothesis that structuralism was the appropriate designation for science "in its most various manifestations".[25]

Likewise, the concept of function could be applied in more than one scientific discipline. Turning to Prague structuralism, Steiner (1976) has argued that the three basic theoretical concepts – structure, function and sign – were complementary notions interwoven into a cohesive approach. This is because structures have to be differentiated according to their dominant functions, and the semiotic function has the capacity to turn every object it dominates into a sign. Elsewhere Steiner explains how the formalist primary concept of function was redefined in semiotic terms (Steiner 1984: 264–266). He argues that structuralists needed the notion of function because they considered all of reality, from sensory perception to the most abstract mental construction, as a vast and complex realm of signs. There was therefore a need for some criterion to differentiate individual semiotic structures from each other. In structuralism the guiding thought is that every element in language exists because it has a function to fulfil. A function is

---

[23]Toman (1995: 88–94) mentions that Jakobson ordered a number of French books in 1921 when he was studying in Prague which included the *Cours.* Also his first investigations into phonological systems were accompanied by references to Albert Sechehaye (1870–1946).

[24]The economic theory is discussed in Joseph (2014). For the chemistry case, see Culler (1976), Clark (2008) and Silverstein (2016).

[25]A position that was fully vindicated through Cassirer's wide-ranging philosophical discussion of structuralism in Cassirer (1945).

defined as an active relation between an object and the goal for which the object is used.[26] In this way we can distinguish between the communicative, practical (or social) function of language and poetic, or artistic/aesthetic function. Function in this sense thus does not apply to the function of an element in a literary text, but rather to the dominant function of a particular semiotic structure. On my estimation, this does not exclude functional interpretation in the former sense. The semiotic understanding of functions just adds another dimension to the application of the function concept of systemic formalism.

Structuralism, like formalism and Saussure before, aimed to establish an independent science of language. The claim for independence prompted an alignment with models and theories stemming from a great variety of directions, including the natural sciences. I hope to have shown that systemic formalism provided a number of key elements of structuralism. If these elements partially overlapped with other sources of inspiration, this would only provide an extra assurance that they were rightly elected as being part of the structuralist programme.

6 Conclusion

Steiner (1984) wittily presents the formalist movement as a *polemos*. Formalists shared the common goal of changing the scholarly practice of literary studies and establishing a new autonomous realm for the discipline, but disagreed about how to achieve that goal. The formalists themselves were each other's fiercest critics. Boris Ejchenbaum (1886–1959) embraced this state of affairs in 1922, exclaiming: "Enough of monism! We are pluralists. Life is diverse and cannot be reduced to a single principle" (quoted in English in Steiner 1984: 259).

In general, three main types of formalism can be distinguished. Two of these, mechanical and organic formalism, differed at crucial points from structuralism, but with a third variant, systemic formalism, such a clear distinction cannot be drawn. In structuralism we can therefore find a number of key aspects of systemic formalism, such as the application of the notion of function, the importance of the systematic recurrence of forms in language, the idea of analysing manifestations of language use with reference to a deeper system, and placing the linguistic system within broader social and cultural systems; that is, thinking in terms of systems within systems. These points of continuity came about in part through a direct collaboration between Tynjanov, the leading systemic formalist, and Jakobson, the leading linguistic structuralist.

---

[26]Note that this teleology is anathema to a mechanistic worldview.

Systemic formalism was constitutive of the new direction in which general linguistics headed, as it helped to define object, aim and task of linguistic study. In structuralism, formalist ideas merged with constituents stemming from other directions, including phenomenology, biology, mathematics and Saussurian linguistics. Mukarovsky tended to consider structuralism as an attitude instead of a distinct linguistic theory. This attitude was synthetic rather than pluralistic. Structuralists wanted to overcome oppositions between form and content, data and interpretation, synchrony and diachrony, *langue* and *parole*, etc. It was therefore natural to combine ideas from all kinds of directions to achieve the sought-after synthesis.[27] We find this attitude most clearly in Roman Jakobson, who was an extremely versatile scholar and who was instrumental in carrying structuralist ideas to the Western world. I agree with Steiner (1984) that Russian formalism is best considered a transitory phase in the history of literary studies and linguistics. While the formalist programme as a whole came to an end, components of it did not, and this was in no small part due to the rise of structuralism as a major approach in linguistics.

Acknowledgements

I would like thank my colleagues Emma Mojet and Sjang ten Hagen for their careful reading of a draft version of this paper.

References

Bod, Rens, Jeroen van Dongen, Bart Karstens, Emma Mojet & Sjang ten Hagen. In Press. The flow of cognitive goods: A gistoriographical framework for the study of epistemic transfer. *Isis* 110(3).

Brik, Osip. 1923. T.n. 'Formal'nyi metod. *LEF* 1(1). 213–215.

Cassirer, Ernst. 1945. Structuralism in modern linguistics. *Word* 2(1). 99–120. DOI:10.1080/00437956.1945.11659249

Clark, A. Cernea. 2008. *Linguistic coins*. https://howtodrawanowl.wordpress.com/.

Culler, Jonathan D. 1976. *Saussure*. Glasgow: Fontana Collins.

Flack, Patrick. 2016. Roman Jakobson and the transition of German thought to the structuralist paradigm. *Acta Structuralica* 1(1). 1–15.

---

[27]Toman (1995: 150–152) includes a section on the "Courage to synthesize". He firmly places the synthetic attitude in the context of dialectics but this is perhaps unnecessary. A synthetic attitude may just involve fusing things together from different directions.

Galan, Frantisek W. 1985. *Historic structures. The Prague School project, 1928–1946.* Austin: University of Texas Press.

Gasparov, Boris. 2014. Futurism and phonology: The futurist roots of Jakobson's approach to language. *Ulbandus Review* 16. 84–112.

Graff, Harvey J. 2015. *Undisciplining knowledge. Interdisciplinarity in the twentieth century.* Baltimore: Johns Hopkins University Press.

Holenstein, Elmar. 1975. *Roman Jakobsons phänomenologischer Strukturalismus.* Frankfurt am Main: Suhrkamp.

Jakobson, Roman O. 1929. Romantické všeslovanství-nová slavistika [Romantic pan-Slavism: A new Slavistics]. *Čin* 1(1). 10–12.

Jakobson, Roman O. 1979. Новейшая русская поэзия: Подступы к Хлебникову [Modern Russian poetry. Sketch 1: Approaching Khlebnikov]. In Martha Taylor Stephen Rudy (ed.), *Roman Jakobson. Selected writings V. On verse, its masters and explorers*, 299–354. The Hague, Paris: Mouton.

Jakobson, Roman O. 1981a. Linguistics and poetics. In Roman O. Jakobson Stephen Rudy (ed.), *Roman Jakobson. Selected writings III. Poetry of grammar and grammar of poetry*, 18–51. The Hague, Paris: Mouton, De Gruyter.

Jakobson, Roman O. 1981b. Poetry of grammar and grammar of poetry. In Roman O. Jakobson Stephen Rudy (ed.), *Roman Jakobson. Selected writings III. Poetry of grammar and grammar of poetry*, 87–97. The Hague, Paris: Mouton, De Gruyter.

Joseph, John E. 2001. The exportation of structuralist ideas from linguistics to other fields: An overview. In Sylvain Auroux, E. F. K. Koerner, Hans-Josef Niederehe & Kees Versteegh (eds.), *History of the language sciences: An international handbook on the evolution of the study of language from the beginnings to the present*, vol. 2, 1880–1908. Berlin: Walter de Gruyter.

Joseph, John E. 2010. *Saussure.* Oxford: Oxford University Press.

Joseph, John E. 2014. Saussure's value(s). *Recherches Sémiotiques* 34(1-2-3). 191–208.

Karstens, Bart. 2012. Bopp the Builder. In Rens Bod, Jaap Maat & Thijs Weststeijn (eds.), *The making of the humanities*, vol. 2, 103–127. Amsterdam: Amsterdam University Press.

Karstens, Bart. 2017a. "The lonely form dies": How epistemic virtues connect Roman Jakobson's new science of language and his personality. In Jeroen van Dongen Herman Paul (ed.), *Epistemic virtues in the sciences and the humanities* (Boston Studies in the History and Philosophy of Science 321), 149–171. Springer.

Karstens, Bart. 2017b. The Prague Linguistic Circle and the analogy between musicology and linguistics. *History and Philosophy of the Language Sciences.* https://hiphilangsci.net/2017/03/07/prague-musicology-linguistics/.

Koerner, E. F. Konrad. 1989. On the problem of "influence" in linguistic historiography. In E. F. Konrad Koerner (ed.), *Practicing linguistic historiography* (Studies in the History of the Language Sciences 50), 61–68. Amsterdam: John Benjamins.

Kohrt, Manfred & Kerstin Kucharczik. 2001. Die Wurzeln des Strukturalismus in der Sprachwissenschaft des 19. Jahrhunderts. In Sylvain Auroux, E. F. Konrad Koerner, Hans-Josef Niederehe & Kees Versteegh (eds.), *History of the language sciences. An international handbook on the evolution of the study of language from the beginnings to the present*, vol. 2, 1719–1735. Berlin, New York: Walter de Gruyter.

Lévi-Strauss, Claude. 1984. Structure and form: Reflections on a work by Vladimir Propp. In Anatoly Liberman (ed.), *Theory and history of folklore* (Theory and History of Literature Volume 5), 167–188. Minneapolis: University of Minnesota Press.

Marinetti, Filippo T. 1909. Manifesto del futurismo. *Gazzetta dell'Emilia di Bologna.* 5 February 1909, front page.

Oppel, Horst. 1947. *Morphologische Literaturwissenschaft: Goethes Ansicht und Methode.* Mainz: Kirchheim.

Percival, Keith W. 2011. Roman Jakobson and the birth of linguistic structuralism. *Sign Systems Studies* 1. 236–262.

Petrovskij, Mikhail. 1927. Morfologija novelly. *Ars Poetica* 1. 69–100.

Propp, Vladimir Y. 1928. Transformacii volsebnyx skazok. *Poètika* 4. 70–89.

Propp, Vladimir Y. 1968 [1928]. *Morphology of the folktale. 2nd revised and edited edition with a preface by Louis A. Wagner and a new introduction by Alan Dundes.* Austin: University of Texas Press.

Saussure, Ferdinand de. 1922 [1916]. *Cours de linguistique générale.* Paris: Payot. Edited by Charles Bally and Albert Sechehaye.

Silverstein, Michael. 2016. Thinking about the "teleologies of structuralism". *HAU: Journal of Ethnographic Theory* 6(3). 79–84.

Steiner, Peter. 1976. *From formalism to structuralism: A comparative study of Russian formalism and Prague structuralism.* Yale University dissertation.

Steiner, Peter. 1984. *Russian formalism. A metapoetics.* London, Ithaca: Cornell University Press.

Toman, Jindrich. 1995. *The magic of the common language. Jakobson, Mathesius, Trubetzkoy, and the Prague Linguistic Circle.* Boston: MIT Press.

Tynjanov, Yuri & Roman O. Jakobson. 1928. Problemy izučenija literatury i jazyka. *Novyj Lef* 12. 35–37.

van Spaendonck, Jan. 1977. *Belle époque en anti-kunst: De geschiedenis van een opstand tegen de burgerlijke cultuur.* Meppel: Boom.

Chapter 6

The resistant embrace of formalism in the work of Émile Benveniste and Aurélien Sauvageot

John E. Joseph

University of Edinburgh

Rarely claimed by linguists as labels for their own work, "structuralist" and "structuralism" have been more often hurled at others as criticisms. Yet those doing the hurling were themselves often pursuing a similarly formalist analysis, and were not averse to claiming their share of the academic capital that structuralism brought to linguistics. Work by Émile Benveniste (1902–1976) and Aurélien Sauvageot (1897–1988) shows different modes of a "resistant embrace" to structuralist formalism, with their resistance centred on a perceived abandonment of attention to phonological and philological detail; and to the role of speakers, a concern that culminates with Benveniste's concept of enunciation. Their reactions are examined here within the framework of two different ways in which structuralism was conceived, one based on holism, the other on universalism.

1 Introduction

Quentin Skinner (1969) expressed concern about the growing use in the history of ideas of the notion of paradigm, which had emerged in the history of art (Gombrich 1960) and of science (Kuhn 1962). Skinner argued that it fosters a mythology that how people thought at any given period was more unified than has ever historically been the case. Insofar as we buy into this "mythology of doctrines", Skinner writes, quoting Voltaire, "History then indeed becomes a pack of tricks we play on the dead" (Skinner 1969: 7, 13–14).[1]

---

[1] The quote is from Voltaire's letter to Pierre-Robert Le Cornier de Cideville, 9 Feb. 1757: "l'histoire [...] n'est, après tout, qu'un ramas de tracasseries qu'on fait aux morts".

John E. Joseph. 2019. The resistant embrace of formalism in the work of Émile Benveniste and Aurélien Sauvageot. In James McElvenny (ed.), *Form and formalism in linguistics*, 141–174. Berlin: Language Science Press. DOI.10.5281/zenodo.2654359

We are ninety years on from the first uses of the term "structuralism" by linguists,[2] first to manifest, then to identify a paradigm, to which some subscribed wholeheartedly, while others resisted no less strongly, and others still, a majority perhaps, were ambivalent. This is not always easy to determine, making it all the more tempting to use the mythology of doctrines to unify the middle decades of the twentieth century into a structuralist period.

Not only do linguists no longer apply "structuralist" to our work, we even struggle to remember what exactly it represented, and why it had the power it did.[3] Actually, "structuralist" and "structuralism" were more often hurled at others as criticisms than claimed as methodological labels. Yet those doing the hurling were themselves often pursuing a recognizably structuralist form of analysis, and were not averse to taking their share of the academic capital that structuralism brought to linguistics. This paper examines some of the modes of resistance to the formalist commitments of structural linguistics in mid-twentieth-century France — before the onset of a "post-structuralist" period — and explores what drove it.

---

[2] Joseph (2001) gives details on these early uses, and later ones, as well as on the "structuralism" proclaimed in psychology starting in 1907.

[3] Having detected recently that younger colleagues in my department were using the term "generative" in a way that struck me as different from my own use of it, I went around to some of them and asked, "Are you a generativist?" This included phoneticians and phonologists as well as people who work in pragmatics and syntax, none of them committed Chomskyans like the people with whom I worked at the University of Maryland in the 1980s. Each of my present colleagues whom I queried hesitated for a few seconds, then answered "yes". I then asked what "generativist" means to them. None of them mentioned innateness, or universal grammar, or rules and representations, or principles and parameters, or infinite creativity or any other of the ideas which I associate with generativism. Rather, all said that they are generativists because they believe in the existence of a language system which speakers know, and which is the basis of language production and comprehension. This, to me, does not a generativist make. It is structuralism, part of the considerable structuralist heritage that continued into generativism. But to make it the criterion for being a generativist is like being asked to define Episcopalianism, and answering that it means believing in God. I have argued for a long time now (since Joseph 1999, and most fully in Joseph 2002) that "American structuralism" actually begins not with Bloomfield and Sapir but with Chomsky, or else perhaps the day in 1942 when Jakobson landed in New York. Yet one now meets linguists who think that the idea of a mental language system originated with Chomsky. When it comes to meaning in language, my colleagues often prove to be pre-Saussurean, conceiving of a language as an encoding of a pre-existing external reality — what Saussure rejected as "nomenclaturism". They are divided over whether the sound side is essentially mental or acoustic. In these respects they are not yet structuralists, let alone generativists. But they value the label.

2 Benveniste and structuralism

Émile Benveniste (1902–1976) was the most important French linguist of the "structuralist period". When asked about structuralism in interviews, he did not keep his distance, but answered the question as though he embraced the term and what it stood for (Benveniste 1974 [1968](a), Benveniste 1974 [1968](b)). His linguistic work became progressively less structural in some senses of that term, starting from when he resumed it after his Swiss exile during the war. Starting in the 1950s and culminating in 1969, he introduced his concept of "enunciation", which is the direct opposite to the structuralist approach in key respects. As discussed in section §6 below, his stated aim was not to replace structuralism, but to supplement it — to provide a parallel mode of enquiry in which the focus is not on the structure of the *langue*, nor on *parole*, but on speakers; on the "semantic" rather than the "semiotic", in his terms, which seems to make him pre-Saussurean, as does his placing of writing at the centre of language.

He continued to publish prolifically on ancient Indo-European languages, as he had done since the 1920s, and also undertook fieldwork on American Indian languages in Alaska and the Yukon, though he published little of this research. He also produced a small but steady number of papers offering radical revisions to key concepts of linguistic analysis such as person, deixis and performatives, the sort of thing that his teacher Antoine Meillet (1866–1936) had often done. A number of these papers were republished in 1966 in a volume entitled *Problems in General Linguistics*, of which a second volume appeared in 1974. The 1966 volume (henceforth referred to as PLG 1, and the 1974 follow-up as PLG 2) appeared just at the time when "structuralism" as a generalized mode of enquiry was getting established as dominant across the fields that comprise what in France are called the "human sciences", and indeed beyond.

The focus of Benveniste (1969) on words, rather than sounds and forms (although they come into the picture in a secondary role), gives it a precarious place within linguistics *tout court*, let alone structural linguistics, which treated words as a pre-scientific concept, necessary to refer to when communicating with the general public and specialists in other academic fields, but kept at bay in their formal analyses. This despite two of the core figures of structural linguistics, Roman Jakobson (1896–1982) and André Martinet (1908–1999), giving the title *Word* to the journal which they co-founded in New York in 1945. The 1969 book is his attempt at the sort of structuralism that had spread beyond linguistics. He read the work of his contemporaries such as Georges Dumézil (1898–1986) and Georges Canguilhem (1904–1995) with admiration mixed with an awareness that the philological knowledge they brought to bear in their enquiries was shallow in comparison with his own. Claude Lévi-Strauss (1908–2009) could not see anywhere near so deeply into the cultures he studied as Benveniste could into the remote Indo-European past.

Yet Benveniste, in spite of all his work aimed directly or indirectly at subverting structuralism, never rejected it. In contemplating why, I have been inclined to attribute it to practical concerns: his awareness that structuralism, in promoting linguistics to master science, had brought considerable advantages to the French linguistics establishment and to him as its leader. That may sound like a cynical motive, except that Benveniste was not a Jakobson or a Martinet, men with flamboyant personalities who strove to attract followers and worried about their place in the academic pecking order. Benveniste's place at the top was assured institutionally, from Meillet's death until his own forty years later, even during the last seven years when he was paralysed by a stroke and could not speak or write. The advantages which the wide attention to structuralism brought were ones that he personally did not need, but they offered benefits to his students and the other French linguists of whom he was the acknowledged leader.

There was still more to his ongoing semi-commitment to structuralism than the pragmatic benefits for others. Even his late work contains signs that he was drawn to what structuralism promised, in an almost religious way — like an agnostic who never misses church, drawn to the vision and promise he aches to believe in.[4]

It is striking how in a 1968 address (Benveniste 1974 [1970][b]: 95), and again in a lecture the following January (Benveniste 2012: 79), Benveniste insists that "the language contains the society".[5] Meillet (1905–1906) had been the first to state in print, more than sixty years earlier, that "a language is a social fact". But Benveniste is asserting much more than that. To understand why, we can look for example at the brief chapter headed *thémis* in his *Vocabulaire des institutions indo-européennes*:

> The general structure of society, defined in its broad divisions by a certain number of concepts, rests on an assemblage of norms which add up to

---

[4]No links to traditional religious thinking are apparent in Benveniste's work, but see Dosse (1997 [1991]: 245–247) on Christian interpretations of the semiology of Jacques Lacan (1901–1981), to whom Benveniste was sufficiently close to have contributed an article to the first issue of his journal *La Psychanalyse* (Benveniste 1966 [1956][b]), and on displaced Christianity in the work of Louis Althusser (1918–1990), Lacan's ally in the École Normale Supérieure (pp. 294–295).

[5]"[...] la langue contient la société." He adds that "la langue inclut la société, mais elle n'est pas incluse par elle" (the language includes the society, but is not included by it) (Benveniste 1974 [1970][b]: 96). Translations are mine unless otherwise indicated.

"law". All societies, even the most primitive [...] are governed by principles of law relating both to persons and to goods. The rules and these norms are traceable in the vocabulary.

[...] We can in the first place posit for common Indo-European an extremely important concept, that of "order". It is represented by Vedic *ṛta*, Iranian *arta* (Armenian *aša*, by a special phonetic development). We have here one of the cardinal notions of the legal world of the Indo-European to say nothing of their religious and moral ideas: this is the concept of "Order" which governs also the orderliness of the universe, the movement of the stars, the regularity of the seasons and the years; and further the relations of gods and men, and finally the relations of men to one another. Nothing which concerns man or the world falls outside the realm of "Order". It is thus the foundation, both religious and moral, of every society. Without this principle everything would revert to chaos. (Benveniste 2016 [1973]: 379–380)[6]

Benveniste is attuned to the differences among Indo-European societies. Words that are not shared across the languages are interpreted as representing later historical developments. Through close study of texts in which the words occur, Benveniste works to establish their precise meanings, and in so doing to reconstruct the societies themselves. In the case of words shared across all or the great bulk of the family, he is reconstructing the earliest recoverable Indo-European social stratum. The language contains the society.

His remarks about the nature of law are grounded in the findings of this linguistic method, but also apply to the method itself, particularly to the guiding principle of Benveniste's training, which he embraces even as he resists it. Structuralism is the search for the system that is "an assemblage of norms which add

---

[6]"La structure générale de la société, définie dans ses grandes divisions par un certain nombre de concepts, repose sur un ensemble de normes qui constituent un droit. Toutes les sociétés, mêmes les plus primitives, [...] sont régies par des principes de droit quant aux personnes et aux biens. Ces règles et ces normes se marquent dans le vocabulaire. [...] On peut poser, dès l'état indo-européen, un concept extrêmement important : celui de l'ordre'. Il est représenté par le védique *ṛta*, iranien *arta* (avestique *aša*, par une évolution phonétique particulière). C'est là une des notions cardinales de l'univers juridique et aussi religieux et moral des Indo-Européens : c'est l'Ordre' qui règle aussi bien l'ordonnance de l'univers, le mouvement des astres, la périodicité des saisons et des années que les rapports des hommes et des dieux, enfin des hommes entre eux. Rien de ce qui touche à l'homme, au monde, n'échappe à l'empire de l'Ordre'. C'est donc le fondement tant religieux que moral de toute société; sans ce principe, tout retournerait au chaos" (Benveniste 1969: vol. 2, 99–100).

up to 'law' ". No wonder its draw was so strong: it "is the concept of 'Order' which governs also the orderliness of the universe, the movement of the stars, [...] the relations of men to one another". It is as true of structure in language as of order in law and society that "Without this principle everything would revert to chaos".

Who knows whether Benveniste saw, let alone intended, the reflexivity of his comments? But a few paragraphs on, after going through various Indo-Iranian, Greek and Latin reflexes of this root *ar–*, including Latin *ars* "art" and *ritus* "rite", Latin *artus* "joint" and Greek *árthon* "joint, limb", he remarks: "Everywhere the same notion is still perceptible: order, arrangement, the close mutual adaptation of the parts of a whole to one another [...]" (Benveniste 1969: 101).[7] If you seek a definition of the structuralist view of the language system, look no further.[8]

So why did Benveniste not seek unambivalently to be the Galileo of language, reducing the vast chaos of diversity to Order? The clue is in the word 'reducing'. Reduction is the genius of structuralism. Its ancient and deep-seated appeal in our languages and cultures is evident in Benveniste's analysis of *thémis*. The one small minority to which it might not appeal are those who actually love the vast diversity of languages, who enjoy nothing more than reading ancient texts in barely-known languages and working through their minute details. In other words, linguists, particularly the sort who entered the field in the nineteenth and the first two-thirds of the twentieth centuries, and who still exist, in reduced numbers.

I am suggesting that the founding tension in structuralism was that it was driven by a reductionist search for order, carried out by people who varied considerably in how fast and how far they thought such reduction could legitimately be taken. Indeed, some of them believed that legitimate knowledge required an

---

[7]"Partout, la même notion est encore sensible : l'ordonnance, l'ordre, l'adaptation étroite entre les parties d'un tout [...]". *ar–* is also the root of French *ordre* and English *order*.

[8]The desire to find order in language, with the promise it held out of keeping everything from reverting to chaos, was by no means exclusive to linguists. It was extremely widespread, lying behind movements for language standardization, and for what linguists disparage as prescriptivism. In my view, the descriptivist-prescriptivist dichotomy is ultimately rhetorical, a veneer which masks a shared desire for order — law and order, given how fond linguists have always been of discovering laws comparable to those by which the movement of the stars is explained. One might expect linguists to regard prescriptivism as a phenomenon of language understanding and use, as worthy of study and analysis as their supposedly prescription-free data, but such an outlook is rare. We claim the unique right to define what order is and how it is to be sought, and see it as our duty to stamp out other conceptions of order in language, exposing their ignorance and error and treating them as an even greater threat to order because they decline to acknowledge our unique authority.

accumulation of ever greater data and detail, in direct contrast to the genius of structuralism, and they would form the hard resistance. But my interest here is in the soft resistance of those who embraced the programme even while holding it at bay. Who smoked, but didn't inhale.

3 The issue of discontinuity

I shall start from the end of the structuralist period, and the critique of structuralist linguistics mounted from the 1970s onward by Henri Meschonnic (1932–2000), who belonged to the generation of Benveniste's students.[9] This is well into the period which, outside France, was being labelled as "post-structuralist", characterized by resistance to key aspects of structuralist work being mounted by academics from fields other than linguistics. Such was the din from without that Meschonnic's resistance from within did not have the full impact one might have expected. Like the integrationist critique of linguistics mounted by Roy Harris (1931–2015) at Oxford, it produced a clique of devoted followers, along with rejection and enmity from the linguistics mainstream — which however had by now cut itself off from any commitments to a structuralism henceforth associated with the past. This masked its enduring heritage, and made it inevitable that by the late 2010s linguists would no longer distinguish structuralism from generativism.

For Meschonnic, the tragedy of structuralism lay in what he called its "triumphalism of scientizing the discontinuous" (*triomphalisme d'un scientisme du discontinu*) (Meschonnic 2009: 20). It is true that, if you ask a linguist what linguistics is, the answer you are likely to get is, first, something about the scientific study of language, and then a litany of the sub-specializations, phonology, syntax, semantics, historical linguistics, sociolinguistics etc. and what they are concerned with.[10] The existence of those sub-fields, with their division of the labour of analysing sound, order, meaning and the rest each allotted to specialists, is taken to signify the field's progress to a mature state. Specialists tend to avoid treading on each other's turf; yet no one would deny that the ultimate goal is an understanding of language *as a whole*. The institutionalizing of discontinuity is seen as a means to that end, yet, as Meschonnic shows, it has tended to become an end in itself.

---

[9]His *magnum opus*, Meschonnic (1982), sits within a massive output that branches across the disciplinary boundaries which he rejected.

[10]For an example, see https://www.youtube.com/watch?v=7HOsQDD1Res.

John E. Joseph

Taking inspiration from Benveniste's (1974 [1970](a)) conception of utterance, the perspective which starts from the speaker or writer rather than from the linguistic system, Meschonnic devoted his mature career to exposing the structuralist fetishization of the discontinuous and shifting the focus to the *continu* ("continuous") in language. It is not always clear who did and did not count as a structuralist for him, though Ferdinand de Saussure (1857–1913) definitely did not. In fact, when Meschonnic reads out his charge sheet against structuralism, each of the nine crimes is described in its opposition to Saussure. Here are the first three:

1. when Saussure says "system", a dynamic notion, structuralism says "structure", a formal and ahistorical notion;

2. when Saussure proposes that with language all we have are points of view — a crucial notion: representations — structuralism with the sign presents itself as describing the nature of language;

3. and Saussure constructs the notion of point of view according to an entirely deductive (rational-logical) internal systematicity, but structuralism created descriptive (empirical) sciences of language [...]. (Meschonnic 2009: 20)[11]

Again, he is right about the discontinuous — though it is complicated. Starting in the 1920s, those who got called structuralists, or more rarely, called themselves that, were torn between two urges. One was to reject the methods of an earlier generation who wanted to decompose phenomena into elements. That can be construed as a desire for continuousness. The other was to seek out what connects phenomena to each other, and doing that demanded the decomposition into discontinuous elements that their first urge was to reject.

Early structuralists invoked Gestalt psychology as continuous with what they were trying to achieve. By 1945, the first volume of *Word* contains two articles laying out visions of structuralism that superficially overlap, but in fact embody these complexly opposed urges. For the older writer, Ernst Cassirer (1874–1945),

[11]"1. quand Saussure dit *système*, notion dynamique, le structuralisme dit *structure*, notion formelle et ahistorique ; 2. quand Saussure pose que sur le langage on n'a que des points de vue, notion capitale : des représentations, le structuralisme avec le signe se présente comme décrivant la nature du langage ; 3. et Saussure construit la notion de point de vue selon une systématicité interne toute déductive, mais le structuralisme a fait des sciences du langage descriptives [...]". Saussure's theory of language was famously laid out in the posthumous *Cours de linguistique générale* (Saussure 1922 [1916]).

systems such as language need to be approached holistically. Language for Cassirer (1945: 110) is organic, "in the sense that it does not consist of detached, isolated, segregated facts. It forms a coherent whole in which all parts are interdependent upon each other".

The younger Lévi-Strauss seems at first to be singing from the same hymn sheet when he rejects the analysis of kinship by W. H. R. Rivers (1864–1922) on the grounds that it is concerned merely with an atomistic charting of the details of relationships in some particular society: "Each terminological detail, each special marriage rule, is attached to a different custom, like a consequence or a vestige: we descend into an orgy of discontinuity" (Lévi-Strauss 1945: 37).[12]

But a careful reading shows Lévi-Strauss singing in a different key from Cassirer. His concern is not with organicity, but with the failure to take a *universalist* point of view, one that looks past superficial differences to find how kinship systems are fundamentally the same from culture to culture. They must be so, Lévi-Strauss assumes, because the human relationships they encode are the same. Taking maternal uncles as an example, he writes:

> We see that the avunculate, to be understood, must be treated as a relationship interior to a system, and that it is the system itself which must be considered in its totality, in order to perceive its structure. (Lévi-Strauss 1945: 47)[13]

If this sounds like Cassirer's holism, the resemblance is deceptive because of what Lévi-Strauss understands by "system". It is not like Saussure's language system, which is specific to each particular language. Lévi-Strauss is not talking about the Yoruba kinship system, as distinct from the Inuit one. He means the *human* kinship system, regarded as a product of evolutionary forces.

There is a double continuity-discontinuity tension at work in this defining structuralist moment: on the one hand, holism versus atomism, Cassirer's tension; on the other hand, the universal versus the language-culture-particular, Lévi-Strauss's tension. Meschonnic's discontent with the discontinuous falls within the first type. When he takes up arms against the structuralist dissociation of language from the body, he cites language-culture-particular examples (notably

---

[12] "Chaque détail de terminologie, chaque règle spéciale du mariage, est rattachée à une coutume différente, comme une conséquence ou comme un vestige : on tombe dans une débauche de discontinuité."

[13] "Nous voyons donc que l'avunculat, pour être compris, doit être traité comme une relation intérieure à un système, et que c'est le système lui-même qui doit être considéré dans son ensemble, pour en apercevoir la structure."

from the Hebrew of the Old Testament, but also from modern languages) as evidence for a universal language-body continuity. Any language-culture-particular versus universal tension is left aside, or at least pushed into the background.[14]

Lévi-Strauss sees the development of phonology, as opposed to the merely physical, empirical study of phonetics, as "playing for the social sciences the same renewing role as nuclear physics, for example, has played for the exact sciences" (Lévi-Strauss 1945: 35).[15] He locates the renewal in four fundamental points of method identified in 1933 by Nicolai S. Trubetzkoy (1890–1938):

> [F]irst, phonology passes from the study of *conscious* linguistic phenomena to the study of their *unconscious* linguistic infrastructure; it refuses to treat terms as independent entities, instead taking as the basis of its analysis the *relations* between terms; it introduces the notion of *system* [...]; and finally it aims at discovering *general laws* either by induction or by logical deduction, [...] which gives them an absolute character. (Lévi-Strauss 1945: 35)[16]

The second and third points, concerning relations and system, are ones Cassirer would have endorsed. But the unconscious is not a concept Cassirer deals with. Although he recognises that consciousness "grows" in the child, the dyad suggested by Lévi-Strauss would have been too simplistic for his liking.

When Cassirer talks about atomism and holism, it is on the level of a particular system. Lévi-Strauss talks about atomism and totality of the general system, for example the avunculate, considered universally. The two approaches are not always at cross purposes, only sometimes, but enough to generate an enduring tension within structuralism. A defining moment came in 1955, when the *succès fou* of Lévi-Strauss's *Tristes Tropiques* defined structuralism for the public at large and for the next generation of scholars. Cassirer's worries about internal discontinuity were shunted aside, not to vanish but to fester.

For Meschonnic and his contemporaries who took up academic posts with the expansion of the Parisian university system after May 1968, structuralism stood

---

[14]The tensions we repress can come back to haunt us, and this, I argue in Joseph (2018b), is potentially the case with Meschonnic's approach to the Hebrew-language body.

[15]"[...] vis-à-vis des sciences sociales, le même rôle rénovateur que la physique nucléaire, par exemple, a joué pour l'ensemble des sciences exactes."

[16]"[E]n premier lieu, la phonologie passe de l'étude des phénomènes linguistiques *conscients* à celle de leur infrastructure *inconsciente* ; elle refuse de traiter les *termes* comme des entités indépendantes, prenant au contraire comme base de son analyse les *relations* entres les termes ; elle introduit la notion de *système* [...] ; enfin elle vise à la découverte de *lois générales* soit trouvées par induction, soit déduites logiquement, [...] ce qui leur donne un caractère absolu."

for discontinuity. In linguistics, that meant treating phonology, prosody, morphology, syntax, semantics, semiology and so on as separate levels of language and distinct areas of specialization; and divorcing linguistics from poetics or applied areas such as translation, and ultimately even semiology, though linguistics continued to focus on the sign and combinations of signs as the essence of language. This never sat well with Meschonnic, but since he was teaching linguistics, he could only go so far in opposing it in these early years of his career, though later he would attack it relentlessly.

The greatest damage wrought by this discontinuity, as Meschonnic saw it, was that it resulted in the unifying core of language — rhythm — being relegated to a minor corner, when it should be at the very centre of an investigative enterprise where everything connects to everything else. Meschonnic's rejection of structuralist linguistics can be read as an assertion that structuralism itself was not structuralist enough.

4 Benveniste's early work: in what sense is it structuralist?

Can Benveniste's earlier work really be called structuralist? It is, after all, diachronic rather than synchronic in orientation, where structuralism is usually characterized as having replaced diachronic with synchronic enquiry. But that characterization is flawed — it is based on a misunderstanding of "diachronic" as a synonym of "historical", when Saussure's intention in calling for a diachronic linguistics was for it to replace the historical tracing of sound and forms through time with, instead, the comparison of *états de langue* at different points in time, each analysed synchronically. Saussure's 1879 *Mémoire* on the primitive vowel system of the Indo-European languages is really a synchronic study, a reconstruction of the system at some indeterminate point in the past. Benveniste's doctoral thesis and first published book (1935) follows the model of Saussure's *Mémoire* to the extent possible, given that it is a morphological rather than a phonological system that he is reconstructing.

The first three-quarters of Benveniste's book consists of focussed surveys of forms and alternations that appear to have been written as separate studies. Not until Chapter 9 does Benveniste explain how they fit together.

> All the lines of facts we have traced have led us progressively and by ultimately converging paths to recognize in neuters and adjectives a coherent structure and rule-governed alternations. In turn, these nominal forms

posited in their most ancient state reveal principles which, once defined, confronted and grouped, constitute a theory of the Indo-European root. (Benveniste 1935: 147)[17]

Before explaining what that theory is, however, Benveniste sets out his structuralist stall, with a sweeping attack on everything written on the subject heretofore:

> What has been taught up to now about the nature and modalities of the root is, in truth, a heteroclite assemblage of empirical notions, provisional recipes, archaic and recent forms, all with an irregularity and complexity which defy ordering. (Benveniste 1935: 147)[18]

He illustrates this with a catalogue of reconstructed roots varying from one to five phonemes in length, monosyllabic or disyllabic, with either a vowel or a diphthong as their nucleus,

> with an initial vowel (*ar–) or a final vowel (*po–); in long degree (*sēd–) or zero degree (*dhǝk–); with a long diphthong (*srēig–) or a short diphthong (*bheudh–), with a suffix or a lengthening, etc. It would be difficult to justify or even to enumerate completely all the types of roots that are attributed to Indo-European. (Benveniste 1935: 147)[19]

This is akin to what Lévi-Strauss a decade later will disparage as "an orgy of discontinuity" in Rivers' ethnography, which he wants to replace with a structural analysis (see section §3). One might expect Benveniste to argue that no language could be this complicated, but he does not. His critique extends only to the analysis:

---

[17]"Toutes les lignes de faits que nous avons suivies nous ont acheminé [sic] progressivement et par des voies finalement convergentes à reconnaître aux neutres et aux adjectifs une structure cohérente et des alternances réglées. A leur tour, ces formes nominales posées en leur état le plus ancien révèlent des principes qui, une fois définis, confrontés et groupés, constituent une théorie de la racine indo-européenne."

[18]"Ce qu'on a enseigné jusqu'ici de la nature et des modalités de la racine est, au vrai, un assemblage hétéroclite de notions empiriques, de recettes provisoires, de formes archaïques et récentes, le tout d'une irrégularité et d'une complication qui défient l'ordonnance."

[19]"[...] à voyelle initiale (*ar–) ou à voyelle finale (*po–) ; à degré long (*sēd–) ou à degré zéro (*dhǝk–) ; à diphthongue longue (*srēig–) ou brève (*bheudh–), à suffixe ou à élargissement, etc. On serait en peine de justifier et même d'énumérer complètement tous les types de racines qui sont attribués à l'indo-européen." It is interesting that *ar–, the root of *order* and its congeners in other Indo-European languages as discussed in section §2 above, should figure among the examples here.

There is here an abuse of words that betrays an indecisive doctrine. The way to arrive at Indo-European is not by piling up the various Indo-European forms with a verbal theme, nor by projecting into prehistory the particularities of an attested language state. It is necessary to try, through broad comparisons, to find the initial system in its simplest form, then to see what principles modify its economy. It is this mechanism that we are attempting to define here. (Benveniste 1935: 147–148)[20]

A number of words are striking: Saussure's *système*, and also *mécanisme*, which occurs repeatedly in the *Cours*; but also *économie*, in a sense more reminiscent of Martinet, Benveniste's younger contemporary and, in Martinet's mind at least, his rival. As Benveniste pursues this theme, the word *structure*, absent from the *Cours*, comes to dominate:

The essential thing being the problem of structure, we shall neglect on principle questions of "value", "aspect" etc. If the definition of the root we arrive at is judged to be valid, these notions of value and aspect will have the morphological basis which they now lack. It will then be the right time to re-examine them. (Benveniste 1935: 147–148)[21]

"Value" does not refer here to Saussurean *valeur*, but to a more particular use of the term by Meillet when writing in his proto-sociolinguistic vein, where he talks about the "abstract" and "concrete" value of words, linking the abstract to the aristocratic, and to the oldest, most enduring strain of the Indo-European lexicon, whereas the concrete belongs to the peasantry, is imbued with "affective" value and is historically unstable. As for "aspect", it figures in Meillet's work mainly in its familiar form, referring for instance to perfective versus imperfective in verbs, but more extensively. For example, "verbs bearing preverbs offer a nuance of 'aspect' different from that of the simple verb: they indicate a process, the

---

[20] "Il y a ici un abus de mots qui trahit une doctrine indécise. On n'obtient pas de l'indo-européen en additionnant les diverses formes indo-européennes d'un thème verbal ni en projetant dans la préhistoire les particularités d'un état de langue historique. Il faut essayer, par de larges comparaisons, de retrouver le système initial sous sa forme la plus simple, puis de voir quels principes en modifient l'économie. C'est ce mécanisme que nous cherchons à définir ici."
[21] "L'essentiel étant le problème de la structure, nous négligerons en principe les questions de 'valeur', d'"aspect', etc. Si la définition de la racine à laquelle nous aboutirons est jugée valable, ces notions de valeur et d'aspect auront le fondement morphologique qui leur fait encore défaut. Il sera temps alors d'en reprendre l'étude."

end of which is envisaged" (Meillet 1931: 263–264).[22] Although Benveniste has dismissed, or rather postponed, investigation of aspect in the same breath with that of value, aspect in the more usual, limited sense is actually central to his theory of the Indo-European root. What he is doing here is distancing himself from Meillet's extension of the concept, where Meillet tends to link it with the "mentality" of speakers — this despite the fact that Meillet repeatedly places his analyses in opposition to that of "Mr Vossler and his school" on the grounds that *they* have recourse to mentality. Meillet's accounts are not as different from Karl Vossler's (1872–1949) as his rhetoric would make it appear. Regarding tense and aspect in the development from early Latin to Classical Latin, Meillet writes of how

> with the development of a civilization of intellectual character, in which the thinking of the upper echelon takes an exact philosophical turn, and in which children and youths are educated in schools, the notion of "tense" takes precedence over the notion of "aspect". (Meillet 1931: 270–271)[23]

Again, a matter of sociolinguistics: the thinking of the upper echelon, education in schools being invoked to explain the rise of rational, which is to say abstract, tense – not entirely replacing concrete aspect, but taking precedence over it, quite as the upper echelon, the aristocracy, take precedence over the peasantry.

The development of structural linguistics is then a story of difference, of differentiating oneself from someone else who is perceived as too psychological, insufficiently concerned with establishing the facts of language structure before offering explanations of them, rendering dubious the sustainability of those explanations. Meillet sees Vossler's "idealism" as too, well, idealist, whereas his own approach is better grounded in "concrete" facts. In historical terms Meillet believes that the move from the concrete to the abstract represents progress; and so too in methodological terms, in that his own method proceeds in this

---

[22]"[...] les verbes munis de préverbes offrent une nuance d''aspect' différente de celle du verbe simple : ils indiquent un procès dont le terme est envisagé." He gives the contrasting examples of *Nec* **tacui** *demens* "I was mad enough not to keep silent" (*Aeneid* II, 94) and **Conticuere** *omnes* "All fell silent" (*Aeneid* II, 1), where, since the highlighted verbs have the same root and are both in the perfect tense, the preverb *con*– is analysed as conveying the perfective aspect.

[23]"[...] avec le développement d'une civilisation de caractère intellectuel, où la pensée des hommes dirigeants prend un tour philosophique exact, où les enfants et les jeunes gens se forment dans les écoles, la notion de 'temps' prenne le pas sur la notion d''aspect'". In his review of Vossler (1932), Firth (1933: 234) contrasts Vossler's conception of "inner language form" with Saussure's "'bloodless system of signs' (*langue*)".

way, deducing higher-level explanations from detailed examination of phenomena. Whereas abstraction that is not so deduced, but simply asserted, risks being fantasy, and so is not progress at all; not a nobility destined to rule over the concrete-minded, but a tyranny that the true nobles must resist.

Meillet is polite when rejecting Vossler, keeping his remarks to a minimum. When it comes Benveniste's turn to make a similar move vis-à-vis Meillet, he is more than polite towards his *cher maître*, not even naming him, just two features of his analysis of Latin, value and aspect in its extended sense, which he says he wants not to eliminate, but to postpone, until the structure of Indo-European is better established. This is not even a criticism of Meillet's analysis of Latin, a language the structure of which *is* well established — at least, not an overt criticism. But perhaps he is undertaking some distancing from what is said in the Preface to Meillet (1931), which, after underscoring the role of value and aspect as key features of the analysis, ends with a paragraph thanking Benveniste for helping to revise the text and compiling its index.

One of the curious aspects of Benveniste (1935) is the sizeable gap between the title, "origins of the formation of nouns", and the contents, which are not restricted to nouns, but culminate in a "unitary and constant definition of the Indo-European root and its aspects" (*une définition unitaire et constante de la racine indo-européenne et de ses aspects*) (Benveniste 1935: 170). This definition says that the "Indo-European root is monosyllabic, triliterate, composed of the fundamental vowel *ĕ* between two different consonants", then gives four further specifications about how it may be constituted (Benveniste 1935: 170–171).[24] Benveniste's theory of the Indo-European root was received by Indo-Europeanists somewhat as Saussure's *Mémoire* had been received: with astonishment at its daring brilliance and respect for its command of linguistic data, mixed with a wait-and-see dubiety that is appropriate with any stunningly simple model, to which scholars are bound to respond with examples that do not appear to fit it.

In the longer term, Benveniste's approach to Indo-European reconstruction has not held up,[25] and has even been rejected as "brutally reductionist" (Dunkel 1981: 560). That does at least furnish him with strong credentials as a structuralist — but one determined to supplement the formalist approach with serious consideration of what speakers do with language, redeeming his 1935 promissory note to re-examine notions of value and aspect if his morphological analysis proves valid. This is what he began to do after the war.

---

[24] "La racine indo-européenne est monosyllabique, trilitère, composée de la voyelle fondamentale ĕ entre deux consonnes différentes."

[25] I am grateful to the eminent Indo-Europeanist and Benveniste scholar Georges-Jean Pinault for confirming to me that this is the case.

5 The spirit of philology in Sauvageot

Another French linguist of the "structuralist period", Aurélien Sauvageot (1897–1988) was born in Constantinople, to a Belgian mother and a French father working as an architect for the Sultan. As a student at the British School of Pera the boy, a natural polyglot, learned English and German, and also picked up Greek and Turkish (see Jean-Robert Armogathe's Preface to Sauvageot 2013: 9). In 1911 his family returned to Paris, where, preparing for the competitive examination for entry into the École Normale Supérieure, he came to Meillet's attention. Many years later Sauvageot would recall his first summons to a private meeting at Meillet's home, in September 1914. The seventeen-year-old made a confession:

> "Look, Professor, I should tell you straightaway that I have no visual memory".
>
> "What?"
>
> "No, with me everything happens only with phonic memory, or acoustic if you prefer. I have only auditory images. So I'm really bad at linking what I hear with what's written, and I can only work on a language insofar as I know how it's pronounced".
>
> "Oh, how extraordinary," he said to me, "because I, you see, never hear any auditory image".
>
> And I said to him: "But, then, how do you think?".
>
> And he said to me: "Well, by sequences of written signs".
>
> With that a lot of things made sense to me. It was one of the first discoveries I made about Meillet. (Sauvageot 1992: 193)[26]

Both are rather extreme cases. Sauvageot's mind worked as one might expect a blind lad's to, Meillet's a deaf man's. There are deep differences in how people think, differences we tend to erase, or sort into normal and pathological cases. I shall come back round to Sauvageot's acute acoustic sensitivity and memory.

---

[26] "Je lui dis : 'Ecoutez, Monsieur le Professeur, je vous dis tout de suite que je n'ai pas de mémoire visuelle.' 'Comment?' 'Non, chez moi tout se passe uniquement avec la mémoire phonique ou si vous voulez acoustique. Je n'ai que des images auditives. Alors, je suis très malheureux pour lier ce que j'entends à ce qui s'écrit et que je ne peux travailler sur une langue que dans la mesure où je sais comment elle se prononce.' 'Oh, c'est extraordinaire, me dit-il, parce que moi, alors, voyez-vous, je n'entends jamais une image auditive.' Et je lui dis : 'Mais, alors, comment pensez-vous?' Et il me dit : 'Eh bien, par séquences de signes écrits.' Alors là, j'ai compris bien des choses. Cela a été une des premières découvertes que j'ai faites de MEILLET."

In April 1917 Sauvageot received another summons, this time to Meillet's office. The only French linguist covering Finno-Ugric, Robert Gauthiot (1876–1916), had been killed in the war, and it was decided that Sauvageot would have to replace him, even though he knew no Finno-Ugric language at the time. He asked why he had been chosen, and Meillet replied, "Why, that's simple, because you were born in Constantinople, you spoke Turkish and you still know a fair bit of Turkish, that's why, and because Turkish is a language whose mechanism is very similar to that of the Finno-Ugric languages" (Sauvageot 1992: 194).[27]

Meillet sensed the young Sauvageot's lack of enthusiasm at the prospect, but assured him that it would come. And come it did, very much so, from his arrival in Finland in the summer of 1919 (the date is from Perrot 2007: 296), where he began studying Finnish with Meillet's friend Emil Nestor Setälä (1864–1935). For the rest of Sauvageot's long life, Setälä would remain one of his principal touchstones not just for Finnish but for the understanding of language generally, rivalled only by Setälä's Hungarian friend Zoltán Gombocz (1877–1935), along with, of course, Meillet, and the linguist Meillet revered above all others, his own teacher Saussure. These four were not a foursome, but a pair of twosomes; and we can see throughout Sauvageot's career a tension between what "structural" linguistics came to represent, versus the sometimes diametrically opposed concerns of the Finnish and Hungarian philologists.

Jump ahead now thirty years. Meillet had died in 1936. Benveniste, who succeeded him in his chair in the Collège de France, that last surviving royal institution, was king of the nation's linguists. The dauphin, Martinet, had exiled himself to New York after being hounded from the Sorbonne under suspicion of having been a collaborator (see Joseph 2016). Beneath Benveniste were the barons, including Sauvageot. He had occupied the first chair of Finno-Ugric languages in France, in the École Nationale des Langues Orientales Vivantes, Paris, since it was established in 1931, with an interruption from 1941–43 at the insistence of the Vichy government (Perrot 2007: 296), probably because for years he had been a prominent and outspoken member of the Communist Party (see Chevalier 2006: 158).

Sauvageot was also active in the Institut de Linguistique, which held monthly lectures by the linguistic aristocracy, many of them aimed at surveying the structures of non-Indo-European languages. In 1946 Sauvageot published his *Esquisse de la langue finnoise* (Sketch of the Finnish language) in a series called "L'Homme

---

[27]"'Mais c'est simple, parce que vous êtes né à Constantinople, que vous avez parlé le turc et que vous savez encore pas mal de turc, voilà, et que le turc est une langue dont le mécanisme est très semblable à celui des langues finno-ougriennes'."

et Son Langage" (Man and his language) put out by La Nouvelle Édition in Paris. Three years later, the same book was published by Klincksieck, as the first volume in a new series that Sauvageot started called "Les langues et leurs structures" (Languages and their structures).[28] The 1949 Avertissement (Preface) announces three other volumes as forthcoming in the series, on Modern Greek, Tamil and Berber, and explains that the aim is to create "a series of descriptive studies bearing on idioms as diverse as possible, each envisaged in isolation, taken in itself" (Sauvageot 1946: 7).[29] Each book will "extricate through an appropriate analysis the characteristics inherent to a given language, grasped at a given moment of its evolution, and reveal the mechanism of the system of functions of which it is constituted" (Sauvageot 1946: 7).[30]

That sounds quite structural — but "mechanism" is a loose concept. Used as a metaphor in linguistic work since the nineteenth century (see Joseph 2018a), it seems to have meant something rather specific to Sauvageot, and perhaps idiosyncratic to him. Sauvageot's life's work had been determined because, as Meillet said, "Turkish is a language whose mechanism is very similar to that of the Finno-Ugric languages". The Preface continues:

> Up to now it has often been affirmed that a language is an ensemble in which all the parts fit together and the categories that supposedly form the foundation of the structure of a language have been much evoked. Only there has been a negligence in adding to the debate the concrete testimony that must be brought in by the descriptive study of a given state of language. (Sauvageot 1946: 7)[31]

What has been affirmed "up to now" is the Saussurean conception of the language system. The *toutes les parties se tiennent* is a slight rewording of the famous

---

[28]Not only were the title and text unchanged, but they bear the copyright and printing date 1946, so apparently the unsold copies were simply given a new cover with the fresher date of 1949. Curiously, the cover and copyright page both give the year 1949, and yet the legally required final page gives the date of printing 24 August 1946, and the legal deposition as the third trimester of 1946 ("Achevé d'imprimer [...] le 24 août 1946. Dépôt légal: 3ᵉ trimestre 1946"). The book must therefore have been completed by mid-1946.

[29]"[...] une série d'études descriptives portant sur des idiomes aussi divers que possible, envisagés chacun isolément, pris en soi."

[30]"Il s'agit de dégager par une analyse appropriée les caractères inhérents à une langue donnée, saisie à un moment donné de son évolution et d'exposer le mécanisme du système de fonctions dont elle est constituée."

[31]"Jusqu'à présent il a été souvent affirmé qu'une langue est un ensemble où toutes les parties se tiennent et l'on a beaucoup évoqué les catégories qui formeraient le fondement de la structure d'une langue. Seulement on a négligé de verser au débat le témoignage concret que doit apporter l'étude descriptive d'un état de langue donné."

motto *tout se tient* (everything supports everything else), attributed to Saussure though first used in print by Meillet (1903: 407). It is probably fair to say that structural linguistics does indeed make "categories" the foundation of the structure of a language, if categories are put into a binary contrast with "concrete testimony", and if that testimony means actual sounds and utterances: phonetics as opposed to phonology, and *parole* as opposed to *langue*. By taking up Saussure's *état de langue*, state of language, as the place where this concrete testimony is to be found, Sauvageot hints that it is not against Saussure that he is positioning himself, but against later structuralists who claim to be following Saussure's programme but are perhaps instead betraying it.

Sauvageot specifies that by "descriptive study" he does not mean simply enumerating grammatical processes or inventorying the most used paradigms, but rather "a prospecting effort to penetrate beyond simple grammatical analysis into the domain of expression of which grammar is so to speak only the more or less schematic skeleton" (Sauvageot 1946: 7).[32] This domain of expression includes "syntax, semantics and vocabulary", all of which are, he rightly notes, neglected in structural grammars. He wants to get to them through "sufficiently detailed analytic descriptions of concrete examples of the behaviour of a certain number of linguistic structures" (Sauvageot 1946: 7).[33] Here nearly every word is charged with potentially polemical meaning: Sauvageot is implicitly accusing structural linguistics of being insufficiently detailed in its analysis of individual linguistic structures, of failing to use concrete examples, of taking a broad-brush approach rather than focussing on "a certain number" of structures in depth, and of neglecting the "behaviour" of the structures, in favour of simple inventories. What he means by behaviour is expanded upon at the start of the book proper:

> What makes the originality of an idiom is not the presence of this or that particular structural feature but how the structure as a whole is arranged, the use that is made of it and the performance that is obtained from it for the needs of the expression of thought. (Sauvageot 1946: 13)[34]

The concern with "arrangement" is an embrace of the core principle of Saussurean linguistics, which Sauvageot thought however had not been adequately

---

[32]"[...] un effort de prospection pour pénétrer par delà la simple analyse grammaticale dans le domaine de l'expression dont la grammaire n'est pour ainsi dire que le squelette plus ou moins schématique."

[33]"[...] des descriptions analytiques suffisamment poussées, des exemples concrets du comportement d'un certain nombre de structures linguistiques."

[34]"Ce qui fait l'originalité d'un idiome, ce n'est pas la présence de tel ou tel trait particulier de structure mais la façon dont l'ensemble de cette structure est agencée, l'usage qui en est fait et le rendement qui en est obtenu pour les besoins de l'expression de la pensée."

buttressed with attention to particular features. The concern with "performance" may again be his embrace of Saussure's all-but-forgotten call for a linguistics of *parole*. The concern with expression of thought reveals a tension within Sauvageot himself, in that he will often insist that language must be understood as a tool of communication, the traditional alternative to representation or self-expression as the primal and formative purpose of language.

The strongest evidence that Sauvageot is taking a polemical stance comes when he claims to be "observation" personified: "In doing this, we have not the least intention of diffusing the theories of a school. We are focussed above all on describing the facts as they present themselves to observation, by disregarding any preconceptions" (Sauvageot 1946: 7–8).[35] But the language he has used up to this point already belongs to a school, that of structural linguistics, and its underlying theory is not immediately dissociable from that language, even when he is positioning himself against aspects of that theory. That positioning is itself a theory, and since this Preface is for a whole series of books by different authors, it looks as though Sauvageot is trying to form a school and to diffuse its theories.

How his treatment of Finnish is distinct from a structural one can be seen from the opening sentence.

> To the ear, Finnish seems "loud", a bit hoarse and abrupt, the whole spouted rapidly in a rhythm with rather close beats, modulated according to a musical phrasing with rather sharp but descending notes that appear to follow an almost unvarying curve. Finnish discourse knows only a few melodic deviations between the peaks and troughs of modulation. The monotonous repetition of these modulations makes one think right away that the language modulates not in order to express, but only to mark out the elements of the flow.
>
> The vowels "mark"; they burst joyfully on speakers' lips, whereas the consonants are muffled sometimes to the point of being whispered. (Sauvageot 1946: 15)[36]

---

[35] "Ce faisant, nous n'avons aucunement l'intention de diffuser les théories d'une école. Nous nous attachons avant tout à décrire les faits tels qu'ils se présentent à l'observation, en faisant abstraction de toute idée préconçue."

[36] "A l'oreille, le finnois fait 'sonore', un peu rauque et saccadé, le tout débité rapidement sur un rythme aux alternances assez rapprochées, modulées selon une phrase musicale aux notes plutôt aiguës mais descendantes, qui semble suivre une courbe à peu près invariable. Le discours finnois ne connaît que peu d'écarts mélodiques entre les sommets et les creux de modulation. La répétition monotone de ces modulations fait tout de suite penser que la langue ne module pas pour exprimer, mais seulement, pour démarquer les éléments du débit. Les voyelles 'marquent' ; elles éclatent joyeusement sur les lèvres des sujets parlants, tandis que les consonnes sont assourdies parfois jusqu'au chuintement."

To his French colleagues this impressionism would have sounded like a throwback to the nineteenth century, maybe even to Rousseau (1782 [written 1755–1761]). In some respects it is — one way to resist the mainstream is to hark back to an earlier age and represent its discourse as a lost truth, as Chomsky would do with his "Cartesian linguistics" (2009 [1966]). Sauvageot is rescuing a musicality in linguistic analysis that in fact had not been absent in twentieth-century French linguistics, but was always a minority concern and was marginalized with the rise of structural linguistics, until its re-emergence with Meschonnic.[37]

But by the late 1940s, Sauvageot found himself unable actually to get the promised books on Tamil and Berber out of their signed-up authors, let alone sign up any further authors.[38] In his Klincksieck series there finally appeared only his own "Sketches" of Finnish and Hungarian (1951). Given the eccentricity of Sauvageot's vision, one can imagine that other authors may have felt themselves caught between maintaining their standing among more conventional linguists and producing what he wanted from them, which perhaps could only be managed by someone with his rare "auditory memory", plus his double saturation in structuralism and the Finnish and Hungarian philological traditions of Setälä and Gombocz.

The Canadian philosopher Charles Taylor (2016) contrasts what he terms the H-L-C and the H-H-H, where the H-L-C is the Enlightenment outlook inherited by analytic philosphers from Hobbes, Locke and Condillac. The H-H-H is the Counter-Enlightenment "Romantic" outlook of Hamann, Herder and Humboldt to which Taylor strives to draw philosophers' attention. These two perspectives are present in modern linguistics, mainly as a result of Saussure's inclusion in his lectures of both semiology, an Enlightenment inheritance from the *grammaire générale* tradition, and the self-contained language system impervious to change by any individual, an inheritance from German linguists, most directly the Neogrammarians. Their conception of sound laws that followed an exceptionless path "insofar as they are mechanical", which is to say physical, represented a neo-Romantic Counter-Enlightenment tradition in which language is something extra-rational, that follows its own organic path, even though the Neogrammarians and Saussure did not go the full naturalist route of Max Müller and others. They however also opened up a breach to allow in some Enlightenment through the role that they allotted to analogy as the only admissible explanation for ap-

---

[37]Saussy (2016) revives the history of this alternative tradition, in which Meillet figures as, among other things, supervisor of the doctoral thesis of Milman Parry (1902–1935), whose studies of contemporary oral recitation in the Balkans would revolutionize the understanding of Homeric epic.

[38]The books announced were *Esquisse de la langue tamoule* by Pierre Meile (1911–1963) and *Esquisse de la langue berbère* by André Basset (1895–1956).

parent exceptions to the sound laws. Analogy is a mental rather than a physical process, and rational in nature.

On the theoretical level, Meillet's structuralism was universalist. He argued that small European languages such as Finnish and Hungarian were doomed by a sort of natural selection that would limit the number of "languages of civilization" in Europe (Meillet 1918: 279; see also Sauvageot 2013: 209–210). That was an Enlightenment position. But unlike Meillet, Sauvageot was H-H-H to the bone. His personal experiences in Finland and Hungary had proved to him that what really determined the present and future vitality of a language was its expressive power. In a book manuscript published posthumously in 1992, he wrote, "If a language succumbs, it is because it failed in its expressive task" (*Si une langue succombe, c'est qu'elle faillit à sa tâche expressive*) (Sauvageot 1992: 160). Sauvageot was torn between loyalty to the man to whom he owed everything in career terms, and the Finnish and Hungarian philologists whose view of their language was so much more in accord with his own.

Hence his embracing and resisting of a structural linguistics that, in France, saw Meillet as its head. But outside France, it was developing in various directions, above all in Prague, where the terms "structural" and "structuralism" were being explicitly proclaimed by the start of the 1930s. In the English and French speaking worlds, 1940 is the year when "structural linguistics" starts to appear regularly (see Joseph 2015). Martinet was the one French linguist in regular contact with the Prague Linguistic Circle, as well as with Copenhagen, where Louis Hjelmslev (1899–1965) and Viggo Brøndal (1887–1942) were laying the ground for glossematics. Perhaps it was Meillet's death in 1936 that licensed French linguists to be more directly critical of, even hostile to structuralism, particularly as it was being developed in Prague. Meillet's successor, Benveniste, was himself ambivalent towards it, as became apparent with the article on the arbitrariness of the sign that he contributed to the first issue of Hjelmslev's *Acta Linguistica* in 1939.

What exactly about structuralism was repellent to Sauvageot? We got some clues earlier in the Avertissement to the *Esquisse de la langue finnoise*, when he wrote about "a negligence in adding to the debate the concrete testimony that must be brought in by the descriptive study of a given state of language", and the neglect of syntax, semantics and vocabulary in favour of inventories of phonemes and morphemes. More generally, he objected to the "dogmatism" of the structuralists, as his student and later colleague Jean Perrot would report that

> Sauvageot was not indulgent towards his colleagues and his hostility to dogmatism led him to severe judgements about these dogmatic theoreticians whom he readily called "these gentlemen", and whom he readily mal-

treated with irony, for example denouncing a manifest error as "a simple blunder". In particular he was rather hard with regard to the "phonologists", for instance reproaching Lazicius for behaving as a "disciple of Trubetzkoy and the Prague phonologists, whose excesses and dogmatism he espoused". (Perrot 2009: 16)[39]

French linguists from 1925 to 1950 seem on the one hand to want to claim that they are, along with the Geneva School, the keepers of the Saussurean structuralist flame, while on the other hand acting as if structuralism is a foreign perversion. This aspect of linguistic history has to be read in the context of how nationalist feeling was developing in the inter-war period, and again with the anti-imperial wars in Indochina and Algeria in the 1950s, when the Cold War is also central to the plot; as is the ambivalence of linguists to the massive increase in attention and status they gained starting with the success of Lévi-Strauss's *Tristes tropiques* in 1955, and the continuing rise of structuralism as the master science informing the work of Lacan, Merleau-Ponty, Barthes, Greimas and soon the next generation of French intellectuals who became prominent in the 1960s. Among the linguists themselves new tensions arose when Martinet returned in 1955 from his self-imposed exile, distancing himself from structuralism in favour of a "functionalism" that combined an ultra-structuralist analytical method with genuine challenges to the how structuralists dealt with dialects, bilingualism and social differentiation, challenges that were being pushed further by Martinet's American student Uriel Weinreich (1926–1967) (see, e.g., Weinreich 1954 and Joseph 2016).

But Weinreich also had strong allegiances to Jakobson, who had been the first to use the word structuralism in print in the 1920s, and had gone on to redefine it, in conjunction with Trubetzkoy and the Prague School, in ways that directly contradicted some of Saussure's core principles. This is what made French linguists resistant to structuralism as redefined by Prague — partly on intellectual grounds, partly on nationalist ones, in which some degree of jealousy at the success of Jakobson and the Prague School in other parts of Europe and America cannot be ruled out. Sauvageot, and to a lesser degree Benveniste, were more

---

[39]"Sauvageot n'était pas indulgent à l'égard de ses confrères et son hostilité au dogmatisme lui inspirait des jugements sévères sur ces théoriciens dogmatiques qu'il appelait volontiers 'ces messieurs', et qu'il malmenait volontiers ironiquement, dénonçant par exemple comme 'une simple bévue' une erreur manifeste. Il était en particulier assez dur à l'égard des 'phonologistes', reprochant par exemple à Lazicius son comportement de 'disciple de Troubetzkoï et des phonologistes de Prague, dont il a épousé les outrances et le dogmatisme'." Perrot does not indicate sources for the citations which he indicates. On the Hungarian phonologist Gyula Lazicius (1896–1957), see Voigt (1986: 288).

forthright about their resistance to structuralism than others of their contemporaries in France, who may have feared being even more marginalized internationally if they overtly challenged Prague, Jakobson, Trubetzkoy, Hjelmslev et al.

But it was not just the formalism, the "structural" part of structural linguistics, that Sauvageot resisted. It was also "linguistics", insofar as it had pushed philology out from the forefront of academic enquiry, to become yesterday's dusty, antiquarian pursuit. With it went attention to the fine details of a language, including how individual writers discovered and exploited its potential resources. *Philology* — the *love* of language. Linguistics — its cold, clinical study.

It was a loss that Sauvageot, with his heritage from the philologists who taught him Finnish and Hungarian, sought to rectify — above all in his last major work (Sauvageot 1973), by which time he no longer needed to be concerned with his position within the French linguistic establishment. Even so, he had the reputation of his students to think of; and that may explain why he never published the book manuscript he entitled *La structure du langage* (The structure of language) that appeared in 1992, four years after his death. This book seems determined to subvert some of the basic principles of Saussurean structuralism, let alone its later variants, and offer in their place a vision of language grounded in his long experience of Finnish and Hungarian language and culture, including the ideas of Setälä and Gombocz and the other great linguists and literary figures whose individual impact on the languages he had witnessed. Yet Sauvageot can never escape the shadow of his first linguistics teacher, Meillet, nor does he want to. In this book he aims at a reconciliation in which we find a rare trace of his apparently avowed Marxism. He distinguishes the "invariants" of a language, which are its "structure", from the "variants" which he calls its "superstructure" (Sauvageot 1992: 18).

Sauvageot's encounter with Finno-Ugric philology would limit his embrace of structuralism — a doctrine whose historical nuances we, starting with me, have glossed over. We assume that embracing and resisting are either/or options. History is more complicated than that, which is what makes it interesting. The resisting embrace can have strategic force: someone who only embraces will not push the science forward; someone who only resists will struggle to get a hearing. The resisting embrace can give one an audience for resistant innovations that are heard as progress within the status quo, even if, in his heart, the innovator is committed to overturning it.

6 Benveniste's later work: enunciation

Normand (1986) traces the development of "enunciation" in Benveniste's work back to papers he published in 1946 and 1949, and notes in particular that his 1954 paper on current trends in linguistics defines a linguist's three principal tasks as being to identify what is described using the word language (*langue*), how to describe this object (linguistic methodology), and thirdly, to confront "the problem of signification". Quoting Benveniste, "Language (*langage*) has as its function to say something. What exactly is this something in view of which language is articulated and how do we delimit it in relation to language itself? The problem of signification is posed" (Benveniste 1966 [1954]: 7).[40]

Signification — essentially, meaning — is implicitly conceived here as lying outside the language system (*langue*), while being its *raison d'être*. Signification and enunciation occupy a "semantic" realm, distinct from the "semiotic" one of the language (see the Editors' Introduction to Benveniste 2012: 49–51). Understanding the semantic is the linguist's third task. The wording makes clear that signification lies outside language not just as a *langue* but as the more general *langage* as well, being the something that it is the "function" of language and languages to say. The challenge is to identify and delimit meaning with relation to language, which is made difficult because language is itself articulated with this function in view.

Benveniste's initial presentation of his approach incorporates a question which it provoked in the minds of other structural linguists, as to whether enunciation, as use, was not what Saussure meant by *parole*, speech. He does not directly answer the question, but indicates how his focus is a different one.

> Enunciation is putting the language to work through an individual act of use.
>
> But isn't this manifestation of enunciation simply *parole*, the discourse which is produced each time one speaks? — We must take care to focus on the specific condition of enunciation: it is the act itself of producing an utterance, and not the text of the utterance, that is our object. This act is the fact of the

---

[40] "Le langage a pour fonction de dire quelque chose. Qu'est exactement ce quelque chose en vue de quoi le langage est articulé et comment le délimiter par rapport au langage lui-même? Le problème de la signification est posé." Ono (2007: 27–57) has shown how in Benveniste's writings from 1945 until the definitive formulations in 1974 [1969] and 1974 [1970](a), the meaning of *énonciation* is often ambiguous, or even indicates quite clearly what he will eventually refer to as *énoncé*. See also Coquet (1987) and Joseph (In Press).

speaker who mobilizes the language on his or her own behalf. The relationship of the speaker to the language determines the linguistic features of the enunciation. (Benveniste 1974 [1970][a]: 80)[41]

The speaker is not "speaker" before the act of enunciation. With enunciation, speaker becomes both speaker and subject; the enunciation positions him or her vis-à-vis the language, while at the same time that relationship shapes the enunciation.

In presenting enunciation not as an alternative to structuralist analysis, but as a parallel track, Benveniste can be said to fulfil a wish expressed by the Neogrammarians Hermann Osthoff (1847–1909) and Karl Brugmann (1849–1919), when they remarked that, in the past, "Languages were indeed investigated most eagerly, but people speaking, much too little" (*Man erforschte zwar eifrigst die* sprachen, *aber viel zu wenig* den sprechenden menschen.) (Osthoff & Brugmann 1878: iii). But more striking is how far forward looking the approach is, anticipating ideas of decades later on stance, voice, identity, indexicality, in addition to the direct continuations of enunciation in the work of Antoine Culioli and others in France. Pierre Bourdieu's (1930–2002) conceptions of language and symbolic power are also grounded in Benveniste, and in fact it was Bourdieu who in 1969 coordinated the assembling and publication of perhaps Benveniste's most influential book, the *Vocabulaire des institutions indo-européennes*. It provides the context for understanding what Benveniste means when he says that "the language contains the society" (see above, p. 144). When he traces the history of a social institution such as "personal loyalty" back through each of the branches of the Indo-European language family, adducing precise etymological evidence to show the very different ways in which loyalty was conceived among Celtic, Germanic, Baltic, Slavic, Italo-Roman, Greek and Persian tribes and peoples, the conclusion seems inescapable that the institutional differences among them are historically bound to the language of their enunciation, so deeply as to be "contained" not just in the sense of residing within, but in the stronger sense of being prevented from escaping.

Benveniste's third task of 1966 [1954] can be read as an attempt at responding to the problematizing of meaning that was at the heart of behaviourism, the same

---

[41]"L'énonciation est cette mise en fonction de la langue par un acte individuel d'utilisation. Le discours, dira-t-on, qui est produit chaque fois qu'on parle, cette manifestation de l'énonciation, n'est-ce pas simplement la 'parole'? — Il faut prendre garde à la condition spécifique de l'énonciation : c'est l'acte même de produire un énoncé et non le texte de l'énoncé qui est notre objet. Cet acte est le fait du locuteur qui mobilise la langue pour son compte. La relation du locuteur à la langue détermine les caractères linguistiques de l'énonciation."

problem that motivated Bloomfield to de-psychologize his linguistics, though Benveniste attacks the problem with a different strategy. The insight particular to Benveniste is that the language system and the speaking person occupy different conceptual spheres that nevertheless intersect with one another. He explores this initially, and in greatest detail, in his papers on person and deixis.[42] Benveniste's semiology as laid out in the second half of his 1974 [1969] paper and the lectures of late 1968 and early 1969 combines the systematicity of a *langue* as conceived by Saussure with the *inter*systematicity assumed by Charles Sanders Peirce (1839–1914). "There is no trans-systematic sign", Benveniste (1974 [1969]: 53) writes;[43] the value of each sign "is defined solely within the system which integrates it", which is perfectly Saussurean. Nevertheless, every signifying system other than a language must be interpreted through a language. "Every semiology of a non-linguistic system must make use of a language to translate it; thus it can exist only through and in the semiology of a language, [...] which is the interpretant of all other systems, linguistic and non-linguistic" (Benveniste 1974 [1969]: 60).[44] And from his last lectures: "It is the language as system of expression that is the interpretant of all institutions and of all culture" (Benveniste 2012: 83).[45] One could argue that this core Benvenistean axiom is implicit in both Saussure and Peirce, but Peirce in particular might have resisted it. It reflects the way a linguist thinks, rather than a psychologist.

The turn the lectures then take, which the article did not, is one that Saussure would certainly have resisted. To say as I have done that Benveniste's semiology combines the systematicity of a *langue* as conceived by Saussure with the inter-systematicity assumed by Peirce is potentially deceptive, because systematicity must be understood in a strong sense for Saussure, and in a weaker sense for Peirce, who places the stress on the "inter-". Benveniste criticizes Peirce for "mis-

---

[42]These include, following on from the 1966 [1946] and 1966 [1949] papers cited above, Benveniste (1966 [1956][a]) and Benveniste (1966 [1958]). It is surprising that, in his review of Benveniste (1966), Winfred P. Lehmann (1916–2007) categorized these papers as "psycholinguistics" (Lehmann 1968). Equally surprising is Lehmann's view that "If in any of his essays Benveniste discusses linguistic theory as such, it is in the first three, which treat the development of linguistics". In other words, for Lehmann, what Benveniste is doing is not linguistic theory at all, which was a compliment from the pen of a non-Chomskyan American linguist like Lehmann in 1968.

[43]"Il n'y a pas de signe trans-systématique."

[44]"Toute sémiologie d'un système non-linguistique doit emprunter le truchement de la langue, ne peut donc exister que par et dans la sémiologie de la langue [...] ; la langue est l'interprétant de tous les autres systèmes, linguistiques et non-linguistiques."

[45]"C'est la langue comme système d'expression qui est l'interprétant de toutes les institutions et de toute la culture."

taking" words for being the whole of language. It is not words, not lexicon, not semantics or even syntax that is the foundation of structural linguistics, but phonology and morphology. And yet, when Saussure is teaching semiology, words are what he uses to exemplify the sign; he brings in morphology in his discussion of the associative axis and relative motivation, but sounds hardly figure. Phonemes do not appear to be signs, just constituents of signifiers, even though the differences between phonemes are the ultimate source of signification, and that poses a puzzle: what differentiates a phoneme from a non-speech sound is some sort of signification that this is a signifying sound.

Here Peirce's idea of "interpretance" offers a valuable insight: that the very first meaning of every sign is: "I am a sign. Interpret me". And even if Benveniste is right that Peirce only thinks about signification at the level of words, nothing in principle prevents us from extending this insight to the level of phonemes.

Regarding his critique of Peirce for reducing languages to words, it is worth noting how widely known Benveniste's revered teacher Meillet was for his Latin etymological work, and that Benveniste himself had his broadest impact through his 1969 *Vocabulaire*, which is word-based. Its focus is on the semantic, and it can be seen as his major practical achievement in the linguistics of enunciation. Yet it shows on every page how understanding the semantic at a deep level requires detailed examination of the semiotic, and how such semantic understanding is in turn what allows us to weigh up alternative analyses of phonological and morphological facts in the semiotic system. Benveniste underscores in his lecture notes "*the impossibility of reaching the semantic in language without passing through the semiotic plus the grammar*" (Benveniste 1969: 114).[46] Peirce tried to reach the semantic through words alone, without signs, without the language system. Saussure did not deny the self-evident link between the semiotic and the semantic, but observed methodological scruples whereby he, as a grammarian (the term he usually applied to himself), could only pronounce on the semiotic, the semantic being the realm of expertise of psychologists and philosophers.

Saussure and Peirce are for Benveniste the key innovative thinkers of two orders of language and signification. With Peirce, Benveniste folds in the later phenomenology of Edmund Husserl (1859–1938) and of the Husserlian linguist Hendrik Joseph Pos (1898–1955). Saussure stands at the head of the tradition of modern linguistics in which Benveniste himself was trained. For Benveniste,

---

[46] "*l'impossibilité d'atteindre le sémantique en langue sans passer par le sémiotique plus la grammaire.*"

Peirce and phenomenology represent the order	Saussure and structural linguistics represent the order
semantic	semiotic
intention/intended	signifier/signified
enunciation	language system
utterance	speech
words and things in the world	signs and social structure

Structural linguistics is based on the Saussurean order, which excludes consideration of writing. The new linguistics of enunciation envisioned by Benveniste would combine the two orders, and one of the main aims of his last lectures is to understand how they are bridged by writing.

Insofar as the marginalization of writing is an aspect of structuralism, Benveniste's last lectures pass unhesitatingly beyond it. The fundamentally philological nature of his etymological work makes it pre-structuralist, though in his explanations of the history of individual words the spirit and basic approach of structural method come through. And if the central roles he accords to writing and enunciation make him a post-structuralist, that is certainly not a flag he wanted to wave. Benveniste strove to reconcile his vision of the future path of linguistics with its present and past. Or, more precisely, its pasts.

7 Conclusion

This study has focused on a small set of linguists whom histories of linguistics place in the structuralist period, and who embraced formalist principles to a greater or lesser extent while also resisting them. It has examined some of the motives for their resistance, which include a perceived abandonment of attention to phonological and philological detail (Benveniste and Sauvageot), as well as to speakers (the same two, plus Martinet), along with a proclivity towards atomism and discontinuity (Meschonnic). Interpersonal relations, political affiliations and national identity have also come into the picture.

There are other chapters to be added to this story, including the polemic between Bloomfield and Leo Spitzer (1887–1960), with Spitzer (1944) calling out Bloomfield's mechanism for the reductionism it entailed; C. K. Ogden and the associated figures studied by McElvenny (2018); Hjelmslev, who never renounced his early Saussurean commitments but moved progressively away from what he saw as the prioritizing of form over function and meaning (Joseph 2018a); and of course Chomsky, who did battle with the methodological and epistemological commitments of the older generation of linguists who are generally classed as "American structuralists", but where Chomsky attacked from a more deeply structuralist position.

My aim may seem counter-structuralist in trying to undo the paradigm. Yet, deep down, what is this enterprise if not a search for the Order which governs the movement of the stars of the modern science of language, and which is the foundation of our society as its practitioners? Without this principle, everything would revert to chaos.

References

Benveniste, Émile. 1935. *Origines de la formation des noms en indo-européen.* Paris: Adrien-Maisonneuve.

Benveniste, Émile. 1966 [1946]. Structures des relations de personne dans le verbe. In *Problèmes de linguistique générale*, vol. 1, 224–236. Paris: Gallimard. Original in *Bulletin de la Société de Linguistique de Paris* 43.1.

Benveniste, Émile. 1966 [1949]. Le système sublogique des prépositions en latin. In *Problèmes de linguistique générale*, vol. 1, 132–139. Paris: Gallimard. Original in *Travaux de Cercle Linguistique de Copenhague 5: Recherches structurales.*

Benveniste, Émile. 1966 [1954]. Tendances récentes en linguistique générale. In *Problèmes de linguistique générale*, vol. 1, 3–17. Paris: Gallimard. Original in *Journal de Psychologie Normale et Pathologique* 47–51.1–2: 130–145.

Benveniste, Émile. 1966 [1956](a). La nature des pronoms. In *Problèmes de linguistique générale*, vol. 1, 251–257. Paris: Gallimard. Original in *For Roman Jakobson.* Morris Halle, Horace G. Lunt and Hugh McLean (eds.), 34–37.

Benveniste, Émile. 1966 [1956](b). Remarques sur la fonction du langage dans la découverte freudienne. In *Problèmes de linguistique générale*, vol. 1, 75–87. Paris: Gallimard. Original in *La Psychanalyse* 1.3–16.

Benveniste, Émile. 1966 [1958]. De la subjectivité dans le langage. In *Problèmes de linguistique générale*, vol. 1, 258–266. Paris: Gallimard. Original in *Journal de Psychologie Normale et Pathologique* 55, 257–265.

Benveniste, Émile. 1966. *Problèmes de linguistique générale.* Vol. 1. Paris: Gallimard.

Benveniste, Émile. 1974 [1968](a). Ce langage qui fait l'histoire (interview with Guy Dumur). In *Problèmes de linguistique générale*, vol. 2, 29–40. Paris: Gallimard. Original in *Le nouvel observateur, spécial littéraire* 210 bis, 28–34.

Benveniste, Émile. 1974 [1968](b). Structuralisme et linguistique (interview with Pierre Daix). In *Problèmes de linguistique générale*, vol. 2, 11–28. Paris: Gallimard. Original in *Les lettres modernes* 1242, 10–13.

Benveniste, Émile. 1974 [1969]. Sémiologie de la langue. In *Problèmes de linguistique générale*, vol. 2, 43–66. Paris: Gallimard. Original in *Semiotica* 1.1–12, 2.127–135.

Benveniste, Émile. 1969. *Vocabulaire des institutions indo-européennes*. Paris: Minuit. 2 vols.

Benveniste, Émile. 1974 [1970](a). L'appareil formel de l'énonciation. In *Problèmes de linguistique générale*, vol. 2, 79–88. Paris: Gallimard. Original in *Langages* 17, 12–18.

Benveniste, Émile. 1974 [1970](b). Structure de la langue et structure de la société. In *Problèmes de linguistique générale*, vol. 2, 91–102. Paris: Gallimard. Original in *Linguaggi nella società e nella tecnica (Congresso Internazionale Olivetti, Milano, 14–17 ottobre 1968)*, 459–460. Milan: Edizioni di Comunità.

Benveniste, Émile. 2016 [1973]. *Dictionary of Indo-European concepts and society*. Trans. by Elizabeth Palmer. Chicago: University of Chicago Press. First published as *Indo-European language and society*, Coral Gables, Florida: University of Miami Press, 1973. Translation of Benveniste (1969).

Benveniste, Émile. 1974. *Problèmes de linguistique générale*. Vol. 2. Paris: Gallimard.

Benveniste, Émile. 2012. *Dernières leçons: Collège de France, 1968 et 1969*. Paris: École des Hautes Études en Sciences Sociales, Éditions Gallimard & Éditions du Seuil. English version, *Last Lectures: Collège de France, 1968 and 1969*, John E. Joseph, trans. Edinburgh: Edinburgh University Press, in press.

Bloomfield, Leonard. 1945. Secondary and tertiary responses to language. *Language* 20(2). 45–55.

Cassirer, Ernst. 1945. Structuralism in modern linguistics. *Word* 2(1). 99–120. DOI:10.1080/00437956.1945.11659249

Chevalier, Jean-Claude with Pierre Encrevé. 2006. *Combats pour la linguistique, de Martinet à Kristeva: Essai de dramaturgie épistémologique*. Lyons: ENS éditions.

Chomsky, Noam. 2009 [1966]. *Cartesian linguistics: A chapter in the history of rationalist thought*. Cambridge: Cambridge University Press. Edited by James McGilvray.

Coquet, Jean-Claude. 1987. Linguistique et sémiologie. *Actes sémiotiques–Documents IX* 88. 5–20.

Dosse, François. 1997 [1991]. *History of structuralism, vol. 1, The rising sign: 1945–1966.* Trans. by Deborah Glassman. Minneapolis & London: University of Minnesota Press. Original published *Histoire du structuralisme, I: Le champ du signe, 1945–1966,* Paris: La Découverte, 1991.

Dunkel, George. 1981. Typology versus reconstruction. In Yoel L. Arbeitman & Allan R. Bomhard (eds.), *Bono homini donum: Essays in historical linguistics in memory of J. Alexander Kerns,* 559–570. Amsterdam: Benjamins.

Firth, John R. 1933. Rev. of Vossler (1932). *Philosophy* 8(30). 234–236.

Gombrich, Ernst H. 1960. *Art and illusion: A study in the psychology of pictorial representation.* London: Phaidon.

Joseph, John E. 1999. How structuralist was "American structuralism"? *Bulletin of the Henry Sweet Society for the History of Linguistic Ideas* (33). 23–28.

Joseph, John E. 2001. The exportation of structuralist ideas from linguistics to other fields: An overview. In Sylvain Auroux, E. F. K. Koerner, Hans-Josef Niederehe & Kees Versteegh (eds.), *History of the language sciences: An international handbook on the evolution of the study of language from the beginnings to the present,* vol. 2, 1880–1908. Berlin: Walter de Gruyter.

Joseph, John E. 2002. *From Whitney to Chomsky: Essays in the history of American linguistics.* Amsterdam: Benjamins.

Joseph, John E. 2015. Structural linguistics. In Keith Allan (ed.), *Routledge handbook of linguistics,* 431–446. London: Routledge.

Joseph, John E. 2016. Divided allegiance: Martinet's preface to Weinreich's *Languages in contact* (1953). *Historiographia Linguistica* 43(3). 343–362.

Joseph, John E. 2018a. From Saussure to Rask: The curious trajectory of Louis Hjelmslev. In M. W. Bruno, F. Cimatti, D. Chiricò, A. De Marco, E. Fadda, G. Lo Feudo, M. Mazzeo & C. Stancati (eds.), *Linguistica e filosofia del linguaggio: Studi in onore di Daniele Gambarara,* 295–305. Milan: Mimesis.

Joseph, John E. 2018b. Language-body continuity in the linguistics-semiology-poetics-traductology of Henri Meschonnic. *Comparative Critical Studies* 18(3). 311–329.

Joseph, John E. In Press. "Énonciation" en anglais: Émile Benveniste et la (re)traduction d'une *utterance* ambigüe. In Giuseppe d'Ottavi & Valentina Chepiga (eds.), *Traduire la linguistique, traduire les linguistes.* Louvain-la-Neuve: Academia.

Kuhn, Thomas S. 1962. *The structure of scientific revolutions.* Chicago: University of Chicago Press.

Lehmann, Winfred P. 1968. Rev. of Benveniste (1966). *Language* 44(1). 91–96.

Lévi-Strauss, Claude. 1945. L'analyse structurale en linguistique et en anthropolo-gie. *Word* 1. 33–53. Repr. as opening chapter of Lévi-Strauss, *Anthropologie structurale*, vol. 1, Paris: Plon, 1958. English version, *Structural anthropology*, Claire Jacobson and Brooke Grundfest Schoepf, trans. New York: Basic Books, 1963.

McElvenny, James. 2018. *Language and meaning in the age of modernism: C. K. Ogden and his contemporaries.* Edinburgh: Edinburgh University Press.

Meillet, Antoine. 1903. *Introduction à l'étude comparative des langues indo-européennes.* Paris: Hachette.

Meillet, Antoine. 1918. *Les langues dans l'Europe nouvelle.* Paris: Payot.

Meillet, Antoine. 1931. *Esquisse d'une histoire de la langue latine, II ed.* Paris: Ha-chette.

Meillet, Antoine. 1905–1906. Comment les mots changent de sens. *Année soci-ologique* 9. 1–38.

Meschonnic, Henri. 1982. *Critique du rhythme: Anthropologie historique du lan-gage.* Paris: Verdier.

Meschonnic, Henri. 2009. Traduire, et la Bible, dans la théorie du langage et de la société. *Nouvelle revue d'esthétique* 3. 19–26. English version, Translating, and the Bible, in the theory of language and of society, John E. Joseph, trans., in Marko Pajević, ed., *The Henri Meschonnic Reader.* Edinburgh: Edinburgh Uni-versity Press, in press.

Normand, Claudine. 1986. Les termes de l'énonciation de Benveniste. *Histoire-Epistémologie-Langage* 8(2). 191–206.

Ono, Aya. 2007. *La notion d'énonciation chez Émile Benveniste.* Limoges: Lambert-Lucas.

Osthoff, Hermann & Karl Brugmann. 1878. Vorwort. *Morphologische Untersuchun-gen auf dem Gebiete der indogermanischen Sprachen* 1. iii–xx.

Perrot, Jean. 2007. Aurélien Sauvageot: L'homme et l'œuvre. *Revue d'études françaises* 12. 295–307.

Perrot, Jean. 2009. La carrière et l'œuvre d'Aurélien Sauvageot: Engagement et retenue dans les options linguistiques. *Études finno-ougriennes* 41. 9–25.

Rousseau, Jean-Jacques. 1782 [written 1755–1761]. Essai sur l'origine des langues, où il est parlé de la mélodie et de l'imitation musicale. In *Collection complète des œuvres de J. J. Rousseau, citoyen de Genève*, vol. 8, 355–434. Geneva.

Saussure, Ferdinand de. 1879. *Mémoire sur le système primitif des voyelles dans les langues indo-européennes.* Leipzig: Teubner.

Saussure, Ferdinand de. 1922 [1916]. *Cours de linguistique générale.* Paris: Payot. Edited by Charles Bally and Albert Sechehaye.

Saussy, Haun. 2016. *The ethnography of rhythm: Orality and its technologies*. New York: Fordham University Press.

Sauvageot, Aurélien. 1946. *Esquisse de la langue finnoise*. Paris: La Nouvelle Édition. Reissued Paris: Klincksieck, 1949.

Sauvageot, Aurélien. 1951. *Esquisse de la langue hongroise*. Paris: Klincksieck.

Sauvageot, Aurélien. 1973. *L'élaboration de la langue finnoise*. Paris: Klincksieck.

Sauvageot, Aurélien. 1992. *La structure du langage*. Aix-en-Provence: Publications de l'Université de Provence.

Sauvageot, Aurélien. 2013. *Souvenirs de ma vie hongroise. New Ed.* Budapest: Collège Eötvös József ELTE — Institut Français de Budapest. Orig. publ. Budapest: Corvina, 1988.

Skinner, Quentin. 1969. Meaning and understanding in the history of ideas. *History and Theory* 8(1). 3–53.

Spitzer, Leo. 1944. Answer to Mr. Bloomfield (Language 20.45). *Language* 20(4). 245–251. Referring to Bloomfield (1945).

Taylor, Charles. 2016. *The language animal: The full shape of the human linguistic capacity*. Cambridge, Mass.: Belknap Press of the Harvard University Press.

Voigt, Vilmos. 1986. Semiotics in Hungary. In Thomas A. Sebeok & Jean Umiker-Sebeok (eds.), *The semiotic sphere*, 279–292. New York: Plenum.

Vossler, Karl. 1932. *The spirit of language in civilization*. Trans. by Oscar Oeser. London: Kegan Paul, Trench, Trübner & Co. Original: *Geist und Kultur in der Sprache*, Heidelberg: Carl Winter, 1925.

Weinreich, Uriel. 1954. Is a structural dialectology possible? *Word* 10. 388–400.

Chapter 7

Linguistics as a science of structure

Ryan M. Nefdt

University of the Western Cape

Generative linguistics has rapidly changed during the course of a relatively short period. This has caused many to question its scientific status as a realist scientific theory (Stokhof & van Lambalgen 2011; Lappin et al. 2000). In this chapter, I argue against this conclusion. Specifically, I claim that the mathematical foundations of the science present a different story below the surface. I agree with critics that due to the major shifts in theory over the past 80 years, linguistics is indeed opened up to the problem of pessimistic meta-induction or radical theory change. However, I further argue that a structural realist approach (Ladyman 1998; French 2006) can save the field from this problem and at the same time capture its structural nature. I discuss particular historical instances of theory change in generative grammar as evidence for this interpretation and finally attempt to extend it beyond the generative tradition to encompass previous frameworks in linguistics.

1 Introduction

The generativist revolution in linguistics started in the mid-1950s, inspired in large part by insights from mathematical logic and in particular proof theory. Since then, generative linguistics has become a dominant paradigm, with many connections to both the formal and natural sciences. At the centre of the newly established discipline was the syntactic or formal engine, the structures of which were revealed through modelling grammatical form. The generativist paradigm in linguistics initially relied heavily upon the proof-theoretic techniques introduced by Emil Post and other formal logicians to model the form language takes (Tomalin 2006; Pullum 2011; 2013).[1] Yet despite these aforementioned formal beginnings, the generative theory of linguistics has changed its commitments quite

---

[1] Here my focus will largely be on the formal history of generative syntax but I will make some comments on other aspects of linguistics along the way.

Ryan M. Nefdt. 2019. Linguistics as a science of structure. In James McElvenny (ed.), *Form and formalism in linguistics*, 175–195. Berlin: Language Science Press. DOI:10.5281/zenodo.2654361

drastically over the intervening years, eschewing among other things formalization, cognitive science for evolutionary biology, derivations for constraints, rules for schemata, phrase structure for cyclic phases of the merge operation and other theoretical choices.

Given significant theory change, the fecundity of the enterprise and its so-called discoveries are inevitably called into question (Stokhof & van Lambalgen 2011; Lappin et al. 2000; Jackendoff 2002). A related, more ontological, question is, if the grammars of linguistics are scientific theories (as Chomsky and others have insisted over the years), then what are the objects being explained by these grammars? The former question has received little attention as compared to the latter.[2] I will not directly add to the ontological debate here, but I do hope to draw some needed attention to the question of theory change in linguistics.

Thus, in this chapter, I argue that linguistics as a science faces the problem of pessimistic meta-induction, more generally discussed in the philosophy of the hard science such as physics. In addition, I claim that the focus on the ontology of linguistic objects, such as words, phrases, sentences etc. belies the formal nature of the field, which is at base a structural undertaking. Both of these claims, I argue, lead to the interpretation of linguistics in terms of ontic structural realism in the philosophy of science (Ladyman 1998; French 2006). Thus, to be realist in this sense is to accept the existence of linguistic structures (not their content) defined internally through the operations of the grammars, and what remains relatively stable across various theoretical shifts in the generative paradigm, from Standard Theory (1957–1980) to the Minimalist Program (1995–present), are the formal structures so defined.

The chapter is separated into three parts. In the first part, I discuss the various theoretical changes which the generative linguistic tradition has undergone since its inception in the late 1950s. For instance, the move from rewriting systems with transformations to X-bar representation (Chomsky 1970) with theta roles to the current single movement operator Merge contained only by constraints. Despite appearances, I hope to show that the structure of these representations has remained relatively constant. In the second part, I discuss structural realism in the philosophy of science more generally and why it might serve as an illuminating foundation for linguistics. Linguistics here is interpreted structurally without recourse to the independent existence of individual objects or contents in that

---

[2]See Chomsky (1986) for the received psychological view on the ontology of linguistics, Katz & Postal (1991) for a Platonist interpretation, Devitt (2006) for a non-psychological physicalist view, and Stainton (2014) for a mixture of all the above. See Nefdt (2018) for an alternative mixture of these views.

structure (along the lines of Shapiro 1997 for mathematics). In other words, there are no phrases, clauses or sentences outside the overarching linguistic structure described by the grammar. Lastly, I briefly show that once a structural realist framework is adopted for the study of language, connections and continuity beyond current generative paradigms become apparent.

2 Theory change in generative linguistics

The history of science has seen a number of radical theory changes, from Newtonian to Relativistic physics, from Euclidean to Riemannian geometry as a characterization of physical space, from phlogiston theory to Lavoiser's oxygen theory, among many others. In the course of such changes, one might easily dismiss the old theory as simply false. However, as Laudan (1981) convincingly showed, there is a deeper issue looming in the passage of time, namely what has become known as pessimistic meta-induction (PMI). PMI can be defined as follows for present purposes.

pmi : If all (most) previous scientific theories have been shown to be false, then what reason do we have to believe in the truth of current theories?

The problem with radical theory change is that it causes serious tension for any realist theory of science, which aims to hold to the truth or approximate truth of current theories. Of course, false theories can be responsible for true ones through some sort of trial-and-error process. But the idea that our best current theories are of mere instrumental value for later truth is hard to accept.[3] Furthermore, at no point will certainty naturally force itself upon us, especially since success is not a guarantee of truth (e.g. classical mechanics is still a useful tool for modelling physical phenomena). PMI has an ontological component as well. When theories do change, they often propose distinct and incompatible entities in their respective ontologies. Consider the move from phlogiston theory to oxygen theory. In fact, the term "phlogiston" has become synonymous with a theoretical term which does not refer to anything. Essentially, the ontological status of the objects of the theories are rendered problematic when radical theory change occurs, which prompts a challenge again to the realist. "[I]f she can't establish the metaphysical status of the objects at the heart of her ontology, how can she adopt a realist attitude towards them?" (French 2011: 165).

---

[3]There are such instrumentalist theories on the market. Van Fraassen's (1980) constructive empiricism is one prominent example. A general problem for such views is that they tend to make miraculous the explanatory and predictive successes of scientific theory.

Linguistics, too, has seen its fair share of radical shifts in theory and perspective over the past few decades. In fact, the early generative tradition of Chomsky (1957) had a more formal mathematical outlook. Drawing inspiration from the work of Emil Post on canonical production systems, which are distinctively proof-theoretic devices in which symbols are manipulated via rules of inference in order to arrive at particular formulas (not unlike natural deduction systems), linguistics approached language from a more syntactic perspective.[4] This was due in part to two assumptions, namely (1) that syntax is autonomous from semantics, phonology etc. and (2) that syntax or the form of language is more amenable, than say semantic meaning, to precise mathematical elucidation. However, it must be added that as early as *Syntactic Structures* (1) had often been advanced as a necessary condition for progress in semantics.[5] Mathematical models of this sort would be a key tool in early generative linguistic analysis. Chomsky states the formal position in the following way at the time:[6]

> Precisely constructed models for linguistic structure can play an important role, both positive and negative, in the process of discovery itself. By pushing a precise but inadequate formulation to an unacceptable conclusion, we can often expose the exact source of this inadequacy and, consequently, gain a deeper understanding of the linguistic data. More positively, a formalized theory may automatically provide solutions for many problems other than those for which it was explicitly designed. (Chomsky 1957: 5)

He goes on to chastise linguists who are sceptical of formal methods. However, as we shall see, the course of linguistic theory saw a decrease in formalization and an increased resistance to it (partly inspired by Chomsky's later views). In fact, a generative grammar in the early stages was expressly noncommittal on ontological questions: "Each such grammar is simply a description of a certain set of utterances, namely, those which it generates" (Chomsky 1957: 48). By the 1960s, grammars were reconceived as tools for revealing linguistic competence or the idealized mental states of language users. With mentalism, linguistics looked

---

[4] For a thorough discussion of the influence of Post on generative grammar, see Pullum (2011) and Lobina (2017).

[5] I thank Michael Kac for emphasizing this point to me.

[6] I attempt to follow Pullum & Scholz (2007) throughout in slaloming my way through the minefield of the distinctions between "formalization", "formal", and "Formalism". The senses expressed here are related to "formal" as a term used for systems which abstract over meaning and "formalization" as a tool for converting statements of theory into precise mathematical representations. Early generative grammar can be seen as a theory which aimed to achieve both distinct goals.

towards sciences such as psychology, physics, and biology for methodological guidance as opposed to logic and mathematics as it did before. As Cowie (1999: 167) states of the time after *Aspects*, Chomsky "seemed also to have found a new methodology for the psychological study of language and created a new job description for linguists". The psychological interpretation of linguistic theory held sway until the 1990s, when the biolinguistic program emerged as yet another new way of theorizing about language. The *Minimalist Program* (1995b) pushed the field towards understanding language as a "natural object", in which questions of its optimal design and evolution take centre-stage.[7]

Each new foundation distanced itself from the methodology of its predecessor, postulated different objects and advocated different ends. Thus, PMI takes on special significance for linguistics and an answer to the puzzles it presents become especially peremptory in this light. In the following sections, I will focus on some specific cases of the methodological changes which underlie the picture sketched above.

3 From phrases to phases

In this section, I aim to provide a story of the mathematical formalisms employed in the service of an ever-changing landscape of theory in linguistics. I will not, however, directly discuss theoretical postulates such as Universal Grammar or modularity etc., which lie outside the scope of the present purview.

The early generative approach had a particular notion of a language and accompanying grammar at its core. On this view, a language L is modelled on a formal language which is a set of strings characterizable in terms of a grammar G or a rule-bound device responsible for generating well-formed formulas (i.e. grammatical expressions). In LSLT, Chomsky (1975: 5) writes of a language that it is "a set (in general infinite) of finite strings of symbols drawn from a finite 'alphabet'". In formal language theory (FLT) (which took inspiration from this period), assuming a start symbol S, set of terminals (words) T, nonterminals NT (syntactic categories) and production rules R, we can define a grammar in the following way:

> G will be said to *generate* a string w consisting of symbols from Σ if and only if it is possible to start with S and produce w through some finite sequence

---

[7]Of course, matters are rarely this simple or clear. For instance, Bickerton (2014) stresses that the peculiarity of the situation in linguistics is that the field at present still contains scholars working in various versions of the generative programme concurrently.

Ryan M. Nefdt

of rule applications. The sequence of modified strings that proceeds from S to w is called a *derivation* of w. The set of all strings that G can generate is called the *language* of G, and is notated $\mathscr{L}(G)$ (Jäger & Rogers 2012: 1957).

In Chomsky (1956), natural languages were shown to be beyond the scope of languages with production rules such as $A \rightarrow a$, $A \rightarrow aB$ or $A \rightarrow \varepsilon$ (ε is the empty string) such that $A, B \in NT$ and $a \in T$ (i.e. regular languages).[8] This result lead to the advent of phrase-structure or context-free grammars with production rules of the following sort: either $S \rightarrow ab$ or $S \rightarrow aSb$ (read the arrow as "replace with" or rewrite). These grammars can handle recursive structures and contain the regular languages as a proper subset. For many years, phrase-structure grammars were the standard way of describing linguistic phenomena. Essentially, phrase structure grammars are rewriting systems in which symbols are replaced with others such as $S \rightarrow NP, VP$ or $NP \rightarrow det, N'$. As Freidin (2012: 897) notes, "phrase structure rules are based on a top-down analysis where a sentence is divided into its major constituent parts and then these parts are further divided into constituents, and so on until we reach lexical items". There are a number of equivalent means of representing the structure of sentences in this way. The most common is *via* hierarchical diagrams, shown below.

(1)

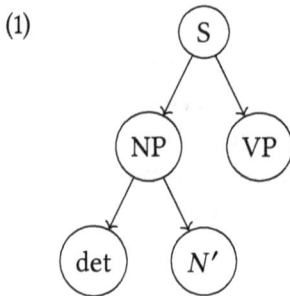

Alternatively one can capture the same information as:

(2) $[_S[_{NP}[_{det}][_{N'}]][_{VP}]]$

This basic structure, however, proved inadequate as a means of capturing the structure of passives and certain verbal auxiliary constructions as shown originally in Postal (1964).[9] Transformations were meant to buttress the phrase struc-

---

[8] One issue is that regular grammars cannot capture centre embeddings such as *The boy the girl loved left*.

[9] This picture of the trajectory of the grammatical formalization is necessarily sketchy. A fuller story would include formal results such as Shieber (1985), which showed from the cross serial dependencies of Swiss-German that natural language syntax cannot be captured by a context-free grammar.

ture system in order to bridge this gap in explanation. Transformation rules operate on the output of the phrase structure rules and create a derived structure, as in (3) below for passivization.

(3) NP_1 V $NP_2 \rightarrow NP_2$ be-en (AUX) V NP_1

The combined expressive power of phrase structure and transformations proved very productive in characterizing myriad linguistic structures. This productivity, with its increased complexity, however, came at a cost to learnability. "[I]f a linguistic theory is to be explanatorily adequate it must not merely describe the facts, but must do so in a way that *explains* how humans are able to learn languages" (Ludlow 2011: 15). The move to more generality led in part to the Extended Standard Theory and the X-bar schema.

Since the continued proliferation of transformations and phrase structure rules was considered to be cognitively unrealistic, linguistic structures needed more sparse mathematical representation. Although, as Bickerton (2014: 24) states, "rule proliferation and 'ordering paradoxes' were only two of a number of problems that led to the eventual replacement of the Standard Theory".[10]

There was also a theoretical push for more general structure from the Universal Grammar (UG) postulate assumed to be the natural linguistic endowment of every language user. UG needed to contain more general rule schemata in order to account for the diversity of constructions across the world's languages. This structural agenda dovetailed well with the Principles and Parameters (P&P) framework, which posited that the architecture of the language faculty constituted a limited number of universal principles constrained by individual parametric settings, where "parameters" were roughly the set of possible variations of a given structure. For instance, some languages, such as English, require a mandatory NP/DP in the subject position of sentences, whereas in pro-drop languages, such as Spanish, empty categories can do the job.

(4)   It is raining.

(5)   Llueve.

These kinds of differences could be expressed in the language of parametric settings. The so-called Extended Projection Principle might be universal, but certain languages can contain distinct parameters with relation to it (such as fulfilling it with a null determiner). In other words, a child in the process of acquiring her

---

[10]"Ordering paradoxes" here refer to the situation in which there are equally valid reasons for orderings from X to Y and Y to X despite the grammar requiring a particular order to pertain.

first language can "set" the parameter based on the available linguistic environment in which she finds herself, like the flicking of a switch. Furthermore, this kind of structural picture is represented well in the X-bar schema (Jackendoff 1977), which contains only three basic rules. There is (1) a specifier, (2) an adjunct, and (3) a complement rule. The specifier rule is given below (where X' is a head-variable and XP and YP are arbitrary phrasal categories determined by that head).

(6) Specifier rule: XP⟶ (Spec)X' or XP⟶ X'(YP)

Or equivalently:

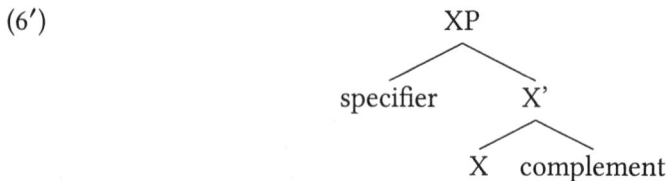

(6')

$$XP$$

specifier   X'

X   complement

A vast amount of linguistic structure can be modelled by means of this formalism. In fact, X-bar theory overgenerates structural descriptions (which need to be reined in by various constraints). But the underlying idea is that our mental competence is more likely to contain generalized rule schemata such as those above than individual phrase structure rules and countless transformations for each natural language. In a sense, X-bar merely smooths over the individual hierarchical structures of before and homes in on a more abstract structural representation for language. As Poole mentions:

> [W]e discovered that your language faculty appears to structure phrases into three levels: the maximal projections or XP level, the intermediate X' level, and the head or $X°$. (Poole 2002: 50)

These rules subsume the previous *ad hoc* phrase structure rules. Importantly, however, the representation only allows for binary rules (unlike the possible n-ary branches of phrase structure trees). Freidin (2012) further claims that X-bar theory represented a shift from top-down to bottom-up analysis, despite being formulated in a top-down manner a decade after its inception. Here, the idea is that the rules stated above are projections from lexical items to syntactic category labels, not the other way around.

Unfortunately, history has a way of repeating itself. Where in the previous instantiation of generative grammar, the proliferation of transformations became unwieldy, parameters would soon see a similar fate befall its fecundity. Briefly, UG was assumed to be extremely rich during this period: "the available devices must be rich and diverse enough to deal with the phenomena exhibited in the possible human languages" (Chomsky 1986: 55). However, what was innate and what was learned or set by experience relied in part on a distinction between "core" grammar and "periphery", which was never explicitly provided by the theory (see Pullum 1983 and Culicover 2011 for discussion). Although formally all previous transformations were reduced to the "move alpha" operation, the multiplication of parameters took similar shape to its transformational predecessor. Newmeyer describes this period as one of instability and confusion:

> In the worst-case scenario, an investigation of the properties of hundreds of languages around the world deepens the amount of parametric variation postulated among languages, and the number of possible settings for each parameter could grow so large that the term 'parameter' could end up being nothing more than jargon for language-particular rule. (Newmeyer 1996: 64)

In addition, these parameters seemed to force the violation of the binary requirement set by the X-bar formalism and with it the cognitive plausibility transiently acquired after the Standard Theory. There needed to be a better way of capturing the movement toward simplifying the grammatical representation and theory of natural language syntax. This and other theoretical motivations led to the Minimalist Program (Chomsky 1995b), which pushed the new biolinguistic agenda and a call for further simplicity.

As mentioned in §2, the question of the evolution of language reset the agenda in theoretical linguistics at this time. The grammatical formalisms assumed to underlie the cognitive aspects of linguistic competence were forced to change with this new perspective, with the result that many of the advances made by the P&P and Government and Binding (Chomsky 1981) theories needed to be abandoned. The rationale was something of the following sort:

> Evolutionarily speaking, it is hard to explain the appearance of highly detailed, highly language-specific mental mechanisms. Conversely, it would be much easier to explain language's evolution in humans if it were composed of just a few very simple mechanisms (Johnson 2015: 175).

The Merge operation represented the goal of reducing structure to these simple mechanisms. In the Standard and Extended theories, grammars followed the structures set by the proof theory of the early twentieth century (see above), which often resulted in grammars "of roughly the order of complexity of what is to be explained" (Chomsky 1995a: 233). In the Minimalist programme, this apparatus was reduced to a simple set-theoretic operation which takes two syntactic objects and creates a labelled output of their composition (the label to be determined by the features of the objects thereby replacing the projection from heads of X-bar theory).[11] The formulation is given below:

(7) $\text{Merge}(\alpha, \beta) = \{\gamma, \{\alpha, \beta\}\}$

Or again, equivalently:

(7′)

$$\begin{array}{c} \gamma \\ | \\ \overset{\textstyle\wedge}{} \\ \alpha \quad \beta \end{array}$$

The above is an example of external set merge (where γ is a label projected from one of the elements). Internal merge accounts for recursive structures since it applies to its own output (as in if β is already contained in α). Consider the following sentence.

(8)   The driver will speed recklessly.

In a bottom-up fashion, *speed* and *recklessly* will merge to form a vp, and thereafter this union will merge with the auxiliary *will* to form a TP or Tense Phrase. Merge will independently take *the* and *driver* and create an NP which will merge to form the final TP to deliver (8) above (the T is the label projected for the entire syntactic object). Importantly for the proposal I will present, "[t]his last step merges two independent phrases in essentially the same way that generalized transformations operated in the earliest transformational grammars" (Freidin 2012: 911).[12] Thus, although the phrase structure rules had been replaced by the less complex merge operation with *phases*, which are cyclic stages applying to the

---

[11]Technically, as Langendoen (2003: 307) notes, "Merge is not a single operation, but a family of operations. To belong to the merge family, an operation must be able to yield an infinite set of objects from a finite basis". However, by this definition, the phrase structure rules with recursive components would be invited to Thanksgiving dinner. The structural similarities of various versions of this infinity requirement on grammars will be discussed in the next section.

[12]Of course, the practice of taking ideas or insights in disguised form from early frameworks was not uncommon. For instance, the binding theory of Government and Binding is very close (if not identical) to principles governing anaphora (like the Ross-Langacker constraints) that were first articulated in the 1960s. Similarly, the trace theory of movement is closely tied to the earlier idea of global derivational constraints. I thank Michael Kac for drawing my attention to these cases.

innermost constituents of the entire process (Chomsky 2008), there is a similar structure to the derivation.

Of course, unlike the top-down analysis of early generative grammar, Merge operates from lexical items in the opposite direction (Merge and the "lexical array" constituting "narrow syntax", see Langendoen 2003). However, as Lobina (2017: 84) cautions, "talk of top-down and bottom-up derivations is clearly metaphorical".[13] It might add something in appreciating the flavour of the computational process at hand, but often the overall structural picture is unchanged by such parlance.

Let this serve as an account, albeit incomplete, of some of the formal and theoretical changes of generative grammar over the 60-year period since its inception. Below, I will draw on the picture developed here to argue for the structural continuity of linguistics despite the theoretical shifts the overarching theory might have taken during this time.

4 Structural realism and linguistics

The previous two sections showed a theoretical landscape in flux with each new stage abandoning the commitments of its predecessor. In such a scenario, PMI takes on a strong force. Not only this, but as mentioned before, the situation in linguistics is unique, since practitioners of each epoch of the theory can still be found working within the remit of their chosen formalism. In §2, I described some of the theoretical shifts in the generative paradigm since the 1950s. In §3, I described the underlying mathematical formalisms utilized in service of the changing theory at each junction. In this section, I want to use a structural realist analysis of linguistics to show that despite the former, the structures of the latter remained relatively constant or at least commensurable.

What is structural realism? One way of thinking of it is as the "best of both worlds" strategy for dealing with PMI. Realists, as we have seen, have trouble holding on to the objects of their theories once better theories come along. Anti-realists, on the other hand, have trouble accounting for the unparalleled predictive and explanatory success of theories (whose objects do not refer to objects in reality). Structural realism offers a conciliatory intermediary position between these choices. Ladyman describes the position as follows:

---

[13]Compare this metaphorical language to a similar caution in Pullum (2013: 496), "[t]he fact that derivational steps come in a sequence has encouraged the practice of talking about them in procedural terms. Although this is merely a metaphor, it has come to have a firm grip on linguists thinking about syntax".

> Rather we should adopt the structural realist emphasis on the mathematical or structural content of our theories. Since there is (says Worrall) retention of structure across theory change, structural realism both (a) avoids the force of the pessimistic meta-induction (by not committing us to belief in the theory's description of the furniture of the world), and (b) does not make the success of science [...] seem miraculous (by committing us to the claim that the theory's structure, over and above its empirical content, describes the world). (Ladyman 1998: 410)

There are two versions of structural realism in the philosophy of science. The first, initially proposed by Worall (1989), is epistemic in nature. The second, championed by French & Ladyman (2003), is an ontological proposal. The former involves the idea that all we can *know* is structure, while the latter is a claim about all *there is*. In other words, what is preserved across theory change is a kind of structure posited by the underlying equations, laws, models or other mathematical representations of the theories. Part of the reason I opt here for ontic structural realism is that there is an ontological component to PMI, as mentioned before. Thus, we are not only interested in what is communicated or epistemically accessible between different theories over time but what these theories say exists as well. The ontological answer to PMI is therefore that if we cannot be realists about the objects of our scientific theories, we can be realists about the structures that they posit.[14]

From here, it is not hard to see what the argument of the present section is going to be, namely that different generations of generative grammar display structural continuity notwithstanding variation in theoretical commitment. The means by which we can appreciate this continuity is by considering features of the mathematical representations employed during the course of history which could affect my proposed analysis. Moss has a similar idea when he discusses the contribution made by mathematical models to linguistic theory.

> [L]anguage comes to us without any evident structure. It is up to theoreticians to propose whatever structures they think are useful [...] Mathematical models are the primary way that scientists in any field get at structure. (Moss 2012: 534)

---

[14] At this point, one can glean how such a picture might enter into the debate concerning the ontological foundations of linguistics mentioned earlier. Unlike Platonists, who claim among other things that languages are individual abstract objects like sets, or mentalists, who claim they are psychological or internal states of the brain, a structuralist could argue that languages are complex structures in part identified by abstract rules and physical properties. See Nefdt (2018) for precisely such a view.

In the previous section, I told a story about how the proof-theoretic grammars of the Standard Theory were transformed into X-bar representations, which eventually led to the Merge operation in Minimalism. However, a remarkable fact about the structural descriptions generated by these various formalisms is that they share a number of essential features: (1) they generate the same sets of sentences (also called "weak generative capacity"),[15] (2) they take a finite input and generate an infinite output, and (3) they can be represented hierarchically through tree structures (not to mention actual structural similarities such as the way in which Merge joins two independent clauses and the way it was proposed in early transformational grammar). None of these latter properties are trivial. For instance, dependency grammars can be shown to be weakly equivalent to phrase structure grammars but are represented by means of flat structures. Model-theoretic grammars, such as Head-Driven Phrase Structure Grammar, are usually hierarchically represented and can generate the same sets of sentences but do not have any cardinality commitments.

It is important to note that there were a number of formal shifts present in the transitions from transformational grammars to Merge which might challenge the framework put forward here. I have already mentioned the top-down to bottom-up change and argued that, from a structural point of view, this is largely a metaphorical distinction. There is, however, another property of formal representations of syntax which also shifted from early to later generative grammar, namely from derivational approaches to representational or constraint-based ones. Simply put, derivational approaches follow the proof-theoretic model discussed earlier, where given a certain finite input and a certain set of rules, a particular structured output is generated. Constraint-based formalisms operate differently. Rather than 'deriving' an expression as output from a rule-bound grammar, these formalisms define certain conditions upon expression-hood or what counts as a grammatical sentence of the language. Chomsky discusses this shift in thought in the following way:

> If the question is real, and subject to inquiry, then the [strong minimalist thesis] might turn out to be an even more radical break from the tradition than [the principles-and-parameters model] seemed to be. Not only does it abandon traditional conceptions of "rule of grammar" and "grammatical construction" that were carried over in some form into generative grammar,

---

[15]In fact, these equivalences go beyond the generative grammars. Minimalist Syntax (or the Stabler 1997 version), Phrase-Structure grammars, Tree-substitution grammars, Head-Driven Phrase Structure grammars (HPSG), and Dependency grammars have been shown to share weak generative capacity. See Mönnich (2007).

but it may also set the stage for asking novel questions that have no real counterpart in the earlier study of language. (Chomsky 2000: 92)

Indeed, with the Minimalist agenda and the Merge operation, more constraint-based grammar formalisms were embraced and adopted. This latter approach involves a different idea of "rule of grammar" and indeed "grammar construction". The formal difference can be understood in terms of how each type of formalism answers the so-called "membership problem". Decidability is an important aspect of formal language theory. Given a string w and a formal language $\mathscr{L}(G)$, there is a finite procedure for deciding whether $w \in \mathscr{L}(G)$, i.e. a Turing machine which outputs "yes" or "no" in finite time. In other words, a language $\mathscr{L}(G)$ is decidable if G is a decidable grammar. This is called the membership problem. What determines membership in a traditional proof-theoretic grammar is whether or not that string can be generated from the start symbol S and the production rules R. In other words, whether that string is recursively enumerable in that language (set of strings). What determines membership in a constraint-based grammar is whether the expression fulfils the constraints set by the grammar (which are like axioms of the system). "An MTS [model-theoretic syntax] grammar does not recursively define a set of expressions; it merely states necessary conditions on the syntactic structures of individual expressions" (Pullum & Scholz 2001: 19). As mentioned above, Generalized Phrase Structure Grammar and Head-Driven Phrase Structure Grammar are formalisms of the latter variety. While phrase structure grammars can be found in the average syntax textbook, tree-adjoining grammars fall within the former camp.

The interesting fact for our purposes is that Merge and Minimalism represent the fruition of the gradual shift from derivational grammars to constraint-based ones. However, Chomsky (2000) does not initially put much stock in this formal transition, despite the strong statement quoted above. He considers the old derivational or "step-by-step procedure for constructing Exps" approach and the "direct definition [...] where E is an expression of L iff ...E..., where ...-... is some condition on E" approach to be "mostly intertranslatable" (Chomsky 2000: 99).[16] Here he holds these formalism types to have few empirical differences.

From a mathematical point of view, the same formal languages and the structures of which they are composed are definable through both generative enumerative and model-theoretic means. Traditionally, the formal languages of the

---

[16]He goes on to "suspect" that the adoption of the derivational approach is more than expository and might indeed be "correct".

Chomsky Hierarchy were defined in terms of the kinds of grammars specified at the beginning of the previous section. However, there are other ways of demarcating the formal languages without recourse to generative grammars. For instance, they can be defined according to monadic second-order logic in the model-theoretic way. Büchi (1960) showed that a set of strings forms a regular language if and only if it can be defined in the weak monadic second-order theory of the natural numbers with a successor. Thatcher & Wright (1968) then showed that context-free languages "were all and only the sets of strings forming the yield of sets of finite trees definable in the weak monadic second-order theory of multiple successors" (Rogers 1998: 1117).

The point is that the same structures can be characterized by means of either proof-theoretic or model-theoretic techniques. Thus, the move from the former to the latter should not be seen as a hazard to the structural realist account of linguistic theory I am proffering here.[17]

5 In search of lost paradigms

The picture painted above is perhaps rather parochial. I consider theoretical shifts within the generative paradigm exclusively as a means of demonstrating the advantages of a structural realist interpretation of the science. There were a number of reasons for this narrow focus. One reason was that, with the centrality of syntax in the early generative tradition, the idea of form over content naturally led to a structural picture. Another reason was related to various criticisms levelled against the theoretical changes and the threat of PMI specific to contemporary generative grammar.

Nevertheless, despite this focus, the structural realist analysis offered here allows the possibility of a broader perspective on the history and development of linguistics, one that goes beyond the inception of generative grammar in the 1950s. The advent of generative linguistics is often characterized as a sharp paradigm shift eschewing the tenets of what was known as "structural linguistics" (or "American structuralism") which came before. Some of these alleged tenets include (1) the limitation to classificatory or taxonomic methods of study, (2) the

---

[17]In terms of the nature of structural properties themselves, there are at least two possible ways in which to identify a structural property in the literature, one in terms of direct *definability* and another *via* a particular notion of *invariance* across structures. See Korbmacher & Schiemer (2017) for a formal comparison between these two options and Johnson (2015) for an application of the latter to linguistic theory.

restriction of data to language corpora (producing only so-called "observationally adequate grammars"), and (3) a local limit on language-specific rules and generalizations (i.e. no Universal Grammar).[18]

However, there is strong evidence to suggest that pre-generative linguists were thinking along similar mathematical lines. As early as Bloomfield (1926), a methodological shift towards the axiomatic method of Hilbert in the sciences is advocated. It is this move towards mathematical (proof-theoretic) structure that took shape in the generative paradigm, but also connects the latter to early work in American structuralism (again despite some theoretical shifts).

> In addition (and more specifically), Bloomfield was an early proponent (possibly the earliest?) of the use of the axiomatic-deductive method in linguistics, an approach that was revived first by Bloch in the 1940s, and then by Bar-Hillel, Harwood, and others in the 1950s, and which gradually became the dominant method of syntactic analysis after the appearance of [*Syntactic Structures*]. (Tomalin 2006: 184)

Bar-Hillel (1953) took this idea even further in providing the first attempt at incorporating recursion theory in mathematics into linguistics (and with it the first generative grammar of sorts). As Tomalin notes:

> Bar-Hillel's use of recursive definitions to analyse the structure of sentences in natural language can be viewed as one manifestation of this pervasive desire for the mathematisation of syntactic analysis, which became such a characteristic feature of certain kinds of linguistic research in the mid-twentieth century. (Tomalin 2006: 67)

Thus, in terms of structural realism, there is ample evidence of continuity across paradigms. In terms of individual structures, Chomsky's mentor Zellig Harris (1951) advocated adoption of what he called "transformations" within his structuralist linguistic theory.

> A different linguistic analysis can be obtained if we try to characterize each sentence as derived, in accordance with a set of transformational rules, from one or more (generally simpler) sentences [...]. Such an analysis produces a more compact yet more detailed description of language and brings out the

---

[18]One might also add scepticism of meaning to the list. Interestingly, meaning-scepticism persisted long into the generative movement and in part resulted in the so-called "Linguistics Wars" (see Newmeyer 1996 for discussion).

more subtle formal and semantic relations among sentences. (Harris 1951: iv).

According to Matthews (2001) structural linguistics is still present within contemporary research on language, depending on how one defines "structuralism". Specifically, the interpretations that involve claims that languages are distinct systems of relations, sets of sentences, and linguistics is the science of such structures (over and above the elements of the systems) show continuity between the past and the present. For Firth (1957: 181), commenting on Saussure, one of the forefathers of structuralism, "true Saussureans, like true Durkheimians, regard the structures formulated by linguistics or sociology as *in rebus* [...]. The structure is existent and is treated as a thing". This idea of being realist about structure and the formalist mathematics of this early paradigm carried through into Chomskyan generative linguistics. In fact, for Joseph (1999: 26), it was Chomsky himself who "introduced structuralism into American linguistics, more fully than any of his predecessors". Nevertheless, the idea of linguistics treating structure as an object of theory directly is also very close in spirit (and word) to the motivations behind structural realism in the philosophy of science which takes the underlying mathematical structures of theories to be transmitted across frameworks and paradigms. For instance, as Pullum (Forthcoming) observes of one of the core mathematical notions of generative grammar,

> [t]he idea that a linguistic description can be viewed as providing instructions for "generating" sentences had been advanced by both Hockett (1954) ("principles by which one can generate any number of utterances in the language," 1954, 390) and Harris (1954) ("A grammar may be viewed as a set of instructions which generates the sentences of a language," 1954, 260). (Pullum Forthcoming)

With Bar-Hillel's recursive grammars, Bloomfield's axiomatic method, and the transformations and generative work of Hockett and Harris, the structures which would find fruition in the generative paradigm were present in its predecessors so much so that, again despite significant theory change, mathematical and therefore structural continuity can be appreciated across paradigms.

6 Conclusion

In this chapter, I have argued that understanding generative linguistics in structural realist terms brings a number of philosophical advantages. Not only does it offer an answer to worries concerning the radical theoretical shifts which the programme has undergone, but it also provides a more sound philosophical understanding of the scientific nature of linguistics and its history. I further extended this analysis beyond the paradigm to include insights from the erstwhile American structural linguistics tradition.

Abbreviations

AUX	Auxiliary category
GPSG	Generalized Phrase Structure Grammar
HPSG	Head-Driven Phrase Structure Grammar
LSLT	Logical Structure of Linguistic Theory
SBCG	Sign-based Construction Grammar
UG	Universal Grammar postulate

Acknowledgements

I would like to thank Geoff Pullum and Michael Kac for their insights into the historical and technical linguistic details as well as Steven French for offering needed guidance on the philosophy of science aspects of the chapter.

References

Bar-Hillel, Yehoshua. 1953. On recursive definitions in empirical science. *11th Natural Congress of Philosophy* 5. 160–165.

Bickerton, Derek. 2014. *More than nature needs: Language, mind, and evolution.* Cambridge, MA: Harvard University Press.

Bloomfield, Leonard. 1926. Set of postulates for the science of language. *Language* 2. 156–164.

Büchi, Richard. 1960. Weak second-order arithmetic and finite automata. *Zeitschrift für mathematische Logik und Grundlagen der Mathematik* 6. 66–92.

Chomsky, Noam. 1956. Three models for the description of language. *IRE Transactions on Information Theory* 2. 113–123.

Chomsky, Noam. 1957. *Syntactic structures.* The Hague: Mouton.

Chomsky, Noam. 1970. Remarks on nominalization. In R. Jacobs & P. Rosenbaum (eds.), *Readings in English transformational grammar*, 184–221. Waltham, MA: Ginn.

Chomsky, Noam. 1975. *The logical structure of linguistic theory.* Netherlands: Springer.

Chomsky, Noam. 1981. *Lectures on government and binding.* Berlin: De Gruyter Mouton.

Chomsky, Noam. 1986. *Knowledge of language: Its nature, origin, and use.* New York: Praeger.

Chomsky, Noam. 1995a. Language and nature. *Mind* 104. 1–61.

Chomsky, Noam. 1995b. *The minimalist program.* Cambridge, MA: MIT Press.

Chomsky, Noam. 2000. Minimalist inquiries. In R. Martin, D. Michaels & J. Uriagereka (eds.), *Step by step: Essays on minimalist syntax in honor of Howard Lasnik*, 89–155. Cambridge, MA: MIT Press.

Chomsky, Noam. 2008. On phases. In R. Freiden, C. P. Otero & M. Zubizarreta (eds.), *Foundational issues in linguistic theory*, 133–166. Cambridge, MA: MIT Press.

Cowie, Fiona. 1999. *What's within? Nativism reconsidered.* Oxford: Oxford University Press.

Culicover, Peter. 2011. Core and periphery. In P. Hogan (ed.), *The Cambridge encyclopedia of the language sciences*, 227–230. Cambridge University Press.

Devitt, Michael. 2006. *Ignorance of language.* Oxford: Oxford University Press.

Firth, John R. 1957. *Papers in linguistics 1934-1951.* London: Oxford University Press.

Freidin, Robert. 2012. A brief history of generative grammar. In G. Russell & D. Fara (eds.), *The Routledge companion to philosophy of language*, 895–916. New York: Routledge.

French, Steven. 2006. Structure as a weapon of the realist. *Proceedings of the Aristotelian Society* 106. 167–185.

French, Steven. 2011. Shifting the structures in physics and biology: A prophylactic promiscuous realism. *Studies in History and Philosophy of Biological and Biomedical Sciences* 42. 164–173.

French, Steven & James Ladyman. 2003. Remodelling structural realism: Quantum physics and the metaphysics of structure. *Synthese* 136. 31–56.

Harris, Zellig. 1951. *Methods in structural linguistics.* Chicago: Chicago University Press.

Harris, Zellig S. 1954. Transfer grammar. *International Journal of American Linguistics* 20. 259–270.

Hockett, Charles F. 1954. Two models of grammatical description. *Word* 10. 210–231. Page references are to the reprinting in Joos (ed.) 1966, 386–399.

Jackendoff, Ray. 1977. X' *syntax.* Cambridge, MA: MIT Press.

Jackendoff, Ray. 2002. *Foundations of language: Brain, meaning, grammar, evolution.* Oxford: Oxford University Press.

Jäger, Gerhard & James Rogers. 2012. Formal language theory: Refining the Chomsky hierarchy. *Philosophical Transactions of the Royal Society B: Biological Sciences* 367. 1956–1970.

Johnson, Kent. 2015. Notational variants and invariance in linguistics. *Mind & Language* 30(2). 162–186.

Joseph, John E. 1999. How structuralist was "American structuralism"? *Bulletin of the Henry Sweet Society for the History of Linguistic Ideas* (33). 23–28.

Katz, Jerrold J. & Paul M. Postal. 1991. Realism vs. conceptualism in linguistics. *Linguistics and Philosophy* 14(5). 515–554.

Korbmacher, Johannes & Georg Schiemer. 2017. What are structural properties? *Philosophia Mathematica.* 1–29.

Ladyman, James. 1998. What is structural realism? *Studies in the History and Philosophy of Science* 29(3). 403–424.

Langendoen, Terence. 2003. Merge. In A. Carnie, H. Hayley & M. Willie (eds.), *Formal approaches to function in grammar: In honor of Eloise Jelinek*, 307–318. Amsterdam: John Benjamins.

Lappin, Shalom, Robert Levine & David Johnson. 2000. The structure of unscientific revolutions. *Natural language and linguistic theory* 18(3). 665–671.

Laudan, Larry. 1981. A confutation of convergent realism. *Philosophy of Science* 48. 19–49.

Lobina, David. 2017. *Recursion: A computational investigation into the representation and processing of language.* Oxford: Oxford University Press.

Ludlow, Peter. 2011. *The philosophy of generative linguistics.* Oxford: Oxford University Press.

Matthews, Peter. 2001. *A short history of structural linguistics.* Cambridge: Cambridge University Press.

Mönnich, Uwe. 2007. Minimalist syntax, multiple regular tree grammars, and direction preserving tree transducers. In J. Rogers & S. Kepser (eds.), *Model theoretic syntax at 10. ESSLLI'07 workshop proceedings*, 68–95. Berlin: Springer.

Moss, Lawrence. 2012. The role of mathematical methods. In G. Russell & D. Fara (eds.), *The Routledge companion to philosophy of language*, 533–553. New York: Routledge.

Nefdt, Ryan. 2018. Languages and other abstract structures. In C. Christina & M. Neef (eds.), *Essays on linguistic realism*, 139–184. Amsterdam: John Benjamins.

Newmeyer, Frederick J. 1996. *Generative linguistics: A historical perspective.* New York: Routledge.

Poole, Geoffrey. 2002. *Syntactic theory*. Great Britain: Palgrave.

Postal, Paul M. 1964. Constituent structure: A study of contemporary models of syntactic description.

Pullum, Geoffrey. Forthcoming. Philosophy of linguistics. In K. Becker. & I. Thomson (eds.), *The Cambridge history of philosophy, 1945–2015*. Cambridge: Cambridge University Press.

Pullum, Geoffrey K. 1983. How many possible human languages are there? *Linguistic Inquiry* 14(3). 447–467.

Pullum, Geoffrey K. 2011. The mathematical foundations of *Syntactic Structures*. *The Journal of Logic, Language and Information* 20(3). 277–296.

Pullum, Geoffrey K. 2013. The central question in comparative syntactic metatheory. *Mind & Language* 28(4). 492–521.

Pullum, Geoffrey & Barbara C. Scholz. 2001. On the distinction between model-theoretic and generative-enumerative syntactic frameworks. In P. de Groote, G. Morril & C. Retoré (eds.), *Logical aspects of computational linguistics: 4th international conference*, 17–43. Berlin: Springer.

Pullum, Geoffrey & Barbara C. Scholz. 2007. Tracking the origins of transformational generative grammar. *Journal of Linguistics* 43(3). 701–723.

Rogers, James. 1998. A descriptive characterization of tree-adjoining languages. In, 1117–1121.

Shapiro, Stewart. 1997. *Philosophy of mathematics: Structure and ontology*. Oxford: Oxford University Press.

Shieber, Stuart. 1985. Evidence against the context-freeness of natural language. *Linguistics and Philosophy* 8. 333–343.

Stabler, Edward. 1997. Derivational minimalism. In C. Restoré (ed.), *Logical aspects of computational linguistics*, 68–95. Berlin: Springer.

Stainton, Robert. 2014. Philosophy of linguistics. *Oxford Handbooks Online*. https://doi.org/10.1093/oxfordhb/9780199935314.013.002.

Stokhof, Martin & Michiel van Lambalgen. 2011. Abstractions and idealisations: the construction of modern linguistics. *Theoretical Linguistics* 37(1/2). 1–26.

Thatcher, James & Jesse Wright. 1968. Generalized finite automata theory with an application to a decision problem of second-order logic. *Mathematical systems theory* 2(1). 57–81.

Tomalin, Marcus. 2006. *Linguistics and the formal sciences*. Cambridge: Cambridge University Press.

Van Fraassen, Bas. 1980. *The scientific image*. Oxford: Oxford University Press.

Worall, John. 1989. The best of both worlds? *Dialectica* 43(1/2). 99–124.

Chapter 8

Formalism, grammatical rules, and normativity

Geoffrey K. Pullum

University of Edinburgh

Formalism within logic and mathematics has indirect connections to modern formal linguistics in that the earliest attempt at realizing the formalist program for logic had the side effect of leading to the development of what today we call generative grammars. Syntactic theory has been dominated by the generative conception for six decades. Despite reference in the literature to "rules", generative grammars do not contain rules in the usual sense (under which a rule can be followed or disobeyed). It is not clear how work on generative grammars could make sense of the idea of normative principles of grammar. But the subject matter of grammar is indeed best taken to be normative: a grammar expresses statements about what is correct or incorrect, not claims directly about phenomena in the empirical world. Grammatical rules with normative force can nonetheless be rendered mathematically precise through a type of formalization that does not involve generative grammars, and normativity can be understood in a way that does not imply anything about obligations or duties. Thus there is some hope of reconciling the normativity of grammar with the enterprise of formalizing grammars for human languages and the view that linguistics is an empirical science.

1 Introduction

The school of thought known as "formalism" in logic and mathematics takes these disciplines to be concerned solely with procedures for manipulating strings over a finite inventory of meaningless symbols. Put like that, it sounds pointless: logic and mathematics were surely supposed to be *about* something, not just meaningless games. But formalism has a point: its aim is to ensure that proofs of theoremhood are constructed in a way that is scoured clean of any question-begging hint of meaning or truth. Then, if what is provable turns out to coincide

Geoffrey K. Pullum. 2019. Formalism, grammatical rules, and normativity. In James McElvenny (ed.), *Form and formalism in linguistics*, 197–223. Berlin: Language Science Press. DOI:10.5281/zenodo.2654367

with what is semantically tautologous, it can be shown that proof in the syntactic sense truly accomplishes something.

That is, ideally we want everything logically provable from true premises to turn out to be true given those premises, and everything that is logically true to be provable. To show that this has been achieved, without circularity, we need first a method of proof that pays no regard to meaning or truth, and second a way of demonstrating that it proves all and only the logical truths. In technical terms, we want a consistent and complete method of proof.

A crucial contribution to the formalist program in logic, just over a century old, was presented in an important book by Clarence Irving Lewis (1883–1964): *A Survey of Symbolic Logic*.[1] Lewis clearly saw that the crucially important work on reducing mathematics to logic, *Principia Mathematica* (1910–1913, henceforth PM) by Alfred North Whitehead (1861–1947) and Bertrand Russell (1872–1970), had failed to separate syntax from semantics in the logical system it assumed. The distinction between axioms and inference rules had not yet emerged: Whitehead and Russell subsumed them both under "primitive propositions". In consequence Modus Ponens was framed in a way that, from the formalist viewpoint, is shockingly confused, because it is semantically contaminated. It says: "Anything implied by a true elementary proposition is true" and, where x is a real variable, "When φx can be asserted [...] and $\varphi x \supset \psi x$ can be asserted [...] then ψx can be asserted".

This precludes making legitimate use of the claim that p implies q, unless we take p to be true. But p might of course be a proposition we are by no means sure of. Using logic to see what follows from a false assumption is an important technique of discovery that Whitehead and Russell's statement of Modus Ponens appears to disallow. Lewis understood that, if we want to be sure that our symbolic reasoning is trustworthy, we must have a purely syntactical method of deriving strings, one that does not in any way depend on meaning, and we must then show that the strings it derives are the right ones – the ones that are true if and only if the initially adopted premises are true. Lewis sketched in ordinary English a statement of Modus Ponens that ruthlessly excluded any talk of meaning or truth, referring solely to positions of symbols in strings.

The program for making logic truly formal that Lewis urged was taken up in earnest by a PhD student in the Department of Mathematics at Columbia Uni-

---

[1] See section III of Chapter 6 in the first edition, 1918; the edition is crucial, because when the second edition by Dover was authorized, Lewis stipulated that Chapters 5 and 6 of his book were to be omitted; he felt that whatever value the book had did not depend on those two somewhat more speculative and heterodox chapters.

versity. Emil Leon Post (1897–1954) graduated with a mathematics BA from the City College of New York in 1917, and went on to do a PhD at Columbia under the philosopher and mathematician Cassius Jackson Keyser (1862–1947).[2] Lewis's book appeared during Post's first year as a graduate student, and appears to have influenced him considerably. The plan for a doctoral dissertation that he conceived involved turning Lewis's informally presented "heterodox" approach into a program within pure mathematics. Post aimed to construct:

(I) a way of testing a formula of the propositional calculus used in PM to determine (via truth tables for connectives) whether it was a tautology (i.e., a logical truth);

(II) a system for deriving new formulæ (intuitively, the theorems) from given formulæ (PM's axioms) that was totally independent of semantic or logical categories like "constant" or "variable" or "connective", working on strings of symbols without reference to their potential meaning; and

(III) a proof that the set of tautologies as determined by (I) coincided with the set of derivable strings defined by (II).

For the limited portion of Whitehead and Russell's logic that he tackled, the propositional part, Post actually achieved that goal (see the abridged version of his PhD dissertation published as Post 1921). He planned to go on and complete the job of dealing with the whole of PM's logic, including its quantificational reasoning, in a postdoctoral year at Princeton, where he had obtained a Procter fellowship. In pursuit of that goal, he generalized his syntactical proof system further, and created a type of formal system that would revolutionize theoretical linguistics nearly 40 years later.

The system Post worked out in 1921 was not described in a publication until 1943, but there were reasons for that. The reasons had to do with a long battle against severe manic-depressive mental illness (now usually called bipolar disorder). Suffice it to say that the system was general enough that it could express any imaginable set of rules for deriving strings from other strings. Indeed, Post rapidly came to regard it as fully capturing the intuitive notion "set for which it is possible to envisage a way of systematically enumerating the membership". Today such a set is usually referred to as *recursively enumerable* (*r.e.*).

---

[2] Post's intellectual and personal biography is well documented in broad outline. Sources that I have consulted include Davis (1994a), Stillwell (2004), De Mol (2006), Urquhart (2009), and Jackson (2018).

Formalizing the inference rule Modus Ponens is a very simple application of Post's system. Assume a symbol inventory containing "⊃", ")", "(", and letters like p and q, and P_i are to be interpreted as indexed variables over unbounded strings. Assume that we have already been given some strings that do not need to be proved (intuitively, those correspond to axioms), and we are trying to build a list of other strings using them (those are the theorems). Then Modus Ponens says that if we can find a string on our list that has a "(" followed by some other stuff which we will call P_1, followed by the symbol "⊃", followed by some further stuff which we will call P_2, followed by a ")", and the stuff that we called P_1, on its own, is also on the list, then the stuff that we called P_2 can be added to the list.

The way Post put it was that a string of the form "(P_1 ⊃ P_2)" together with a string of the form "P_1" *produce* a string of the form "P_2".

Modus Ponens is an extremely simple application of the idea of building strings systematically on the basis of already obtained strings (though it was crucial for Post's PhD dissertation project). But in 1920–1921 as a Procter fellow at Princeton, Post started working on doing the rest of Whitehead and Russell's logic – the reasoning that involved quantifiers – and in connection with that he worked out a radical generalization of the notion of a rule of inference. There could be any finite number of "premise" lines, and both the premises and the conclusion could be of any finite length and contain any number of specified symbol strings and/or the variables over strings (P_1, P_2, etc.). He presented his generalized metaschema in a truly bewildering tableau. I give it here in a slightly modified form due to Davis (1982), which (believe it or not) makes things slightly clearer:

$$
\begin{array}{cccccccc}
g_{1,0} & P_{1,1} & g_{1,1} & P_{1,2} & \cdots & P_{1,n_1} & g_{1,n_1} \\
g_{2,0} & P_{2,1} & g_{2,1} & P_{2,2} & \cdots & P_{2,n_2} & g_{2,n_2} \\
& & \vdots & & \cdots & & \vdots \\
g_{k,0} & P_{k,1} & g_{k,1} & P_{k,2} & \cdots & P_{k,n_k} & g_{k,n_k} \\
& & & \Downarrow & & &
\end{array}
$$

$$
h_1 \; P_{r_1,s_1} \; h_2 \; P_{r_2,s_2} \quad \cdots \quad h_j \; P_{r_j,s_j} \; h_{j+1}
$$

Each of the g_i and h_i stand for specific strings of symbols that would be given in the production. The down arrow "$\Downarrow$" means "produce" in Post's sense. The r_i variables tell us which premise line a variable comes from, and the s_i tell us which variable we are talking about (counting from the left), so requiring the r_i to be between 1 and k (where k is the total number of premises) and requiring the s_i to be between 0 and n_{r_i} (where n_{r_i} is the total number of variables in the relevant line) guarantees that the last line will call only P_i variables that are present somewhere in the earlier lines. Thus everything in the conclusion must be either an explicitly specified string or something drawn from the material covered by the P variables of the premises. Hence the conclusion can say things like "put the content of the xth variable in premise number y into the conclusion at this point", while not allowing it to say "put in some random stuff at this point", which would make nonsense of the idea of representing logical reasoning.

I exhibit the above tableau merely to make the point that it represents a schema fully general enough to express arbitrary string edits. It is more than general enough to state anything from simple phrase structure rules (immediate constituent analysis), or categorial grammar rules, or Chomsky's most elaborate generalized transformations.

Thus a chapter of the history of formalism in mathematical logic turns out to relate to a crucial part of the prehistory of generative linguistics. For Post's specific design of a formalist proof system with axioms as inputs was to emerge later in Noam Chomsky's work under a new name: generative grammar.

Chomsky hit upon the idea of rewriting systems as a mathematical technique for giving syntactic descriptions of human languages some thirty years after Post developed his production systems. Late in 1951, in the revised version of his MA thesis,[3] Chomsky (1951: 3) used the verb "generate" for the relation between a grammar and a string of symbols – for the first time in linguistics, as far as I have been able to determine. By 1954 both Zellig Harris (1909–1992) and Charles Hockett (1916–2000) had used "generate" in the same way (see Harris 1954: 260 and Hockett 1954: 390). It is not clear whether they were influenced by Chomsky's usage, for although Chomsky had close contacts with Harris up to summer 1951, his December 1951 revision of the MA thesis was done during his first six months at the Society of Junior Fellows at Harvard (see Chomsky 1975: 26), and was little known before its publication by Garland in 1979 (Chomsky 1975: 30 says it met with an "almost total lack of interest"). By 1955 Chomsky had completed a first draft of *The Logical Structure of Linguistic Theory*, which proposed a theory of "generative grammars" in detail (though it was very little read at that time, and did not appear in print until twenty years later, as Chomsky 1975).

There is no citation or mention of Emil Post in Chomsky (1955–1956), but from 1959 onward Chomsky has occasionally mentioned Post's name as an earlier source for the prior use of "generate" in the mathematical literature. Chomsky (1959: 137n) notes that he is "following a familiar technical use of the term

---

[3]On the two versions of Chomsky's MA thesis *The Morphophonemics of Modern Hebrew*, see the very careful comparative study by Daniels (2010).

'generate' ", citing Post (1944), a paper that says almost nothing about how production systems work. The locus classicus on production systems is Post (1943), a paper which Chomsky has never cited, probably because (as conjectured by Urquhart 2009: 471), he learned about Post's work mainly or entirely from secondary sources like the 1950 mathematical logic text by Paul C. Rosenbloom (1920–2005), which is cited in Chomsky (1975). In Chomsky's hands over the following six decades, production systems, under the new name "generative grammars", became the overwhelmingly dominant type of framework for the study of syntax.

2 Rules

With generative grammars firmly established as mainstream in linguistics, both linguists and philosophers commonly speak as if generative grammars of the sort that Chomsky advocates contain something like rules of grammar of the traditional kind – "The verb agrees with the subject" and so on. Chomsky even had an early paper called "On the notion 'rule of grammar' ", which might tempt anyone to think that he was dealing with rules in some antecedently understood sense. I am not aware of anyone who has pointed out that it is simply not true. Linguists have completely overlooked a key fact about generative grammars: that they do not consist of rules in any sense that would be recognized by traditional grammarians or non-linguists like philosophers.

The ordinary intuitive understanding of a rule is something that we can follow (that is, behave in a way that complies with it) or break (that is, violate or disobey it). It defines a regular pattern or practice, a way of "going on in the same way". But nothing of the content of a generative grammar has anything like this character. Chomsky actually recognizes this when he comes to respond to the discussion of rule-following in Kripke (1982) and observes that "we would not say, as scientists, that a person follows the rule of phrase structure" formulated as "VP → V NP Clause" (Chomsky 1986: 243). A rule of this sort (a context-free phrase structure rule, to be technical about it) is often thought of as saying "a verb phrase may consist of a verb followed by a noun phrase followed by a complement clause", but in fact it means nothing of the kind. The presence of such a "rule" in a generative grammar neither says nor implies that a VP always contains a V followed by a NP and a Clause in that order. It does not even say that this is possible. It does not entail that a VP always contains a V, or even that it may contain a V. These things may be true in a grammar with such a "rule", or they may not. Everything depends on what the rest of the grammar says.

There could be a transformational "rule" that always shifts v to the end of vp (as with the "universal base" analyses of the early 1970s that derived even sov languages from vso underlying structures), or the v could be shifted out of the vp altogether (as in much more recent transformational analyses). In either case there would never be a vp containing a v with an np following it. Nothing is fixed by any individual statement in the grammar. Only the entire grammar, taken holistically, does anything at all; and what it does is to provide an instantaneous description of the entire set of well-formed sentences. No part of the grammar expresses any generalization about the shape of expressions in the language.

Through all of the last 60 years of linguistics, and especially the discussion of linguistics among philosophers, there has been talk of Chomsky-style generative grammars containing "rules" that is completely counter to the way generative grammars actually work. If we take a rule to be a statement that expresses some generalization about the form of linguistic expressions, then no proper subpart of a generative grammar, of any scope or size, is a rule or contains a rule.[4]

What I have said about phrase structure rules holds also for transformations. *Wh*-movement cannot be followed or complied with. A transformation saying "move a *wh*-marked phrase to the beginning of the clause" does *not* say that the language has clause-initial *wh*-words. The language might or might not exhibit them: there could be another transformation that moves them back again (the device known as "reconstruction" in post-1980 transformational grammar does exactly that when mapping s-structures to logical form), or a transformation that moves them to the very end of the sentence, or a rule that simply expunges them completely (which is actually what happens in bare relatives like *the one I want*). Everything depends on the rest of the grammar and how all of its components interact.

It is very important, therefore, not to assume when we talk about people following particular rules, or languages having particular rules, that "rule" refers to anything found in a generative grammar. The non-technical and informal notion

---

[4]We can see a partial exception in the case of Chomsky (1981), *Lectures on Government and Binding* (lgb), but that is precisely because it is not fully generative (in the narrow sense of that term I assume here). In lgb, modules of grammar of a completely different sort are introduced. When the "binding theory" says that anaphors (like reflexive pronouns) must be bound in their governing category, it actually is talking about something that has to hold within the structure of any expression. It says that an np node with a reflexive pronoun as its lexical realization always has a coindexed node that c-commands it in the tree (roughly, is closer to the root, and dominated by a node that also dominates the reflexive pronoun). This use in lgb of what linguists often call "constraints" is a departure that Chomsky made from his earlier theoretical work. It disappeared again after 1990 with the appearance of his "minimalist program".

of a rule is valuable (indeed, in my view it is essential), but it simply cannot be equated with any pieces or elements of generative grammars.

3 Normativity

What I have just said entails that we are in a certain amount of difficulty when we come to consider the issue of whether the claims made by a grammar are (or are not) *normative*. A normative statement is one that deals not with how things are but how they ought to be, or how it is appropriate for them to be given some set of values. Nothing in a generative grammar has that property.

Some philosophers in effect question whether normativity can arise in a physical universe. How could any physical distribution of elementary particles constitute a situation in which some things (drawn from an indefinitely large range) are objectively "good", or "beautiful", or "right"? Such reflections lead to moral antirealist views under which ethical statements like "That is morally wrong" or "You should apologize" are regarded as having more in common with grunts or cries of pain than truth-evaluable statements like "This is made of gold".

My own views in metaethics incline towards moral realism. But at least one philosophically inclined linguist assumes we have to accept antirealist error theories of ethics. Replying to an article in which I mentioned that I think claims about grammaticality are normative (Pullum 2007), Geoffrey Sampson remarked:

> I was at least assuming that grammatical description consists of statements that are correct or incorrect: but correctness is not a concept applicable to the domains of ethics or aesthetics. (As it is often put in the case of ethics, "you cannot derive an ought from an is".) (Sampson 2007: 112)

Sampson is assuming that claims like "Torturing children is wrong" or "Bach's music is beautiful" are not even truth-apt, and he thinks that my passing mention of ethics and aesthetics has committed me to the view that claims about grammaticality are likewise not statements of objective fact. This is of course nothing like what I believe. But it is instructive to read Sampson's views (restated in Sampson and Babarczy 2014: 96–99), because they are a reminder of how difficult the philosophical clarification of descriptive linguistics is going to be. While extreme prescriptivists seem to think that a construction can be held to be grammatically incorrect no matter how much natural usage conflicts with that claim, Sampson represents the opposite pole, apparently holding that the only objective claims about language concern what has occurred in a corpus, and statements about what is grammatical or ungrammatical do not even have truth conditions.

Let me start by attempting to be clear about what I think normativity is. Normativity is generally taken primarily as a property of statements, and then derivatively as a property of domains or subject matters in which normative statements are the appropriate mode of discourse (see Millar 2004: 93–96 for a careful discussion of how the two are related).

The claims of geology are not normative; the system of table manners is. Number theory is not a normative discipline; ethics is. Aeronautical engineering is not normative; aesthetics is.[5]

Millar (2004: 92–99) points out that all the classic cases of normativity involve normative statements providing reasons for doing, feeling, believing, desiring, or intending something. I believe grammatical normativity falls together with the classic cases. "It is not good table manners to lick your knife" offers a reason for not licking your knife; "Torturing children is wrong" implies a reason for not torturing children; "Bach's music is beautiful" suggests a reason for planning to attend a Bach concert; "Attributive adjectives expressing colour always follow the noun in French" provides a reason for positioning colour adjectives after the noun when seeking to be regarded as using normal French.

4 Prescriptivism

Touching on a rule of grammar that defines how to a speaker ought to position French adjectives brings us inevitably to a consideration of prescriptive grammars. Some discussion cannot be avoided, though in fact I will not have much truck with prescriptivism here. I make a terminological distinction that is not standard: although many have referred to old-fashioned "don't-do-this" grammar and usage books as "normative grammar", and many have said that normative statements are prescriptive rather than descriptive, I am going to use "normative" and "prescriptive" quite differently.

With respect to the grammatical rules for a human language (especially one with a high-prestige standard variety), there is a crucial distinction between two stances or attitudes:

- *descriptive* grammar involves the identification and statement of the rules or constraints that define the linguistic system (rules and constraints that I am going to argue are normative);

---

[5]Logic is a rather interesting case, since on the one hand we want to say that it is a plain and undeniable fact that $P \rightarrow Q$ is logically equivalent to $Q \vee \neg P$, but on the other hand it also seems right and proper to reason logically rather than illogically. There is a philosophical literature on this but, regrettably, exploring it is beyond the scope of this chapter.

   – *prescriptive* grammar involves the issuing of injunctions or opinions or exhortations about what system ought to be used, or judging how well or poorly some use of language complies with a given system.

Prescriptivist grammarians certainly see language as a normative domain, but not in the way I am interested in. What primarily marks out prescriptivists is that they see their role as advising or instructing or cajoling other language users to alter their linguistic behaviour. They want to change the way we speak and write, to lead us out of error and towards the correct path.

We can set aside here the fact that prescriptivists often have the rules wrongly conceived or wrongly formulated. They often doggedly maintain the validity of rules that do not match what they profess to regard as excellent usage, such as the usage of people they explicitly admire (Orwell, Strunk, White, whoever). Often it can be shown that they defend a rule which they unknowingly and constantly violate in their own writing, which one might have thought was a knock-down drag-out argument that the rule cannot be right, at least for their own English. They never accept such arguments, preferring to insist, irrationally, that even their own usage is to be condemned if it does not comply with the fictive rule. And they invariably ignore grammatical differences between dialects, treating non-standard English *He don't never come here no more* as simply incorrect standard English, as if it were a poorly executed attempt at saying *He does not ever come here any more*, when in truth languages or dialects that have negative concord working-class and low-prestige dialects of English around the world fall together with standard Italian, standard Polish, and other languages in which repeated morphological expressions of negation reinforce each other rather than cancelling out.

But all of this is basically a side issue, because even if the prescriptivists had all the rules exactly right, their enterprise would still be quite distinct from that of descriptive linguistics. They are in the critical and advisory business of evaluating language use as good or bad. I am not.

John Searle draws a relevant distinction (in his book *Speech Acts*, 1969) between *constitutive* and *regulative* rules. Constitutive rules define or set up the activities to which they apply; regulative rules are established to govern an activity that can proceed independently of them and in defiance of them. Knocking other marathon runners down in order to get ahead of them is still clearly running in a marathon, because the rule that we should not use physical violence against other runners in a marathon is regulative. But moving a knight six squares directly towards the other end of the board is not playing chess: the rule that a knight moves to a second-nearest square of opposite colour is constitutive.

Prescriptivists take grammatical rules to be regulative. Criticizing other people's linguistic behaviour and attempting to get them to modify it is the goal. That has nothing to do with my topic here, so I want to simply set the prescriptive stance aside.

The question I am concerned with is whether the *descriptive* view of grammar also involves a normative perspective of what the subject matter is.

What suggests normativity in the subject matter of grammar, more specifically syntax, is the fact that there is (or at least, linguists assume there is) a distinction between well-formed and ill-formed expressions, and it holds over an indefinitely large range, certainly far too large for it to be a matter of list membership.

What a grammar has to do is not to summarize some finite set of observations or facts, but to use all available evidence to discover a definition, over an indefinitely large class of candidate objects (potential expressions), of the difference between those that are good or properly structured in the language under study and those that are bad or improperly structured.

This does not mean that linguistics fails to be empirical (contrary to Sampson's assumption). Its task is to find out what the right constraints are, and that is not an a priori matter. It can only be done empirically, ultimately by reference to the usual behaviours and reactions of the native users of the language when distractions and irrelevant extraneous factors do not intrude. This is true despite the fact that both intuitions and corpus attestations are fallible sources of evidence. The epistemology is therefore subtle. I have suggested elsewhere (see Pullum 2017) that it should be seen as based on the method of reflective equilibrium.

The way generative linguists usually view it, the grammar has to cover all the expressions of the language, and only those expressions, and it must do it in a way that tells us the status of novel expressions – expressions we have never encountered before. That means making a description that is fully explicit about how the expressions of the language – all of them, however many there may be – are structured. And that calls for some kind of formalization of both the representation mode and the grammatical rule system.

5 Formalization

What I mean when I refer to formalization in syntax is simply *the use of mathematical and logical tools to make theoretical claims more explicit*. Talk about formalization is therefore not essentially connected to the "formalist" programme. It has nothing to do with de-emphasizing the semantic, pragmatic, rhetorical, or aesthetic aspects of human languages, or with assigning more importance to form than to function, or with Carnap's project of eliminating meaning from the language of science, or with Hilbert's doomed project of reducing all of mathematics to questions of logical truth in some decidable formal logic.

The tools that formally inclined linguists have borrowed from logic for use in framing syntactic theories over the last few decades have included rewriting systems, automata, graphs (most importantly trees), and model theory. More recently, 21st-century linguistics has been increasingly employing tools from statistics and probability theory.

But there is truth in the familiar remark about how to a three-year-old with a hammer everything looks like a nail. Syntacticians have become so completely engrossed in working with generative grammars that they see everything in terms of derivations, and cannot conceive of what life would be like in any other terms.

They have paid very little attention to the fact that a generative grammar of *L* says absolutely nothing about the structural properties of any non-sentence of *L*. They have ignored the fact that the sharp boundaries of any set defined by a generative grammar fly in the face of the widely accepted intuitive view of ill-formedness as gradient – the fact that one ungrammatical sentence can be more ungrammatical than another.

They have also paid little or no attention to the fact that a generative grammar makes syntactic properties depend crucially on the contents of a finite lexicon: a derivation that does not terminate in a string of items belonging to the relevant lexicon is not a derivation at all, so there is no way for a generative grammar to represent an example like Carnap's *Pirots karulize elatically* as grammatical unless the lexicon contains a noun *pirot*, a verb *karulize*, and an adverb *elatically* – which for standard English it does not.

These are not problems for formalized syntax in general. For one thing, when we are talking about the invented languages of logic and computer programming, the worries I just expressed about generative grammars turn into virtues. For proving theorems about logical systems – completeness, consistency, compactness – it is absolutely crucial that the formulæ of the logic should be sharply defined to form a specific set with a known cardinality. And for proving correctness of a computer program, the same is true. There can be no gradient levels of ill-formedness, or potential tolerance of minor deviance, or uncertainty about the finite list of allowable symbols, when we are talking about logics or programming languages. This is the grain of truth in Michael Tomasello's capsule summary of "Chomskian generative grammar" (2003: 5), which he says is "a 'formal' theory, meaning that it is based on the supposition that natural languages are like formal languages". In a way, though I suspect not in the way he intended, he is correct.[6]

The sense in which generative grammars do treat natural languages like formal languages has to do with the origins of their formal machinery, as already outlined. It was developed for a specific purpose within mathematical logic (formalizing formation rules and inference rules in a fully general way), and it is perfectly suited to the description of the invented languages for logic, metalogic, and computer programming. But it is important that there are ways of making grammars mathematically explicit that are quite distinct from the generative one. Chomsky has sometimes confusingly denied this point, claiming (as in, e.g., Chomsky 1966: 12) that for him the term "generative grammar" means nothing more than "explicit account of sound/meaning correspondences", but this does not square at all with his actual usage (Ney 1993 argues this point at length). Pullum & Scholz (2001) use the term "generative-enumerative syntax" to stress that the referent is syntax formalized in terms of nondeterministic random enumerators; their paper discusses certain types of explicit grammar that are not generative in this sense.

The non-generative mode of formalizing grammars that Pullum and Scholz discuss uses model theory rather than rewriting systems to formalize syntactic description. Grammatical rules are taken to be constraints on the structure sentences, in a straightforward and informally comprehensible sense: the constraints in a model-theoretic grammar for English would say things that for convenience we can readily paraphrase in English. A few examples:

- A preposition phrase has a preposition as head.

- A lexical head is the initial subconstituent of its parent.

- A pronoun subject of a finite clause takes its nominative case form.

Such constraints can be stated more precisely as formulæ of a logic; a grammar can be defined as a finite set of such formulæ; structures of sentences can be taken to be the models for the interpretation of that logic; and grammaticality can be reconstructed as satisfaction of the constraints in the grammar, in the model-theoretic sense.

---

[6]The rest of his summary is inaccurate and confused. He says generative grammar uses "a unified set of abstract algebraic rules" (they are actually of diverse types, not at all unified); and they "are both meaningless themselves and insensitive to the meanings of the elements they algorithmically combine" (but algebraic operations always need interpretations, as McCawley 1968 carefully shows, and grammar rules can be written to build semantic representations simultaneously with syntactic ones, as in Montague 1973, Montague 1974 or Gazdar et al. 1985). Finally he says the rules come with "a lexicon containing meaningful linguistic elements that serve as variables in the rules" (but I see no sense in which lexical items serve as variables).

For additional concreteness, we can look very briefly at the syntax of preposition phrases (PPs) in English. A typical old-fashioned generative grammar would include a phrase structure rule like this:

(1)   PP $\longrightarrow$ P   NP

Under its standard interpretation this licenses derivational steps in which the symbol "PP" is replaced by the sequence "P NP", and derivatively licenses the building of (part of) a tree diagram that looks like this:

(2)

$$
\begin{array}{c}
\text{PP} \\
\diagup\diagdown \\
\text{P} \quad \text{NP}
\end{array}
$$

We might easily think that the rule entails that prepositions always have NP complements. It does not. There could be (and in fact for English there will need to be) other rules in the grammar saying things like this:

(3)   a. PP $\longrightarrow$ P   PP
      b. PP $\longrightarrow$ P   Clause

So some PPs will not have NP right branches. And we might easily think that the rule at least says that those prepositions that do take NP complements precede their NP complements. But it does not entail that either. There could be another rule in the grammar saying this (where ε is a symbol representing the null string):

(4)   PP $\longrightarrow$ ε

In that case there might be no prepositions appearing in the language at all. Or there could be a transformational rule like this:

(5)   X   -   P   -   NP   -   Y
      1   -   2   -   3   -   4 $\Longrightarrow$ 1   -   3   +   2   -   4

In that case prepositions would always be suffixed to their NP complements – unless some other rule in the grammar tampered with things further. This is what I am referring to when I say that the grammar provides its definition holistically: in the same way that we are told that in the Brexit negotiations nothing is agreed until everything is agreed, with a generative grammar we do not know anything about what any part of the grammar determines about any part of a sentence until we know what the entire grammar yields.

We might easily fall into the error of thinking that the rule "PP → P NP" does say that a PP always contains a P. But it does not do that either. It does not guarantee anything about the interior of PPs. There could be another rule in the grammar saying "PP → A B C".

Under the view I favour, the conditions on PPs would be stated directly as constraints – and for concreteness we can take them to be constraints on the structure of trees.

Assume a predicate logic in which we quantify over nodes with variables $x, y, z \ldots$ and have a vocabulary of monadic predicates for category labels and binary relations for grammatical functions. We write "$B(x)$" to mean "node x is labelled with category label B" and "$F(x, y)$" to mean "the F of node x is node y" (i.e., "node y bears the grammatical function F to its parent node x"). Then the constraint saying that PPs have P heads would be expressed precisely in this way:

(6) $\forall x[PP(x) \rightarrow \exists y[\text{Head}(x, y) \wedge P(y)]]$

And if we write Lexical(x) to mean "node x bears a lexical category label", "Parent(y, x)" to mean "x immediately dominates y", and "$x < y$" to mean "node x is to the left of node y", then the second constraint above, stating that lexical category nodes are initial in their phrases, can be stated like this:

(7) $\forall x, y[\text{Head}(x, y) \wedge \text{Lexical}(y) \rightarrow \forall z[\text{Parent}(z, x) \rightarrow x < z]]$

Any set of trees characterized by a set of first-order logic formulæ in this sort of way will be a regular set of trees (recognizable by a finite-state tree automaton) and its string yield will be a context-free stringset (these results are corollaries of theorems now found in textbooks of finite model theory like Ebbinghaus & Flum 1999 and Libkin 2004). By giving a finite set of first-order logic statements interpreted on tree models in this way, we explicitly characterize a set of trees and thereby a context-free set of strings. We are in effect giving a formally explicit model for a context-free language without using a context-free generative grammar. I argue elsewhere (Pullum 2013) that this yields significant advantages.

I point all this out merely in order to establish the point that normative principles like those stated informally in English above can be made fully precise and become, without change, a formalized grammar with precise consequences, known parsability results, etc. I am in no doubt that it is worth pursuing the goal of making the syntactic structural principles for human languages fully explicit – formalizing them using the tools of logic and mathematics.

On the other hand, I do not believe that by formalizing some version of the grammar rules for a language we are thereby defining a hypothesis about the mind – ultimately the brain structure – of an idealized native speaker of that language. Kripke (1982) believes there are profound difficulties for this basically Chomskyan view, because there seems to be no way to identify the unique set of rules that guides a given speaker's grasp of their native language: indefinitely many grammars would account for all of the utterances they have produced (or judged acceptable) in the past, and nothing identifiable about the speaker in question can be said to fix the structure that will be revealed in further utterances as the speaker goes on.

I think Scholz (1990) was right to elaborate on Kripke's worry, and argue that we do not obtain an explanation of *S*'s linguistic capabilities simply by saying "*S* has a mentally inscribed representation of the generative grammar *G* in his brain". And I think Chomsky is wrong in responding to Kripke by denying that there is any normative aspect to grammar (see Chomsky 1986: chap. 4).

What I am suggesting is that we are better placed to see how there can be a normative conception of grammar that is not prey to Kripke's metphysical worries if we conceptualize grammar in model-theoretic terms, as approximate compliance with certain structural constraints on the form of sentences.

It might also assuage the worries expressed by Riemer (Chapter 9, this volume) concerning a kind of authoritarianism that he sees as stemming from the ideas of generative grammar. Imagining that there is some unique generative mechanism that is the mental and ultimately neurophysiological reality underlying the capacity to use English, and teaching students about it as if it were unique, he feels, is inimical to the idea that this complex world can be viewed from many divergent perspectives. It might even militate against our students feeling that they have the intellectual freedom to explore alternatives, and to encourage belief in an authority that could be "argued to replicate and so to normalize, in the domain of education, the kinds of relations of social domination on which contemporary political orders rest" (this volume, p. 225).

The relevance of the model-theoretic approach to Riemer's problem is that it is by no means necessary that to adopt the "unique form hypothesis" that he sees as implicit in standard generativism. Indeed, I see absolutely no reason to believe that one unique, correct set of constraints defines English (or any other language), or that there is one correct way of formally expressing the content of such a set. What is needed for someone to be a competent user of English is not that they have some ideal and perfect constraint set (or generative system) neurochemically implanted in their brain, but merely that they have developed a set of constraints on grammatical form that, to a good approximation, leads them to structure their utterances in ways much like the way other speakers of

English structure theirs. There will be indefinitely many ways to do this, and indefinitely many ways to represent formally what has been done. Let a hundred flowers blossom and a hundred schools of thought contend. I regard it as eminently plausible that among the vast population of native speakers of English, millions of slightly different systems of constraints contend. The reason this is not problematic is that all we need for linguistically expressed communication to be possible is substantial overlap in the consequences of the different systems. And the slight differences between the ways the constraints are defined and realized will of course be the seeds of future linguistic change.

One further thing I should say about normativity concerns the notion of universal grammar. Here the issue of normativity may not be relevant at all. Modern linguistics since Chomsky (1965) has stressed the goal of formulating a theory of *universal* grammar (UG). This theory has been taken to be not just a systematization of the facts that have been discovered to hold for all human languages, but a kind of ideal model of the human infant's capacity for learning languages. And it is important that UG could in principle be an entirely non-normative domain: it could be a description of a set of neurophysiologically instantiated devices or of a psychological organization.

I do not regard this as plausible or well supported, because of the lack of any account of mechanisms. How does UG constrain the growth of grammars? We know how the curved horns of a ram grow (faster-growing cells on one side and slower-growing on the other), but nothing at all about how UG works or develops in the brain. And more recent work tells us nothing that helps (the literature on what some have been calling "biolinguistics" over the past decade seems to me increasingly to be parodying itself).

But we can set aside the issue of whether there might be a serious theory of the biological aspects of the human language acquisition capacity. I am concerned here simply with understanding grammars of individual languages. This will be necessary regardless of whether the human capacity to form and use them is constrained by a built-in UG. It is by no means clear to me that any non-normative, naturalistic, neurophysiological account of the parochial grammars of specific languages makes sense.

It is uncontroversial that the mentally inscribed grammar that Chomsky posits does not (i) describe all the utterances that have occurred in the past, or (ii) predict what utterances will occur in the future, or (iii) identify the probabilities of occurrence for future utterances, or (iv) make us do whatever it is we do when we produce an utterance or understand one. Assuming that *Fetch quickly it* is ungrammatical, for example, the correct statement of the grammatical rules of

English does not imply (i) that no one has ever said it, or (ii) that no one will ever say it, or (iii) that the probability of its being uttered is low, or (iv) that we ought not to utter it.

The implication of a grammar defining something as ungrammatical is closer to being that no one *should* say it if they want to be taken as speaking English as it is usually spoken. What kind of "should" is that? Well, it should be clear enough that we are not talking about anything closely analogous to the moral sense of "should". Moral philosophers standardly take morality to be universal. Certainly for a moral realist (and moral realism is the metaethical view that I would subscribe to), torturing a child is not immoral just for certain people in certain circumstances though possibly moral in other cultures or under other circumstances; it is morally wrong for everyone. Someone who disagrees is simply mistaken. Societies and cultures can evolve, and come to see that moral views they held earlier were mistaken,

But essentially none of the rules in the grammar of a particular language can be taken to hold universally. There are some 7,000 extant languages, differing quite radically in grammar as well as lexicon. No one of them is more grammatically correct in its structures than any of the others. In matters of grammar we have to be radically relativist.

Morality also relates to behaviour in a way that has consequences for human actions. From the fact that torturing a child is immoral it follows that we ought not to torture a child. But from the fact that *Fetch quickly it* is ungrammatical in English nothing at all follows concerning what anyone ought to do or not do. Whether we ought to utter it will depend entirely on the circumstances. During a minute of silence at a funeral, we ought not to utter it, or anything else. But if we are playing a foreign character in a play and the script has your character saying *Fetch quickly it*, then at the relevant point we ought to utter it.

This issue has sometimes been discussed in the philosophy literature, in the context of the normativity of meaning. Philosophers of language are in fact maddeningly uniform in their habit of talking only about reference of words – as if all we ever do with our language were pronounce the word "cat" and successfully achieve reference thereby to a creature of the species *Felis silvestris catus*, and as if that were the deepest and most interesting thing about language. But even there, saying that *cat* refers to a certain animal species in the Felidae family does not mean that we ought to describe cats by using that word. Even if we do want to refer to the creatures, we might want to use *moggy* or *pussy* or *foul razor-clawed mewing beast from hell*. And we have no obligation to talk about cats or refer to them at all if we do not choose to.

My concern here is not with elementary lexical meaning but with syntax. How-ever, it just as clear that no syntactic rule or constraint or principle conveys any obligation or presumption about how we should act.

For one thing, the constraints of syntax mostly involve categories and restric-tions and classifications of which we have no conscious knowledge whatsoever, so typically we could never know whether we had violated them or not. And almost everyone agrees that "ought" implies "can", of course: it is generally not taken as coherent to assert that we have a duty to do something that we are totally incapable of doing.

This point offers a clue to some understanding of what the prescriptivists are up to. They peddle rules that, while not a correct reflection of the actual syn-tax of the language, are fairly easy for even linguistically unsophisticated people to check: never place an adverb between infinitival *to* and a plain-form verb (*to boldly go*), never end a sentence with a preposition (*What are you looking at?*), never begin a sentence with *however*, avoid the passive, etc. Such rules are hope-less as a guide to how to actually use the language like a normal person, but they have become cultural markers of attention to grammar. Most people are not aware of how inaccurate they are or how much they are ignored by truly accomplished writers, and it is moderately easy to identify violations.

Prescriptivists fail in some of their identifications: they mistake particles for prepositions, and mistake existentials or predicative adjective constructions for passives, and so on; but they *think* they are correctly applying genuine rules, and they see a kind of quasi-moral force to the rules: they see the people who do not respect the rules as falling short of the standards of behaviour that society ought to maintain and enforce. In other words, they see the rules of grammar as regulative.

Domains involving obligations on agents to act (or not act) in certain ways are not the only domain for normativity. Neither constitutive nor regulative rules of a game have any connection to anything about obligations. We are not obliged to play the game at all, for one thing, so the rule defining a knight's move certainly does not say we should or should not move any particular knight.

Moreover, making an illegal move is not something we "shouldn't do" in abso-lute terms; whether we should do it depends on the circumstances. We might be playing against a sadistic jailer, with the life of a fellow prisoner forfeited if we lose, in which case we *should* make the illegal move if we can get away with it and it will ensure a win.

What we should *do*, if "should" has anything like the sense it has in connection with morality or similar kinds of obligation, has nothing whatever to do with the normative force of linguistic rules.

I should also note that the rules of syntax do not have normative force in any *instrumental* way: it is not that they should be obeyed because bad things will happen if they are not obeyed, or because following them will enable one to get things that one needs. There is sometimes hint of this in naive talk about language and how we learn it: people talk about needing to make oneself understood in order to interact satisfactorily with other people. But in fact there is very little pressure to get things right grammatically. There are people who live most of their lives speaking mostly in a language that is not their native language, and speaking it very badly. They still find ways to get what they want.

And perhaps the starkest and most obvious refutation of the instrumental view comes from looking at the actual facts of human infants' experience: while they are incapable of speech they are constantly looked after, and all their needs are met, but once they are four or five and can speak and understand they start being expected to do things that other people want them to do. The idea that we speak the way we do because we have to on instrumental grounds is nonsense.

6 Understanding

The normative rules of games and linguistic systems do not define anything as unethical, or contemptible, or inadvisable, or evil. But I think what they do can be elucidated in terms of the very interesting work of Alan Millar in *Understanding People* (2004), cited above. Millar stresses the notion of a *commitment* to follow rules: he separates the *following* of rules from the *commitment* to follow them.

It is important that there can be tacitly acknowledged rules that no one has set down in detail. Management of phone calls is an example. Nowhere is it set down that when a call is connected the recipient of the call is supposed to speak first, or that normally the maker of the call is supposed to instigate the ending of the call, or that the recipient speaks last (echoing the goodbye of the maker of the call). The fact that a certain set of rules is tacit does not preclude the existence of a practice based on them.

This is the potential answer to the problem with Crispin Wright's observation about effortless first-person authority: we do not appear to have that for syntax, in the general case. We can have tacit command of a rule that one cannot state, and the fact that we cannot state it does not mean we cannot recognize departures from what it requires.

What the tacitly acknowledged rules of grammar do is to define certain ways of structuring expressions and associating them with meanings. Millar put it this way in the handout for a talk at the University of Edinburgh in 2010:

The commitments incurred by participation in a practice have a closely analogous structure to those incurred by beliefs and intentions. Participating in a practice, G, incurs a commitment to following the rules of G. To a first approximation that amounts to it being the case that one ought to avoid continuing to participate in G while not following the rules of G. [... T]here are two ways to discharge the commitment – by withdrawing from the practice and by complying with the rules.

Rules of grammar that define expressions as being structured in certain ways do not entail that we ought to structure our expressions in those ways.

We do incur a commitment to structure our expressions in the English way when we decide to speak English. But incurring a commitment to do something does not entail that we ought to do it. Sometimes the way to deal with a commitment that we incur by engaging in a certain practice is to cease engaging in the practice.

Millar uses the example of offensive ethnic terms to illustrate the point that the existence of a practice says nothing about what we ought to do: *Chink* in English is an offensive epithet meaning "Chinese person". But the existence of a practice of saying *Chink* to mean "Chinese person" does not imply that anyone ought to use the term: most would say the opposite is true.

It is not by any means as easy to illustrate the same sort of thing in syntax, but I think it is possible. Consider the fact that it is usual for the direct object to follow the verb in what the *Cambridge Grammar of the English Language* (Huddleston & Pullum 2002) calls canonical clauses:

(8) a. The old tree shades the house.
  b. * The old tree the house shades.

That rule codifies a certain practice, applying the generalization to an indefinitely large range of expressions, not just recording properties of previous utterances. It has normative force in that it defines it as syntactically incorrect to put the object before the verb. If we do not put the object before the verb, other things being equal, we are not respecting the constraints of English syntax. But it does not follow that anyone ought to place any direct object before any verb. A person might have reason not to respect the constraints of English syntax. For example, someone might be imitating the poetry of the eighteenth or nineteenth centuries, where the long-extinct order with object before verb was often employed.

One might well ask what point there could be to having rules that do not have to be obeyed. This would be like having rules of the road that nobody has to follow. The rules of the road at least have instrumental motivation relating to safety, but in the case of grammar we do not even have that. Millar (handout) in effect answers that question when he says:

> On the view I am promoting it is our participation in practices and our ability to recognize what these require in particular situations that enables us both to make reasonable predictions about, and make sense of, what people think and do. The basic idea is simple. Because we know how people are supposed to act we can often make sense of how they do act and how they are likely to act.

In talking about making sense Millar is not necessarily to be interpreted as referring to the understanding of meaning, either semantic or pragmatic. The point has nothing inherently to do with the correct apprehension of literal meaning or perceiving the utterer's intended meaning, though it may apply to those accomplishments, and it may not even imply those abilities. I am breaking with the usual practice among philosophers of language in wanting to talk about syntax.

The understanding I am alluding to is simply a matter of making sense of what is going on linguistically: what sort of system the interlocutor is using, what to expect, what to infer about the intent of a speaker or the likely form of further utterances.

Understanding of meaning is neither necessary nor sufficient for the syntactic ability I am talking about. It is not necessary because it is often possible to grasp the structure of an uttered sentence without having the vaguest clue as to its meaning. Faced with something like *I doubt whether that is not necessarily not untrue*, most people are aware that they have heard something grammatical but they cannot work out the truth conditions of a quadruple negation. And we can immediately perceive the grammaticality of *Appearances are not deceptive, it only seems as if they are*; working out from its meaning whether it is sensible or contradictory is much harder. But it is also not sufficient: being able to extract the meaning does not imply grasping the syntactic structure. We often correctly identify intended meanings despite massive non-compliance with syntax: if a worried stranger says "*Me need you help! Me house go fire!*" we would know what was meant.

However, it remains true that if we follow the practice of ordering words and structuring phrases and clauses in the English manner, and our interlocutor understands us to be following that practice, they can make sense of certain aspects of our intentions that otherwise would be inscrutable to them, and they can make much better guesses at why our linguistic behaviour is the way it is, and what to expect in future utterances. They can assume that if we begin an utterance with an auxiliary verb and continue with a nominative pronoun (*Can we...*; *Is he...*; *Will they...*) we are beginning a closed interrogative, and thus that we will probably continue with a verb phrase, and are probably about to ask a question with a yes/no answer, and are likely to have made the assumption that they know the answer to the question, and so on.

If we depart from the usual practices, that does not necessarily mean that we should not have, or that we have made a mistake. If our interlocutor detects that we have departed from the usual grammatical practices, they can simply regard us as having ceased to operate in accord with the usual rules, and they can reason about why that might be and what they should assume from now on. A normal context is one where we appear to be respecting the same constraints on sentence structure as they would, and using words they have encountered before, so they assume we are using the same language, and they turn out to be right. But there are also anomalous contexts, such as one in which a native speaker who is required to draft a forced confession by the agents of a foreign dictatorship puts subtle syntactic mistakes into the text to signal that he is under duress, intending people back home to spot that he is not complying with the usual constraints.

There are any number of reasons why we might depart from normal syntax: we might be half asleep, drunk, delirious, brain-damaged, interrupted, distracted, foreign, playful, joking, impersonating someone. But if our interlocutor can see *why* we have departed from the usual grammatical practices, they may be able to understand what is going on with us. Otherwise, we become mysterious. But it is of course our right to be mysterious if we want to: the fact that grammatical constraints have normative force does not impose on us, even as a default, any obligation to obey.

7 Conclusion

What I have tried to do in this rather wide-ranging survey is to make the following points. I have stressed that the formalist movement in logic had an important rationale: representing logical proof in a totally syntactic way so that the completeness and consistency of a logical language (the correspondence between its resources for proof and its efficacy in preserving truth under inference) could be mathematically verified. It was in pursuit of this goal that Emil Post invented the systems we now call generative grammars, the systems that were repurposed three decades later for use in linguistics.

Though talk of "rules of grammar" persisted in linguistics, even in Chomsky's work, it did not really make sense within a generative perspective (as Chomsky himself noticed): rewriting operations are *not* rules in the sense that we can follow them, behave in accordance with them, be guided by them, or violate them. Yet we do need a conception of rules with normative force in the ordinary sense of rules that can be respected or violated, for the point of linguistic grammars is not to compactly represent a corpus or to characterize a mental organ, but to define well-formedness over an indefinitely large class of sentences.

The claim that rules of grammar have normative force should not be confused with the bid to change people's linguistic habits and practices represented by the prescriptive grammar tradition. And it should also not be taken to be at odds with the empirical character of linguistics (there is a fact of the matter about whether English is a prepositional or a postpositional language), or to be in conflict with the goal of making the predictions of grammars fully clear and explicit, with help from tools from logic and mathematics.

I believe that generative grammars (the systems that Post invented) were the wrong tool to pick, but there are alternatives. Repurposing model theory for syntactic description, for example, is a better idea. Under that view grammars are finite sets of constraints on structure, and well-formedness is construed as model-theoretic satisfaction. An early work advocating this view was Johnson & Postal (1980). Rogers (1998) develops it in a much more technically sophisticated way, and uses the model-theoretic perspective to derive some fascinating insights concerning what generative grammars of early 1980s vintage actually claimed (they were in fact strongly equivalent to context-free phrase structure grammars). A small but growing minority of syntacticians have been further developing the idea that formal grammars could be developed along model-theoretic lines (see Pullum & Scholz 2001 and Pullum 2013 for discussion and references).

As to how formalized constraints on sentence structure can have normative force without in any sense implying anything about what anyone should do, or implying any judgment on a person that they have done something wrong (or right), I think the work to turn to is that of Millar (2004), who (as briefly recounted above) relates the normativity of rules in certain kinds of systems not in what we ought to do but in what can make our words or actions more predictable to others. Weaving together the strands I have briefly surveyed here offers what I believe might be a productive line of work in the steadily unifying disciplines of philosophy, psychology, and linguistic science.

References

Chomsky, Noam. 1951. *Morphophonemics of modern Hebrew.* Typescript of a radical revision of Chomsky's MA thesis, dated December 1951; retyped and published by Garland, New York, in 1979.

Chomsky, Noam. 1959. On certain formal properties of grammars. *Information and Control* 2. 137–167. Reprinted in R. Duncan Luce, Robert R. Bush, and Eugene Galanter (eds.), *Readings in Mathematical Psychology*, Vol. II, 125–155, New York: John Wiley and Sons, 1965 (citation to the original on p. 125 of this reprinting is incorrect).

Chomsky, Noam. 1965. *Aspects of the theory of syntax.* Cambridge, MA: MIT Press.

Chomsky, Noam. 1966. *Topics in the theory of generative grammar.* The Hague: Mouton.

Chomsky, Noam. 1975. *The logical structure of linguistic theory.* New York: Plenum. Published version of Chomsky (1955).

Chomsky, Noam. 1981. *Lectures on government and binding.* Dordrecht: Foris.

Chomsky, Noam. 1986. *Knowledge of language: Its origins, nature, and use.* New York: Praeger.

Chomsky, Noam. 1955–1956. *The logical structure of linguistic theory.* Manuscript, mimeographed 1955; revised 1956 and distributed on microfilm by MIT Library, Cambridge, MA; ultimately published as Chomsky 1975.

Daniels, Peter T. 2010. Chomsky 1951a and Chomsky 1951b. In Douglas A. Kibbee (ed.), *Chomskyan (r)evolutions*, 169–214. Amsterdam: John Benjamins.

Davis, Martin. 1982. Why Godel didn't have Church's thesis. *Information and Control* 54. 3–24.

Davis, Martin. 1994a. Emil L. Post: His life and work. In Martin Davis (ed.), xi–xxviii. Boston, Mass.: Birkhäuser.

Davis, Martin (ed.). 1994b. *Solvability, provability, definability: The collected works of Emil L. Post.* Boston, Mass.: Birkhäuser.

De Mol, Liesbeth. 2006. Closing the circle: An analysis of Emil Post's early work. *Bulletin of Symbolic Logic* 12(2). 267–289.

Ebbinghaus, Heinz-Dieter & Jorg Flum. 1999. *Finite model theory. 2nd edition.* Berlin & New York: Springer.

Gazdar, Gerald, Ewan Klein, Geoffrey K. Pullum & Ivan A. Sag. 1985. *Generalized phrase structure grammar.* Oxford: Basil Blackwell.

Harris, Zellig S. 1954. Transfer grammar. *International Journal of American Linguistics* 20. 259–270.

Hockett, Charles F. 1954. Two models of grammatical description. *Word* 10. 210–231. Page references are to the reprinting in Joos (ed.) 1966, 386–399.

Huddleston, Rodney D. & Geoffrey K. Pullum (eds.). 2002. *Cambridge grammar of the English language.* Cambridge: Cambridge University Press.

Jackson, Allyn. 2018. Emil Post: Psychological fidelity. *Inference: International Review of Science* 4(2). https : / / inference - review . com / article / psychological - fidelity.

Johnson, David E. & Paul M. Postal. 1980. *Arc pair grammar.* Princeton, NJ: Princeton University Press.

Kripke, Saul. 1982. *Wittgenstein on rules and private language: An elementary exposition.* Cambridge, MA: Harvard University Press.

Lewis, C. I. 1918. *A survey of symbolic logic.* Berkeley, CA: University of California Press.

Libkin, Leonid. 2004. *Elements of finite model theory* (Texts in Theoretical Computer Science). Heidelberg: Springer.

McCawley, James D. 1968. Concerning the base component of a transformational grammar. *Foundations of Language* 4. 243–269. Reprinted in James D. McCawley, *Grammar and meaning,* 35–58, New York: Academic Press; Tokyo: Taishukan, 1973.

Millar, Alan. 2004. *Understanding people: Normativity and rationalizing explanation.* Oxford: Oxford University Press.

Montague, Richard. 1973. The proper treatment of quantification in ordinary english. In Jaakko Hintikka, Julius Moravcsik & Patrick Suppes (eds.), *Approaches to natural language,* 221–242. Dordrecht: D. Reidel. Reprinted in Montague (1974), 247–270.

Montague, Richard. 1974. *Formal philosophy.* New Haven, CT: Yale University Press. Edited by Richmond Thomason.

Ney, James. 1993. On generativity: The history of a notion that never was. *Historiographia Linguistica* 20. 441–454.

Post, Emil L. 1921. Introduction to a general theory of elementary propositions. *American Journal of Mathematics* 43. 163–185. Reprinted in Davis (1994b), 21–43.

Post, Emil L. 1943. Formal reductions of the general combinatory decision problem. *American Journal of Mathematics* 65. 197–215. Reprinted in Davis (1994b), 442–460.

Post, Emil L. 1944. Recursively enumerable sets of positive integers and their decision problems. *Bulletin of the American Mathematical Society* 50. 284–316. Reprinted in Davis (1994b), 461–494.

Pullum, Geoffrey K. 2007. Ungrammaticality, rarity, and corpus use. *Corpus Linguistics and Linguistic Theory* 3. 33–47.

Pullum, Geoffrey K. 2013. The central question in comparative syntactic metatheory. *Mind and Language* 28. 492–521.

Pullum, Geoffrey K. 2017. Theory, data, and the epistemology of syntax. In Marek Konopka & Angelika Wöllstein (eds.), *Grammatische Variation: Empirische Zugänge und theorische Modellierung* (Institut für Deutsche Sprache, Jahrbuch 2016), 283–298. Berlin: Walter de Gruyter.

Pullum, Geoffrey K. & Barbara C. Scholz. 2001. On the distinction between model-theoretic and generative-enumerative syntactic frameworks. In Philippe de Groote, Glyn Morrill & Christian Retoré (eds.), *Logical aspects of computational linguistics: 4th international conference* (Lecture Notes in Artificial Intelligence 2099), 17–43. Berlin & New York: Springer.

Rogers, James. 1998. *A descriptive approach to language-theoretic complexity.* Stanford, CA: CSLI Publications.

Rosenbloom, Paul. 1950. *The elements of mathematical logic.* New York: Dover.

Sampson, Geoffrey. 2007. Reply. *Corpus Linguistics and Linguistic Theory* 3. 111–129.

Sampson, Geoffrey & Anna Babarczy. 2014. *Grammar without grammaticality: Growth and limits of grammatical precision* (Trends in Linguistics: Studies and Monographs 254). Berlin: Walter de Gruyter.

Scholz, Barbara C. 1990. *Kripke's Wittgensteinian paradox.* Columbus, OH: The Ohio State University dissertation. Published by University Microfilms, Ann Arbor, Michigan.

Searle, John. 1969. *Speech acts: An essay in the philosophy of language.* Cambridge: Cambridge University Press.

Stillwell, John. 2004. Emil Post and his anticipation of Gödel and Turing. *Mathematics Magazine* 77(1). 3–14.

Tomasello, Michael. 2003. *Constructing a language.* Cambridge, MA: Harvard University Press.

Urquhart, Alasdair. 2009. Emil Post. In Dov Gabbay & John Woods (eds.), *The handbook of the history of logic,* vol. 5, 617–666. Amsterdam: Elsevier.

Whitehead, Alfred North & Bertrand Russell. 1910–1913. *Principia mathematica.* Cambridge: Cambridge University Press.

Chapter 9

Linguistic form: A political epistemology

Nick Riemer

The University of Sydney & Laboratoire d'histoire des théories linguistiques, Université Paris-Diderot

This chapter explores ideological dimensions of contemporary mainstream linguistics, especially with reference to the "unique form hypothesis": the assumption that each language has a single form, which it is the role of linguistics to characterize. The chapter surveys grounds for scepticism about the hypothesis, reviews some recent ideological critiques of linguistics, and sketches the contours of a speculative "political epistemology" of the unique form hypothesis, suggesting how well-known critiques of the other social sciences might apply to structural linguistics research. It pays special attention to the unique form hypothesis' role as a vehicle for the discretionary intellectual authority of the linguistic expert – in the pedagogical context, the lecturer who serves as the origin and authority of the ideas about language structure transmitted to the linguistics student. This authority is argued to replicate and so to normalize, in the domain of education, the kinds of relations of social domination on which contemporary political orders rest. As a result of this discussion, the theoretical biases of contemporary linguistics are replaced in the broader socio-ideological context to which they belong, and considered with respect to some classic political critiques of "bourgeois" social science.

1 Introduction

What might it mean to assert that a language has a form, and what political and ideological consequences, broadly conceived, might such an assertion currently entail? If, with Konrad Koerner (1999), we accept that linguists in the past have been "particularly prone to cater, consciously or not, to ideas and interests outside their discipline and, as history shows, allowed at times their findings to be used for purposes they were not originally intended", then the question arises

Nick Riemer. 2019. Linguistic form: A political epistemology. In James McElvenny (ed.), *Form and formalism in linguistics*, 225–264. Berlin: Language Science Press. DOI:10.5281/zenodo.2654369

as to whether, and if so how, this may also happen today.[1] One of the functions of the humanities and social sciences in general, it has often been argued, is to supply an apologetics of the dominant political order and the ideologies that accompany it (Nizan 1971 [1932], Chomsky 1978 [1967], Ingleby 1972, Baudrillard 2001 [1972], Bourdieu 1991). What role in this apologetics might linguistics play? What insights might the "critical" tradition in the reflexive social sciences bring to our understanding of the nature of formalist linguistics as an intellectual, disciplinary and ideological project? In exploring these questions, this contribution starts not with the substantives *language* and *form*, but with the indefinite articles accompanying them, and the implications of singularity they introduce. Those articles express central intellectual and ideological characteristics of contemporary "structural" or "formal" linguistics – those varieties of the discipline, that is, that posit a unique underlying "form" of language and set out to characterize it.[2] In its mapping of grammatical form, this kind of linguistics deploys reductive, objectivizing and centripetal procedures in order to discern a single structural unity underlying the diversity of observable manifestations of language. The rules, generalizations, and categorizations deployed in describing grammar tend in a single direction: almost exclusively, intellectual effort is devoted to bringing complex facts under the scope of general rules, and to deriving the diverse manifestations of speech, sign and text from the operations of a unique and singular grammar – the Platonic form that underlies the variety of human language, guarantor of the "scientificity" of linguistics.

"There is a single French language, a single grammar, a single Republic", the French Education Minister, Jean-Michel Blanquer tweeted in November 2017 in the context of calls for French spelling reform in the interests of gender inclusiveness.[3] But while traditional grammar has always sought to discern – or, more frequently, establish – forms (plural) in language, the "unique form hypothesis" – the idea that each language has *a single* form, which linguists scientifically re-

---

[1] An earlier version of some of these ideas was published as Riemer (2016b).

[2] It is important for what follows to note that, as I use it here, "formal linguistics" has a far wider extension than usual. Whereas in its typical use "formal" denotes a feature of linguistic methodology – the use of mathematizable techniques in grammatical analysis – here it is simply used to refer to any theoretical endeavour that assumes that a language has a unique underlying form. Approaches that avoid this hypothesis are, needless to say, in a distinct minority in the discipline: the most obvious example, no doubt, is integrational linguistics, which rejects the assumption of "a single vantage point from which language presents itself as forming a unified or homogeneous system", along with "the idea of a scientific search for the single best model or set of procedures for analyzing language and communication" (Pablé & Hutton 2015: 4, 15).

[3] "Il y a une seule langue française, une seule grammaire, une seule République." See https://twitter.com/jmblanquer/status/930813255211208707.

veal – has not been a permanent feature of the discipline, and it is not a necessary one. Its dominance in our period therefore deserves to be critically analysed. In this chapter, I propose to explore the ideological dimensions of the unique form hypothesis in linguistics, particularly with respect to its political and ideological affordances in the era of contemporary "platform" capitalism (Srnicek 2017). Koerner (2000: 19) observes that "linguistics, past and present, has never been 'value free', but has often been subject to a variety of external influences and opinions, not all of them beneficial to either the discipline itself or the society that sustains it". In the spirit of this remark, I will ask what might lend the unique form hypothesis plausibility in the context of the overarching ideological climate in which linguistics research and teaching currently unfold, understanding ideology in Slavoj Žižek's sense of ideas that are "functional with regard to some relation of social domination ('power', 'exploitation') in an inherently non-transparent way" (Žižek 1994: 8).

According to Christopher Hutton, "linguists [...] generally associate their discipline and the practice of linguistic analysis with a vague form of liberal progressiveness" (Hutton 2001: 295). A corresponding progressivism of some kind no doubt also characterizes most linguists' political orientation: right-wing political views are probably distinctly in the minority in the profession. Yet ideological critiques identifying political aspects of linguistics, whether progressive or anti-progressive, are only rarely acknowledged in the discipline itself. Many linguists, working under the assumption that they are doing "normal science", often hesitate to take ideological analysis seriously, and linguistics' scientific aspirations regularly serve to inhibit any critical reflection on either the epistemological status or political import of the discipline's theoretical results.

Such reflection is nevertheless both important and interesting. As Talbot Taylor notes,

> if purportedly descriptive discourse on language is best reconceived as a (covertly authoritarian mode of) normative discourse, then the assertion of the political irrelevance and ideological neutrality of linguistic science can no longer be maintained. (Taylor 1990: 25)

Examining the ideological dimensions of linguistics in order to propose a "political epistemology" of the discipline – an account of the political and ideological conditions that help secure acceptance of theoretical propositions – can only enrich the way in which linguistics understands itself. Linguists may often prefer to maintain the illusion of a wholly independent and isolated discipline, but we are ourselves well and truly members of the body politic. Understanding how linguistics works also means understanding its connections to society, illuminating the ways in which external stakes can feed into linguistic research, and, correspondingly, how linguistic theories themselves can act on the world outside theory.[4]

I begin by briefly surveying a number of the ways in which the reductive and formalizing energies embodied in the unique form hypothesis have been or could be called into question, thereby establishing that the unique form *hypothesis* is, precisely, just that. I then review a number of ideological critiques of linguistics from the past several decades, before sketching the contours of a speculative "political epistemology" of the unique form hypothesis, which shows how well-known critiques of the other social sciences might apply to structural linguistics research. In particular, I consider the unique form hypothesis from the point of view of an aspect of the discipline often neglected by historians: its function in undergraduate education. This pedagogical function is essential for an accurate grasp of the ideological dimensions of linguistics as a discipline. I pay special attention to the unique form hypothesis' role as a vehicle for the discretionary authority of the linguistic expert – in the pedagogical context, the lecturer who serves as the origin and guarantor of the ideas about language structure transmitted to the student. I consider an interpretation of this authority as prefiguring and normalizing, in the symbolic register, the kinds of relations of social domination on which contemporary political orders rest, and to which linguistics undergraduates, like those in other disciplines, must learn, as one of the key functions of a university education, to accommodate themselves. As a result of this discussion, the theoretical biases of contemporary linguistics are replaced in the broader socio-ideological context to which they belong, and considered with respect to some classic political critiques of "bourgeois" social science.

2 Must language have a single form?

To raise the question is, of course, to bring linguistics' very disciplinary identity into question. In a striking example of the way in which the formal presuppositions of theories can be ignored by their own proponents, however, linguists sometimes react negatively to the suggestion that they are involved in characterizing *the* form of languages, and protest against the dogmatism and epistemological closure that such a claim might be taken to entail. So it is important, at the outset, to register precisely that the very idea of *the grammar, the structure,*

---

[4]I have explored an aspect of this latter question in Riemer (2019).

or *the form* of a language, particularly when coupled with the empirical procedures of modern linguistic "science", carries exactly this implication of singularity. To characterize the phonological structure of a language is to claim that the
language has – until, of course, improvements in phonological theory prompt
revisions – *this* phonology, and not some other. Equivalent remarks apply to the
other grammatical subfields. Regardless of the open-mindedness or tolerance for
different perspectives with which any particular researcher approaches the subject matter, it is intrinsic to the theoretical enterprise of formal linguistics in its
contemporary guise that any paradigm within it advances a claim of uniqueness
for its current best analysis of a particular grammatical phenomenon. This does
not mean formal linguists are epistemic zealots: like any empirical researchers,
they replace their current conception of what form is like when a better theory
presents itself, all things being equal. But it is only if the unique form hypothesis is adopted that this process of theoretical replacement can be understood.
If the presumption was that a multitude of different analyses of a grammatical
phenomenon was possible, and that any number of different interpretations of
the grammar could be equally "correct", or correct in different ways or for different purposes, formal linguistics' basic operational norms could not be sustained.
Without the premise that languages have a unique form, monopolistic theoretical
competition over the right way to characterize that form becomes meaningless.

The assumption that any language has a single form is, then, necessary to the
very practice of the discipline. But the history, and even just the recent history,
of reflection on language, within linguistics and outside it, offers ample grounds
for calling that assumption into question.

Doing so does not mean denying that languages have forms at all or denying
that they can be represented structurally; it just means denying that those forms
and representations are necessarily unique. In this section, I will briefly review
a handful of considerations which militate against the unique form hypothesis.
These considerations do not always contradict the hypothesis directly; but their
effect is to weaken its plausibility by calling into question many of the ideas
about language or its structure which accompany it. The aim of my review of
these considerations is therefore to illustrate that the unique form hypothesis is
not self-evidently correct: that it has a case to answer. And if the hypothesis can
at least be doubted, then we have good reason to enquire into the forces that
quarantine it from that doubt so thoroughly in the modern discipline.

The most serious obstacle to the unique form hypothesis comes, no doubt, from
the failure of linguistic theory to reach consensus on what such a form might be.
This is more than the necessary "failure" intrinsic to ongoing empirical enquiry,

in which the inadequacy of the previous best theory and its replacement by a successor is the very mark of scientific progress. This continual renovation of the best theory is not the case in linguistics, since even cursory inspection of the major subfields shows that linguists do not agree even on the premises on which the search for a unique form is to be conducted. Whatever its practitioners might think, linguistics is not characterized in a Kuhnian fashion by a contrast between periods of "normal science" in which the details of accepted paradigms are being refined, and wholesale paradigm shifts which thoroughly change the field's basic apparatus. Instead, "formal" linguistics is the site of numerous jockeying paradigms, none of which is the object of consensus, investigators not even sharing a single set of metatheoretical criteria on which the relative adequacy of different explanatory models could be judged (for example, only some researchers accept that a theory of syntax should be "generative" in the Chomskyan sense). In a situation like this, the idea that language does, in fact, *have* a unique form available for investigators to discover, seems incongruous.

For the purposes of linguistics, a language has a form if it can be reduced to a series of rules (generalizations) which demarcate units which are fully part of the language ("grammatical" ones) from ungrammatical or less grammatical ones. The true "form" of the language ("grammar", "competence", "*langue*"), then, is the one for which the grammatical theory accounts, the others ("usage", "performance", "*parole*") being understood as derivative of this. One does not have to be a generativist to accept this elementary definition: it is implicit in essentially all attempts to explain "surface" well-formedness by reference to "underlying" grammatical rules. The role of underlying rules in grammar allows us to recognize a second obstacle to the unique form hypothesis. As acknowledged by Chomsky (1986), among others, the second Wittgenstein's (2001 [1953]: §§139, 40) sceptical critique of the notion of rule-following, especially in the version popularized by Saul Kripke (1982), poses a serious challenge to any attempt to ground grammar in rules. There is not the space here to go into the detail needed to develop the arguments that underlie the Wittgensteinian critique properly, or to address the numerous difficult questions it raises.[5] We will instead briefly sketch one aspect of it.

Wittgenstein establishes that what constitutes following a rule or being in conformity with a rule is indeterminate: for any given rule, there is any number of different and indeed contradictory behaviours which might be described as following, or as in conformity with it. Applied to language, this means that a

---

[5]For an attempt to do the question greater justice, see section 3.3 of Riemer (2005) and the references there.

grammatical rule cannot correspond to, mandate or "generate" any single surface output; and, conversely, that the well-formedness of an utterance in a language cannot be exhaustively explained by any single rule or set of rules. The reason is the following: since, as Wittgenstein demonstrates, the *way* in which a rule is to be followed is always ambiguous, and numerous *different* and contradictory behaviours can all count as conforming to the rule, no rule or set of rules is sufficient on its own to specify a unique output. Any grammatical rule requires a set of further rules which governs the way in which it is to be applied – yet this combination of first and second-order rules is itself powerless to specify any determinate set of grammatical sentences as its output, since the second-order rule is just as much in need of principles of interpretation setting how it is to be applied, as was the original rule itself. Second-order rules need third-order ones to set their application, third-order ones need fourth-order ones, and so on. An infinite interpretative regress is set in train that has been argued to undermine any attempt to conceive of rule systems such as grammars as anything other than heuristically convenient representations of aspects of language.

The conclusion I have drawn elsewhere about the effect of the "rule-following argument" in semantics generalizes to *any* domain of formal structure: the rule-following argument renders *all* competing rule-based explanations of a linguistic regularity equivalent (Riemer 2005: 52). In proposing rules as part of the analysis of language structure, the linguist is relying on a tacit "background" of practices which allows her to apply those rules with confidence and generate the output in an apparently definite way, effectively ignoring the interpretative indeterminacy that attaches to any given rule, and even though the rule itself radically underdetermines the "correct" result.

The fact that *any* rule relies on an *infinite* number of interpretative meta-rules radically levels the status of the theoretical metalanguages in which grammatical rules are stated vis-à-vis the object languages which they supposedly explain: rather than standing *over* our ordinary language practices in a relation of *theoretical explanation* to them, the metalinguistic enunciation of grammatical rules emerges as simply a *different kind* of linguistic practice, equally reliant on an unexplicated background as the object language practices for which it purports to account, and to which no explanatory priority can therefore be attached. There is, for the later Wittgenstein, simply no more fundamental level of simplicity in the explanatory order than our everyday language use: to seek out some more basic level of theoretical explanation underlying it is to substitute a deluded search for unattainable "philosophical" certainty for the (confusingly named) "grammatical" description of our everyday practices that is, he believes, the real, therapeutic task of reflection. If to have a form is to be characterized by rules exhaustively explaining well-formedness, Wittgenstein offers a critique of the very possibility of that explanatory project.

Another important line of objection to the unique form hypothesis takes its inspiration from the broad phenomenological tradition, and can be constructed through appeal to a range of thinkers such as Heidegger, Gadamer, Hubert Dreyfus and – with a very different critical sociological twist – Bourdieu.[6] The premise of this line of thought can be captured in the proposition that "philosophy [and so linguistics] has from the start systematically ignored or distorted the everyday context of human activity" and that the everyday world cannot be represented by a "theory [that] formulates the relationships among objective, context-free elements (simples, primitives, features, attributes, factors, data points, cues, etc.) in terms of abstract principles (covering laws, rules, programs, etc.)" (Dreyfus & Dreyfus 1988: 25, 28). Applied to linguistics, the essence of this critique can be summed up in the proposition that the formal structure which linguistic science sees as the basis of linguistic competence does not reflect any underlying linguistic "essence", but should be understood instead as a product of artificial situations of "breakdown" in which our ordinary relation to our linguistic practices has been suspended. The formal rules and categories posited to underlie speech do not, on this account, reflect anything deep about the nature of language: they are, instead, theorists' elaborations of the heuristics to which speakers appeal *post hoc* in order to consciously and artificially rationalize aspects of their unreflective linguistic behaviour. For Gadamer, for instance, outside situations of breakdown, speakers are not just unaware of language as form: they are even unaware of language as *language*:

> No individual has a real consciousness of his speaking when he speaks. Only in exceptional situations does one become conscious of the language in which he is speaking. It happens, for instance, when someone starts to say something but hesitates because what he is about to say seems strange or funny. He wonders, "Can one really say that?" Here for a moment the language we speak becomes conscious because it does not do what is peculiar to it. (Gadamer 1976 [1966]: 64)

Form is what is left when meaning has been emptied out. Many phenomenologically inspired thinkers like Gadamer, accordingly, maintain that speaker-hearers

---

[6]Christopher Lawn's (2004) comparison of Gadamer and Wittgenstein can usefully be consulted here as an indication of the continuities between this and the previous line of critique.

are simply not aware of language as form, in the sense of a dimension of speech separated from meaning. In *The phenomenology of perception*, Merleau-Ponty denies that speech and thought (meaning) are "thematically given" to the speaker independently of each other: in fact, he says, "they are intervolved, the sense being held within the word, and the word being the external existence of the sense" (Merleau-Ponty 1962 [1945]: 182). The speaker is not aware of *two* things when speaking, the form (the word) and its meanings (her thoughts); the very division between the two only emerges when the speaker steps out of their unmonitored, prereflective linguistic habitus and adopts an artificially external attitude to it – Bourdieu's (2003 [1997]: 12) "scholastic disposition".

In this situation of what Gadamer calls the intrinsic "self-forgetfulness" of language, the idea that structural form underlies linguistic action represents a serious misconstrual: language is, first and foremost, the activity of speaking, and structure – "form" – is an artificial domain of constructed regularity carved out from it *a posteriori* (for some interesting illustration, see Preston 1996). Language is not, therefore, fundamentally semiotic: it should not be seen as a code uniting (more or less) fixed forms with (more or less) fixed meanings:

> Signs [...] are a means to an end. They are put to use as one desires and then laid aside just as are all other means to the ends of human activity. [... A]ctual speaking is more than the choice of means to achieve some purpose in communication. The language one masters is such that one lives within it, that is "knows" what one wishes to communicate in no way other than in linguistic form. "Choosing" one's words is an appearance or effect created in communication when speaking is inhibited. "Free" speaking flows forward in forgetfulness of oneself and in self-surrender to the subject-matter made present in the medium of language. (Gadamer 1976 [1972]: 87)

If language is not a system of signs, and if speech is not to be theoretically conceptualized as the mere *implementation* of an antecedent grammatical structure, then the interest of formal approaches to characterizing this structure is immediately diminished. In terms largely compatible with Gadamer's, Bourdieu (1991: 37, italics original) criticizes "the *intellectualist philosophy* which treats language as an object of contemplation rather than as an instrument of action and power", a treatment he sees as perfectly instantiated in the word-plus-definition conception of the vocabulary embodied in dictionaries. The postulation of structure on which formal linguistics depends can be criticized, that is, for a fundamental, intellectualist misconstrual of the nature of our relationship to language, and hence

Nick Riemer

of the nature of language itself. In *Pascalian meditations*, Bourdieu pursues a similar line of thought:

> Projecting his theoretical thinking into the heads of acting agents, the researcher presents the world as he thinks it (that is, as an object of contemplation, a representation, a spectacle) as if it were the world as it presents itself to those who do not have the leisure (or the desire) to withdraw from it in order to think it. He sets at the origin of their practices, that is to say, in their "consciousnesses", his own spontaneous or elaborated representations, or, worse, the models he has had to construct (sometimes against his own naive experience) to account for their practices. (Bourdieu 2003 [1997]: 51)

Bourdieu emphasises the intrinsic distortion that this kind of theoretical modelling introduces:

> simply because we pause in thought over our practice, because we turn back to it to consider it, describe it, analyse it, we become in a sense absent from it; we tend to substitute for the active agent the reflecting "subject", for practical knowledge the theoretical knowledge which selects significant features, pertinent indices (as in autobiographical narratives) and which, more profoundly, performs an essential alteration of experience. (Bourdieu 2003 [1997]: 51–52)

He concludes that "it is very unlikely that anyone who is immersed in the scholastic 'language game' will be able to come and point out that the very fact of thought and discourse about practice separates us from practice" (Bourdieu 2003 [1997]: 52). If, *simply in virtue of their status as representation and explanation*, theoretical models must be understood as "distortions" of the reality they model, there is even less justification for seeing any one particular theoretical model as uniquely accurate. On Bourdieu's account, theoretical knowledge of language, with the forms it posits, is something intrinsically different from the practical knowledge that speaking deploys; there is therefore even less reason to anoint a *single* theoretical representation as the definitive unique body of forms underlying linguistic practice.

The final source of doubt about the unique form hypothesis that I will briefly mention comes from the work of researchers in the "translanguaging" movement:

The point is simple: a named national language is the same kind of thing as a named national cuisine. Like a named national cuisine, a named language is defined by the social, political or ethnic affiliation of its speakers. Although the idea of the social construction of named languages is old in the language fields, it is often not understood. The point that needs repeating is that a named language cannot be defined linguistically, cannot be defined, that is, in grammatical (lexical or structural) terms. And because a named language cannot be defined linguistically, it is not, strictly speaking, a linguistic object; it is not something that a person speaks. (Otheguy & Reid 2015: 286)

As is the case in generativism (see, e.g., Chomsky 2000), translanguaging scholars only recognize the existence of idiolects, "the system that underlies what a person actually speaks, ... [consisting] of ordered and categorized lexical and grammatical features" (Otheguy & Reid 2015: 289). Insofar as "linguistic form" is understood as the form of a *language*, where the latter is defined pretheoretically and exemplified by such things as "French", "Turkish" or "Arabic", translanguaging scholars explicitly reject the proposition that such form exists.

3 Ideological critiques of linguistics: a sampler

There are, then, many reasons for which the unique form hypothesis might be doubted. But it will be clear that the grounds for scepticism that we have just surveyed are either highly marginal within linguistics, or come from disciplinary traditions outside it. The analytical task that faces us, therefore, is to understand why this is the case. Why is questioning of the unique form hypothesis so alien to mainstream linguistics itself?

In looking to what I am calling a "political epistemology" of the discipline, my presupposition is that the answer is, in part at least, ideological. Linguistics occupies a highly independent – sometimes, indeed, isolated – position within the contemporary humanities and social sciences. That intellectual autonomy, however, does not entail social, political, or ideological innocence or neutrality. Nor does it mean that linguistics has no effect on the world beyond its own intellectual frontiers, still less that it is not influenced by the overall context in which research is conducted (see Joseph 2002: 182 for some pertinent observations). So linguists must not, in Talbot Taylor's (1990: 20) words, "continue to mistake theories of the nature of languages and linguistic competence as culturally neutral and value-free, conceiving of ourselves as unbiased conveyors of scientific objectivity". This is particularly the case given that *acceptable* ideological objectives of grammatical and linguistic analysis are not infrequently avowed perfectly openly. Linguistic description, especially, has often been framed as a progressive intellectual project designed to loosen the arbitrary grammatical authority of social elites.[7]

On the other side of the ledger, reactionary ideological consequences of modern models of grammar have also often been denounced, though mainly from outside linguistics itself. To generalize massively, the main line of critique can be summarized in the proposition that linguistics' semiotic and cognitive premises entail an instrumentalist, asocial vision of language and humanity, well suited to the liberal ideology of capitalist exploitation. As far as I know, however, the history – a fascinating one – of ideological critiques of linguistics remains to be written. In order to situate the ideas that follow, in this section I will briefly mention some more recent critiques, before considering their relation to the unique form hypothesis in the next. Because these critiques are often not well known, I will not hesitate to quote from them generously.

Arguably the most important ideological effects of linguistics are those which it shares with the social sciences and humanities more generally. A common line of critique targets the historical role of disciplines in this category, linguistics included, in promoting norms of bourgeois liberalism, understood as the dominant ideology of competitive capitalism. Applied to linguistics, the core of this critique would focus on the discipline's near-universal construal of language as a sign system, along with the model of autonomous subjecthood that accompanies it. The significance of the semiotic framing of language derives from the status of signs as things which people autonomously and rationally *use* to further their ends:

> When you speak, you are using a form of telemetry, not so different from the remote control of your television [...] Just as we use the infrared device to alter some electronic setting within a television so that it tunes to a different channel that suits our mood, we use our language to alter the settings inside someone else's brain in a way that will serve our interests. (Pagel 2012: 275–276, quoted by Enfield & Sidnell 2017: 75)

The semiotic view of language entails that speakers' and hearers' relation to language is essentially instrumental, but not only in the way acknowledged in the

---

[7]This is by no means a uniquely modern framing. According to Talbot Taylor (1990: 11), the 18th century grammarian Horne "Tooke argued for a descriptive approach to language in part because he felt it would help to free language from the control of political authorities and would thereby offer access to the use of that powerful instrument by the politically oppressed."

quotation: quite aside from any effect produced by signs on hearers ("alter[ing] the settings inside someone else's brain in a way that will serve our interests"), the speaker uses signs in order to convey the coded meanings which correspond to the conceptual or denotational content they wish to express, following the rational determinations of an underlying code. This semiotic-instrumental conception of language as code locates the source of speech uniquely in the individual, and wholly obfuscates social determinants of linguistic acts.[8] Structural linguists, Bourdieu (1991: 44) says, "merely incorporate into their theory a pre-constructed object, ignoring its social laws of construction and masking its social genesis". This asocial vision elevates the individual's means-end rationality as the all-important parameter governing speech. It thereby promotes the fantasy of a rational, sovereign, and unfettered subject with a uniform code at her disposal, free of the constraints introduced by class, gender or ethnicity, either in the speech situations in which she might participate, or in her access to the code itself. This is the very ideology of autonomous rational agenthood that accompanied, for instance in Locke, the development of bourgeois liberalism and the market economy, and that is essential to their justification (Losurdo 2014). The ideological rationale for the "free" market rests on the fiction of the subject as *homo economicus*, a maximally informed, rational and independent agent of commodity transactions in an individualized, competitive market – a fiction obligingly affirmed not only by the semiotic conception of language and its various philosophical elaborations, but by the premises of much other work in the humanities and social sciences.

The advent of the forms of heavily authoritarian capitalism characteristic of the administered economies of the twentieth century elicited a famous ideological critique from members of the Frankfurt School. This critique of "instrumental reason" – the term is Horkheimer's (1992 [1947]) – has clearly been of significant influence on the more specific critiques of linguistics we will consider shortly. The modern West, Horkheimer and Adorno claimed, perverts reason, reifies domination as law and organization, and leads to a "nullification" of the individual in the face of dominant economic powers (Horkheimer & Adorno 2002 [1944]: xvii). "Bourgeois society," they say

> is ruled by equivalence. It makes dissimilar things comparable by reducing them to abstract quantities. For the Enlightenment, anything which cannot be resolved into numbers, and ultimately into one, is illusion; modern

---

[8] The individualist bias of theories in pragmatics has been a particular object of criticism by scholars working on non-Western and postcolonial communities: see Anchimbe & Janney (2017) for a summary.

positivism consigns it to poetry. Unity remains the watchword from Par-
menides to Russell. All gods and qualities must be destroyed. (Horkheimer
& Adorno 2002 [1944]: 4–5)

The effect is that individuals, in all their particularity, contradictions and *anomie*,
"are tolerated only as far as their wholehearted identity with the universal is beyond question" (Horkheimer & Adorno 2002 [1944]: 124), where "the universal"
stands for the permanence of social compulsion, the form in which the inex-
orable power of the modern socioeconomic order confronts individuals, "who
must mold themselves to the technical apparatus [of the economy] body and
soul" (Horkheimer & Adorno 2002 [1944]: 23). The principle of universality or
identity, in this vision, "strives to suppress all contradiction", a process which, as
Terry Eagleton (1991: 127) puts it, "has been brought to perfection in the reified,
bureaucratized, administered world of advanced capitalism".

This process of universalization and suppression of difference is reflected in
linguistics' construal of the activity of speech as selection from a shared, formal-
izable semiotic code: rather than intersubjective expressions of ourselves, meanings are reified (commodified) components of a formal calculus which we freely
exchange to accomplish certain goals, and from which we are therefore essentially alienated. By installing the same formal code in the head of every speaker,
grammatical theory accomplishes a wholesale cognitive uniformization, offering
a striking illustration of Horkheimer and Adorno's (2002 [1944]: 3) claim that for
the modern sensibility "anything which does not conform to the standard of cal-
culability and utility must be viewed with suspicion". Rationality is domination's
nom de guerre: "the impartiality of scientific language," Horkheimer & Adorno
(2002 [1944]: 17) say, "[...] merely provide[s] the existing order with a neutral
sign for itself". Christopher Hutton's (1999) demonstration of the links between
German "mother tongue" linguistics and National Socialism provides sobering
empirical illustration of Horkheimer and Adorno's ideas, in a mode inflected by
vitalistic and mystical sensibilities.

The structuralist emphasis on the unique form underlying speech forces the
contingency of linguistic convention into the background and thereby displaces
attention from its changeable character. This displacement is, indeed, intrinsic to
the very project of writing *a* grammar of *a* language, where both are thought of
as inherently singular. The totalizing and singularizing picture of language that
emerges contributes to what has sometimes been identified as the wider ideological purpose of the social sciences in general: to distract attention from the
alterability of human social arrangements, thereby affirming the inevitability of
the status quo, reflecting "a world of objects frozen in their monotonously self-
same being, [...] thus binding us to what is, to the purely 'given'" (Eagleton 1991:

126, on Adorno). Linguistics' structural universalizing, on this vision, has the effect of dematerializing the conception of humanity by abstracting it from local circumstances. By stressing what is supposedly necessary to an undifferentiated human nature, it forces the contingency of the social order into the background and displaces attention from their volatile and hence politically modifiable character. In a similar vein, Blommaert and Verschueren (1991, 1992) have characterized the assumptions lying behind much work in linguistics as "the dogma of homogeneism": "a view of society in which differences are seen as dangerous and centrifugal, and in which the 'best' society is suggested to be one without intergroup differences" (Blommaert & Verschueren 1992: 362). In enforcing a singular vision of linguistic structure, theoretically suppressing linguistic variation, and tacitly canonizing the standard (often, national) language, the unique form hypothesis contributes centrally to the homogeneist dogma.

Critiques along these lines have a long pedigree. Almost forty years ago, Deleuze and Guattari highlighted what they took to be the political implications of the modern linguistic project. "Since," they asked, "everybody knows that language is a heterogeneous, variable reality, what is the meaning of the linguists' insistence on carving out a homogeneous system in order to make a scientific study possible?" Their answer deserves to be quoted in full:

> It is a question of extracting a set of constants from the variables, or of determining constant relations between variables (this is already evident in the phonologists' concept of commutativity). But the scientific model taking language as an object of study is one with the political model by which language is homogenized, centralized, standardized, becoming a language of power, a major or dominant language. Linguistics can claim all it wants to be science, nothing but pure science – it wouldn't be the first time that the order of pure science was used to secure the requirements of another order. What is grammaticality, and the sign S, the categorical symbol that dominates statements? It is a power marker before it is a syntactical marker, and Chomsky's trees establish constant relations between power variables. Forming grammatically correct sentences is for the normal individual the prerequisite for any submission to social laws. No one is supposed to be ignorant of grammaticality; those who are belong in special institutions. The unity of language is fundamentally political. (Deleuze & Guattari 1987 [1980]: 100–101)

"Linguistics," Deleuze (1977: 21) comments elsewhere, "has triumphed at the same time that information has been developing as power, and imposed its own image of language and thought, suitable for the transmission of slogans and the organisation of redundancies".

Recognition of an underside of theoretical analysis – its ideological links with socio-political domination – is a constant in modern analysis of instrumental reason. Deleuze and Guattari's remarks recall Althusser's (2015 [1976]) discussion of the ideological import of idealist philosophy. For Althusser, the very project of "philosophical languages" à la Descartes or Leibniz – a tradition well and truly alive in contemporary linguistics – unwittingly serves an inherently authoritarian and conformist political stance. The "vertiginous exercises" of philosophical analysis, Althusser tells us, "are not neutral", but intrinsically beholden to the power of the status quo:

> Even if they have no object, they have well known objectives, or, at least, stakes. Since they speak of order, they speak of authority and thus of power, and since there is no power other than the established one, that of the dominant class, its power is the one they serve, even if they don't know it, and especially if they believe they are combatting it. (Althusser 2015 [1976]: 107)[9]

Sandrine Sorlin follows a similar line in criticizing the totalizing and reductive vision of linguistic theory:

> The common denominator of philosophical and universal language, standard languages, and [...] the Saussurean concept of "langue" could be a single attempt at reduction and autonomization. [...] Like the universal languages which linguistically take account of the world in a single "glance", grammatical and linguistic activity is motivated by the same "aim of linguistic unity" consisting in making language "single and visible". (Sorlin 2012: 103)[10]

– for her, a highly ideological result:

---

[9] Original: "S'ils n'ont pas d'objet, ils ont des objectifs, ou, à tout le moins, des enjeux bien connus. Comme ils parlent d'ordre, c'est qu'ils parlent d'autorité, donc de pouvoir, et comme il n'est de pouvoir qu'établi, celui de la classe dominante, c'est le sien qu'ils servent, même s'ils ne le savent pas, et surtout s'ils pensent le combattre." In all cases where no translation is cited in the bibliography, translations are my own.

[10] "Ce qui pourrait être le dénominateur commun des diverses entreprises linguistiques étudiées, à savoir les langues philosophiques et universelles, les langues standard, et, ici, le concept saussurien de 'langue', c'est une même tentative de réduction et d'autonomisation. [...] À l'image des langues universelles qui rendent linguistiquement compte du monde d'un seul 'coup d'œil', l'activité grammaticale et linguistique est animée par la même 'visée d'unité langagière' consistant à rendre la langue 'une et visible'."

While "pure" linguistics believes itself to be neutral from the political and social point of view, without being conscious of it, it is at base eminently ideological. Its implicit acceptance of pre-established political categories is masked by its methodological rigour. (Sorlin 2012: 113)[11]

Even more recently, Philippe Blanchet (2016: 73) has drawn attention to linguistics' disciplinary role in maintaining "glottophobia" – "the directly human, social, political and ethical dimensions of linguistic discrimination" – by promoting "a dissociation [...] between language and society, between linguistic practices and speakers, between linguistic forms and individual and collective forms of existence". The debt of this analysis to the Frankfurt School is clear:

This dissociation has been effected by a long western intellectual – including philosophical and scientific – tradition, which has conceptualized "language" [*la langue*] as a cognitive tool: as a *tool*, it is therefore supposedly exterior to the human and able to be evaluated, changed, validated or invalidated from a strictly technical point of view; as a set of cognitive operations, it is supposedly exterior to the social and able to be evaluated, developed, implemented or corrected from a strict neurological and mathematical point of view. (Blanchet 2016: 73–73)[12]

Finally, it is necessary to mention critiques of the well-known links between linguistics and colonialism. Christopher Hutton has emphasized that "the history of modern linguistics [...] is coextensive with that of high colonialism and inextricably tied to it." "The practices of descriptive linguistics," Hutton (2001: 291) writes, "require forms of privileged social access, and the attempt to set up a typology in which the relationships between the world's languages are laid out is an expression of a universal 'panoptic vision' ". This theme will be taken up in the following sections.

---

[11]"[...] alors même que la linguistique 'pure et dure' se croit neutre du point de vue politique et social, sans en être consciente, elle est au fond éminemment idéologique. Son acceptation implicite des catégories politiques préétablies est masquée par sa rigueur méthodologique."

[12]"Au-delà de l'adhésion cynique à un projet de société inique, ce qui rend possible le masquage de la glottophobie, c'est-à-dire des dimensions directement humaines, sociales, politiques, éthiques, des discriminations linguistiques, c'est une dissociation opérée entre langue et société, entre pratiques linguistiques et locuteurs, entre formes linguistiques et formes d'existence individuelle et collective. Cette dissociation a été réalisée par une longue tradition intellectuelle occidentale, y compris philosophique et scientifique, qui a conceptualisé 'la langue' comme un outil cognitif: comme *outil*, elle serait extérieure à l'humain et pourrait être évaluée, modifiée, validée ou invalidée d'un point de vue strictement technique; comme ensemble d'opérations cognitives, elle serait extérieure au social et pourrait être évaluée, élaborée, implémentée ou corrigée d'un strict point de vue neurologique et mathématique."

4 Ideology as process or as magic

The critiques of orthodox linguistics we have now surveyed should be taken seriously. Yet, when they are not simply ignored, most of them are likely to be characterized as arbitrary or unbalanced. Penelope Brown (2017: 391), for instance, summarily dismisses Bourdieu-inspired objections to the Brown and Levinson politeness framework as "postmodern posturing" which, she thinks, conveys the ultimatum "study a phenomenon my way or not at all". By no means all linguists would assent to Brown and Levinson's politeness theory. By contrast, the unwillingness to entertain foundational challenge evident in Brown's reaction is, unfortunately, far more characteristic of the discipline.

It is nevertheless true, in so far as it is possible to judge, that most linguists would explicitly oppose the universalizing and dominating politics which the critiques we have surveyed associate with the discipline. That is only to be expected: ideology would not exist if consciously held intentions and beliefs were transparently reflected in their holders' intellectual and discursive practices.

In any case, the totalizing, hegemonic dimensions of linguistic theory that critics have identified are certainly not the only ones which students will retain from their undergraduate training. The intellectual climate of linguistics is, as I have already noted, surely mostly progressive, opposed to discrimination and, above all, antiracist. As one American textbook expresses it, "looking more closely at languages, and in particular at languages that might seem exotic to us, can make us more tolerant" (Gasser 2012). Opposition to "prescriptivism", which is hammered into students from the first moments of their linguistic study, is the most concrete manifestation of this kind of "tolerance". As for another core aspect of linguistics pedagogy, structural analysis of unfamiliar languages, there is no doubt that this can offer powerful lessons in human diversity. Linguistics also fosters values like curiosity, logical rigour, and appreciation of difference, along with other mental capacities which can be harnessed for anti-reactionary and critical ends. It is surely not among linguistics graduates that one should seek virulent racists.

These considerations are certainly relevant, but they do not disprove the existence of the ideological effects discussed in the previous section. Instead, they suggest that linguistics is not ideologically uniform, and that those effects are not the only ones which need to be taken into account. In its intellectual and educational practices, linguistics is, like any complex intellectual institution, heterogeneous: on the one hand, its practitioners are mostly characterized by an open, liberal, vaguely left-leaning political ethos which the discipline's content cannot but reflect in some ways; on the other, linguists' theoretical assumptions are inherited from longstanding, often more conservative, intellectual traditions which should not be expected to be in phase with this encompassing political culture, and which allow the discipline to be valued precisely *as* an autonomous field with its own traditional modes of internal validation.

However, for the purposes of the ideological critique of a discipline, it is not enough to reason solely from the *content* taught to students. Doing so would leave us open to Baudrillard's important objection against what he calls a "magical" conception of ideology. In standard ideological critique, Baudrillard (2001 [1972]: 79, italics original) says, "ideology [...] always appears as the overblown discourse of some great theme, content, or value [...] whose *allegorical* power somehow insinuates itself into consciousness (this has never been explained) in order to integrate them. These become, in turn, the *contents of thought* that come into play in real situations". But critique of this kind of ideological effect, he says,

> feeds off a magical conception of its object. It does not unravel ideology as form, but as content, as given, transcendent value – a sort of mana that attaches itself to several global representations that magically impregnate those floating and mystified subjectivities called "consciousnesses." (Baudrillard 2001 [1972]: 79)[13]

As we have seen, "instrumental reason", "rationalism", "individualism", "homogeneism", "ethnocentrism" or "colonialism", are among the "great themes, contents or values" that have been argued to be conveyed by linguistics or the social sciences in general. Baudrillard's critique would consist in asking exactly *how* these themes come to *actually affect* linguistics students' beliefs and practices, as well as their consciousness: the failure to address this point no doubt accounts for the tenuous, far-fetched, or arbitrary impression that the critiques discussed in the last section may have left on some readers.

In order to develop a non-magical, non-allegorical account of the effect of ideological content, Baudrillard insists that attention must be paid to the *forms* and *processes* of that content's transmission. Ideology, Baudrillard (2001 [1972]: 80) claims, *is* nothing less than "the process of reducing and abstracting symbolic material into a *form*" (italics added). This means that the analytical challenge is to account for ideological effects in a way that explains how abstract doctrines influence practice and consciousness not by simply positing a black box, but by taking into account the *processes* involved in the generation of ideological effects

---

[13]See Larrain (1994) for a discussion of Baudrillard on ideology.

at their point of production. If we want to critique linguistics effectively, we have to do better than solely discerning abstract analogies or "allegories" between linguistic and political ideas. Neither bourgeois individualism, nor colonialism, nor any of the other ideological values purportedly conveyed by linguistic theorizing can be claimed to be automatically induced in students simply because linguistic theory can be described as "individualist" or "colonialist" in certain respects. If they could, it would be possible to detect harmful ideological effects under any disciplinary bed, justifying the impression of arbitrariness that ideological critiques risk giving.

To properly establish an argument about the ideological tenor of a discipline, analysis of content must be linked to analysis of the discursive and other material forms in which that content is transmitted (cf. Debray 1996 [1994]). Attention to linguistics as a set of *educational forms, processes or practices* therefore calls for analysis, since it is through exposure to those forms and participation in those practices in the course of disciplinary socialization that new audiences of students are brought to take on the attitudes and practices of ideological interest. The different effects that linguistics might have on students constitute the most significant concrete influence that the discipline has, but they are almost never discussed seriously. When it comes to analysis of the real effects of education in linguistics, the discipline typically does not come closer than conventional rhapsodic claims of linguistics' ability to equip students for the needs of the information economy:

> Students who major in linguistics acquire valuable intellectual skills, such as analytical reasoning, critical thinking, argumentation, and clarity of expression. This means making insightful observations, formulating clear, testable hypotheses, generating predictions, making arguments and drawing conclusions, and communicating findings to a wider community. Linguistics majors are therefore well equipped for a variety of graduate-level and professional programs and careers. (Linguistic Society of America, "Why major in Linguistics?"
> https://www.linguisticsociety.org/content/why-major-linguistics, 10 April 2018)

How, then, might a more serious, non-"magical" account of the ideological effects of linguistics pedagogy advance beyond the kind of marketing discourse evident in this claim?

To answer, we can start with the epistemic or justificatory status which students are encouraged to attribute to linguistic knowledge. As I have emphasized, this knowledge does not command a similar level of disciplinary consensus to the results taught to students in the "hard" sciences – far from it. Nevertheless, linguistic theory, particularly those parts of it constituting the core of the discipline – those, in other words, in which the unique form hypothesis is asserted most categorically – are regularly presented to students as "scientific", and therefore as enjoying an epistemic authority *qualitatively* similar to that of the natural sciences – not as great, certainly, but nevertheless of the same basic kind. Some linguists would no doubt hesitate to make that claim openly, substituting for "scientific" expressions like "empirical" or "systematic", but the idea is always there in the background, as can be easily confirmed by an inspection of Linguistics websites, including that of my own department, with their explicit references to "science", or to unmistakably "scientific" methodologies ("discovering the common properties" of languages or of "the human language capacity"; italics below are added):

> Linguistics is the *scientific study of language*, aimed at finding out what language is like, and why. Each of the world's 6000 languages is a rich and textured system, with its own sounds, its own grammar, and its own identity and style. From the Amazon to Africa, from Southeast Asia to Aboriginal Australia, we use language to think with, to persuade others, to gather information, to organize our activities, to gossip, and ultimately to structure our societies. (http://sydney.edu.au/arts/linguistics/, 25 July 2018)

> *Sciences of language* degree. Linguistics sets itself the task of discovering the common properties of languages by studying their formal properties, their history, their diversity, their acquisition, and their pathologies.
> (http://www.linguist.univ-paris-diderot.fr/_media/plaquette_licence_sciences_du_langage_nov_2016.pdf, 25 July 2018)[14]

> Yes, *linguistics is a science*! [...] *Linguists develop* and *test scientific hypotheses.* Many linguists appeal to statistical analysis, mathematics, and logical formalism to account for the patterns they observe.
> (http://www.linguisticsociety.org/content/why-major-linguistics, 24 July 2018)

> It is impossible to overstate the fundamental importance of language to individuals and society. Linguistics—the *scientific study of language structure*—explores this complex relationship by asking questions about acquisition, production, comprehension and evolution.
> (https://arts-sciences.buffalo.edu/linguistics.html, 24 July 2018)

---

[14] "Licence *Sciences du langage* SDL. La linguistique s'efforce de dégager les propriétés communes des langues en étudiant leurs propriétés formelles, leur histoire, leur diversité, leur apprentissage, leurs pathologies."

Linguistics is the *science of language.* It is not about learning a new language; rather, we study everything about language itself, ranging from how speech is produced to the relationship between language and the human mind / brain, and the role language plays in society.

(http://www.humanities.uct.ac.za/hum/departments/linguistics, 24 July 2018)

Linguistics is the *scientific study of human language,* from the sounds and gestures of speech up to the organization of words, sentences, and meaning. Linguistics is also concerned with the relationship between language and cognition, society, and history.

(https://www.ling.upenn.edu/, 24 July 2018)

General Linguistics cross-linguistically explores the structures of the sound systems, morphology, phrase construction, meaning and use of linguistic expressions and attempts to derive these from general laws of communication and the human capacity for language

(https://www.linguistik.hu-berlin.de/de/institut/professuren/allgemeine-sprachwissenschaft/allgemeine-sprachwissenschaft-s-prof/, 25 July 2018)[15]

The ideology of scientificity reflected here is not just a matter of academic marketing: it remains embedded in linguistics education throughout undergraduate studies in the subject and, in generativism, is strongly asserted in the form of opposition to "methodological dualism" (Chomsky 1995; see Johnson 2007: 367 for a defence of the claim that there is "a remarkably tight point-by-point agreement between the relevant aspects of linguistic methods and the underlying logic of the other sciences"). Whatever the paradigm in question, approaching languages "scientifically" means discovering a unique form underlying the diversity of speech.

In the context of their "scientific" study of language, students are explicitly or implicitly encouraged to accept the following broad presuppositions:

Totalizing objectivity. The language practices of human communities should be approached from the point of view of their formal and structural coherence, with the aim of reducing them to the single (ideational) reality of linguistic structure (grammar). The structural reality thereby discovered is factual and objective on every level of linguistic analysis: every language has a unique, precise and discoverable level of semantic content, a unique representation of morphosyntax and

---

[15]"Die Allgemeine Sprachwissenschaft untersucht einzelsprachübergreifend die Strukturen der Lautsysteme, der Wortbildung, des Satzbaus, der Bedeutung und der Verwendung sprachlicher Ausdrücke und versucht diese aus allgemeinen Gesetzmäßigkeiten der Kommunikation und der menschlichen Sprachfähigkeit abzuleiten."

phonology; a unique information structure, etc. It is the job of linguistic theory to reveal all these levels, with the overall aim of bringing to light *the* grammar of *the* language.

Reducibility. Actually observed utterances are therefore the imperfect realizations of a level of underlying, more regular structure. The flux of "performance", replete with non-normative structures, is mined to extract fixed categories, on the hypothesis that variation is not essential to language, but the cloak in which an invariant structure is concealed. Actual utterances, with their numerous "ungrammatical" phrases, "sentence fragments" and "production errors", are thus degraded in comparison to the underlying representations which they imperfectly realize, and which can be captured in a unique and stable metalanguage in a way which reconciles cultural and cognitive diversity. The recognition of variation is not consistent throughout the discipline: as is often admitted by variationists, the study of linguistic variation is principally concerned with dominant languages.[16] In one's own language, variation can therefore be studied, but in someone else's, uniformity is assumed.

Formalizibility. Languages lend themselves to a formal or quasi-formal description through rule-systems.

Transparency. This formalization is, most often, transparent (intuitive, shallow), in the sense that the rules believed to underlie the object-language can be expressed in the theorist's native language without any need for this to be enriched with an extended apparatus of technical concepts. For instance, "thematic roles" (agent, patient, recipient, etc.), a core component of descriptive and theoretical grammar, are defined through ordinary language expressions ("move", "action", "place", "possession", etc.), and definitions of Vendlerian aspectual categories make reference to commonsense notions like "limited", "instantaneous", and so on. Wierzbicka and Goddard's well known Natural Semantic Metalanguage (NSM) framework is a striking example: in this theory, all possible word meanings are reduced to intuitive definitions in "natural" language, supposedly without the least technical accretions (see Wierzbicka 1996). To analyse semantics in NSM, there is therefore no need to develop a sophisticated technical apparatus: ordinary language suffices. Not all semantic theories, of course, are as

---

[16]Cf. the "Widening horizons: cross-cultural approaches to linguistic variation" workshop at NWAV 45 in 2016, whose abstract starts with the words: "Despite great advances in variationist sociolinguistics in the last decades, a major limitation is the fact that the great majority of studies are done on relatively few languages; existing work in our discipline also leaves non-Western societies massively under-represented. Hence the accepted wisdom and prevailing theories and models in sociolinguistics actually rest on a culturally narrow base" (conference booklet, pp. 32–33, http://web.uvic.ca/~ddenis/NWAV%2045%20Booklet.pdf).

reluctant as NSM to adopt a technical metalanguage. Neverthlesss, transparency is characteristic of a large part of linguistics, especially as it is presented to students.

The authority of linguistics. Thanks to the properties of objectivity, reducibility and formalizability, linguistics is a science, and linguists hold an intellectual authority which qualifies them to pronounce on human linguistic nature in their own right, without mastering the technical competencies of the biological or brain sciences.

None of the principles I have listed would be accepted without qualification by all linguists. Nonetheless, they constitute a reasonably accurate summary of the hypotheses that most students studying "mainstream" linguistics, especially in the English-speaking world, are encouraged to embrace during the early years of their linguistics study. These years are, of course, the operative period for the purposes of analysing the discipline's most important ideological effects, because most students never advance to a stage where the premises of linguistic research are seriously challenged or complexified: in order to study the ideological effects of linguistics, it is undergraduates, not doctoral students, who should be observed.

From the beginning of their linguistic studies, students learn that language can legitimately be approached in the highly systematizing and totalizing way that is necessary if a unique form underlying the plurality of a speech community's linguistic practices is to be revealed. In thinking about language within their own society or outside it, students are trained in an essentially reductive and classificatory approach to human diversity. This framework defines a unique, idealized, normative model of language and meaning (the "language faculty", "linguistic universals", "grammatical structure", "semantic/conceptual structure"), with reference to which linguistic variability is conceptualized. Almost always, intellectual effort in linguistics is devoted to referring complex and multifaceted facts to a framework of general rules, in order to reduce the motley variety of human languages to the operations of a unique and singular structure. The reductive, universalizing and classificatory mental habits formed during this training constitute, I believe, the principal mechanisms by which the ideological effects identified in the previous section are created.

In fostering their capacities of abstraction and idealization in the context of the unique form hypothesis, students are trained and examined in formal techniques of reduction and analysis much more than in hermeneutic ones of interpretation or complexification. In line with this orientation, students are often taught that:

- Predicates belong to a small handful of semantic categories (those of Vendler 1957);

- A language's vocabulary can be exhaustively categorized into a finite set of lexical categories;

- Discourse has a basic unit — the phrase, utterance, or turn;

- Some phrases are grammatical, others ungrammatical;

- Propositions (truth-conditional statements) are at the base of meaning;

- Conversation is governed by a small number of conversational maxims or similar principles;

- Speech acts can be taxonomized into a finite number of specific categories;

- Words' diverse uses can be reduced to a meaning or definition, or a finite set of these, reducible in turn to a set of conceptual primitives.

Behind the variety and complexity of human speech acts, a kind of underlying force or power can therefore be identified: abstract linguistic reason, the essential properties of the linguistic "system", deriving from psychological, biological or quite simply grammatical constants.

On the whole, the concepts I have just listed are not approached as *partial interpretative perspectives* on linguistic facts, useful for certain specific purposes. Instead, they are reified, and claimed to constitute the permanent essence of linguistic structure. Linguistic diversity ends up being understood as what is left after the maximum number of cross-linguistic generalizations have been extracted. Linguistic aspects of human life are presented as the rational products of underlying rule-systems. For this to be plausible, significant idealization is necessary: what is studied are "grammar", "vocabularies", "language families" – imaginary, idealized constructs remote from, and not easily de-idealized to, situated acts of speech.

It is precisely because they have been idealized that languages admit the generalizations about them that students are encouraged to make. It goes without saying that both generalization and idealization are necessary and unavoidable in intellectual activity and there could be no question of studying language without them. But they can be presented to students in different ways, and the universalizing and reductive manner in which they are currently understood in linguistics is only one of them (cf. Stokhof & van Lambalgen 2011).

What ideological effect might this kind of training have? There are two aspects that are worth exploring: the implications of the fact that the universalizing and reductive theorization of unique form is conducted in a Western, usually English, metalanguage; and the meaning of the universalizing and reductive energies themselves that students are trained to channel. We will deal with these in turn in the next two sections. First, however, it is worth emphasizing the modernity of this intellectual configuration. Experts on language have not always claimed that grammatical knowledge encompassed human language in an exhaustive, scientific way. Eighteenth-century English grammarians, for instance, quite frequently acknowledged that at least some aspects of the grammatical structure of English simply could not be summed up in neat rules. In such cases it is not the "head" – the seat of rationally statable, rule-based grammatical knowledge – which is the judge of what the correct construction is, but the "ear", which "will overrule judgement and theory", as the English grammarian Anselm Bayly put it in his 1772 *Plain and complete grammar of the English Language* (Bayly 1772: 61).[17] As well as the rational principles governing language structure, then, Bayly recognized the influence of a whole domain of different ones, connected with aesthetic or perhaps stylistic, rather than strictly rational, principles, and reinforced by usage. These mark out a territory into which grammar is represented as unable to venture, and which escapes from the possibility of description by objective rules. Bayly's vision is characteristic of the period: language is hybrid in nature, largely constituted by rational, orderly principles which can be described and submitted to conscious regulation, while at the same time containing aspects which evade the grip of rule-based formalization, and which are a matter of "taste and judgement", as William Cobbett expressed the point (Cobbett 1983 [1818]: 56).[18] Far from a formal theory being able to account for the entirety of discourse, grammarians acknowledged that there were some regions into which their expertise could not penetrate.

Bayly and Cobbett's present-day successors do not have the luxury of being able simply to declare some aspects of grammatical organization off-limits. The centralizing and universalizing intellectual dynamic of formal linguistics has the goal of reducing *all* of a community's language practices to a single struc-

---

[17] See Bayly (1772: 26, 44) for some illustrative passages.

[18] The ear, then, occasionally trumps the head. But this principle of the sovereignty of the ear was applied only selectively, to those cases where the grammarian could not devise any rules to neatly describe the particular aspect of grammar in question. Where such rules could be invented, no amount of appeal to the "natural demand" of the ear would be countenanced. For Lowth, for instance, even though ordinary language use is sanctioned by the ear, this in itself gives it no grammatical warrant; as he explains (Lowth 1762: 9), English is very often spoken inaccurately, no matter how good it sounds to the ear. The contradiction of allowing that some aspects of language could be left to the discernment of the ear, but that in other apparently similar cases the ear had to be ignored, seems not to have been noticed.

ture, a grammar – and often then to claim that a single set of theoretical categories is capable of accounting for *all* languages (universal grammar, "the basic blueprint that all languages follow", as it is put by a well-known linguistics textbook, Fromkin et al. 2010: 18). This theoretical process frames the structure of language and languages, including the "structure" of meaning, as a unique and determinate object open to empirical methods of discovery, aspiring to the imagined epistemology of the natural sciences (see Zwicky 1973 for a striking example).[19]

5 Western ethnocentrism

The first of the two ideological effects of linguistics pedagogy that we will discuss lies in the implications of the metalanguage in which this kind of analysis is conducted. It is no doubt in semantics – a domain presupposed by a great deal of linguistic description and theory – that the relevant effects can be most clearly observed. Semantics depends on the proposition that the linguist's native language is an adequate medium for the representation of meaning cross-linguistically. If, like most linguistic semanticists, I hold a mentalist theory of meaning, then I am justified in using a minimally enriched version of my own native language to reveal what others have in mind when they speak, regardless of what language they happen to be using. Semantic theory, as expressed in English, reveals both the content of others' semantic representations, and the conceptual structures on which this content rests.

The very tool of cross-linguistic semantic research – a Western metalanguage, usually English – therefore participates in what Anchimbe & Janney (2017: 109) have called "the ad hoc transformation of the West's emic research perspectives into the prescribed etic standards for the rest of the world". This entails some uncomfortable consequences: even if "exotic" languages are configured differently from the researcher's metalanguage, they can nevertheless, at base, be "contained" in the latter. The point is not limited to semantics: in all domains of grammar, the mainly Western languages which serve as metalanguages for comparative research do not assume the status of languages like any other, into which "exotic" languages can be translated in necessarily approximate, rudimentary, contextually variable ways: they are, on the contrary, master-codes in which fixed, context-independent, explanatory representations of exotic meaning can be definitively supplied. The universe of meaning in non-Western languages turns out to be completely "legible" or "decipherable" in Western metalanguages.

---

[19]I am grateful to Geoff Pullum for this reference.

In a discussion of informant-training in his once well-known 1967 handbook on linguistic fieldwork, William Samarin (1967: 41) states that "the ultimate goal is to get the informant to think about language as the investigator does [and to answer questions in] the way he should respond". Such a frank admission that the goal of fieldwork is to substitute Western metalinguistic categories for indigenous ones, even in the consciousness of the informant, would not, of course, be easily avowable today. Nevertheless, contemporary glossing practices have exactly the same effect, as though Samarin's instructions to field-workers – to aim for the native informant to wholly assimilate the linguist's metalinguistic categories – were still in full effect. The most visible semantic theories, such as cognitive semantics or Wierzbicka's Natural Semantic Metalanguage (see Wierzbicka 1996) give the impression that English, in which research in these frameworks is mostly presented, is not just spoken in every airport and hotel in the world, but in every head as well. The uncomfortable conclusion is that this arrangement is, in short, a striking example of Christine Delphy's (2008: 31) definition of racism: the idea that "the characteristics of the dominant are not seen as specific characteristics but as the [...] normal way of being" — normal, in the sense that it is the vocabulary of dominant languages which provides the universally valid metalanguage in which the significations of any language can be represented.[20]

Charles Taylor observes that

> We are always in danger of seeing our ways of acting and thinking as the only conceivable ones. This is exactly what ethnocentrism consists in. Understanding other societies ought to wrench us out of this; it ought to alter our self-understanding. (Taylor 1985: 129)

However, current semantic theories are not meant to entail any alteration to their users' self-understanding. From the moment that one presents expressions in English as markers of invariant semantic "primitives", the possibility is excluded that their meanings could be changed by their analytical function. Semantic analysis is not dialectical: an object-language expression is analysed through a known, usually native-language expression, whose meaning is presumed to be fixed and settled, and which can therefore serve as a point of reference for the representation of exotic meanings.

It is one thing to state – incontestably – that different languages can be translated and understood for the purposes of a very wide range of practices and

---

[20] "Les caractéristiques des dominants ne sont pas vues comme des caractéristiques spécifiques mais comme la façon d'être [...] normale."

interactions. It is quite another to imagine that that reflects a cognitive identity in meaning, and that a single language – most often, English – provides an all-encompassing metalanguage capable of representing all other languages' meanings. John Lucy's (1997: 333) critique of the Berlin and Kay colour typology, that it "dictated in advance the possible meanings the terms could have since no other meanings were embodied in the [Munsell colour] samples", can be generalized to all of semantics: the use of English as a metalanguage also dictates in advance the possible meanings of object-language terms.

Descriptive linguists who engage in fieldwork know very well, and frequently mention, how far their metalinguistic tools are provisional and inadequate to theoretical expectations, unable to account definitively for languages' structural and semantic reality. Linguistic theory, by contrast, conveys an entirely different idea. For the epistemology of theoretical linguistics, it is more or less inconceivable that our own linguistic categories might be inappropriate for the representation of foreign meanings. Of course, it is freely admitted that certain parts of the vocabulary – words for colours, for emotional states, etc. – wholly or partly resist metalinguistic definition, but those very parts are problematic for the semantic analysis of our own languages too. For everything which *can* be represented metasemantically, English – the dominant language of metalinguistic analysis – works. For metalinguistic purposes, there are no areas in which English turns out to be less adequate than others. Difference is abolished, with the English-speaking student in semantics being trained in an analytical technique that rests on the presupposition that *their* language and *their* meanings are, in a sense, the only ones that exist, since they can serve as a universal metalanguage for the representation of foreign or exotic meanings. There is a significant symbolic violence in this position: not only does the world *speak* English, it thinks in it too.

6 Theoretical domination?

Anglophone ethnocentrism is not the only ideological value reinforced by undergraduate linguistics education. The second ideological consequence of linguistics pedagogy derives from the reductive intellectual dynamic of the unique form hypothesis itself and the claims to scientificity that accompany it. The field of theoretical competition over language in undergraduate linguistics education, I suggest, inducts students into practices which will be reengaged when, after graduation, they enter the labour market and come to participate fully in the competition of differing social interests that that entails. This induction operates on two levels. Fields of linguistics (phonology, morphology, syntax, historical linguistics, and much of semantics and pragmatics) in which instruction is mainly based around problem sets and concrete analysis model the norms of orderly, rule-governed and dispassionate decision-making essential to the ideology of contemporary technocratic administration. This much is more or less explicitly admitted in the marketing many linguistics departments regularly undertake. The spirit of disciplined, hierarchical reasoning characteristic of formal linguistics recalls Horkheimer's (1992 [1947]: 22) critique of the reduction of language in modernity "to just another tool in the gigantic apparatus of production in modern society". It is, consistently, also strongly reminiscent of Max Weber's principles of bureaucracy (Weber 1947: 329–341), which I present here in a selective and summarized form (Blackburn 1967: 177–178):

1. All official actions are bound by rules with the official subject to strict and systematic control from above.

2. Each functionary has a limited and defined sphere of competence.

3. The organization of offices follows a principle of hierarchy with each lower one subordinate to each higher one.

In drumming a procedural, rule-based approach to complexity into students, linguistics education trains them in the habits of streamlined rational organisation well suited to the demands of administrative work in many domains.

The second way in which the reductive training of scientific linguistics operates ideologically is through a tension created by the unique form hypothesis itself: the clash between the search for a single, definitive representation of language structure, and the fact that multiple analyses of any theoretical problem can always be envisaged (this is, of course, just one instance of the more general underdetermination of theory by evidence in empirical enquiry). Theoretical linguistic analyses are perspectives on or interpretations of languages. Any grammatical analysis depends on a multitude of little decisions about how a chaos of variable performance data is to be idealized and normalized in order to be turned into the imaginary constructs of "language" and "grammar". As acknowledged by Hockett (1958: 147) in the passage quoted by Kaplan (this volume, p. 17), these depend on creative decisions informed by a myriad of considerations on which opinions can legitimately differ. In this situation, it demands significant intellectual determination to elevate contingent and hermeneutic answers to these questions into unique, "scientific" and definitive analyses. In fields like semantics and

pragmatics, where the role of the investigator's subjective, discretionary judgement is determinant in arriving at a definitive theoretical analysis, analytical
indeterminacy is overwhelming, though typically not fully acknowledged, with
claims of the empirical authority and uniqueness of the researcher's preferred
analysis remaining largely unqualified by any recognition of theoretical pluralism. When the availability of more than one theoretical solution is acknowledged,
it is typically resolved by appeal to values of "parsimoniousness", "elegance", or
"explanatory" capacity. The claim of any one analysis to empirical or scientific authority therefore depends on a hermeneutic – subjective, discretionary, aesthetic
– judgement *par excellence*, the judgement that solution x is "simpler", more "ele-
gant", "economic", or "explanatory" than solution y.[21] Althusser (2015 [1976]: 105)
refers to the formalist or taxonomic tradition in idealist philosophy as the "mania for domination through categorisation". Exactly such a mania characterizes
linguistics in its pursuit of the unique form hypothesis. Students learn that the
manifest diversity of possible solutions to analytical problems cannot be maintained: despite appearances, only one of the many possible analyses of a phonological, syntactic or semantic problem can be endorsed as accurate, and dominate
theoretically.

Hermeneutic considerations therefore underlie claims of empirical accuracy
in core linguistics subfields. The same hermeneutic foundation is evident on the
higher level of framework selection. Questions of choice between theoretical
frameworks (generativism versus "West Coast" functionalism in syntax, Relevance Theory versus more classically Gricean approaches in pragmatics, Wierz-
bickian versus cognitive, or truth-functional versus definitional semantics) cannot be resolved by objective considerations, and the role of essentially discretionary and interpretative judgement in preferring one approach to another is
inescapable. Yet the proponents of different frameworks rarely find the need to
justify their theoretical choices in depth, and certainly do not engage in detailed
theory comparison, but still enjoy the full force of claims of empirical uniqueness.
The student of a Chomskyan will benefit from demonstrations of the "scientific"
or "empirical" accuracy of generativism and of the mistakenness of alternative
paradigms like Cognitive Linguistics. Cognitive linguists, in turn, claim a scientific authority for their own, different analyses. And so on: despite the courtesy
and collegial respect evident in the majority of linguistics departments that I have

---

[21]From this perspective, it is striking to note that Ludlow (2011: 159) denies that "there is a genuine
notion of simplicity apart from the notion of 'simple for us to use' ": simplicity, he says, "is in
the eye of the theorist" (Ludlow 2011: 161), and varies from one research community to the next,
and over time.

Nick Riemer

observed, each "academic lobby" (Rastier 1993: 155) presents its own approach to language as the correct, and most often, as the only really legitimate one, despite the self-evident fact that it is only ever one among a number of theoretical alternatives, with choice between them being established on essentially discretionary grounds.[22] Bourdieu's (2003 [1997]: 44) reference, in the context of philosophy, to "the contradiction [...] which arises from the existence of a plurality of philosophical visions, each claiming exclusive access to a truth which they claim to be single" carries over to linguistics perfectly.

Undergraduate textbooks, accordingly, most often shelter their preferred theory and methodology from the threat of alternative perspectives through claims of the disciplinary longevity, influence, or institutional entrenchment of the favoured approach: "a longstanding and influential view about language", states Kearns (2008: 6) at the start of her introduction to truth-functional, formal semantics, "is that the meaningfulness of language amounts to its 'aboutness'". Adger's (2003: 14) stipulation of theoretical assumptions at the start of *Core Syntax* is similarly discretionary: "[t]he approach to syntax that we will take in this book, and which is taken more generally in generative grammar, assumes that certain aspects of human psychology are similar to phenomena of the natural world, and that linguistic structure is one of those aspects"; challenges to this assumption are not even mentioned. Frameworks are taught not so much because they and their assumptions are "right", though this is certainly implied, but because they are more "influential" or "general" than their competitors. No greater accountability from teachers for their choices of theoretical perspective is expected. Lawson (2001: 9) notes that "[t]he rhetoric of dismissing a theory as 'uninteresting' [...] seems to be one of the stock-in-trade notions of introductory, as well as advanced, texts in linguistics". Twentieth-century textbooks of linguistics, he notes, "present the historically most-highly contested elements of their theories simply as fact", and "the most tenuous and problematic premises of a linguistic theory have tended to be presented to the reader of introductory linguistics texts as a natural assumption, true by definition or out of common sense" (Lawson 2001: 12).

Whether within frameworks or between them, it is the institutional authority held by an academic in the classroom setting that allows the arbitrariness of these theoretical choices to be obscured, the existence of analytical indeterminacy and competing theoretical frameworks to be rejected in an essentially voluntaristic

---

[22]See McElvenny's discussion (this volume, p. 42) of Boas' "domineering role in the world of Americanist anthropology, freely blocking the work of researchers who did not meet his frequently quite arbitrary standards".

way, and the threat these pose to the academic's own theoretical preferences and hence authority to be obviated. Students quickly learn that linguistic experts can claim authoritative "scientific" or "empirical" uniqueness for their preferred theoretical framework, even in the absence of disciplinary consensus.[23]

This exercise of discretionary theoretical power, we might speculate, constitutes the most important ideological consequence of the unique form hypothesis as an educational practice in linguistics. The spectacle of theoretical justification to which students are exposed in their linguistics training habituates them to a certain acceptance of arbitrary symbolic authority – their lecturer's – which will be rapidly reactivated outside the university in the figure of their employer, landlord or political "representative". This authority is at its most obvious when students sit examinations or submit work to be marked: here, the extent to which academic success is a function of their lecturer's discretionary judgement is clear. In submitting to their lecturer's theoretical authority over the thoroughly material stakes of their academic results, students reinforce dispositions that will be reengaged in the far more coercive world of labour-market exploitation which they will soon fully (try to) join.

For academics, too, the stakes of theoretical competition are not just immaterial or intellectual, confined to a world immune from any extra-disciplinary considerations. Theories are also the instruments of careers, and enable the acquisition and exercise of institutional power and professional advancement. Theoretical pluralism and the evaluative equivalence it suggests between different frameworks sits uneasily in a rigidly hierarchical institutional context like that of the university. In such a world, theoretical competition is natural. Only if the unique form hypothesis is in place can intellectual competition for the best theory of language be aligned with material competition for professional rewards.

I have suggested, then, that linguistics education ends up prefiguring the conflict of interests in society. It does not do this, however, by conveying any explicit theoretical content: asserting that would be precisely the "magical" or "allegorical" view of ideology criticized by Baudrillard. Rather, the ideological import of linguistics education should be located in its pedagogical *processes* and *forms* of

---

[23]The discretionary authority detained by the academic is, perhaps, nowhere in greater evidence than in the grammaticality assignments on which syntactic theorizing rests. There can be no rules to determine whether a sentence is grammatical: the native speaker's intuition is the only judge, and one of the most commented-on features of syntax classes is the regularity of disagreements. These inevitable disputes are a prime arena for the imposition of the linguist's own preferences: for the purposes of a syntax class, a sentence is grammatical if the lecturer says it is. The discretionary authority exerted by the linguist in stipulations about grammaticality is a microcosm of the authority they detain more generally.

transmission. In studying linguistics students learn to submit to – and to assume – a certain way of exercising arbitrary symbolic power in the domain of theory, by gradually accepting the scientistic pretensions of a basically discretionary, subjective institutional practice. Students studying linguistics are encouraged to develop generalizations and theories about linguistic aspects of the human world in a highly reductive and abstract way, subject to fairly lax empirical controls. The verification procedures they are trained to employ rarely go beyond the idealized and hence hypothetical representations under study, and are strongly conditioned by their lecturer's interpretative preferences. By validating their own theoretical preferences in the context of the unique form hypothesis and by effectively sheltering them from serious contestation, academics model for students the way that claims of scientificity, reason and empirical responsibility can be deployed to legitimate individual sovereign interests.

The arbitrariness of justification in the theoretical order, embodied in the regimes of authority of the university, comes therefore to correspond to the arbitrariness of the material and political order outside it. In giving students, at an important stage of their intellectual development, and at the very moment when they are on the point of entering the full-time labour-market, the authorization to claim scientific status, in the context of the unique form hypothesis, for what remain essentially discretionary and unoperationalized interpretations, linguistics education, whatever its other effects, normalizes the unjustifiable exercise of power.

The fact that the ideological properties of linguistics are rooted in the wider institutional context of higher education means that commonalities between linguistics and other "human sciences" should exist. This is, indeed, the case: habituation to the arbitrariness of intellectual power is arguably a hallmark of education in the humanities in general (see Riemer 2016a for some preliminary discussion). It is commonplace to insist on the capacity of the humanities to foster students' critical capacities, but the complement of this process is a risk that is often ignored – the possibility that humanities disciplines, linguistics included, end up habituating students to different kinds of arbitrary symbolic domination, forerunners of the very real forms of domination to which they will soon have to reconcile themselves as job seekers amid the madness of capitalist labour markets, or that they will themselves exert as members of the comparatively privileged Western middle classes (see Pinsker 2015).

7 Education and linguistic 'science' in a post-truth world

If linguistics was a natural or "hard" science – if, that is, theoretical activity was governed by protocols generally accepted throughout the discipline, thereby producing objective and agreed-on results – we would be wholly justified in accepting every theoretical linguistic result, regardless of its apparent ideological tenor. This is not, however, our situation. As we have noted, there is no single theory accepted discipline-wide: linguists do not even agree on how to define the object they study. Unlike the sciences of nature, linguistics, as a human "science", concerns the behaviour of autonomous creatures endowed with their own ways of existing and understanding the world. Given this, it is not self-evident that theoretical understanding is obtained through an objectifying and reductive analytical procedure, assimilating grammar and meaning to a determinate object able to be studied using the empirical techniques of the natural sciences, rather than through a pluralistic process of interpretation, drawing the study of language closer to that of other socio-cultural performances. Anthropology, literary history and sociology are all empirical disciplines which propose explanations, not just descriptions, of the objects they study. But they do not have the ambition of producing reductive and singular analyses of their objects. As far as linguistics is concerned, it is no more obvious that it should advance unique analyses of grammatical and semantic "structure" than it is that literary historians should converge on a unique interpretation of a canonical text.

Linguistic analyses of grammar and meaning intrinsically entail conclusions about the conceptual competencies of speakers and the cultural resources of communities. Sidelining the entire interpretative dimension of linguistics, ignoring the multiplicity of analyses that is always possible, claiming to discover a unique conceptual form underlying speech – this is, as we have seen, what a large part of linguistics education involves. At a time when racist and other identitarian forms of discrimination are strongly on the rise, when many political actors seek to caricature the psychology of entire civilizations and social categories in ways whose reactionary intentions are only too clear, and in the "post-truth" era when the results of scientific research are routinely threatened by pseudo-sciences in the pockets of influential political lobbies, linguists have a responsibility not to insist on the necessity or scientific credentials of their fundamentally wholly hermeneutic analyses, if we do not wish to reinforce the abuses of science and expertise characteristic of our age.

Just as it is important to validate "minor" languages, a challenge which linguists often take up explicitly, minor *linguistics* should be validated too. To do so is natural, given a basically hermeneutic understanding of what the discipline is. In this chapter, I have described some of the ideological factors that entrench the unique form hypothesis in linguistics, especially in its ramifications in undergraduate education, and which obscure the ample reasons to call it into question. The purely speculative, strictly non-"scientific" nature of this "political epistemology" of the unique form hypothesis might strike readers from the mainstream of linguistics as problematic. Such a reaction would be mistaken. A discipline's development does not involve just the collection, analysis and theorization of data, but should also consist in collective reflection on the various aims and effects of those practices. This reflection must not allow itself to be diverted into a purely "academic" and abstract investigation of the sociology of linguistic theory, valuable though that would be in its own right. Linguists are not sociologists, and we do not have to be in order to undertake metatheoretical reflection on the possible social meaning of our practices. In a world disfigured by the ecological, economic and political violence of the neoliberal capitalist order, the value of theoretical understanding and education derives from the contribution they make to harnessing reason for the progress of society. It is therefore incumbent on those of us responsible for the creation and transmission of knowledge to interrogate our own practices in order to assess how far they facilitate or obstruct this goal. As participants in the education of the next generation of workers, unemployed, exploiters and voters, it is difficult to reflect too deeply on our discipline's possible social effects.

This vision entails no dogmatism, and certainly does not threaten, as one might be tempted to think, to coercively subordinate linguistics to any particular political program. On the contrary, it allows us to conceive of the discipline as a site of a pluralistic and reflexive exchange, and justifies a blossoming of different theoretical frameworks and approaches. As a disciplinary practice, that is, as a matter of fact, what linguistics often already is. That the discipline's conventional epistemology can only analyse this as theoretical *competition* is a fact that surely sits uneasily with the solidarity that should be at the origin of intellectual progress, whether in theory or education.

References

Adger, David. 2003. *Core syntax.* Oxford: Oxford University Press.

Althusser, Louis. 2015 [1976]. *Être marxiste en philosophie.* Paris: PUF.

Anchimbe, Eric A. & Richard W. Janney. 2017. Postcolonial pragmatics. In Anne Baron, Yueguo Gu & Gerard Steen (eds.), *The Routledge handbook of pragmatics,* 105–120. Abingdon: Routledge.

Baudrillard, Jean. 2001 [1972]. For a critique of the political economy of the sign. In Mark Poster (ed.), *Jean Baudrillard. Selected writings,* 60–100. Stanford: Stanford University Press.

Bayly, Anselm. 1772. *A plain and complete grammar of the English Language to which is prefixed the English accedence.* London: G. Big.

Blackburn, Robin. 1967. A brief guide to bourgeois ideology. In A. Cockburn & R. Blackburn (eds.), *Student power,* 163–213. Harmondsworth: Penguin.

Blanchet, Philippe. 2016. *Discriminations. Combattre la glottophobie.* Paris: Éditions textuels.

Blommaert, Jan & Jef Verschueren. 1991. The pragmatics of minority politics in Belgium. *Language in Society* 20. 503–531.

Blommaert, Jan & Jef Verschueren. 1992. The role of language in European nationalist ideologies. *Pragmatics* 2. 355–375.

Bourdieu, Pierre. 1991. *Language and symbolic power.* Trans. by Gino Raymond & Matthew Adamson. Cambridge: Polity.

Bourdieu, Pierre. 2003 [1997]. *Pascalian meditations.* Trans. by Richard Nice. Stanford: Stanford University Press.

Brown, Penelope. 2017. Politeness and impoliteness. In Y. Huang (ed.), *The Oxford handbook of pragmatics,* 383–399. Oxford: Oxford University Press.

Chomsky, Noam. 1986. *Knowledge of language: Its nature, origin, and use.* New York: Praeger.

Chomsky, Noam. 1995. Language and nature. *Mind* 104. 1–61.

Chomsky, Noam. 2000. *New horizons in the study of language and mind.* Cambridge: Cambridge University Press.

Chomsky, Noam. 1978 [1967]. The responsibility of intellectuals. In J. Peck (ed.), *The Chomsky reader,* 59–82. New York: Pantheon.

Cobbett, William. 1983 [1818]. *A grammar of the English Language in a series of letters.* Amsterdam: Rodopi. Edited by Charles C. Nickerson and John W. Osborne.

Debray, Régis. 1996 [1994]. *Media manifestos.* Trans. by Eric Rauth. London: Verso.

Deleuze, Gilles. 1977. *Dialogues*. Paris: Flammarion.

Deleuze, Gilles & Félix Guattari. 1987 [1980]. *A thousand plateaus*. Trans. by Brian Masumi. Minneapolis: University of Minnesota Press.

Delphy, Christine. 2008. *Classer, dominer. Qui sont les autres ?* Paris: La Fabrique.

Dreyfus, Hubert L. & Stuart E. Dreyfus. 1988. Making a mind versus modeling the brain: Artificial intelligence back at a branchpoint. *Daedalus* 117. 15–43.

Eagleton, Terry. 1991. *Ideology: An introduction*. London: Verso.

Enfield, Nick J. & Jack Sidnell. 2017. *The concept of action*. Cambridge: Cambridge University Press.

Fromkin, Victoria, Robert Rodman & Nina Hyams. 2010. *An introduction to language*. 9th edition. Wadsworth: Cengage Learning.

Gadamer, Hans-Georg. 1976 [1972]. Semantics and hermeneutics. In David E. Linge (ed.), *Philosophical hermeneutics*, 82–94. Berkeley: University of California Press.

Gadamer, Hans-Georg. 1976 [1966]. Man and language. In David E. Linge (ed.), *Philosophical hermeneutics*, 59–68. Berkeley: University of California Press.

Gasser, Michael. 2012. *How language works. The cognitive science of linguistics*. 3rd edition. http://www.indiana.edu/~hlw/index.html.

Hockett, Charles. 1958. *A course in modern linguistics*. New York: Macmillan.

Horkheimer, Max. 1992 [1947]. *Eclipse of reason*. New York: Continuum.

Horkheimer, Max & Theodor W. Adorno. 2002 [1944]. *Dialectic of Enlightenment. Philosophical fragments*. Trans. by Edmund Jephcott. Stanford: Stanford University Press.

Hutton, Christopher. 1999. *Linguistics and the Third Reich: Mother-tongue fascism, race and the science of language*. London: Routledge.

Hutton, Christopher. 2001. Cultural and conceptual relativism, universalism and the politics of linguistics: Dilemmas of a would-be progressive linguistics. In René Dirven, Bruce Hawkins & Esra Sandikcioglu (eds.), *Language and ideology: Cognitive theoretical approaches*, 277–296. Amsterdam: Benjamins.

Ingleby, David. 1972. Ideology and the human sciences: Some comments on the role of reification in psychology and psychiatry. In Trevor Pateman (ed.), *Counter course. A handbook for course criticism*, 51–81. Harmondsworth: Penguin.

Johnson, Kent. 2007. The legacy of methodological dualism. *Mind and Language* 22. 366–401.

Joseph, John E. 2002. *From Whitney to Chomsky: Essays in the history of American linguistics*. Amsterdam: Benjamins.

Kearns, Kate. 2008. *Semantics*. 2nd edition. Houndmills: Palgrave Macmillan.

Koerner, E. F. Konrad. 1999. *Linguistics and ideology in the study of language. paper delivered at the 6th international cognitive linguistics conference, stockholm university, july 10–16, 1999.* http://www.tulane.edu/~howard/LangIdeo/Koerner/Koerner.html.

Koerner, E. F. Konrad. 2000. Ideology in 19th and 20th century study of language: A neglected aspect of linguistic historiography. *Indogermanische Forschungen* 105. 1–26.

Kripke, Saul. 1982. *Wittgenstein on rules and private language.* Oxford: Basil Blackwell.

Larrain, Jorge. 1994. The postmodern critique of ideology. *The Sociological Review* 42. 289–314.

Lawn, Chris. 2004. *Gadamer and Wittgenstein: Towards a post-analytic philosophy of language.* London: Continuum.

Lawson, Aaron. 2001. Ideology and indoctrination: The framing of language in twentieth-century introductions to linguistics. *Language Sciences* 23. 1–14.

Losurdo, Domenico. 2014. *Contre-histoire du libéralisme.* Paris: La Découverte.

Lowth, Robert. 1762. *A short introduction to English grammar.* London: J. Hughs.

Lucy, John. 1997. The linguistics of color. In C. L. Hardin & Luisa Maffi (eds.), *Color categories in thought and language,* 320–346. Cambridge: Cambridge University Press.

Ludlow, Peter. 2011. *The philosophy of generative linguistics.* Oxford: Oxford University Press.

Merleau-Ponty, Maurice. 1962 [1945]. *Phenomenology of perception.* Trans. by Colin Smith. London: Routledge & Kegan Paul.

Nizan, Paul. 1971 [1932]. *The watchdogs. Philosophers of the established order.* Trans. by Paul Fittingoff. New York: Monthly Review.

Otheguy, Ricardo & Wallis Reid. 2015. Clarifying translanguaging and deconstructing named languages: A perspective from linguistics. *Applied Linguistics Review* 6. 281–307.

Pablé, André & Christopher Hutton. 2015. *Signs, meaning and experience. Integrational approaches to linguistics and semiotics.* Berlin: De Gruyter.

Pagel, M. 2012. *Wired for culture: Origins of the human social mind.* New York: Norton.

Pinsker, Joe. 2015. Rich kids study english. *The Atlantic.* https://www.theatlantic.com/business/archive/2015/07/college-major-rich-families-liberal-arts/397439/. 6 July 2015.

Preston, Dennis R. 1996. "Whaddayaknow?": The modes of folk linguistic awareness. *Language awareness* 5. 40–74.

Rastier, François. 1993. La sémantique cognitive: Éléments d'histoire et d'épistémologie. *Histoire Épistémologie Langage* 15. 153–187.

Riemer, Nick. 2005. *The semantics of polysemy.* Berlin: Mouton.

Riemer, Nick. 2016a. Academics, the humanities and the enclosure of knowledge: The worm in the fruit. *Australian Universities' Review* 58. 33–41.

Riemer, Nick. 2016b. Diversity, linguistics and domination: How linguistic theory can feed a kind of politics most linguists would oppose. *History and Philosophy of the Language Sciences.* https://hiphilangsci.net/2016/05/11/diversity-linguistics-and-domination-how-linguistic-theory-can-feed-a-kind-of-politics-most-linguists-would-oppose.

Riemer, Nick. 2019. Cognitive linguistics and the public mind: Idealist doctrines, materialist histories. *Language and Communication* 64. 38–52.

Samarin, William J. 1967. *Field linguistics. A guide to linguistic field work.* New York: Holt, Rhinehart & Winston.

Sorlin, Sandrine. 2012. *Langue et autorité.* Rennes: Presses Universitaires de Rennes.

Srnicek, Nick. 2017. The challenges of platform capitalism. *Juncture* 23. 254–257.

Stokhof, Martin & Michiel van Lambalgen. 2011. Abstractions and idealisations: The construction of modern linguistics. *Theoretical Linguistics* 37. 1–26.

Taylor, Charles. 1985. *Philosophy and the human sciences. Philosophical papers II.* Cambridge: Cambridge University Press.

Taylor, Talbot. 1990. Normativity and linguistic form. In H. G. Davis & T. J. Taylor (eds.), *Redefining linguistics*, 118–148. London: Routledge.

Vendler, Zeno. 1957. Verbs and times. *Philosophical Review* 66. 143–160.

Weber, Max. 1947. *The theory of social and economic organization.* Trans. by A. M. Henderson & Talcott Parsons. Glencoe: Free Press & Falcon's Wing Press.

Wierzbicka, Anna. 1996. *Semantics. Primes and universals.* Oxford: Oxford University Press.

Wittgenstein, Ludwig. 2001 [1953]. *Philosophical investigations.* Trans. by G. Elizabeth M. Anscombe. Oxford: Blackwell.

Žižek, Slavoj. 1994. The spectre of ideology. In Slavoj Žižek (ed.), *Mapping ideology*, 1–33. London: Verso.

Zwicky, Arnold M. 1973. Linguistics as chemistry: The substance theory of semantic primes. In Stephen R. Anderson & Paul Kiparsky (eds.), *A Festschrift for Morris Halle*, 467–485. New York: Rinehart & Winston.

Name index

Subject index

www.ingramcontent.com/pod-product-compliance
Lightning Source LLC
Chambersburg PA
CBHW080916100426
42812CB00007B/2291